A History of
THE
METHODIST
CHURCH
in Great Britain

———◦◉◦———

VOLUME TWO

LONDON
EPWORTH PRESS

First published 1978
by Epworth Press
Room 195
1 Central Buildings
Westminster
London SW1H 9NR

Third impression 1992

7162 0301 4

Typeset by Ebenezer Baylis and Son Ltd
Printed and bound in Great Britain by
Mackays of Chatham PLC, *Chatham, Kent*

CONTENTS

ABBREVIATIONS

H.M.G.B., i. *A History of the Methodist Church in Great Britain,* Volume I (London 1965).

L.Q.H.R. *The London Quarterly and Holborn Review* (London 1932–   ).

N.H.M. *The New History of Methodism,* ed. W. J. Townsend, H. B. Workman, and G. Eayrs, 2 vols. (London 1909).

Wesley:

Journal *The Journal of John Wesley,* standard edn. in 8 vols., ed. N. Curnock (London 1909–16).

Letters *The Letters of John Wesley,* standard edn. in 8 vols., ed. J. Telford (London 1931).

Works 14 vols., 3rd edn., ed. T. Jackson (London 1831ff.).

W.H.S. Proc. *The Proceedings of the Wesley Historical Society,* 1899–

PREFACE

—⊃◦⊖◦⊂——

Thirteen years is a long time to elapse between the appearance of the first and second volumes of a consecutive work. Certainly in the case of this *History* great patience has been required from both authors and prospective readers, and some explanation of the delay is needed from the Editors. There have been the usual unavoidable problems involved in the recruiting of many overworked writers and the assembling and scrutiny of their chapters. But there has been an additional impediment. The stream of learned works on Methodism, its nature, its social context, and its effects on personal and corporate life, has continued unabated since the middle of the century and shows no signs of drying up. It has seemed necessary to some of our authors to delay their writing until certain important studies have appeared and been assessed. The Editors have thought it right not to press too hard on these contributors, lest the results of valuable research be lost. But they acknowledge that the postponement of publication, however caused, may result in giving the totally false impression that those who adhered to the deadline they were given were unwilling to take account of later findings and theories.

This volume, constituted on the same lines as its predecessor, consists of substantial essays on those features of Methodism in Great Britain, from the death of Wesley to the middle of the nineteenth century, which seem to us to be the most significant for its own history and the most important from an ecumenical standpoint. The third volume, which is already well on its way to publication, will bring the story, as was promised in the Preface to Volume I, 'within sight of the present day'. The fourth volume, also in preparation, will contain the documents and other sources most likely to be useful to teachers and students.

The original Editors are glad to welcome the addition of Mr Raymond George, with his meticulous scholarship, to their ranks. And they record their thanks to the Rev. Gordon S. Wakéfield, who has kept the same supervisory eye on the whole project as he did when he was the Connexional Editor of the Methodist Church. We are very grateful also to Herbert Rees for his careful preparation of the typescripts for publication.

RUPERT E. DAVIES

January 1978

A. RAYMOND GEORGE

E. GORDON RUPP

I

Church and Society in the First Half
of the Nineteenth Century

W. R. WARD

ENGLAND in the first half of the nineteenth century
was the scene of unprecedented social and economic
developments, and yet always bore the marks of her
kinship with Europe, and her still closer kinship with the
democracy in America. It was not just that, as Carlyle taught,
disease powerfully enforced the doctrine of the brotherhood
of man, as typhus continued its ravages, and cholera became
a new and dreadful herald of revolution or renewed religious
seriousness.[1] Nor was it just that this country shared to an
explosive degree in the great increases in population which,
for reasons almost totally obscure, took place over much of
the globe. The great contest of ideas between the apostles of
the Enlightenment and their challengers was fought as keenly
in England as anywhere. In religion the Unitarians maintained
an influential witness to the cause of 'reason' in religion, and
by the 'thirties, when their power in the Nonconformist
world had begun to wane, the Church itself had been powerfully infected by the development of the old English enlightenment in Germany. On the other hand Evangelicals and
Tractarians protested furiously in the name of older doctrinal
inspirations, and in this period enormously outweighed the
liberals in influence and constructive power. In the economic
and administrative fields, however, the English enlightenment

[1] Charles Girdlestone, *Seven sermons, preached during the prevalence of cholera, in the parish
of Sedgley* (London 1833); cf. Asa Briggs, 'Cholera and Society in the Nineteenth
Century', in *Past and Present*, xix (Kendal 1961), 76–96.

grew steadily in vitality. The reformers who drew their inspiration from Bentham had no use for the wisdom of their ancestors, and after 1830 they made a powerful mark on English law and government. Still more impressive was the development of the individualism and rationalism of the enlightenment in the classical liberal political economy. It is true that, as the performance of the economy after 1810 failed to justify Adam Smith's assumption that the free play of market forces would produce a natural social order, political economy became a dismal science. Malthus demonstrated that the poor would be always with us, and Ricardo admitted that the introduction of machinery might not be to the interest of displaced workers. But vocal as were the opponents of political economy, they had to depend on moral repugnance and sentimentality rather than on intellectual weapons of the calibre of the economists. In economic movements as well as ideas, England was closely knit to the Continent and the United States. The secular price trends, showing a rapid rise from 1790 to 1814 or 1815 and then a long decline to 1847, closely match those of France, for example, and the cyclical turning-points, such as the important trough of 1829-30, often correspond as well. Vital for the general movement of the economy as the harvest remained until the middle of the nineteenth century, England's dependence on foreign trade also exposed her to the consequences of economic movements abroad. The good years for the British economy during the Napoleonic wars were those in which foreign trade throve on subsidies and loans granted to foreign powers; again in the 'thirties British exports to the United States varied directly with the movement of the American economy and increased the amplitude of the trade cycle at home. England's experience of the Industrial Revolution was in this period unique, yet at every point English society was linked to and influenced by developments abroad. The history of Methodism has a similar character. Methodism was so English a phenomenon that it obtained no substantial foothold in any other part of Great Britain, and in America it developed on substantially different lines. Yet Methodism was a conscious protest against the theological modernisms of the Enlightenment, of a sort which was being made in one shape or another in many parts of Europe and America; and at the unconscious level, Methodist pietism, in rejecting a scholastic theology and believing that a religious community could be invented, was continuing the work of the Enlightenment itself. Similarly English Methodism was both stimulated and vexed by the activities of American revivalists; in the 'thirties and 'forties many Methodists were caught up in the agitations for peace and against slavery, popery and strong liquor, put on by the Anglo-American evangelical front with its 'world' conventions, and Jabez Bunting found that he could no more keep Methodism insular than he could keep it conservative. Likewise Methodism responded to the great international economic tides as did other social movements; the long-term economic processes at work in England were continually multiplying the number of people among whom Methodism might obtain a hearing, and, as we shall see, the cyclical movements also marked its progress from year to year.

I

Within the limits of this introduction, however, we must concentrate upon the local rather than the international bearings of the English Churches and society. The English establishment – to use the phrase in its general sense – was not only unlike every other; it was new even in England. The establishment was made up of the aristocracy, the country gentry, the Anglican Church, the legal profession, the older and privileged commercial and financial interests, the fighting services and the permanent civil service. This group of interests had only lately been so bound together. For most of the eighteenth century the bulk of the gentry had been in opposition, and among them and in the universities there had been a current of Jacobitism or subversive revolutionary politics. In the same way a great many of the clergy had gone into opposition soon after the Hanoverian accession, and the breach between them and the Court was not healed until the reign of George III. The new political issues of that reign, however, induced many dons, parsons and gentry gradually to surrender their opposition politics for fear that worse things than government influence might befall them. In the age of Hoadly, high-church clergy and Tory gentry had harboured the suspicion that liberal rationalism had been a device of Whig ministers to undermine the Church; but early in the reign of George III liberal rationalism was the badge of an outsider like Wilkes against whom Court influence might be turned. Conservative opinion swung further in the government's favour during the American War of Independence, even while radical criticism hardened. After the Hanoverian accession the Dissenters had been hand in glove with a wicked government, but now they vocally supported their brethren across the seas against the authority of the Crown in Parliament, and derived from their notion of the Church as a federation of gathered congregations the analogy of an imperial system providing for Home Rule. If the Dissenters were again going into opposition, the Church came back to court and profited from the revulsion of imperial sentiment, losing nothing when the outworks of the ascendancy were whittled away to facilitate the recruitment of Irish Catholics to the armed forces. The discontent of Dissenters was revealed again after the American war in agitations for the repeal of the Test and Corporation Acts, and Church and Court again drew closer. The agitations of the Dissenters, and the parliamentary weakness of Pitt's government were both ended by the horror of the upper classes at the development of the Revolution in France. Some of the Dissenters and their political sympathizers were bold enough to associate themselves with revolution abroad, and to churchmen it seemed that liberal rationalism led in both countries to unbelief, anarchy and revolution.[2] The English bishops denounced the French Revolution as they had not denounced anything for years, and the revival of high-church sentiment was encouraged by the atrocity stories brought over by a trickle of Catholic priests from France. No more telling argument

[2] There was some ground for this view. In 1790 a Unitarian attempt to lead the Dissenters of Lancashire and Cheshire against the Test and Corporation Acts foundered when the Independents and Baptists discovered that the agitation was being used to cloak an effort to abolish the liturgy and the tithes of the Church of England: *Manchester Mercury*, 2 March, 9 March, 6 April, 1790.

could have been devised for the need of Church and State to stand together than the events of the revolutionary epoch. The Revolution finally completed the growth of a party of order in England of a kind which had not been seen before, and cemented the union of the Church with the other elements of the establishment. Gentry and parish clergy felt at home with bishops and government to a degree unknown since the latter days of good Queen Anne, and striking changes were evident among the erstwhile anarchists of the University of Oxford. Not only were the dons and their burgesses ministerial politicians, but they forgot their old animosity against episcopal Visitors, and their college claims to be lay corporations, and blossomed out as the conscience and right arm of the Church. When in 1800 they reformed their examinations, they demanded one new thing, a compulsory examination in the elements of religion and doctrinal articles, which, so far as anyone knew, no other university in the world required for an arts degree. The high-church press acclaimed this means of checking the plague which had issued from the seminaries abroad to overthrow the dearest interests of the human race, 'the sophisms of that reptile philosophy, which would materialise and brutify the whole intellectual system'.[3] Oxford, like the rest of the establishment, was pledged against revolution, and, at the time of Pusey's and Newman's birth, had made a bow to the notion of church education which they as young men were to claim as an indelible character.

The new establishment was subject to two great challenges, one immediate and overt, the other subterranean and unplanned but no less radical in the end. The open challenge came from the Irish Catholics and their English allies, the covert challenge from the astonishing social development of the next thirty years.

II

The Act of Union of 1801 transformed Ireland from an imperial into a domestic problem, and the new Irish Catholic

[3] *British Magazine*, i (1800), 425-6.

vote, which in the short run had been fatal to government from Dublin Castle, was in the long run very nearly fatal to government from Westminster. Over the past generation events had done much to draw together the denominational factions lying at the root of Irish political life, and the Enlightenment had so blurred the lines between Catholic and Protestant as to persuade the optimists that within a short time their beliefs would be indistinguishable. No one, more-over, could be more firmly pledged against the French Revolution than the Catholics, so that recent history conspired with present embarrassments to secure the vote for the Irish Catholics in 1793, and negotiations for emancipation after the Union. The old English squirearchical Catholicism was now at its lowest ebb,[4] and, to men of conservative inclina-tions like William Windham, the only threat to the English Church came from the might of Napoleon and revolutionary France. To save Ireland and England from that threat, emancipation was a small price. To the Whigs too, casting about for some issue to revive their flagging fortunes, the cause of emancipation seemed to offer new hope. It was true that the conscience of George III, stiffened by interested parties, brought down Pitt's government in the midst of emancipation negotiations in 1801, and wrecked the Talents ministry on the score of much smaller concessions in 1807. But no one suspected that the King would live as long as he did, still less that in office the conscience of the Prince Regent would turn stoutly Protestant; and in a period of very weak government, a conjunction of circumstances like those which brought about the election of the pro-Catholic Grenville as Chancellor of the Protestant University of Oxford in 1809, might land the country with a ministry able and willing to grant Catholic relief. After 1812, Grenville and the Whigs proved to be a spent force, but emancipation remained an open issue in the cabinet. After the death of Castlereagh in 1822 ministerial Toryism became more liberal, and emancipa-tion at the hands of Canning and his friends became an imminent prospect. Scarcely had the clergy generally come to

[4] For details of its distribution in one of its old strongholds, Lancashire, see Cheshire County Record Office: MS. account of papists within the diocese [of Chester].

court than they found professional politicians willing to seek salvation at the expense of the Ascendancy.

Thus the nineteenth century opened with churchmen having to justify their privileges in what was evidently a plural society, and a process of argument and adjustment began which proved during the next hundred years one of the most interesting features of English politics. The arguments of the great constitutional writers of the last century were now given a specifically anti-Catholic twist and men of letters such as Southey, Coleridge and Wordsworth, and later churchmen such as Newman, Keble and Blomfield set themselves to restate the theory of the Protestant constitution. The crux of the matter was that the subordination of Catholics was the fundamental law of the constitution. The British constitution was of unrivalled excellence, and it had taken shape after an open challenge from popery had been rebuffed under James II and measures had been taken to prevent its recurrence. The religious and secular advantages secured by the constitution could not be separated, and this made it impossible to change the constitutional status of the Church. Moreover, while lay authority in the Church was represented by Parliament it was absurd to admit Roman Catholics. No one believed that religion and politics were separable issues; religious liberty was guaranteed for all parties by the combination of Anglican ascendancy with toleration for minorities. It was Rome's evident intention to subordinate the State to the Church; the loyalties of the Catholic were therefore bound to be divided. This belief underlay the repeated efforts to obtain from the Catholics certain 'securities', one of the chief of which was a royal veto upon the appointment of their bishops. None of these views was in principle foolish, and if the disasters which emancipation portended to the Protestant constitutionists were long in fulfilment, they were ultimately fulfilled to the letter.

Liberal churchmen shared too many of the assumptions on which this view was based to be able readily to frame a cogent reply, and too often contented themselves with arguments from expediency or with abusing their opponents as backwoodsmen. In 1810, however, Edward Copleston, fellow of Oriel, and the chief pillar of the politics of Grenville and Canning in the University of Oxford, put the case that the basic documents of the constitution so cherished by the Protestants must be construed in the light of a higher principle:

> The argument of *abstract right and justice* has always appeared to me untenable, and inconsistent with the principle, that the Church establishment is an essential part of the Constitution. That principle I maintain in its fullest extent; . . .
>
> Still it is an undisputed maxim of English government, that an equal participation of civil rights shall be enjoyed by all ranks and persuasions, as far as is consistent with the public good. The imposition, therefore, or the relaxation of these disabilities, will ever be a varying and not a fundamental rule of policy. . . . Unless this position were admitted, with what conscience could we carry up an Address to the Throne, talking of the *wisdom of our forefathers* who imposed restraints on Catholics, and yet expressing satisfaction *at the repeal of the greatest part of them* within the present reign?[5]

The pragmatic considerations urged by Copleston proved ultimately decisive. In 1823 Daniel O'Connell established in the Catholic Association a pressure group to challenge English authority at every point. His activities would in any case have made it impossible for the British government to maintain its neutral attitude to the Catholic claims, but they were set against the mounting tempo of the Irish agrarian crisis. In 1828 and 1829 violence was widespread and civil war seemed imminent. Any prospect that the British government might try to restore the situation by strong tactics was ruled out by the final disintegration of the Pittite Tory party which had ruled England for so long.

The stresses within the party had grown up over a number of issues of policy, of which emancipation was one of the chief, and were exacerbated by Peel's and Wellington's distrust of Canning, whom they rightly suspected of pursuing

[5] [E. Copleston] *A letter to John Coker, of New College, Esq.* (Oxford 1810), pp. 13–15. On these grounds Copleston seems to have favoured the admission of Jews to civil rights: *Remains of the late Edward Copleston D.D., Bishop of Llandaff*, ed. R. Whately (London 1854), pp. 36–7. Copleston, who in 1814 became Provost, was the leading light among the Oriel Noetics, against whose influence Newman and Keble eventually rebelled.

the succession to Liverpool with Whig support. On Liverpool's resignation in February 1827 they finally refused to serve with him, and the Tory party broke in half. Six months later Canning died, and at the beginning of 1828 the succession fell to Peel and Wellington with a cabinet composed partly of Canningites and partly of old friends from the Liverpool ministry. Immediately the constitution in Church and State was in danger. A united pressure group of Nonconformist bodies had taken advantage of Canning's accession to office to stage an agitation for the repeal of the Test and Corporation Acts, which in form at least restricted their access to office. The Catholic issue was now so overwhelming that there was not much hostility to concessions to Dissenters even in Oxford,[6] and the motion for repeal was carried against the government. But this ill omen did not exhaust the legacy of Canning. On a question of Parliamentary reform the Canningites led by Huskisson resigned; Vesey Fitzgerald, the minister who succeeded him, had to stand for re-election in County Clare and was overwhelmed by Daniel O'Connell. The government was now faced with the alternatives of emancipation or civil war in Ireland, and, to the utter disgust of the Protestant constitutionists and the young high-church friends of Newman and Keble, made the only possible choice.

From now on events followed thick and fast. The Catholic Emancipation crisis produced the party chaos which gave the Whigs a wholly unexpected chance to return to power in 1830, and which was never remedied for long under the reformed constitution. It was also a tremendous shock to the Church and her political supporters. For years the Church had clung to the establishment, and yet now a government in which the chief figure was M.P. for the University of Oxford had purchased the survival of the unreformed political system at the expense of the unreformed Church. A bitter resentment at this betrayal flared up in Oxford and elsewhere, a fierce Toryism which none the less regarded the official Tory leaders as exemplars of a lack of political principle, and a realization that if the Church and its privileges were to

<hr>

[6] B.M. Add. MSS. 40343, fo. 189. Cf. Colchester diary, iii, 553.

be defended it must be on grounds quite other than those of the 'Church-and-State men'. Nor had the Protestant constitution party fired their last shot. They concluded that if the unreformed political system could produce such a result it was time to change the system. In the elections of 1830 Lord Eldon had his Northumberland tenants voting for Lord Grey, and on 25 November a meeting of the 'Ultras' decided to support Brougham's motion on reform. That very night Peel was beaten, and Lord Grey formed a government which included four Canningites, four friends of Lord Liverpool, and the ultra-Tory Duke of Richmond.

III

The Reform crisis, however, bore a much closer resemblance to revolution than to the crises produced by the shifting of political factions in the previous century. In order to see how this came about, and how the Church, having lost its old constitutional standing, was threatened with disestablishment or even worse, we must examine the social developments of the previous generation; for both agrarian and industrial developments threatened the Church with unparalleled ruin.

The Industrial Revolution was preceded and accompanied by important changes in British agriculture. By the 1830s the population had at least doubled since the middle of the previous century, yet the great bulk of the grain which sustained them was still produced at home. Commercial attitudes in English agriculture had set in early and were driven deep by the demands of the new market. Output was increased by better farming, by extending the area of cultivation, and by changes in agricultural organization. Inevitably these developments deeply concerned a Church which was primarily a confederation of country parishes. On the economic side, endowed chiefly by full or partial ownership of land, the Church had the largest stake in the prosperity of the agricultural industry. Nor was this simply a matter for bishops and chapters, cathedrals and colleges; it struck home in every parish. The parson's three chief sources of income were his glebe, the fees he earned for spiritual services, and the tithes which he drew as co-parcenary owner of the land and which, particularly in the case of rectories, were generally the staple of his living. In 1836, when the residue of the tithe was compulsorily commuted for a corn-rent, tithe was still worth £4,000,000 per annum, three-quarters of which was in church hands. This sum in purchasing power very greatly exceeded the present revenues of the Church Commissioners, and in defending and increasing a regressive tax on gross output which bore particularly hardly on the yield of expensive improvements, or on reduced income in bad times, the Church had become seriously embarrassed in the countryside.

The most spectacular change in English agriculture after the middle of the eighteenth century came with the piecemeal enclosure by Acts of Parliament of the great belt of open-field country which stretched right across the south Midlands and went up through Lincolnshire into Yorkshire. Substantial landowners everywhere in this region assumed that they would get the best return from the new market only by enclosing the land and safeguarding the improvers from the interference of their neighbours. The result was that in 1759 a spate of enclosure Acts began which swelled to a torrent whenever food prices rose or money was cheap. But, profitable as it was expected to be, enclosure was a costly business, and the legal and parliamentary expenses, the payment of surveyors, the making of fences, roads and drains, consumed immense sums. Improving landlords, therefore, aimed at getting rid of the burden which tithe imposed upon their expected increase in output.

The result was that in the great majority of enclosure Acts tithe was commuted. In the early enclosure Acts in the Holderness area the tithe was commuted for cash payments, but before long price increases showed how this could operate to the disadvantage of the clergy. Subsequently the tithe was commuted half for money and half for land, and later still for land alone,[7] a solution to which landowners and tithe-owners alike pinned their hopes. The only exceptions to this

[7] *Parliamentary papers*, H.C. 1836, XLIV: H. E. Strickland, *A General View of the Agriculture of the East Riding of Yorkshire* (York 1812), p. 55. For a further treatment of this theme, see my paper in *The Journal of Ecclesiastical History*, xvi (1965), 67–81: 'The Tithe Question in England in the Early Nineteenth Century'.

general rule were firstly that, in parishes where there was a large number of small proprietors whose holdings were too small for parcels to be conveniently removed and added to the glebe, the small men often commuted their tithe for cash payments, and secondly that when food prices soared during the war years some canny tithe-owners provided for commutation in whole or in part for a corn-rent, that is the cash value of a given output of corn.

The terms of commutation were remarkably generous to the clergy. In the early Acts one-seventh or one-eighth of the acreage of the parish was regarded as the equivalent for tithes of all kinds; during the war years the equivalent sometimes rose to one-fifth of the arable and one-eighth of the pasture, and there were exceptional cases like the enclosure at Shipton Bellinger in Hampshire in 1792 where the tithe-owner received three-tenths of the land in the parish, and the vicarial tithes were still to remain payable.[8] It is not entirely clear how the church and lay impropriators managed to drive so hard a bargain. However, no enclosure Act could be obtained without the consent of the tithe-owners as co-parcenary proprietors of the land; the bishops encouraged the parsons to stick out for an equivalent to the full improved value of the tithe as it might be expected to stand after enclosure, and proprietors normally wanted their enclosures and their exemption from tithe sufficiently to pay a high price in land and to relieve the tithe-owner of all expense, even to ring-fencing his property for him.

These changes in the distribution of property were the more important because they were concentrated in particular areas. There was no significant amount of commutation in the old enclosed areas of Lancashire and Cheshire, or in the south-east or the south-west of the country. On the other hand there was much enclosure right through the south Midlands, and a great amount in the eastern belt stretching north from Cambridgeshire and Bedfordshire to Lincolnshire and Yorkshire. Thus, at the very time when Churches within reach of Revolutionary France were losing property whole-

[8] For these and subsequent details, see *Parliamentary papers*, H.C. 1831-2, XXX: 1836, XLIV.

sale, the Church of England was gaining it on a substantial scale throughout the Midlands and the east.

It is impossible to define precisely the scale of land transference, but the impression created by the available statistical material[9] is that commutation multiplied the average glebe by a factor of two or three. In addition, spiritual corporations, and colleges of the ancient universities which were now standing forth as church bodies, profited by the commutation of their rectorial tithes.

But the thing which was obvious in the country parishes of the newly enclosed areas was the sudden rise in the standing and affluence of many of the parsons. The stories, in the agricultural improvers' propaganda, of livings doubling or trebling in value overnight were not exaggerated, and right through Yorkshire, Lincolnshire and Northamptonshire there were instances of parsons possessed of many hundred, sometimes more than a thousand, acres of glebe. At a time when respectability in the country could be gauged in terms of acres, the profession as a whole had greatly increased its holdings and, as the average man in the parish could not fail to note, had done so in a measure at the expense of the peasant proprietors. Their part in the whole transaction was only underlined by their frequent appointment as commissioners to carry out enclosure schemes.[10] Moreover, the new affluence (in which the parsons who had extended their tithe rights or broken old compositions also participated, especially during the war years of high food prices) often separated the parson from his people in the most literal sense: the old mud and wattle parsonage which had been good enough in the days when the parson was simply a peasant with a university degree, would do no more; he moved out of the village, sometimes out of the parish altogether. Cobbett never wearied of the gibe that the parsons let their houses fall down in order to find an excuse for non-residence,[11] and certainly the parsons made no bones

[9] *Parliamentary papers*, H.C. 1867, LIV: 1887, LXIV.

[10] M. W. Beresford, 'Commissioners of Enclosure', in *The Economic History Review*, xvi, 139.

[11] William Cobbett, *Rural Rides*, ed. G. D. H. & M. Cole (London 1930), i, 108; ii, 383, 402, 406, 416, 441; cf. [J. Wade] *The Extraordinary Black Book* (London 1832), pp. 34, 37.

about being now too grand for their residences. In 1817 an Act was passed nullifying contracts to let houses in which bishops required clergy to reside, and requiring beneficed clergy to keep their houses in repair;[12] in 1818 the parsons declared that the houses in 2,183 of the 7,700 parishes which had houses were unfit and described them to their bishops in such terms as: 'scarcely fit to be inhabited by labourers'; 'merely a labourer's cottage'; 'small old cottage fit only for a pauper, built of mud, &c.'.[13] It soon became apparent that parsons could not be fixed in their parishes without extensive building of houses, houses which were shockingly symptomatic of the new status assumed by the country clergy and which have been millstones round the necks of their successors ever since. To quote only one tract of enclosure country, the parsonages in 112 out of 178 Oxfordshire parishes were built or extensively repaired in the first half of the century, and the new stipends and houses attracted many more incumbents of gentle birth than before.[14] It became orthodox doctrine that the proper function of pastoral oversight was to induce deference through respectability.[15] From inside the rectory this civilizing mission looked somewhat different; one thinks of the entry in the diary of Benjamin Newton, rector of the recently enclosed Yorkshire parish of Wath, for 6 February 1817:

> Went hunting with Mr Bell's hounds, had tolerable sport, these hounds please me much as they are attended by gentlemen only, no farmers.[16]

While the status of the clergy was thus improving, the lot of the labourers was getting worse. Enclosures often meant loss of amenity, the loss of illegal but valuable advantages in

---

[12] 57 Geo. III c. 99.

[13] *Parliamentary papers*, H.L. 1818, XCIII e.g. pp. 11, 117, 146, 173, 179, 205, 211, 215.

[14] Diana McClatchey, *Oxfordshire Clergy 1777–1869* (Oxford 1960), p. 22. This whole chapter contains much information about Oxfordshire parsonages and the declining willingness of the clergy to admit plebeian origins.

[15] *The Quarterly Review*, xxix, no. 58 (July 1823), p. 551; M. Cove, *An Inquiry into the Necessity, Justice & Policy of a Commutation of Tithes* (Hereford 1800), p. 47.

[16] C. P. Fendall & E. A. Crutchley (eds), *The Diary of Benjamin Newton, Rector of Wath, 1816–1818* (Cambridge 1933), p. 51.

grazing on the common and open-field stubble, and the growth of pauperism. The sheer cost of the poor rate drove the magistrates after the wars to reduce steadily the bread scales which under the original Speenhamland scheme had been supposed to guarantee a bare subsistence. In this process not only the churchwardens but also the clergy took a leading part. The steady concentration of land-ownership was leaving more and more parishes without a resident squire, and in parts of the country the administration of justice and the conduct of county business was imperilled by the fact that lay magistrates lived so far apart. Who better to take their place than the newly arrived squarson? By 1830 a quarter of the entire bench of magistrates were clergy, and while it is true that the fringes of the country where resident squires were thin on the ground had the highest proportion of clerical magistrates, the parsons' steady rise in affluence had given them practical control of the bench throughout large tracts of the area of enclosure where there was no special shortage of gentry. Prominent among the examples given by the Webbs were the East Riding and Lincolnshire.[17] Never before or since has England seen so much clerical government as in the half-century before the Reform Act. The clergy seemed to be profiting from the upheaval in the countryside and to be the instruments of government in pauperizing the labourers. It is not surprising that after 1832 their ranks on the bench were thinned not only by a Whig government which disliked Tories, and by Lords Lieutenant who disliked their tendency towards the 'collective regulation of morality', but by Bishop Blomfield, who knew what damage had been done to their pastoral character by their well-meaning activities in local government.[18] For there is not much doubt that while commutation of tithe greatly reduced the friction between the clergy and the farmers, it helped to alienate them from small freeholders and labourers.

These social changes seem to have underlain the spread of Dissent in great areas innocent of all industry – and also of all

[17] Sidney & Beatrice Webb, *English Local Government from the Revolution to the Municipal Corporations Act: the Parish and the County* (London 1906), p. 384, n.2.
[18] F. C. Mather, *Public Order in the Age of the Chartists* (Manchester 1959), p. 56.

affection for the clergy. At the time of the religious census of 1851 the Dissenters had established a long lead over the Church in the East and North Ridings, in Lincolnshire and Bedfordshire, and were ahead in Huntingdonshire; while in Northamptonshire, Buckinghamshire and Norfolk, they were within striking distance of drawing level. All these areas except Norfolk were great enclosure areas, and all bore out the complaints audible from the 1790s onwards that the clergy were utterly losing their influence in the countryside.[19] What is more interesting is that they were also great revival territories. The Yorkshire and Lincolnshire revivalists had a legendary reputation in the old Wesleyanism,[20] while the East Riding was the scene of the greatest triumphs of the Primitives, the famous Hull circuit giving birth to no less than thirty others. In Huntingdonshire and Bedfordshire the great strength of Dissent was among the Baptists and Independents, old bodies which responded to the tide of revival; the minority Dissent of the other south Midland counties (whose progress was perhaps checked by the fact that large areas here went back to grass after enclosure, and employment consequently diminished)[21] nevertheless formed a significant part of the national strength of those denominations. And in those areas, however much they might differ from the Methodists in theology, they did not differ very much in practice. The Baptists were strong revivalists, and when William Ferguson, the Congregational minister of Bicester, came in the middle of the nineteenth century to prescribe for the ills of the rural Independent congregations created in past revivals and now struggling, he advocated the wholesale adoption of Primitive Methodist preaching methods and the circuit system.[22] But it was not only the Independents who were in difficulties; the rural poverty which Ferguson and that die-hard of disestablishment, Edward Miall, expected to

[19] D. Davies, *The Case of Labourers in Husbandry Stated and Considered* (London 1795), pp. 94–5; W. Cobbett, *Rural Rides*, e.g., i, 212, 217, 290; ii, 381, 443.

[20] Benjamin Gregory, *Side Lights on the Conflicts of Methodism during the Second Quarter of the Nineteenth Century 1827–1852* (London 1899), pp. 179, 247.

[21] W. G. Hoskins, *The Midland Peasant: The Economic and Social History of a Leicestershire Village* (London 1957), p. 261.

[22] W. Ferguson, *Our Rural Churches: Their Perils, and the Remedy* (London 1849), pp. 8–9.

end in revolution, [23] set insoluble problems to the established Church as well. Compulsory conformity in the countryside was about to break down, and the statistics of 1851 flatter the real strength of the rural Church. When deference finally ceased rural Nonconformity had its last real chance. The Primitive Methodists who had transformed themselves from a local revival into a denomination by getting a foothold in Lincolnshire, and proving Lincolnshire methods in the East Riding, were now best placed to take advantage of the opportunity, and had missions going at full blast in areas as widely separated as Shropshire, Wiltshire and Norfolk.[24] The momentum they had acquired in the enclosure areas had carried them beyond its bounds.

IV

Even in the enclosure areas tithe remained on half or more of the land; in the areas of old enclosure and in Wales, where tithe was not commuted on the new enclosures of hill-pasture, payment went on as before. During the great boom in agricultural prices during the war the value of tithe increased,[25] and although some vicars and curates suffered from the increased cost of living,[26] many rectors shared in the generally increased affluence of the clerical estate. Rising rents made a golden age for the land-owning classes and did not prevent the farmers from prospering and enlarging their farms. But in 1814 corn prices broke; they broke again more decisively in 1820, and although the next twenty years were not all gloom for the agricultural industry, things remained difficult until the later 'thirties, and did not become rosy till the middle of the century. After long prosperity the first break seemed catastrophic. Long leases which had been the recipe for

[23] W. Ferguson, *The Impending Dangers of Our Country: or, Hidden Things Brought to Light* (London 1848); Edward Miall, *The Social Influences of the State-Church* (London 1867), pp. 42–6.

[24] cf. J. M. Ludlow & Lloyd Jones, *Progress of the Working Class 1832–1867* (London 1876), pp. 280–1, 289–95; J. W. & Anne Tibble (eds), *The Letters of John Clare* (London 1951), p. 161; and Clare's poem, 'The Parish: a Satire'.

[25] e.g., W. Gooch, *General View of the Agriculture of the County of Cambridge* (London 1813), p. 35.

[26] *Reflections by a layman and a farmer on the present state of certain of the clergy of the established church* (London 1812), pp. 3–4.

progressive farming were a millstone round the necks of tenants who had to pay wartime rents out of post-war prices; those who had borrowed from country banks to enlarge their holdings were in desperate straits; the banks themselves collapsed by the score. Farm labourers had enjoyed little of the prosperity of the industry even in the best years and now faced a deeper decline into pauperism, embittered by the inevitable efforts of the upper classes to restrain the crippling rise in the poor rates. North of a line drawn from south Lincolnshire to central Shropshire opportunities for industrial employment did something to keep up agricultural wage rates, and the pasture land of the west Midlands and the south-west did not suffer as heavily as the corn-growing country further east. The worse effects of agricultural depression were therefore felt in the counties from Dorset to Norfolk, most of which lay to the south and east of the enclosure territory.

The agricultural interest responded to its problems by a violent agitation. Its first concern was for prices. A Corn Law was obtained in 1815 which forbade the import of foreign corn till English prices reached 80 shillings a quarter, and although the law did not save English farmers from much lower prices and was greatly modified in later years, it remained a powerful emotive symbol for the whole agricultural interest, not least because it was very nearly all they obtained. When prices continued to drop, a section of the landed interest joined forces with other business interests and all those who had the interest of debtors at heart. To all these, deflation seemed a consequence of the financial orthodoxy which triumphed with the return to cash payments in 1819. In fact, prices were falling abroad as well as at home, among other reasons because of great technological advances, but paper and credit had something to be said for them, and they became the stock-in-trade of agrarian and radical agitators both in Britain and the United States. English financial policy, however, had come under the influence of the orthodox economists and the leaders of the cotton industry, and they were not to be shifted. The farmers' last resort was to scale down the overheads on the industry. Rent-reductions were unpopular with the landlords, but took place willy-nilly. Where the other overheads, taxes and tithe, were concerned, landlords and farmers could stand together. A great howl went up for reduced taxes, and for the only means of obtaining them, namely, a cut in public spending and in the interest on the national debt. There were explosions of fury against placemen and the moneyed interest, and the cry against tithe led to astonishing outbursts against the Church from its old allies in the agricultural interest.[27] Local meetings of the clergy to defend their interests were sorely abused,[28] and by 1822 radical pamphleteers could see no hope of salvation except from a capital levy beginning with church property, the English being now 'the only people who have a large mass of ecclesiastical wealth in reserve'.[29]

Tithe was burdensome not only on expensive improvements; as a regressive impost it fell cruelly upon diminished agricultural income. It was no longer one of the inevitable hazards. Over a great tract of country the tithe system had been dismantled piecemeal by the enclosure legislation, and in 1799 Pitt had considered allowing land-owners to redeem it; in return the clergy were to be paid from the funds a sum which might be periodically augmented as the cost of living mounted.[30] The bishops defeated this attempt to transform the clergy openly into state pensioners, but it was symptomatic of the fact that no one now took tithe for granted in England – much less in Ireland, where events were moving inexorably towards the catastrophe of the great famine. Tithe-levying was also a source of anxiety. Unless there was a deadlock between parson and farmer, tithe was not often taken in kind at the beginning of the nineteenth century, except in the north-west and the south-east. In Cumberland, in Westmorland, in the great tract of Lancashire from the Ribble to the Mersey, and in Cheshire, at least some of the

[27] L. P. Adams, *Agricultural Depression and Farm Relief in England, 1813–52* (London 1932), pp. 76–7; cf. W. Edmeads, *National Establishment, National Security; or, Thoughts on the Consequences of Commuting the Tithes* (Oxford 1816), p. 2; *The Edinburgh Review*, xxvi, no. 52 (June 1816), 277–81.

[28] *The sacred and indefeasible rights of the clergy* (London 1817).

[29] *Remarks on the consumption of public wealth by the clergy*, 2nd edn (London 1822).

[30] *Anecdotes of the Life of Richard Watson, Bishop of Llandaff; Written by Himself at Different Intervals, and Revised in 1814*, ed. R. Watson (London 1817), pp. 306–9.

produce was tithed in kind, though even here the custom was steadily dying out.[31] The real home of tithes in kind seems to have been in Hampshire, parts of Sussex, Middlesex, Surrey and Kent.[32] But it is unlikely that more than a fifth of the total yield was taken in kind.[33] Most parsons cut out the cost of collection and settled for a cash composition at less than the full value of the tithe, and many leased their tithes to landlord or farmer for a period of years.[34] These leases relieved the improving farmer of the burden upon his marginal increases in production, and had been advantageous during the booming years of the war; but thereafter, when prices tumbled, the boot was on the other foot. Cases were quoted where the tithe became as large as the rent. Of course the parsons, like the landlords, often met the farmers in their distress, and accepted less than their legal due in order to keep farms tenanted;[35] but there were also refusals. To the farmer working for the market, tithe, the reward of a co-parcenary owner of the land who risked no capital in the industry, began to appear intolerable, and the Irish Tithe Composition Act of 1823 indicated a way out for the English. In 1828 an unsuccessful Tithe Commutation Bill was promoted, and early in 1830 the Primate himself was introducing a bill.

By this time the tithe question had broadened and become greatly exacerbated. *The Edinburgh Review* sought to turn

[31] J. Bailey & G. Culley, *General View of the Agriculture of the County of Cumberland* (London 1805), p. 210; A. Pringle, *General View of the Agriculture of the County of Westmorland* (London 1805), p. 305; R. W. Dickson & W. Stevenson, *General View of the Agriculture of Lancashire* (London 1815), pp. 127–30; H. Holland, *General View of the Agriculture of Cheshire* (London 1808), p. 104.

[32] C. Vancouver, *General View of the Agriculture of Hampshire, including the Isle of Wight* (London 1813), pp. 77, 80, 84–5, 87–9; A. Young, *General View of the Agriculture of the County of Sussex* (London 1808), p. 31; J. Middleton, *View of the Agriculture of Middlesex*, 2nd edn (London 1807), p. 66; W. Stevenson, *General View of the Agriculture of the County of Surrey* (London 1809), pp. 92, 94; J. Boys, *General View of the Agriculture of the County of Kent*, 2nd edn (London 1805), pp. 39–43.

[33] In a speech in the Commons in 1835, Peel declared that in the property assessments of 1810 tithe compositions were returned at £1,932,000, and tithe in kind at £421,000 (*Parliamentary debates*, 3rd ser., xxvii, 200). These figures suggest that the parsons were extremely adept at evading their income tax, and it is conceivable that tithe in kind, being harder to conceal than cash, evaded tax less readily, and so formed an even smaller proportion of the real receipts under this heading.

[34] J. Farey, *General View of the Agriculture of Derbyshire* (London 1813), ii, 29; cf. T. Davis, *General View of the Agriculture of Wiltshire* (London 1813), p. 27.

[35] R. C. Gaut, *A History of Worcestershire Agriculture and Rural Evolution* (Worcester 1939), p. 255.

consumers against tithe by the argument that it kept up prices.[36] The radical discovery that a quarter of the tithe had originally been set aside for the poor involved the labourers,[37] and they were now drawn into the question by the inexorable growth of pauperism, a grinding poverty aggravated by the gradual ruin of the domestic textile industries by the competition of the factory. By the end of 1830 even the Tory *Quarterly Review* admitted that tithe must depress the margin of cultivation, hinder investment and reduce agricultural employment, the lack of which was now an urgent social issue.[38]

Rural discontent came to a climax in the autumn of 1830, when the southern farmers determined to use the distress of the labourers as a weapon against their overheads. In rural as well as industrial areas 1830 was one of the decisive years. The leaders of the Church virtually gave up the current system before the farmers' attacks. The arguments for cheap government were now applied to the Church, and a meeting at Penenden Heath in Kent in that year resolved that

> however essential the aid of wealth and honours may have hitherto been to the Church of England, to enable her to lure to her service men of learning and talent, . . . the necessity for such aid happily no longer exists. . . . The well-paid labours of those eminent men, who, attracted by the splendid rewards of the Church, have enlisted in her cause, have so simplified the clerical duties as to make them practicable by persons of ordinary capacities and acquirements; . . . for its comprehensive Liturgy, by supplying all the formularies of devotion, whether for prayer or praise, imprecation or benediction, disavowal or belief, and also strictly enjoining the various occasions upon which they are to be respectively used, affords no opportunity for the exercise of judgment, the exhibition of talent, or the display of learning. . . . Nor do the duties of the preacher, any more than the minister, require an education superior to that which is usually bestowed upon the middling class of society; for the inexhaustible stores of invaluable sermons which have emanated from the labours of those highly-gifted divines who have, at different periods, shed a

---

[36] *The Edinburgh Review*, xxxiv, no. 67 (August 1820), 61–79: 'Plan for a Commutation of Tithes'.
[37] *Extraordinary Black Book*, pp. 11–12.
[38] *The Quarterly Review*, xliii, no. 85 (May 1830), pp. 252–3.

lustre upon the English Church, afford a fund of instruction admirably adapted for every purpose, and to select from which requires but a moderate portion of literary attainments. The qualifications for the proper performance of these functions being few, and the acquisition of them not requiring expense, as they consist principally of propriety of demeanour, and the possession of the natural advantages of suitable voice and delivery, but moderate stipends would be necessary to ensure a sufficient number of competent candidates, and the payment of these stipends might be safely left to the generosity of their respective congregations; . . .[39]

In the autumn of 1830 the labourers' revolt broke out in Kent and spread rapidly through the southern counties as far as Dorset. Demands for higher wages were backed up by rick-burning and machine-breaking. The ominous feature of this jacquerie was that in many places the rural middle class, the farmers, refused to support the tithe.[40] The farmers convinced the labourers that without reductions of tithe they could not increase wages, and the clergy and lay impropriators often suffered personal violence. The labourers were ruthlessly put down by the government, but the farmers were not spared in the comments of the judges or the editorials of *The Times*:

> But the knavery of the farmers! What scoundrels! To induce their labourers to believe that they should receive higher wages if they would but first endanger their lives for them, – if they would but run the slight hazard of the gallows, by murdering the clergyman of the parish if he would not give up his tithes, or a portion thereof, to them, the farmers.[41]

Yet what else could be expected from men driven by agricultural depression to the views expressed on Penenden Heath? By exerting their strength at the crucial moment the farmers carried the day; and the fact that the Reform and Irish crises delayed a settlement until 1836 only injured the

[39] *Parliamentary debates*, new ser., xxiv, 821–2.
[40] For a general account of the revolt, see J. L. & B. Hammond, *The Village Labourer 1760–1832*, Chapters X, XI; J. R. M. Butler, *The Passing of the Great Reform Bill* (London 1914), pp. 113 (n.2), 130–2; *Parliamentary debates*, 3rd ser., i, 1316, 1333–4.
[41] *The Times*, 31 December 1830.

interest of the Church. Once some form of commutation became inevitable, tithe-owners by the hundred began proceedings to establish their full claim;[42] and, most scandalous of all, though tithe upon the profits of labour had not been heard of for centuries, the Rector of Lockington in the East Riding made a claim upon fourteen labourers whose pay ranged from 6 guineas to 18 pounds per year, and upon default of payment lodged one of them in the house of correction at Beverley upon the warrant of a clerical magistrate.[43] When tithe was finally commuted for a corn-rent in 1836 the Church got a very much worse bargain than in the days of enclosure bills: the corn-rent was computed on the average of the last seven years' yield, and where (as in the great majority of cases) there had been a cash composition, the composition rather than the tithe was taken as the basis of assessment.[44] Nor could anyone foresee what a rent-charge varying with the price of corn would cost the Church when prices tumbled again in the 'seventies.

The tithe issue, however, cost more than money. It is true that in the south-east, where the tithe issue was at its worst, Dissent made little progress, notwithstanding reports that the farmers were opening conventicles to spite the parson[45] and that Dissenting or Methodist preachers often spoke for the labourers.[46] The farmers were in no mood to add the expenses of voluntaryism to those of tithe, and neither Methodism nor any other form of Nonconformity ever flourished among men as desperate as the farm-labourers of the south in 1830. Only in Norfolk, which lay full in the track of the Primitive Methodist advance from Lincolnshire and Nottinghamshire, were there any substantial gains. But the Church suffered irrevocable losses nevertheless, and Cobbett's continual

---

[42] Some colleges became notorious for their actions, e.g. at Kendal (*Parliamentary debates*, 3rd ser., vi, 589–90; xx, 880; *Parliamentary papers*, H.C. 1837, VI pp. 58–62; *The Times*, 4 September 1833, p.5) and Hornchurch (*Parliamentary debates*, 3rd ser., ii, 29–38); cf. *Parliamentary debates*, 3rd ser., xx, 608–10, 709–10, 794–6, 831–3, 868–71, 879–84.

[43] *The Times*, 30 August 1833, pp. 2, 3.

[44] Tithe Commutation Act, 6 & 7 William IV, c. 71, cl. xxxvii.

[45] *The Times*, 10 February 1831, p. 5.

[46] *The Times*, 17 November 1830; quoted in J. L. & B. Hammond, op. cit. (London 1911), p. 247.

reports of declining clerical influence in the decisive years were borne out by the Religious Census of 1851. At that date in the south Midland enclosure country, even in counties where there were numerous Dissenters, about two in every seven, and even in Norfolk about a quarter of the population, attended the parish church. But with very little competition from Nonconformity in the south-east and in the Welsh border country, where there had been no great amount of recent enclosure, the Church could attract only about two in every nine.[47] Considerations of the market had in various ways turned a whole generation of farmers and labourers against the Church and already in the 'thirties organized religion was in a very poor way over most of the southern counties. Victorian commentators were bound to be impressed by the virtues of free trade in religion when in rural areas, where Dissent was strong, total church attendances were almost everywhere higher than in the south, where the Church had preserved apparent ascendancy; in the extreme cases, well over half the population of Huntingdonshire or Bedfordshire – virtually every man, woman and child who according to Horace Mann's calculations was free to attend[48] – were in church or chapel, compared with barely a third in Kent and Sussex. But perhaps the real truth is that the sting had been taken from the tithe issue in the newly enclosed areas before the agricultural depression began.

V

In the peculiar conditions of Wales, revival was possible in circumstances which were unfavourable to it in England, albeit revival of a special kind. The Welsh Church was especially vulnerable. Its preferments had long been used as an adjunct to those over the border, and an exceptional proportion of its tithes were in lay hands. In country towns there

[47] Except in the backward county of Dorset, where almost one-third of the population was at church on the census day.

[48] Horace Mann, who organized the census of religious worship in 1851, computed that not more than 58 per cent of the community could attend church on any given Sunday, and that consequently there was no need to provide church accommodation for more than that proportion of the population.

were examples of abuses in the pew system as bad as any in England, while the rapid and relatively late development of the coalfield in Glamorgan and Monmouthshire exposed spectacular defects in the parish system. In 1801 this area was comprised within nine ancient parishes, and had a population of about 17,000; forty years later there were 100,000, but still no more than thirteen Anglican churches, only one of which was in Merthyr.[49] Yet at the beginning of the century the great bulk of the population owed real or nominal allegiance to the Church; not until 1811 did the Calvinistic Methodists establish themselves as a distinct denomination, and not until the post-war years had there come a real breach. The bulk of the land in Wales (like the tithes) was owned by the Anglo-Welsh upper class, while the bulk of the population consisted of Welsh labourers or small tenant farmers. Welsh rural society below the level of the anglicized gentry was much more homogeneous in character than the English country society. Similar national distinctions grew up in the industrial area. Welsh industrialists, sometimes of English Noncon-formist stock, intermarried with the gentry and adopted their Anglicanism; their managers, like the estate agents of many of the gentry, were brought from over the border. The Welsh revival became a mass movement as part of the process by which the homogeneous lower order in the country, and the working class in the industrial areas, asserted themselves against the upper class. After the war, Welsh farming escaped the distresses of the English corn-growers, but suffered bad hay harvests and other troubles. Bitter agitations against tithe began – even the Commutation Act was denounced in Wales as increasing the burden on the country – and the egalitarian character of Welsh society enabled the revivalists to gain a hold rarely approached in England. On the Census Sunday in 1851 almost everyone who could be at church was there, and almost four-fifths of them were Nonconformists. But numerical strength was not the only peculiarity of Nonconformity in Wales. Unlike the English Nonconformists the Welsh denominations had made

[49] W. L. Bevan, *Notes on the Church in Wales* (London 1905), p. 21; D. Williams, *A History of Modern Wales* (London 1950), p. 249.

their gains in a period when on more than one occasion Welshmen had been goaded by desperation to rebellion; under the influence of the Anti-Corn Law League and the Liberation Society, Nonconformity in Wales became much more deeply tainted with political radicalism than was common in England. Behind the Liberal landslide at the election of 1868 lay a long history of preparation, agitation and organization.

VI

The changes in the countryside, though startling enough, were not as surprising as the changes in industry, the causes of which are still matters of acute controversy, and the theoretical apparatus for interpreting which is still crude. In Britain, as in other parts of Western Europe, there had been important developments in large-scale production in the mining and manufacturing industries since the seventeenth century or even earlier. Wherever a large-scale demand could be created or tapped, modern methods of production were introduced in response. State spending for purposes of war encouraged the growth of ship-building and the metallurgical industries; Cornish copper output, for example, increased eightfold between 1729 and 1760. The eighteenth-century John Bull rejoiced in bread, beef and beer, and was encouraged in the last taste not only by nationalists who could see no virtue in foreign wines, but also by temperance reformers who wished to keep him off spirits. The bulkiness of beer limited the brewer's market to the range of his dray, but in London even this range opened the prospect of a mass market; the great London breweries became avid consumers of steam-engines, and with their liquid raw material remained wonders of automation far into the nineteenth century. Nevertheless, in spite of the immense capital which they employed and their advanced methods of production, the great breweries had no power to stimulate general industrial change. Nor, despite their growth, did the mining and metallurgical industries change fundamentally in character. To the point of 'take-off', it has been plausibly suggested, British economic development had followed the balanced growth models usually associated with planned economies; the 'take-off' itself exemplified the unbalanced growth of the 'sectoral' models where the rapid development of the leading sector had a feed-back in other industries.

Radical changes would come only in an industry where a mass market could be reached by relatively simple technical changes. The chief large-scale market for manufactured goods had traditionally been in textiles, and there were now special reasons for the revolutionary advances made by the English cotton industry. English cottons had been produced as cheap imitations of the finer products of India, and the colonial market offered the industry a stimulus which had no counterpart elsewhere. The wars of the eighteenth century had delivered over to England most of the French colonies in America and the West Indies, and most of the trade in slaves. African slaves were partly paid for in Indian cottons, a market which Lancashire seized when trade was interrupted; the West Indian planters produced cotton for Britain and consumed British cotton goods. The African and American markets took the lion's share of Lancashire's booming exports in the middle of the century, and as the demand for raw cotton grew, the southern plantations of America became committed to producing the raw material, and offered in return an immense and growing market for British products. Between 1750 and 1769 British cotton exports multiplied ten times, and thereafter never looked back. During the Napoleonic wars the industry was forced to concentrate upon the American and colonial markets, and afterwards, though enormous quantities were exported to Europe, an ever-growing proportion of a fantastically increasing output went to colonial and similar markets. The monopoly which the naval blockade had given British manufacturers in this field remained unbroken for generations. The competitive power of the Lancashire manufacturers not only broke their rivals in other parts of England, Scotland and Ireland, but eventually killed the Indian industry and opened another subcontinent to their products. Here, for the first time, a mass market on a world scale was opened up, and it called out a crowd of technical innovations, first in weaving and then in spinning.

These technical devices were simple and cheap, and very speedily paid for themselves, so that the industry was able quickly to accumulate the capital it required. The traditional method of raising output was to put more work out to domestic producers, and in weaving this continued for a long time to be the practice; but the speed with which the overseas market opened up encouraged the entrepreneurs who created the cotton industry to begin factory production. And until the middle of the nineteenth century factory production was almost exclusively concentrated in the textile industries and predominantly in cotton. To the men who contrived it, unremarkable as they usually were for any qualities beyond those of organizing ability and drive, immense fortunes accrued. The woollen industry which had been the pride of British manufacture was relatively slow in following the lead of Lancashire. There was no vast market for British woollens in India or the West Indies; the shorter staple of the woollen fibre presented greater technical difficulties to mechanical processes, and in the older industry there was probably greater conservatism. Yet by the beginning of the century the factory system was coming in here too, and the East Anglian worsted industry was already feeling the pressure of West Riding competition. As in cotton, so in the woollen trade, industrial concentration was at work.

In the capital goods industries much heavier investment was needed to begin a new enterprise than in cotton, and it was much more difficult to find a mass market. In many respects the best-placed product was coal. Coal had long been the chief form of domestic fuel in towns, and the growth of large towns and especially of London had led to a great expansion in production since the sixteenth century. Moreover, there were plenty of improving landlords who would not invest in cotton but would develop the coal resources of their own estates. They had also been willing to invest in canals to help shift it, and in the second quarter of the nineteenth century the problem of shifting coal led to fundamental changes in the capital goods industries. The mines used steam engines of great power and in great numbers; in Durham they ran trucks on rails, and there the innovations were combined to provide modern railway transport from the pithead to the shipping point for London. With exemplary enterprise the Lancashire cotton producers seized on the railway as a means of reducing their handling charges between Manchester and the coast, railway manias followed in the middle 'thirties and middle 'forties, and by 1850 a railway system was in being.

In the railways much money was lost and the yield on the average investor's capital was low. The upper classes had long been aware of the advantages of an efficient transport system to the national economy and had often invested in canals more heavily than commercial considerations warranted. Now the upper and middle classes were making more from industrial progress than they could either spend or invest. Neither better living, nor the spate of chapel building which so embarrassed the Wesleyan pundits in the 1830s, nor enormous losses on investments in South and North America, dried up the flood, and the rate of interest dropped slowly but inexorably. From the shareholders' standpoint the wildest English railway project could hardly look more hopeless than many foreign bonds, and money was poured into the new folly in amazing amounts. Moreover, the railway boom had two important consequences which to the community as a whole more than offset the poor dividends which it yielded. The first of these was a startling reduction in production costs over a wide range of industries, which enlarged the market they might hope to meet; the second was a tremendous impulse to the coal and iron industries.

The iron industry had long been expanding slowly and had gradually found the means of breaking the limits imposed upon its growth by its dependence on wood and charcoal; the substitution of coal and coke made it possible for the industry to respond to any sudden increase in demand without mortgaging its whole future. The railway boom provided just such an opportunity. Between 1830 and 1850 more than 5,000 miles of railway were built, many with more than one track; each track-mile required on the average 300 tons of iron for rails alone. In the same period the output of the iron industry trebled, and the output of the coal industry, which

found an enormously expanded market in the smelting and
fining processes and in providing power for the railways,
more than trebled. Thus it came about that the savings
generated in the early stages of the Industrial Revolution
produced revolutionary changes in a whole series of other
industries.

One of the great problems of the leaders of the new
industries was the assembling and training of an adequate
labour force. A population whose industrial experience had
hitherto been confined largely to domestic production, where
bouts of hard work could alternate with bouts of idleness or
drunkenness, did not take kindly to the long haul of regular
factory labour. In any case English labour, in spite of the
great increase in rural pauperism, was extremely immobile,
and the fact that the mobile members picked up by the early
factory masters were regarded (accurately) as tramps did not
help the repute of the factories. Compulsion was the only
other resort, and the early masters contracted with the town
workhouses for the supply of both child and adult labour;
again the repute of the factories suffered. In due course the
manufacturing areas of the Midlands and the North managed
to attract labour from surrounding agricultural regions, but
the bulk of the labour migration seems to have been of a
short-range character, with country towns and villages losing
population to the industrial towns, and in turn acting as
assembly points for fresh migrants from the country near
by. But on the one hand agricultural unemployment in
the south-eastern counties was in no way mitigated by the
demand for labour in the North and the Midlands, and on the
other, although rural families in the North could not for long
keep their children and girls out of the factories, they did
keep them out of the mines. Of all industrial occupations
mining had the worst reputation; in Durham, where there
was little alternative industrial employment, the increase in
the labour force was recruited largely from the natural
growth of a notoriously prolific section of the population.
The other English coalfields were interspersed among textile,
metal and pottery industries which recruited a good deal of
labour, and there must have been immigrant labour when the

South Wales coalfield was developed; but everywhere the coal-mining communities became inbred, as those in Durham had been from the beginning.

One labour force willing to move into mining, and also immensely mobile, was the surplus agricultural population of Ireland. They were used to conditions beside which those of the most hardly-used English agricultural labourer seemed comfortable. There had long been seasonal immigration from Ireland for harvest employment and crowds of Irish vagrants making their way from the west coast ports to London and back again as the Poor Law authorities removed them. But in the last dozen years of the eighteenth century much greater permanent settlement in England began, and the numbers increased till the census of 1851 recorded almost three-quarters of a million residents of Irish birth; there were of course many more born in England of Irish parents and indistinguishable to the English eye from the rest of their kin. Some of these went, as we have seen, into the mines in the north of England and in South Wales, and there were sizeable colonies in London and around Birmingham where Newman pitched his Oratory; but the great bulk poured into the textile trades of south Lancashire and the west of Scotland. As machine competition squeezed the formerly prosperous Lancashire handloom weavers out of the trade in the early decades of the nineteenth century, they were replaced by droves of Irish who quickly acquired the skill, and at a deplorable level of living vastly prolonged the life, of a dying industry. Wherever they went the Irish took the least skilled jobs at the lowest rates of pay; they brought with them an alien religion, ways of life which were alien to even the poorest English classes, and diseases which English workmen would have preferred to be confined to Ireland.[50]

[50] The attitude of even charitably disposed Protestants is sufficiently exemplified by this unambiguous reference to the Irish in the *Annual Report of the Stockport Sunday School, 1824*, p. 13: 'The prosperity of our town and the demands for additional labour, have brought an influx of population that forms a striking contrast to the native inhabitants; the uncivilized manners and squalid appearance of their persons and of their children are only exceeded by the filth and disorder of their habitations. They are evidently come from those darker regions of moral degradation, where society is only one remove from the level of brutish ignorance. The poor children of these families have now claims upon us for protection from the evils and dangers to which they are exposed by parental incapacity and neglect.'

They had the largest and most difficult adjustment to make to urban and industrial life, and their Church could not keep pace with their increase; on census day in 1851 less than a quarter of a million Catholics attended Mass. This great influx of cheap labour balanced what the country lost in overseas emigration and disembarked at points where additional labour was badly needed. Yet some modern scholars have doubted whether employers were wise to employ Irish labour on the scale they did. In town or country, wherever there was labour trouble, the Irish were in the forefront, and in its later stages Chartism almost has the appearance of an Irish movement.

The relatively high mobility of Irish labour was due partly to the fact that the passage was cheap – steam packets sometimes brought in immigrants to Liverpool at 4d. or 5d. a head – and partly to the fact that the Irish were peculiarly susceptible to the inducements of both the carrot and the stick. The existence of a Poor Law in England meant that even at the worst English conditions would compare favourably with Irish, while on the other hand the sudden increase in Irish immigration in the years immediately preceding the great famine of 1846 (years which included some periods of very high unemployment in England) show how that catastrophe was casting its shadow before and driving the Irish abroad.

How savage were the economic pressures upon the much less mobile English working men? The question is difficult to answer, for there were many separate markets for labour even within a particular trade; the farm labourer in south Lancashire or the market gardener around London, for whose services there was urban competition, did much better than his fellow in Norfolk or Dorset. Moreover, even if adequate evidence as to the trend of wages and the cost of living were available (which it is not), it would be misleading to combine the two to produce a curve of real wages for a period like the first half of the nineteenth century; urban growth alone transformed the components of the family budget. Nor are indices of consumption easy to interpret even where they can be reliably constructed, for it is not always clear how to assess changes in the public taste. In

Ireland, for example, the introduction of the potato seems clearly to indicate a declining standard, but when the potato became widespread in south Lancashire in this period it may have brought about an improvement by increasing the variety of the diet, and reducing dependence on barley-bread and oatmeal.

How, again, should we relate living standards to the growth of population? At a time when the birth- and death-rates are high it is much easier to increase the population by reducing the death-rate than by increasing the birth-rate, and the view has been pressed that although the technical progress of the medical profession through the increase in the number of hospitals probably made disease or childbirth more hazardous for the patient, many more people were raised above the margin of subsistence by the filtering down of some portion of the great increase in output. It is possible that this is what happened in the generation before the French wars; but it is also possible that the key factor was inoculation, which was far more widespread than was formerly thought. In either case changes in the age structure of the population might sustain an increase in numbers even during a decline in living standards.

Equally obscure is the extent to which domestic consumption was influenced by its rivals in the division of the national product, namely, war, investment and international trade. Each of these has been regarded by some modern students as a means of depressing the working-class standard of life. The war probably did so; prices rocketed, and wages lagged behind. Furthermore, in the course of the war the national debt more than trebled, and a debt serviced by duties upon articles of popular consumption was a means of transferring purchasing power from ordinary consumers to the investing class. On the other hand, nothing is worse for working men than unemployment, and one of the consequences of deficit war finance was that there were fewer really bad years during the war than there were afterwards; moreover, although the Continental System restricted British access to European markets, the war gave England the monopoly of the world's 'colonial' markets and damaged her competitors. Nor is it clear that investment diverted resources from consumption. It is true that production of producer-goods consistently rose faster than that of consumer-goods, but the disparity was not as great as it was later in the century, when working-class standards were unmistakably rising; in any case the rate of interest dropped steadily from early in the century until the middle 'forties, the investing classes had money to waste on South American mines, North American banks, and unprofitable railways, and it does not seem that pressure exerted by this sector seriously hindered investment in the production of consumer-goods. Similarly with international trade: the terms of trade moved sharply against Britain in the later stages of the French wars and continued adverse down to the middle of the century. It is said that in 1840 Britain had to export twice as many goods to pay for a given volume of imports as she had in 1800. There is no doubt that part of the benefit of industrial efficiency went to foreign consumers, but this is not to say that it went at the expense of British working men. For the terms of trade were changed partly by a change-over in Lancashire to goods of a cheaper type, and partly by enormous reductions in the real costs of production. The interest of the working man lay in the maximum volume of business, and Lancashire's post-war exports could hardly have been sustained on the earlier terms of trade.

None of the chief factors affecting working-class prosperity seems to swing the balance decisively either way, and it may be that neither the advancing nor the declining occupations were clearly in the lead. The army of farm labourers in the south found agricultural employment, domestic textile work and poor relief all harder to come by as time went on, but neither the carrot nor the stick ever got them on the move in the dramatic Irish manner. Still, there was a considerable redistribution of population, and the population of the large towns grew at twice the rate of the country as a whole. By 1850 a much greater proportion of the population was in the industries which were higher paid as long as there was any work at all. That in this sector there was a gradual increase in prosperity is possibly suggested by the Wesleyan and still more by the Primitive Methodist membership figures. It is well-known that it took conditions of extreme distress to interest British working men in politics, and that when the business curve turned upwards, they tended to exploit their bargaining power and their thoughts turned to trade unionism and still more to friendly societies. It was much the same with Methodism, which like trade unionism and friendly societies was an expensive hobby; for even if it meant not a new, but simply an altered religious loyalty, it represented a preference for the expensive voluntary to the cheap endowed established article. Both Wesleyans and Primitives combined great capacity for growth with great responsiveness to the business cycle. Methodism has often been regarded as a recession phenomenon, a competitor with radical politics; but the reverse is true. Bad years for business were almost always bad or indifferent years for Methodism, and years like 1793, 1803, 1816–17, 1819, 1829–30, 1837, 1842 and, worst of all, the years in which the economy slid from the peak of 1845 into the trough of 1848, were all dismal times for the Connexion. The Wesleyanism of Jabez Bunting might well hate democracy as it hated sin, for in the bad years when democracy was abroad in the land not only did the denomination lose steam but it suffered the sharpest internal tensions. The years which saw the Kilhamite agitation (1796–7), the expulsion of Hugh Bourne (1808), the Leeds Protestant schism (1827), the West Cornwall teetotal secession (1841), not to mention the fearful disasters which were brewing up in 1847 and 1848, were all of them bad years. If the point needs any further emphasis it is provided by the fact that none of these Methodist 'depression' secessions showed any great capacity for growth except the Primitive Methodist Connexion, and even here there was no suggestion of its future potentialities until the denomination changed character altogether, and established itself in the east Midland enclosure country a decade after the original schism in the Potteries. If ever a movement was created on a shoestring it was Primitive Methodism, and the years of business upturn which followed the slumps of 1819, 1832 and 1848 were golden ones for the revivalists; on the other hand, the denomination was threatened with collapse during the downturn from the business peak in 1825, and had only one really good year (as business was picking up from the slump of 1842) in the unhappy period between 1837 and 1848. (It is noteworthy that there were also great schisms in the Friendly Society movement in the later 'forties, but the overall picture was of immense growth.)

Methodism failed to take root in the pauperized counties of the south-east, and its poor performance in the bad years suggests that if the level of purchasing power among the working classes had been generally diminishing it would never have established itself at all. In the generation which preceded the religious census of 1851, the Primitives, starting almost from scratch, had acquired a predominantly working-class following of 230,000 and nearly 3,000 buildings. Modest and temporary as many of these were, the record seems hardly consistent with a general decline of working-class purchasing power, and that from an initially low level. Nor can the stupendous growth and extensive coverage of the main Wesleyan body be ascribed exclusively to middle-class support. But, the sceptic may reply, the short-term benefits of the upswing may not demonstrate a long-term amelioration; no people were more determined voluntaryists than the Irish, and the generation in which they created the fabric of Catholic church life was that which ended with the Famine.

VII

The Methodist membership figures, like every other statistical series concerning the mass of the people, illustrate clearly how such benefits as the Industrial Revolution brought were liable to be rudely interrupted by mass unemployment at the low points of the trade cycle. But industrial distress still followed upon agricultural distress, and it is not surprising that the serious rural disorders which began in the autumn of 1830 were accompanied and succeeded by acute trouble in most parts of the country. At the general election in the summer of 1830 there was no great prospect of reform; before the end of the year radical reform was a certainty.

Since the peak of 1825 business had followed a course of irregular recovery and relapse, and there were very low points in 1829 and 1832. At the same time, as we have seen, the governing Tory party had fallen into irreconcilable divisions, and some of its most conservative elements were now looking for the end of the unreformed political system. Moreover, the election itself advanced the cause of reform, for the unreformed electoral system showed signs of breaking down. Lord John Russell was defeated at the family seat of Bedford, and Edward Baines, the famous Congregationalist and proprietor of the *Leeds Mercury*, with the support of hordes of town voters carried Henry Brougham for the West Riding against the Whig magnates. Brougham took up reform and compelled the Whigs to follow him; to increase the number of borough seats might be the only way to prevent town voters from swamping aristocratic influence in the counties. Nor were farmers the only middle-class group showing disaffection to the system; there was trouble in the City, which was soon faced with an outflow of gold, and in the industrial North and Midlands. In Lancashire and the West Riding, where the factory system had set master and man at loggerheads, there could be no united action. The *Manchester Guardian* thought that the object of reform was to enable middle-class electors to put down venal voters from below, while the West Riding operatives countered the reformism of Baines and his friends by a ferocious agitation for the ten-hour day. But the closeness of master and man in the metal trades of Birmingham and Sheffield permitted the growth of a common radicalism, and there was a similar unity in the north-east. Businessmen concluded that their interest could no longer be defended without parliamentary representation, and working men saw a chance to strike for their rights. A lead was given by Attwood and the Birmingham Political Union, and political unions throughout the country followed the Birmingham men in putting pressure on the government, and securing for Grey a great reforming majority at the elections of 1831. It was now absolutely necessary to make an offer to the middle class which would separate them from the forces below. And in whatever else it failed, in this the Reform Bill of 1832 triumphantly succeeded.

Yet the Reform crisis had borne all the marks of revolution:

the combination of urban and rural discontent, of middle-class disaffection and governmental weakness, was the classic recipe. When the old establishment tottered, the Church was in a parlous state. The bishops and the bulk of churchmen had opposed reform and appeared ogres to the radical parliamentary reformers. There were influential Benthamites and others who found the higgledy-piggledy organization of the Church irrational and thought that its temporalities would be better devoted to the support of Mechanics' Institutes. Even before the final crisis was on, as early as 1829, avowed friends of the Church had taken alarm and begun to move for administrative changes. Late in 1829 an Ecclesiastical Commission was appointed which reported many of the facts about pluralities and so forth, and it was widely rumoured that the bishops had been recommended 'from the highest quarter' to revise the liturgy, an unambiguous reference to the King's aversion to the Athanasian Creed. During the Reform crisis the papers teemed with attacks on the bishops, and although there were reports of meetings held in defence of the establishment, these very meetings often demanded a redistribution of church revenues. Where money was concerned, so were the interests of Dissenters, who might have to share the cost of any attempt to restore order in the Church. Some of the Dissenters began to preach disestablishment, and it was ominous for the Church that this doctrine might often be disguised as church reform. The mood of the moment was caught by a Unitarian journal which shortly became a steady defender of the Church against the assaults of rabid evangelical Nonconformists.

That Churchmen will take the lesson so promptly as to derive benefit from their fears, we can scarcely expect; yet we hold it to be impossible that in a nation like this, and at such a period of inquisition into all public matters, any gross error or foul abuse can long be maintained. Besieged as the Church of England is on all sides, her defenders would do well to capitulate whilst honourable terms may be had, and not wait from indolence or obstinacy or false pride until the Establishment is stormed by the popular indignation which is fast gathering round the dilapidated edifice.[51]

[51] *The Christian Reformer, or, Unitarian Magazine and Review*, February 1832, p. 58.

What, then, were the foul abuses in the dilapidated edifice of what had hitherto been regarded as the purest Church in Christendom?

For a generation before the Reform crisis the Church had been involved in controversies about the adequacy of its pastoral organization which matched those concerning its constitutional standing. Reform had begun, but had reached a deadlock as the political situation deteriorated and the establishment itself was called in question. The first group of complaints concerned the distribution and remuneration of the clergy; many of the troubles here went back to the Reformation and beyond, and illustrated the fact that, having escaped the major upheavals which shook the continental Churches in the Reformation, the Counter-Reformation and the French Revolution, the English Church was in many respects the most unreformed Church in Europe. The second group of complaints related to the failure of the Church to cope with the recent growth and movement of the population, problems which have since proved too much for Churches everywhere.

At the beginning of the nineteenth century the incumbents of more than half the parishes of the country were non-resident, and the issue quite suddenly became pressing when some London lawyers, taking advantage of the provisions of the Residence Act which proscribed non-residence, claimed the rewards due to informers. This was notoriously unjust to some London rectors who might live round the corner from their church and yet be technically non-resident. Parliament therefore suspended the operation of the Residence Act and laborious efforts were made to regulate clerical residence for the future. These finally took shape in legislation in 1813. In that year, of the incumbents of 10,558 livings only 4,183 were resident; another 1,641 were doing duty, though non-resident.[52] Of the non-residents, a third were absent on other benefices, a quarter were away owing to the lack or inadequacy of a parsonage house, and more than a tenth were absent without licence or exemption. New legislation, including the

[52] *Parliamentary papers*, H.L. 1816, LXXIX, pp. 42-3. It had been difficult to get the clergy to notify the bishops of their non-residence.

Pluralities Act of 1817, made little impression on the problem; by 1831 the number of residents had risen to only 4,649, and the number of non-residents doing duty to 1,684.[53] The new Acts, indeed, had had to acknowledge that at the root of the trouble lay the intractable problems of clerical poverty and lay patronage, and had enlarged the grounds of non-residence. In 1810 no less than 3,998 livings, nearly two-fifths of the whole, were returned as worth less than £150 p.a., and of these 1,061 were worth less than £50 and a further 1,726 less than £100.[54] The only solution to the problem of the very small livings, then as now, was to allow them to be held in plurality with others, and the Bishop of Norwich, who was particularly plagued with poor livings unendowed with glebe houses, had the unique privilege of granting the personal union of benefices.[55] Pluralities became a notorious abuse – the family of Dr Sparke, who reigned at Ely from 1812 to 1836, were said to draw £40,000 a year in ecclesiastical preferments – but the abuse grew out of an attempt to make better provision for men of learning and chaplains to the aristocracy, the bishops and the Crown. And if the lot of the poor parson (until solaced by an extra benefice) was not a happy one, the lot of the curate whom he installed in the living on which he did not reside was likely to be even worse – though curates doubled up as well as incumbents. Queen Anne's Bounty, it is true, made annual grants of £200 for the capital endowment of poor parishes, but its resources were not sufficient to match the need; and although, by disposing of these grants by lot, the governors avoided the reproach of favouritism, they also destroyed any prospect of deploying their funds where they would be most useful. At the top of the hierarchy there was a similar range of incomes. The Archbishop of Canterbury and the Bishop of Durham both received over £19,000 p.a., but at the other end of the

[53] *Parliamentary papers*, H.C. 1833, XXVII.

[54] *Abstract of returns of livings under the value of £150 p.a.*, in *Parliamentary papers*, H.C. 1810, XIV. This return was fuller than that of the previous year (*Parliamentary papers*, H.C. 1809, IX) but may not have been complete.

[55] *Parliamentary papers*, H.C. 1808, IX. Return of non-resident clergy, p. 22. A recent investigation in the diocese of Ely shows that it was not often that the smallest livings were held in plurality there; cf. R. Mitchison, 'Pluralities and the Poorer Benefices in Eighteenth-Century England', in *The Historical Journal*, v. 2 (1962), pp. 188–90.

scale the Bishop of Rochester received only £1,500, and his lordship of Llandaff £900. These stipends were a good deal smaller than the lusher parish preferments and were too small for men who were expected to be in London for six months of the year voting for the government in the House of Lords. The poorer bishops could only be kept on the job by reinforcing their stipends with other preferments. Thus in the Church, as in English society as a whole, immense wealth was very unevenly distributed.

In the first decade of the century, long before radical iconoclasts had laid hands on all things sacred, the redistribution of church funds had had its advocates. Apart, however, from pessimistic arithmeticians who computed that if stipends were equalized there would only be £167 each, there were two considerations which to the Tory mind seemed decisive against any change and which effectually prevented any radical move until the great inflation of our own time. The first was that the patronage of the majority of church livings was in lay hands and was a freely marketable commodity;[56] Sir William Scott expected and received no answer when he asked in the Commons in 1802,

> upon what ground I can be called upon to give up half the living, the advowson of which I have purchased, upon a price relative to its value, in order that that moiety may be transferred to improve another living, belonging to another patron, who has paid nothing for that moiety, and who has no other title to it, but that he happens to possess the advowson of a smaller living.

Equalization meant the plunder of lay property. The second point was that the hierarchy of revenues made the Church an excellent prop to a hierarchical society; equalization would

[56] The result of a not quite comprehensive survey in 1835 was as follows:

In the gift of the Crown:	934 benefices
In the gift of the Bishops, Deans, Chapters & other ecclesiastical patrons:	3810 benefices
In the gift of the Universities, Colleges and Schools:	939 benefices
In the gift of Private Individuals:	4790 benefices

(*Parliamentary papers*, H.C. 1836, XL: Church Patronage, England and Wales.) If the figures quoted in J. Wade, *Extraordinary Black Book*, p. 22, for 1821 are at all accurate there had been a great transfer of patronage in the interval from lay to ecclesiastical and collegiate patrons, but the probability is that, as on other occasions, his information was wildly inaccurate.

mean presbyterianism, subversion and republicanism. To quote Sir William Scott again,

> As the revenues at present are distributed, the clergy, as a profession, find an easy and independent access to every gradation of society, and maintain a fair equality, as they ought to do, with the other liberal professions; and the elevation of the highest ranks gives something of a dignity to the lowest: alter the mode of distribution, and you run the risk of producing a body of clergy, resembling only the lower orders of society, in their conversation, in their manners, and their habits; and it is well if they are not infected by a popular fondness for some or other species of a gross, a factious, and a fanatical religion.[57]

If equalization were ruled out, only two means of increasing clerical earnings remained; either the state must allocate public funds to their support, or clergy must be encouraged to increase their non-professional profits. Charles Simeon wanted the government to put £40,000–50,000 a year into Queen Anne's Bounty; in 1809, indeed, the first of eleven annual parliamentary grants of £100,000 was made.[58] On the other line, there had always been clergy who were in effect part-time parsons eking out their benefices with lay and often illegal occupations. Wade speaks of a Welsh parson who ran a ferry, shaved the village for a penny on Saturday nights, and taught the children reading and writing on five evenings a week;[59] Wilberforce spoke in the House in 1806 of a curate turned weaver. Education was hallowed by tradition as a clerical profession, and there were clergy who farmed not only their own glebe, but (illegally) were tenant farmers on other men's land as well.[60] To Sir William Scott

> the parish priest is, by the very constitution of his office, in some degree, an agriculturist; he is, *ex officio*, in part a farmer,[61]

[57] *Parliamentary History*, xxxvi, 483–5.

[58] C. Hodgson, *An Account of the Augmentation of Small Livings, by 'The Governors of the Bounty of Queen Anne, for the Augmentation of the Maintenance of the Poor Clergy', and of Benefactions by Corporate Bodies and Individuals, to the End of the Year 1825* (London 1826), p. 32.

[59] *Extraordinary Black Book*, pp. 54–5 n.

[60] W. Pitt, *General View of the Agriculture of the County of Worcester* (London 1813), p. 35.

[61] *Parliamentary History*, xxxvi, 476.

and, inhibited by no later doctrine of a separated ministry, he urged that the clergy be encouraged in this gentlemanly pursuit. The ill-conceived restrictions placed upon glebe farming by the legislation of Henry VIII were, indeed, repealed; in 1817 the clergy were permitted to farm up to 80 acres as tenants,[62] and they were gradually given rights to act as partners in business concerns, especially in those dealing in fire and life assurance.[63] By all these devices the clergy were allowed to reinforce their stipends, and by 1835, when food prices were lower than at the beginning of the century, the average net value of the stipends themselves was raised by state subsidies and other means to £286.[64] Yet little impression was made on the problem of pluralism.

What kind of pastoral provision was the Church making for the new concentrations of population? Nowhere was the dead hand of the past more evident than here. The most rapidly developing part of the country was in the Northern Province, counting only six bishoprics as against twenty in the Southern Province; Norfolk contained 731 parishes and Suffolk 510, but there were only 70 in Lancashire and 193 in the West Riding of Yorkshire. Nor was there any prospect of an improvement while the creation of every new parish required a separate Act of Parliament. This did not necessarily mean that the parish church was the only place in which the Church of England made provision for the needs of souls. The parish of Manchester, for example, was an extreme case of the unwieldy northern parish; between 1801 and 1851 the population increased from 125,911 to 515,581 and the number of Anglican churches from 23 to 56.[65] We may probably assume that where there was an effective demand for Anglican church accommodation the buildings went up; but the existence of concurrent pastoral oversight led to abuses and inconveniences of all kinds. Under Hardwick's Marriage Act marriages might be celebrated only in the parish church, and when marriages in the Manchester district churches became

[62] 57 Geo. III. c. 99 s. 2. They could farm more with the permission of the bishop.
[63] 1 & 2 Vict. c. 106, ss. 29–30.
[64] *Parliamentary papers*, H.C. 1836, XL. Church patronage (England and Wales).
[65] *The Church in Manchester. Report of the Bishop of Manchester's Special Commission 1905–14* (Manchester 1914), p. 66.

legal double fees were payable to compensate the chaplains of the collegiate church. To avoid them the townsfolk still thronged to the parish church, in unmanageable numbers. The publication of the banns was 'equivalent in point of time to the reading of a chapter of the Bible' and

> marriages are very often celebrated on the Sundays, and there is an accumulation of people in the neighbourhood of the church for those marriages. The registration of marriages goes on during Divine service – the issuing of certificates goes on during Divine service. The same with regard to baptisms; there is an accumulation of numbers, who resort to the old parish church; there are meetings in the neighbouring public houses, sponsors assembling there; and, in short, scenes, I do not say of gross scandal, but of indecorum, and certainly a want of reverence, which is extremely painful, and operates very injuriously to the interest of the church at Manchester.

There was unfortunately worse than indecorum in the inevitably hasty conduct of marriages; it was known that no inquiries would be instituted, and couples from miles around wishing to marry in defiance of the law or of family disapproval flocked to the Manchester parish church.[66] When the district clergy felt that their flocks could never comprehend what their status was, and when the Warden and Fellows of the heavily endowed collegiate church disclaimed all pastoral responsibility for the parish, there were vociferous protests from loyal Anglicans.

The parish of Marylebone, where the Duke of Portland was unwilling for his advowson to be reduced by the division of the parish, though the church provided only 200 seats for a population of 40,000, was probably not unique, and in other urban parishes the effective demand for church accommodation was so low as to be a serious reproach to a privileged establishment. In 1816 a computation was made of the number of parishes in which the population exceeded 2,000 and there was Anglican accommodation for less than half. Such parishes were found to contain a population of 5,265,079 and church

---

[66] *Manchester Rectory Division Bill. Report of the evidence given before the Committee of the House of Commons* (Printed for the Manchester Churchwardens, 1850), pp. 6, 109–12.

accommodation for not much more than a million. In eighty such parishes in London there was no provision for eight-ninths of a population exceeding 930,000; in five parishes in Aston, Deritend and Birmingham, church accommodation for 24,000 sufficed for a population of 185,000; in Leeds the church found room for 3,400 of a population of 67,000.[67] In detail these figures are suspect; but the general impression of what was called 'spiritual destitution' in urban areas was beyond question. Moreover, the published figures do not reveal the worst – that by the system of privately owned or rented pews the general public was debarred from much of what accommodation there was. Parishioners had a common law right to accommodation in the nave of their parish church, but in very many parishes they did not get it; pews were often appropriated to particular houses and could be sold or rented by their owners, or, particularly in poorly endowed churches, were rented to provide a stipend for the minister.

> In London where the Churches with few exceptions are blocked up with high pews, and where the system of pew rents is carried to its ultimatum – where the stranger has usually to stand in the aisle until the Psalms, before the mercenary official styled 'the Pew Opener' finds him a sitting, taking care, before the door is closed, to lower the hand expectant of a fee!

In one degree or another this system prevailed all over the country, filling churches higgledy-piggledy with boxes of all shapes, sizes and amenities, and making a mockery of the Anglican claim to be the poor man's Church.[68] In Anglican

[67] *Parliamentary papers*, H.L. 1816, LXXIX. An account of the population and capacity of churches & chapels in all benefices . . . wherein the population consists of 2000 upwards, and the churches & chapels will not contain half. Cf. *Parliamentary papers*, H.L. 1818, XCIII. Abstract of number of benefices and population of each diocese, pp. 48–9.

[68] W. H. Egerton, *The Pew System* (London 1862), pp. 12–13. Few men have ever more consistently bemused the British public than the Cambridge ecclesiologists. They began their work of church building and restoration in the 1840s, and diverted the biggest church building programme this country has ever seen into sham gothic of various kinds; we may, however, be grateful that they helped tremendously to get rid of pews. If the uniform benches they recommended were not comely, they often effected a great increase in the accommodation afforded by the church. On this movement, see James F. White, *The Cambridge Movement: The Ecclesiologists and the Gothic Revival* (Cambridge 1962), and A. G. Lough, *The Influence of John Mason Neale* (London 1962).

chapels in large parishes there were fewer restraints upon the pew system; lack of endowments tied ministers to it, while the public had no common law right to accommodation in a chapel. On the other hand there is not much doubt that in these cases the pew system operated to increase rather than reduce the amount of church accommodation, and that in most places there was a greater demand for rented than for free accommodation. Nonconformists were also heavily dependent on pew rents, but they did not levy church rates on the public they excluded.

In the last years of the Napoleonic wars the cause of church building was promoted energetically by a little knot of high-churchmen whose pressure organization was the nearest thing on their side to the grandiose machine being constructed by the evangelicals. This group was led by two laymen successively, William Stevens, who founded and gave his nickname to the dining club, 'Nobody's Friends', and Joshua Watson, a wine-merchant, who retired from business in 1814 to give himself to church affairs, and was the king-pin of the Hackney Phalanx. This body, a closely-knit group of intermarried Sikeses, Powells, Daubenys and Watsons, with the support of the wider membership of Nobody's Friends, had the ear of the Archbishop of Canterbury, through his domestic chaplain, Christopher Wordsworth, the brother of the poet, and had already been instrumental in the foundation in 1811 of the National Society for the Education of the Poor in the Principles of the Established Church, had obtained a foothold in the S.P.C.K., and through Watson had managed two important relief funds at the end of the war. Watson's first plan, indeed, was to press the premier to build a number of free churches as a sort of war memorial, but no funds could be spared. In 1817, therefore, the Hackney Phalanx launched a church building society, continued social tension convinced the government that money had better be found, and in 1818 a Church Building Commission, upon which the Hackney Phalanx was strongly represented, was established by statute, with a million of public funds to spend. In 1824 a windfall repayment of a wartime loan to Austria, which had been written off, produced another half-million for the Commission, and as state funds were used to prime the pump of private generosity, a considerable programme of church building was begun, costing in the fifteen years following 1818 some six million pounds.

This extension was long overdue, but it is not clear that the Church derived much benefit from it. In the earlier stages particularly, the churches erected were too large and expensive and had too few free pews. Many of them never gathered a reasonable congregation, and provided a telling argument against the provision of religious amenities except by the play of market forces. There were parishes that did not relish the additional maintenance costs, and as the new buildings were opened a new political issue was forced to the front. A not unnatural Anglican reluctance to burden the church rates with new expenses for the benefit of pew-holders was speedily reinforced by Dissenting and popular animosity. Until the 'twenties church rates had never been challenged, and even the Quakers had submitted meekly to the inconveniences of not paying; but now, although church rates were usually trivial in amount, there was a very general reluctance to admit the indefinite extension of liability implied by the church building programme. In 1827 and 1828 there was a concerted attack on the rates for the new churches in the West Riding, and the Leeds vestry proved as troublesome about its new amenities as at that moment the Leeds Brunswick leaders were about their new organ. Already precedents were set for the havoc wrought by 'rabble vestries' in the 'thirties, and for the scandalous clashes which then took place between the people assembled in the vestry and the privileges of the establishment.

Even before the Reform crisis the process had begun by which the methods of church extension had been assimilated to those obtaining in the 'private sector' of Nonconformity. In 1828 the Church Building Society was incorporated by Act of Parliament and was made the official channel for the work; church building was no longer the function of a department of state. Moreover, private munificence had to be stimulated by allowing subscribers the right not only to pews but to patronage; how chapel-like the arrangements might be was in 1831 illustrated in Salford, where an evangelical group obtained an Act[69] enabling them to wrest the patronage from the Warden and Fellows of the Manchester collegiate church, and built Christ Church for the evangelical firebrand Hugh Stowell. Stowell's biographer proudly claimed that he never received any emolument from church endowments, but lived on pew rents.[70] Whatever the inducements, however, Anglican accommodation per hundred of population diminished inexorably with every decade in the first half of the nineteenth century, and the fact that between 1831 and 1851 the total church provision recovered almost all the ground it had lost relative to the growth of population[71] since the beginning of the century was due to the efforts of Nonconformists, to the fact that the industrial revolution had put more money in many middle-class pockets than could readily be spent, and to the unfortunate folklore which grew around the whole question. The Anglican church builders' demand for state assistance had been based more upon what was due to the Church as an establishment than upon the needs of the Church in pastoral oversight; to many Nonconformists the proper reply to this demand seemed to be to show that more church provision could be made through voluntary channels with equal disregard to pastoral requirements. Building became the last resort of churchmen, Anglican and Nonconformist, with no real policy, and the country became saddled with a church system, like the railway system, which later ages could not afford. In 1851 Horace Mann's census showed that almost a third of the population for whom there was church accommodation did not take advantage of it, and he concluded

> that the greatest difficulty is to fill the churches when provided; and that this can only be accomplished by a great addition to the number of efficient, earnest religious *teachers*, clerical and lay, by whose persuasions the reluctant population might be won.[72]

[69] 1 & 2 Wm. IV c. 38.
[70] J. B. Marsden, *Memoirs of the Life and Labours of the Rev. Hugh Stowell, M.A.* (London 1868), p. 168.
[71] *Report of census of religious worship 1851*, pp. cxxxi, cxl.
[72] ibid., p. clxvii.

And yet the denominations continued to vie with one another in conspicuous wastefulness.

VIII

In 1830 this was not yet apparent, and the Nonconformists, having just made one great leap forward and being poised for another, no doubt needed more accommodation. It was this advance which provided a spearhead for the generalized discontent against the Church during the Reform crisis, a threat which seemed unlikely to diminish after parliamentary reform had been obtained. The middle-class electoral qualifications and increased borough representation seemed bound to increase the political strength of Dissent, events in Ireland were there moving towards a fresh crisis, and changes which were inevitable in the standing of the Irish Church might be expected to injure the ascendancy at home. Yet the first decade of the reformed system proved a great disappointment to Nonconformists; at the end of it the Church was relatively much stronger than at the beginning, and the Irish issue proved to be a liability rather than an asset. In 1840 the Wesleyanism of Jabez Bunting might well preen itself on having staked all on the survival of the establishment rather than on its collapse.

The Protestant Dissenting Deputies went into action under the new system with other Dissenting bodies and before the end of 1833 had compiled a minimum programme of five points:

1. a legal registration of births, marriages and deaths, dissenting registers not having the same standing in the courts as parish registers;
2. the right to marry in dissenters' chapels;
3. the right of burial according to nonconformist forms in parochial cemeteries;
4. the removal of university tests;
5. the abolition of church rates.

This was a not unrealistic programme, but by the end of the

decade only the first two items had been obtained, and schemes for disestablishment had begun to look like pipe-dreams. Why, then, as the revolutionary atmosphere of the Reform crisis evaporated, did Dissent begin to look politically so feeble?

The first cause of weakness could not have been foreseen: it was that the Reform Act ushered in a generation of weak government, broken only by the strong ministry of Sir Robert Peel, a ministry from which only Unitarian Dissenters received any benefit. Notwithstanding the excitement of the elections of 1832, even the first Whig government under the new system was a weak one, it rapidly became divided upon Irish policy, and let in the Tories before the first Parliament had run its course. Irish preoccupations postponed the day when the government might pay attention to the grievances of its Nonconformist supporters, and when that time arrived in 1834-5, the legislative capacity of the government was severely curtailed by the opposition. At the elections of 1835 the Whigs lost ground, and after those of 1837 they were a spent force, feebly struggling to maintain a bare majority. The Nonconformist politicians were thus faced with an insoluble problem. From the beginning there had been a cleft between the prosperous Protestant Dissenting Deputies, who represented the congregations of the minority London Dissenters, and the apocalyptic fire of Baptists and Congregationalists in the North or in Wales, who in places represented the ruling orthodoxy. The Deputies limited their purview to the redress of grievances, and would have no truck with visionary schemes like disestablishment. Very shortly they were reinforced in some unlikely quarters. The Unitarian *Christian Reformer*, which had recently been rabidly anti-Anglican, warned Nonconformists in May 1834

> that intemperate language and menacing and violent proceedings are hurtful, if not destructive to their own interests. If on matters of *time* and *degree*, they quarrel with a friendly government, they may soon have to fight a battle of great *principles* with a government decidedly inimical.[73]

[73] *The Christian Reformer*, I (May 1834), 423.

This prophecy was fulfilled within six months, and it became the policy of this journal to urge that the Dissenters' only hope of concessions was to give docile support to their Whig allies in office. In 1838 Robert Vaughan, then professor of history at University College, London, and in 1843 Principal of Lancashire Independent College, recommended that the Congregationalists, who in 1832 had formed the Congregational Union with a view to agitating for disestablishment, should hold their peace.

> If there are Dissenters who, having looked to the monarchy and to the court of England; and to the prepossessions, on this subject, of . . . the upper, and even the lower house of Parliament; and have expected to see these parties concur in any thing approaching towards an extinction of the State Church, such expectation must surely have been indulged in some of those delusive moments when the passions do not allow the understanding to perform its proper office.[74]

With Wesleyans attacking disestablishment in almost Tractarian terms,[75] and exceedingly sore at the interference of other denominations in Connexional affairs, it might be thought that the game was up.[76]

It could, however, be urged that this Dissenting conservatism was totally unconstructive, that crumbs would never fall unsolicited from the Whig table, and that by compromising upon a totally unintelligible principle the Nonconformist leaders were ruining their only hope of translating their strength in the country into political terms. This became the cry of Edward Miall,[77] a Congregational minister who was turned by the church rates issue and his experience of Leicester radicalism into a sworn foe of the establishment and all its

[74] R. Vaughan, *Religious Parties in England: Their Principles, History, and Present Duty* (London 1839), pp. xlv–xlvi; cf. R. Vaughan, *Congregationalism: or, The Polity of Independent Churches, Viewed in Relation to the State and Tendencies of Modern Society* (London 1842), pp. 172–3.

[75] *Wesleyan-Methodist Magazine*, 3rd ser., xv (1836), 26.

[76] This evidence seems to me to require the modification of the argument pressed by Professor Gash, that disestablishment was becoming the dogma of Dissent in these years; Miall's broader programme discussed below was an attempt to find a new basis for a policy which had admittedly failed; cf. N. Gash, *Reaction and Reconstruction in English Politics 1832–1852* (Oxford 1965), p. 74.

[77] E. Miall, *The Nonconformist's Sketch-book* (London 1845), pp. 5–6.

works. In 1841 he launched *The Nonconformist*, the sturdiest of all disestablishment journals, and tried to turn all the forces of movement, Chartism, free trade, Complete Suffrage, rural misery,[78] against the stubborn mass of established religion. The turn taken by the education issue in the early 'forties also renewed support for disestablishment among the more doctrinaire Dissenters; the Congregational Union launched a rabid disestablishment sheet, *The Christian Witness*, in 1844; and the Disruption in Scotland, coinciding as it did with the last agonies of Newman and his Oxford friends, raised hopes that a general break-up might be at hand.

But neither the dissenting agitators, nor the official party organizers, could end the deadlock created by the new electoral structure. In 1847 Baines, Miall and all the voluntaryist doctrinaires urged Dissenters to put up anti-State-education candidates wherever they could carry them, and where they could not find candidates 'prepared to utter their anti-education shibboleth', they were to abstain. A Unitarian commentator reckoned that not more than a dozen boroughs could be carried on this platform, while perhaps fifty seats might be lost to the Whigs through Nonconformist abstention.[79] The insoluble dilemma of the Nonconformist politicians was that if they were docile they would get nothing, while if they agitated they would probably let in the Tories. Not until the electoral deadlock was broken up in 1868 were they able to put the screw upon a Liberal government powerful enough to act. Miall's policy was to break the electoral system and his hopes, like Marx's, were disappointed by the fact that, contrary to all previous experience, agrarian and urban discontent were not again to reach a revolutionary climax together.

Moreover, as the Nonconformists became distracted by this dilemma in the later 'thirties, they began furious efforts to disendow each other. The lawsuits earlier brought by Congregationalists against Unitarian trustees, to recover endowments which they had inherited from their Presbyterian forebears, reached an acrimonious climax. The Unitarians

---

[78] E. Miall, *The Social Influences of the State-Church* (London 1867), Chapter IX.
[79] *The Christian Reformer*, new ser., iii (1847), 377.

were turned out of the Protestant Dissenting Deputies, taking with them valuable financial support and important connexions with the Whigs, and seemed likely to be deprived of most of their chapels. Eventually in 1844 Peel saved the day for them with his Dissenters' Chapels Bill – a bill furiously opposed by the Wesleyans, notwithstanding their habitual complaints at outside interference in their own affairs.[80]

If the Wesleyans were brought nearer to the evangelical Dissenters by these cases, and by the abuse which they suffered from the Tractarians, the education issue revealed how equivocal these improved relations were. In 1839, while most Dissenters were still prepared to support a national education scheme, Russell made the first moves with a plan for a normal and model school under state management; the Wesleyans were prepared to denounce any scheme of the kind as an attempt to gain the whole world at the cost of the nation's soul, and their opposition, added to that of the Church, was sufficient to wreck the scheme.[81] In 1843 they acted strongly with the Nonconformists to defeat Sir James Graham's Factory Education Bill as giving gross preference to the Church, but when Russell moved again with fresh education minutes in 1847, the Conference committees concerned, contrary to all public expectation, infuriated the voluntaryists and the Connexional opposition to Bunting by lending their support, and drove Unitarians speechless with indignation by securing special advantages through a private negotiation with the government carried through by Lord Ashley.[82] Though by this volte-face the Connexional leaders bid up their price to the ministry, they broke up the evangelical Nonconformist front, and brought their own denomination nearer to the disastrous schisms soon to follow.

The crusade for disestablishment was not broken up solely by the electoral dilemma and Nonconformist disunity; there was also the disastrous depression which began in 1837 and reached its bottom in 1842. In these years the Chartist movement rose to its peak and, with society seriously threatened by

[80] *Wesleyan-Methodist Magazine*, 3rd ser., xv (1836), 235; xxiii (1844), 415–17, 660–7.
[81] ibid., xvii (1838), 69, 260–2.
[82] *The Christian Reformer* (1847), 304–5; E. Hodder, *The Life and Work of the Seventh Earl of Shaftesbury, K.G.* (London 1886), ii, 214–15.

the politics of desperation among the lower classes, it was not easy to pretend that the root of all evil lay in a State Church; indeed at this juncture the Church and the bulk of the chapels were on the same side. Moreover, in the minds of many who had been hottest against the Church, the depression created a new symbol for social iniquity, and that symbol was the Corn Laws. Free trade in corn might reduce production costs and give new hope of setting the wheels of business turning again; it might help to choke the slave economy of the American South by encouraging the development of the North as an English granary; it would be a great blow to the nexus of privileged institutions whose selfish interests cramped the development of the country (including, of course, the Church whose corn-rents would be reduced by a fall in prices). In 1841 Cobden set George Thompson, the American anti-slavery agitator, to organize at Manchester a grand synod of Dissenting ministers (from which Wesleyans were conspicuously absent) which obligingly declared the Corn Laws anathema, 'opposed to the law of God . . . anti-scriptural and anti-religious', terms which only lately had been reserved for the State Church. The funds, fervour and organization of the Anti-Corn Law League were in a measure so much lost to the campaign for disestablishment.

The disappointments of these years left a permanent mark on the agitation for disestablishment and associated objects. This is well illustrated by the change which came over the campaign against church rates. The spleen which had been mounting against them in the later 'twenties boiled over after the Reform Bill. Church rates were levied for the last time in Birmingham in 1831, and in Leeds in 1833, in which year the rate was levied in Manchester by one vote in a poll of 7,000. The following year a tremendous battle was joined over a halfpenny rate; the friends of the Church, beaten by armies of unqualified voters whipped in by the Dissenters, never dared levy a compulsory rate again.[83] By comparison with these ferocious struggles parliamentary elections were com-

---

[83] *The Christian Reformer*, I (1834), 727; this thoroughly mendacious Nonconformist account needs to be corrected by those of the *Manchester Guardian*, 6, 13, 27 September 1834, and the *Manchester Courier*, 6 September 1834, 11 July 1835, 11 March 1837.

monly kid-glove affairs. John Bright described how at Rochdale

> he had seen three or four thousand persons assembled in the churchyard, harangued by aspiring orators who denounced the system of church rates. He had seen the church crowded by persons in a temper and state of mind which it was a matter of regret to witness anywhere, but especially in a place of worship. He had known an expenditure take place on such occasions far exceeding the expenditure at contested elections. He had seen the military called out. And he had seen the vicar of the parish exposed to insults to which every man of right feeling must regret that a minister of religion should be subjected.[84]

Peel from the Tory side insisted in 1835 that the church rate question must be cleared up,[85] for various reasons many Anglicans felt no less strongly,[86] and yet year after year no bill could be got through to abolish them or put them on a voluntary basis. Not until the eve of the great Liberal triumph of 1868 was the right of vestries to levy compulsory church rates brought to an end.

Long before this time, although church-rate bills were hardy annuals, the main struggle had gone elsewhere, and already by 1851 it was computed that only three-sevenths of the possible rate-payers were being assessed. This result was brought about partly by the organizing of majorities in the vestries in parts of London and the great industrial towns to refuse the levy of church rates, and partly by putting legal obstacles in the way. Samuel Courtauld, a Unitarian silk and crêpe manufacturer, launched the cases at Braintree in Essex in 1837 which went through court after court, the second of them reaching the Lords only in 1852. The cases showed how far a pertinacious individual might go in putting the Church upon a voluntary basis by catching out the incumbent or churchwardens on points of law. The Liberation Society, Miall's notorious disestablishment body founded in 1844, brought out a tract, on *Illegal Church Rates: being Practical Directions to prevent their Collection*, to show how.

[84] *The Edinburgh Review*, c, no. 204 (October 1854), 308.
[85] *The Edinburgh Review*, c, 306; cix, no. 221 (January 1859), 76.
[86] e.g. *Westminster Review*, new ser., xiv (1 July 1858), 46–7.

To give a specimen: it is now held to be the undoubted legal right of every parishioner to raise a discussion and take a vote on each item of the estimate; and there is no limit to the number of amendments that may be moved prior to going to a poll on the first question, whether any rate shall be levied at all. If the chairman lacks patience or discretion, the odds are that he will fail in some point of form or order, and the slightest aberration may prove fatal to the rate. Indeed, the power of a minority at a vestry meeting may be compared to that of a minority in the House of Commons who are determined to obstruct an obnoxious measure by moving adjournments.[87]

By these methods the battle against church rates had in many places been won long before 1868, and a process had been set in motion of virtual disestablishment by parishes. This process was very characteristic of the later history of the disestablishment movement as a whole, which became concerned with sectional victories like that which wrested a great part of the university endowments from the hands of the Church, and with struggles to secure local triumphs in Ireland, Wales and Scotland. From this standpoint the disestablishment campaign became part of the general movement for administrative local options, and as such became linked with liquor licensing and other quite separate matters. The establishment of the distinct Welsh Sabbath was a step towards the disestablishment of the Welsh Church; it helped to make Wales a special case.

IX

The threat to the establishment was thus dissolved by forces as complex as those by which it had been created. But if the Church was not saved by her own efforts, it would be a great mistake to suppose that no efforts were made at all. The relatively superficial reforms of the pre-Reform era were now succeeded by fundamental administrative changes designed to redeploy the resources of the Church and by efforts to find a new role for the establishment in education.

By the time of the Reform Bill it was clear that an enormous amount of money was needed if the Church was to repair

[87] *The Edinburgh Review*, cix, no. 221 (January 1859), 71.

the deficiencies in its parochial system, root parsons in their parishes by building them houses, and end the abuses of pluralities; it was clear to the discerning that this would not come from the state, and to everyone that it would not come from a Whig ministry. Private generosity in the Church was so closely tied to local objects that it was difficult to use for central policies,[88] even where central policies themselves were not abused as Romanism.[89] The one hope was to free the superfluous wealth of the Church for urgent purposes. Lay patronage excluded any possibility of redistributing parochial endowments, and eyes turned inevitably to the estates of bishops, deans and chapters. When Lord Henley, Peel's brother-in-law, who wrote one of the most successful tracts on church reform in 1832, came to this point he looked favourably upon bishops, who, like parish priests, had useful work to do and a station to keep up. Moreover, the idea speedily got about that more bishops were needed, so that it seemed likely that the whole of the episcopal endowments would be required for the proper functioning of the order. This left to the cathedral chapters a great tangle of patronage, rich and poor, towards which no one was disposed to be sentimental. However valuable the cathedral clergy might be in other benefices, said Henley,

> here they have no sphere or means of usefulness. They are connected with no poor, who look up to them as their protectors and guides; they have no sick or dying to pray with; no children to catechize; no flock towards whom the sympathies and affections of a pastor can be called forth. The most important offering to God's glory and service, is a formal attendance on a cold and pompous ceremonial.

It was true that William Sewell, an Oxford eccentric, who was very often a fellow-traveller of the Tractarians, attempted to defend the very wastefulness of cathedral worship as a fitting return for the prodigal bounty of God,[90]

[88] cf. Peel's admission of this: B.M. Add. MSS. 40533, fo. 12, quoted in Olive J. Brose, *Church and Parliament: The Reshaping of the Church of England 1828–1860* (London 1959), p. 65.

[89] Rev. Edward Duncombe, *The Justice and Centralization: or the Parson and the Constitution* (York 1840), p. 44.

[90] *The Quarterly Review*, lviii, no. 115 (February 1837), 236.

making every faculty of man, the ear, the eye, the fancy, the reason, minister to its purpose; not penurious and thrifty, doling out its pittances for God, while treasures are lavished on our own luxuriousness – but profuse and bountiful, as the great Author of all mercies is bountiful to man; . . .

But even if the economics of the kingdom of God were what Sewell said they were, cathedrals mouldering to ruin, staffed by clergy who for much of their time were sinecurists in both senses, were an odd way to requite the bounty of God. Shortly after the middle of the century, under Cambridge influence, Gothic 'caught on' in the Church in a big way. Cathedrals then became stage properties almost as evocative as ruined monasteries a generation earlier, but as late as 1848 the high-church *Guardian* could declare that[91]

Cathedral Chapters make the Church unpopular wherever they are. We do not overlook the bright examples which individual members of them, in different places, have set and are now setting; but it is impossible to gainsay that universal testimony, which speaks to the spirit of exclusiveness and nepotism which the bodies have exhibited. . . . Everybody who has lived near a cathedral town has a fund of anecdotes illustrative of the prebendal religious and social code. He tells you that the first use which these bodies make of their ecclesiastical wealth and position, is to make a broad and impassable distinction between themselves and the other clergy, whom they cease to treat as equals and almost to recognise as brothers; that they form what are called 'county connexions', set themselves up, give themselves airs, live expensively, keep carriages and horses, and regard themselves as having risen above the rank of clergy into that of lay magnates and men of the world. . . . The cathedral bodies have contrived to get a bad name; and one, we grieve to say, too universal not to be deserved. . . .

Clearly cathedral endowments must be put to some useful purpose or taken away. Durham had prudently endowed a university during the Reform crisis, Wells and Chichester opened theological colleges a few years later, but churchmen like Blomfield could not fail to contrast the spiritual destitution

[91] *Guardian*, 24 May 1848, p. 337.

of London with the inert opulence of St Paul's,[92] and it was simplest to appropriate cathedral revenues for other purposes. Henley recommended that this be done, as preferments became vacant, by a church commission composed partly of salaried staff and partly of great officers in Church and State. This proposal was in great measure followed by Peel when he created the Ecclesiastical Commissioners in 1835.

The Ecclesiastical Commissioners ran true to form. They recommended a revision of episcopal salaries, cuts from the wealthier sees going to reinforce the poorer; two new sees were created at Manchester and Ripon to ease the load upon Chester and York. Cathedral chapters (Oxford excepted) were to be reduced to a common staff of a Dean and four Canons, and the income of the suppressed benefices was to go to the Commissioners, chiefly for the augmentation of poor livings. Capitular patronage should be vested in the Bishop, who as a public personage was thought less susceptible to dubious transactions. These and other recommendations were given legislative force by the Whig government between 1836 and 1840, Melbourne appointed a permanent Ecclesiastical Commission in 1836, and in 1840 gave all the bishops membership of it. They began to end the wasteful leasing of episcopal and capitular property by beneficial leases and to break through the mass of private freeholds in the interests of the Church as a body. One of these interests was, of course, in church extension which Blomfield continued on a vast scale in London, and the additional funds now available enabled the Church further to adapt its methods to those which prospered among the voluntary bodies. The great vice of the Church Building Act of 1818 had been that it had required a church to be built before an ecclesiastical district could be formed, and it had accordingly produced more churches than congregations. Not a little Methodist virtue in church-building arose from the necessity of gathering a congregation first. The Church Pastoral Aid Society, founded in 1836, had acknowledged that man-power was much nearer the core of the problem of spiritual destitution than bricks and mortar, and in its very first year sent a great party of curates and lay

[92] *Parliamentary debates*, 3rd ser., lv, 1137–8.

assistants to the howling wilderness of Yorkshire. In 1843 Peel's New Parishes Act took the whole conception a great deal further by providing that a district could be formed where the population was over 2,000 and that the Ecclesiastical Commissioners could provide a stipend for the minister. It was then up to the minister and congregation to get the church built, and the one snag was that larger endowments than before were locked up in guaranteeing the stipend. While the Ecclesiastical Commissioners were waiting for canons to die, and for leases for life to run out, they had very little money; Peel therefore enabled them to anticipate the profits of their future rack rents by borrowing from Queen Anne's Bounty.

There is no doubt at all that over the next twenty years these new administrative and legislative devices gave the Church a tremendous shot in the arm, and even at the beginning enabled her to take advantage of the great improvement in her political position. Yet from the first they were subject to a great deal of criticism. Manning, whose inelastic mind always moved in rigid antitheses, considered that, as the state rather than the successors of the apostles had taken the lead in all this, total erastianism had taken over; those who complained that a potent new engine had been put at the disposal of the bishops were nearer the mark, but the truth really was that a new church institution had been created which, with others, would in the very long run sensibly modify the initiative accorded by the Prayer Book to bishops, priests and deacons. If these institutions were not apostolical, neither were they erastian. A second group of criticisms came from all those who could not bear to see funds accruing locally being spent elsewhere, though this was what had happened to a large part of capitular funds for centuries, and with little consideration for policy. There were, moreover, abundant complaints of the utter inefficiency of the Commissioners, and of their meeting running expenses from capital.[93] The truth of these comments we cannot now judge, but there was a major scandal at the end of 1849, when the joint secretary and treasurer, C. K. Murray, was found to have

[93] e.g. *Guardian*, 13 February 1850, p. 101.

embezzled funds to the tune of £7,000 for the purpose of gambling in railway shares, and had lost all. His joint office had been created for purposes of economy, but as treasurer he took incoming sums of money, and when the accountant sent out reminders to the parties who appeared to be in arrear, Murray as secretary took the reminders from the office messenger![94]

The basic flaw in the original arrangements of the Ecclesiastical Commissioners, however, was that they contributed nothing to the salvation of the chapters themselves. If the elaborate cathedral establishments of old were too large for sinecure corporations, a dean and four canons were equally too many, and from 1849 onwards there were proposals to put the endowments to other uses. When the challenge was actually put no one seemed to know what the purposes of cathedrals were,[95] and a fresh crop of reports of cathedral abuses [96] made the matter urgent. Even in the deaneries where Gaisford, Milman, Waddington, Peacock, Buckland and Conybeare bore testimony to a wealth of learning, specifically ecclesiastical scholarship was not greatly in evidence. At the end of 1852 a strong cathedral commission was appointed which began by publishing the cathedral statutes. The church world then discovered that there were two distinct types of ancient cathedral, those of the Old Foundation,[97] and conventual[98] and New Foundation cathedrals,[99] with quite different statutes and objects. The cathedrals of the Old Foundation had been in origin missionary colleges, in which the bishop had been the central figure, and had lived in common with his missionary staff; they had been *sine cura animarum* because of their evangelistic functions. The other churches had been of monastic origin and had been given capitular form at the

[94] The history of the Ecclesiastical Commissioners is attractively treated in G. F. A. Best, *Temporal Pillars: Queen Anne's Bounty, the Ecclesiastical Commissioners, and the Church of England* (Cambridge 1964), but no tests of economic efficiency are applied.

[95] See, for example, the extraordinary hodge-podge in *The Edinburgh Review*, xcvii, no. 197 (January 1853), 161.

[96] e.g. R. Whiston, *Cathedral Trusts and Their Fulfilment* (London 1849); *The Christian Reformer*, new ser., v (1849), 189.

[97] York, St Paul's, Chichester, Exeter, Hereford, Lichfield, Lincoln, Salisbury and Wells in England; St Asaph, Bangor, Llandaff and St David's in Wales.

[98] Canterbury, Carlisle, Norwich, Winchester, Durham, Ely, Rochester and Worcester.

[99] Bristol, Oxford, Chester, Peterborough and Gloucester.

Reformation. They had, however, kept their collegiate character, and in some of them the bishop had very little authority indeed. Their statutes bore witness to the objects of a religious community, the promotion of learning, the celebration of perpetual worship and the maintenance of discipline, none of them objects bearing upon diocesan organization.[100] Centres either of evangelism or of ecclesiastical scholarship would have been invaluable to the Church in the middle of the nineteenth century, but neither was likely in chapters enervated by the torpor of centuries, and then truncated by reformers who took them at their own valuation. The objects of cathedrals had been discovered too late, and Walter Kerr Hamilton's pamphlet, *Cathedral Reform*, issued in 1853, was an early move in the still-continuing quest to find something for cathedrals to do – one of the unwritten chapters of modern ecclesiastical history. The raising of the collegiate churches of Manchester and Ripon to cathedral status gave notice that the scale of the problem would grow larger.

The education problem was involved in the same ambiguities as the church-building question, with which indeed it had been connected from the first. Before the end of the eighteenth century there were those who held that the influence of the parson was lost without the school, and that 'the first necessary step towards *restoring the influence of religion* is the making a permanent provision for the *religious education* of poor children'.[101] The schools societies which were founded soon afterwards were to expand the supply of religious education with a view to filling the empty churches, and justifying the efforts of the church-builders to create more. The only question was what sort of religion was to be offered to the children in the schools.[102] The high-church party, which was in full cry against the Bible Society for the heinous sin of offering the scriptures without note or comment, founded the National

---

[100] *Parliamentary papers*, H.C. 1854 XXV; 1854–5 XV; *Guardian*, 2 August 1854, p. 611: art. 'Cathedral Reform'.

[101] D. Davies, *The Case of Labourers in Husbandry Stated and Considered*, p. 94.

[102] This question is admirably treated by G. F. A. Best, 'The religious difficulties of national education in England, 1800–70', in *Cambridge Historical Journal*, xii, 2, pp. 155–73. Mr Best, however, presses his argument too far when he subsumes the question of educational efficiency altogether under the heading of religious difficulties.

Society 'for the Education of the Poor in the Principles of the Established Church' as understood by high-churchmen; other churchmen (especially evangelicals) joined with Dissenters, as they had in the Bible Society, to propagate an undenominational Christianity in the British and Foreign Schools Society. The question of voluntaryism did not at first arise, nor was there a clear cleavage between the Church and Dissent. Still less was there any question, as has lately been suggested,[103] of opposing the 'unity' of education (whatever that might mean in the nineteenth century) or medieval or Tudor conceptions to secularism. The undenominational Christianity of the British and Foreign Schools Society was not a fancy but a fact, and was already embodied in the schools of the Sunday School Union, which were managed by a committee composed half of churchmen and half of Dissenters, and early in the century it attracted not far short of a million children. Each of the societies was 'official', and the one ambiguity was that, by its title, the National Society claimed the privileges of the establishment not only for the Church as a pastoral body but for a party within the Church. This ambiguity was quickly exposed when the public purse became involved.

The first small state grants in 1833 acknowledged the existing position (that national education was the function of official societies) but undermined it by dividing the grant in proportion to money raised by the societies, enabling the National Society, with its access to the pockets of the upper classes, to secure the lion's share of the public funds. If this did not commend it to a Whig ministry in which undenominationalism was incarnate in Lord John Russell, still less did the efforts of a party of high-churchmen to rejuvenate the society in 1838, and develop a teacher-training scheme based on cathedral endowments. Moreover, the cause of undenominational education had not stood still. In 1831 a Board of Education had been successfully established in Ireland on which sat the Anglican and Roman Catholic Archbishops of Dublin, a member of the synod of Ulster, the Lord Lieutenant and three laymen, one of whom was a Unitarian. They made

[103] H. J. Burgess, *Enterprise in Education: the story of the work of the Established Church in the education of the people prior to 1870* (London 1958), pp. 89–90.

arrangements for the clergy to have access to the children in the schools for purposes of denominational education, and for an agreed anthology of selections from the Bible to be used by the teachers in ordinary lessons. By the mid-'thirties the scheme seemed to be well established, and was eagerly taken up by the new Liberal council in the town where English denominational conditions most approximated to Irish, namely Liverpool. In two schools the Irish plan was adopted under the inspiration of the Unitarian, William Rathbone, as a model, it was hoped, for adoption elsewhere. Lord John Russell was not prepared to extend this on a national scale, but when in April 1839 he increased the education grant and set up the Committee of the Council on Education he proposed to erect a pilot project in a normal and model school on the Liverpool pattern.

There were two possible bases for undenominational education: one was the view abused by evangelicals and Tractarians as liberalism, the other was evangelicalism itself, which by the 'thirties was strongly represented in most of the English denominations. As late as 1836, evangelicals had made an essay in undenominational and Pestalozzian infant teaching through the Home and Colonial School Society, and with the ferocious Roman Catholic Archbishop of Tuam, John MacHale, attacking the Irish system, and the Tractarians extending their grip on the National Society, they might have been expected to give their backing to Russell's plan. In fact, on Merseyside, Hugh McNeile in Liverpool and Hugh Stowell in Salford were rejuvenating the Church by violent Orange campaigns, turned against any plan which looked like a concession to Catholics and, following the lead of extreme evangelicals in Ireland, put about the gross calumny that the Liverpool and Irish scheme involved the use of a mutilated version of the scriptures and the exclusion of the Bible as a whole. Behind the front line they were reinforced by Francis Close in Cheltenham and Lord Ashley in London, and went far to establish Anglican unity behind the National Society. With the Wesleyans coming to the conclusion that Russell's scheme involved a state-recognition of Popery and Socinianism, and . . . principles which, if legitimately carried out and fairly applied, would require a state-recognition of Infidelity and Socialism,[104]

even the normal and model school had to be dropped, and the Committee of Council survived a parliamentary challenge only by a hair's breadth.

The effects of this crisis were far-reaching, though hardly constituting the triumph for liberty claimed by recent church writers.[105] In the first place the National Society put forth a tremendous effort to extend its operations, and in the second it pressed its advantage further against the government. School inspectors were for the first time appointed to supervise the expenditure of the increased government grants, and in 1840, by what was known as the Concordat, the Church secured that no inspector of her schools should be appointed without the consent of the Archbishop, who should also receive the inspectors' reports. Church pressure also put a stop to grants to Roman Catholic schools.[106] But even this triumph could not disguise the ambiguity in the high-church use of the National Society, and Joshua Watson resigned in the conviction that too much had been conceded to the state, or, in other words, to the admission that the national religion was not altogether that of the National Society. As the *Edinburgh Review* unkindly put it in 1850 when similar tensions were threatening Archdeacon Denison's connection with the society,

> The real ground of controversy is in the question, who is to teach the people, and what are they to be taught? It is our affair, says the Church, – and ours, too, replies the State. Yes, rejoins the Church, it is your business to pay for it.[107]

The question was taken a stage further in 1843, when, after

---

[104] *Wesleyan-Methodist Magazine*, 3rd ser., xviii (1839), 939.

[105] A. B. Webster, *Joshua Watson: The Story of a Layman 1771-1855* (London 1954), p. 48.

[106] When in 1847 Lord Lansdowne said that Roman Catholics had not pressed a claim since 1840, he was given the lie by *The Tablet*; cf. *The Christian Reformer*, new ser. iii (1847), 373-4.

[107] *The Edinburgh Review*, xcii, no. 185 (July 1850), 118.

pressure from Lord Ashley, Sir James Graham moved the Factory Education Bill which proposed to limit children's working hours and require part-time attendance at schools governed by boards of seven trustees, of whom two were to be churchwardens and the chairman a parish priest. This bill produced a tremendous storm amongst Nonconformists, who now numbered enthusiastic Wesleyans among their ranks. As recently as 1839 one of the Protestant Dissenting Deputies had moved that

> education of the lower classes of society at the public expense is not a legitimate function of the government, which is constituted for the sole purpose of dispensing justice and of securing to the whole community without distinction the fullest enjoyment of liberty and property[108]

but he had been unable to find a seconder. Now voluntaryism, pertinaciously propounded by Baines and Miall, became the official Nonconformist creed, and the favours of the state were set over against the efforts of church bodies in a manner foreign to earlier experience. Moreover, the attitude of the high-church intransigents was not very different. The thing which lashed the Wesleyans to fury was the growth of Tractarianism and the discovery that, having just laid claim to be a Church, they were being unchurched by apostolicals all round the country.[109] Baines ascribed the bill to 'priestly monopoly' and 'Puseyite-Popery'; yet the fact was that many of the high-churchmen held aloof because the bill made some concessions to the consciences of Dissenters, and exposed a little further the impossibility of making the establishment a stalking-horse for high-church principles.

This exposure was skilfully completed when Lord John Russell made the next forward move with the Education minutes of 1846. The devious diplomacy by which the Wesleyans were now induced to support the government scheme must be set forth elsewhere; what is interesting is the crisis which it produced in the National Society, notwithstanding

[108] B. L. Manning, *The Protestant Dissenting Deputies* (Cambridge 1952), p. 339.
[109] *Wesleyan-Methodist Magazine*, 3rd ser., xxii (1843), 615.

the enormous financial advantages which it brought. The government sought to introduce a standard management clause in the Trust Deeds of each new church school built with the aid of state grant, establishing a board of managers including laymen; by this means the public might obtain some continuity of policy (which the patronage system notoriously failed to guarantee in the clergy) and place some bridle on the unfettered control of the parson. This was sufficient to goad Archdeacon Denison into a bitter campaign in favour of the priest's exclusive rights, which finally forced the society to break off its negotiations with the government, but not before Archbishop Sumner had refused to press the society's claims further.

Along with this controversy Denison fought another over the conscience clauses. The original object of the National schools had been to give every child instruction in the Prayer Book Catechism and require church attendance. But from very early days many schools had exempted children of Dissenting parents from these requirements, and no difficulty arose until the 'forties. There was then, under Tractarian influence, pressure to repair this breach in the National Society's logic which evoked efforts by Sir James Kay-Shuttleworth at the Committee of Council to secure a conscience clause in the Trust Deeds as the price of state aid. Again Denison went furiously to war, claiming that to omit Prayer Book teaching would injure children's souls by implying 'that reading writing and arithmetic are essential parts of education, but religious knowledge is not'. This campaign drove Francis Close, the evangelical who had done so much to promote the Church rally of 1839, out of the Society, and eventually raised such opposition that Denison himself was silenced. But Denison had clearly exposed the ambiguity, latent in the National Society from the beginning, that it claimed for the establishment rights which might reasonably have been conceded to the Church as a pastoral body. When in 1860 the Privy Council began to *demand* a conscience clause in selected projects, it skilfully chose schools in Wales where the Church was in a small minority, and where accordingly the principles of the Society implied the forcing of Anglican teaching upon those outside the Church. But as in church-building, so with the schools, the Church had made sacrifices to its ambitions as an establishment which as a pastoral body it could ultimately ill afford. Roman Catholic schools educating Roman Catholic children are a quite different economic proposition from Anglican schools educating children with whom the Church has no other pastoral connection.

Moreover, as at least Edward Higginson, an able Unitarian, recognized,[110] the upheavals of the 'forties had squarely posed the question of educational efficiency. The 'official' voluntary agencies had been primed with public funds, and goaded still more by the prospect of government intervention. The crisis of 1839 had driven the National Society to raise one immense fund, that of 1843 had driven the Wesleyans and Independents to raise another; the Education minutes of 1846 had the same effect again. But

the voluntary principle is of fluctuating and unreliable force. It can make great efforts on great occasions; but the continued, equable, though smaller effort, year by year, is the greater difficulty. It is easier to build a schoolroom once for all, than to maintain its annual expenses, as experience continually shows. Then the voluntary principle is chiefly effective within narrow limits. It may bring the wealthy and educated classes of a moderate-sized town and neighbourhood into joint action on behalf of the poor and ignorant of the same district but it does not proportionately provide for the educational needs of those districts . . . in which the poor and ignorant hold more than the average proportion to the wealthy and educated classes. . . . There is not, we believe, at the present time a single voluntary organization, unless it be Wesleyan Methodism, that has any pretensions to this ubiquity of equalized action. . . . And the same insufficiency of voluntary societies is experienced in the want of adequate provision for the training of masters . . . [which] is now and always has been the weakest part of the voluntary system (so-called), aided though it has been by large state donations.

Thus considerations of efficiency had converted the most nonconforming type of Dissenter to state action, and were to

[110] In an article signed 'E.H.H.', in *The Christian Reformer*, new ser., iii (1847), 65–88.

convert others before 1870. To the growth of undenominational religion a new force had been added.

X

The social developments of the first half of the nineteenth
century were enormously costly to the Church's social
influence, and the Religious Census of 1851 was to drive
home how much furious running churchmen needed to do
simply to stand still in relation to social development. Where
at least some circumstances were favourable, as for example
in Lancashire and Cheshire which suffered little from tithe
commutation and escaped the worst of the agricultural
depression, the Church could still remain on roughly equal
terms with Protestant Dissent (a position strikingly more
favourable than in the West Riding, for example); but rapid
urbanization, bitter social conflict, and a catastrophic tide
of Irish immigration, had reduced the church attendances
respectively to one-ninth and one-seventh of the population.
Nor was Nonconformity, which throve in the industrial
villages of Wales, Cornwall and Durham and in large tracts
of the countryside, better able to meet the need. The financing
of even this reduced scale of operations had helped to make a
church connection, whether in the establishment or out of it,
in a great measure one of the status symbols of the middle
class. And although Churches like the Primitive Methodist
might still be so largely composed of working-class members
as to be much influenced by working-class circumstances and
aspirations, they did not over the country as a whole make
much difference to the general picture. In places with a
considerable urban history behind them, and especially
London, working-class leaders preened themselves on their
rationalism, though it may be questioned whether their
affection for the last dregs of the Enlightenment should be
regarded in the Marxist manner as progressive. From the
Churches' point of view the steady diffusion of middle-class
standards after 1850 was to contribute to the thick veneer of
religiosity of the later Victorian period, and at Norwich nonconformity replaced atheism as the badge of working-class

radical leaders;[111] but in the new towns the passage of time was to produce an alienation from religion among the lower classes similar to that of the Great Wen itself.

This situation was the outcome of complicated social developments with which the Church had been unable to cope. The church parties whose activities fill a good deal of the ecclesiastical literature had only a peripheral bearing upon it. None of them ever managed to carry more than a minority of the clergy with it, and they were never as important as they supposed. Nevertheless behind the shrinking frontiers they left a mark upon the life of the Church which began to be seriously obliterated only in the second quarter of the twentieth century, and we may conclude by saying something of them and of their attitude towards the problem of the Church in mid-century.

First in the field and most influential was the evangelical party, a party which had been largely created by Wilberforce and had taken full advantage of the opportunities which had increased the power of evangelical opinions not only in England, but in America, Scotland and elsewhere. It was the genius of Wilberforce and his coadjutors to launch a vast number of campaigns, and to found or capture immense numbers of societies with worthy objects, so as to draw the upper classes into his programme of national reform, and insert the wedge of sound evangelical doctrine. The most important of these campaigns was that against slavery, which brought into play evangelical forces on both sides of the Atlantic, and displayed to the full the pressure which could be exerted by the evangelical machine. For it was a machine that Wilberforce had created, and the interlocking directorates of the key societies such as the Church Missionary Society, the Religious Tract Society, the British and Foreign Bible Society, the Jews' Society, the General Society for Promoting District Visiting, and the Church Pastoral Aid Society, gave a cohesion to the evangelical party which no other church party possessed. At the same time the influence of Charles Simeon at Cambridge, and lesser lights such as John Hill at St Edmund Hall, gave them a grip on the education of

[111] J. M. Ludlow & Lloyd Jones, *Progress of the Working Class, 1832–1867*, pp. 289–95.

generations of ordinands, an education which in numerous cases was paid for by evangelical benefactors. The lead taken in all this by influential laymen in raising funds, buying livings and generally pressing the cause (a role most strikingly played in the third generation when Shaftesbury became bishop-maker to Lord Palmerston) gave a fright to high-churchmen from very early days. As early as 1799, John Randolph, Bishop of Oxford, denounced the

> *increasing danger*, of which people are scarcely enough aware, which is the adopting and forwarding religious projects without the authority and assistance of the Church and its rulers. The end is ostensibly good, and the intention perhaps is such, but inasmuch as it tends to dissolve or weaken the tie by which the established church is held together, it becomes a cooperation with levellers and reformers.[112]

To denounce the evangelicals as virtual Methodists and Dissenters became common form with high-churchmen, and their abuse has passed into many of the books.

Yet it is obvious that, however impatient they might be with bishops, the great body of the evangelicals were strong establishment men, the more so as time passed. They did as much as any to weaken the ties of the Methodists with the Church,[113] and could not accomplish their work among the upper classes except through the Church. In Ireland in the 'twenties forlorn efforts of government to temper religious conflict seemed evidence to some that the ultimate apostasy of the Church was at hand, while in England the constitutional crisis which followed upon emancipation was too much for others, who began to fraternize with Brethren or dabble in Irvingism, faith-healing and speaking in tongues.[114] But the bulk of the party stood fast, and their unshakeable conviction that evangelicalism was the religion of the Bible and the Thirty-nine Articles appeared to them to give the Church a

[112] Bodleian MS. Top. Oxon. d. 354/2 fo. 74.

[113] See, for example, Arthur Pollard, 'Evangelical Parish Clergy, 1820–1840', in *Church Quarterly Review*, clix (July–September 1958), 392.

[114] H. B. Bulteel was one of the latter; a vivid account of his aberrations, and of the impact of the crisis upon evangelicals, is given in the MS. Diary of John Hill, at St Edmund Hall, under the years 1831 and 1832.

unique title to state support. Hugh McNeile, for example, denied

> that the state fixes our creed, and that we cannot change an article of our creed but by act of parliament. Our creed is fixed, not by the state, but by the Bible. There we find it, and present it in intelligible formulas to the civil ruler. . . . As to the charge that we cannot change an article of our creed, it is our glory that our creed is unchangeable. It is the one, the ancient, the true, the divine creed, which no man can change, . . . Thus the only terms of union, which are at once efficient in themselves, and scriptural in their application, exclude any and every society calling itself a christian church, but refusing to pledge itself to a written standard, or maintaining, in addition to a written standard, some further and undefined rule of faith or practice. The dissenter, therefore, who rejects the primitive formulary, and the papist who adds to it, tradition written and *unwritten*, (unwritten! there is an open door,) stand equally excluded from safe union with the state.[115]

Of course there were always some evangelicals who regarded the common evangelical platform which they shared with many Dissenters as more important than the special position of the Church (as there were always some whose scruples of conscience coincided with the demands of liberal reform); there were always some, of the sort who flocked into the Evangelical Voluntary Church Association, who thought the establishment restricted the power of the party,[116] and some of the great evangelical societies had been founded and continued to be supported by Dissenters; but when Edward Bickersteth and others used the grand furor against the Maynooth grant to launch the interdenominational Evangelical Alliance they received little support from their brethren. Of the 200 ministers who supported the first meeting at Liverpool in 1845 only nineteen were Anglicans; Hugh McNeile

[115] H. McNeile, *Lectures on the Church of England*, 3rd edn (London 1840), pp. 141-2. At this date evangelicals were still able to regard doctrinal development in the Church as evidence of the depravity of Catholics, and this passage helps to explain why many evangelicals in the next generation were so shocked by the discovery that there was doctrinal development in the Bible itself.

[116] On this ground Baptist Wriothesley Noel seceded to the Baptists in 1848; cf. B. W. Noel, *Essay on the Union of Church and State* (London 1849).

denounced the grant,[117] while Hugh Stowell got up a petition of the Manchester clergy against it, partly on the grounds that the Alliance made schism appear unimportant and took for granted that it would continue. At this date, indeed, Stowell had not yet lost hope that the state would save the day for the Church by pouring its resources into the schools of the establishment.

It is easy to caricature the evangelicals as depending either on state action or a well-timed Second Coming, and liberal and Catholic writers repeatedly drew a picture of the evangelical parson doing nothing around his parish except preaching to the elect on the Sabbath and enjoying cross-word puzzle games with clues from the prophetic books. It took more than this to create the influence which evangelicals came to wield in their great suburban centres. It is worth quoting at length a description of Stowell's methods given by his son.[118]

With the aid of two curates, five services were held every Sunday in the parish; three in the church and two elsewhere; Mr. Stowell himself always preaching morning and evening, and once a month publicly catechising in the church in the afternoon. On Wednesday evenings there was service, followed by an expository lecture; each of the Gospels and Epistles being in turn plainly and practically explained. Schoolroom and cottage lectures were frequent during the week. On the Saturday evening, previous to the monthly celebration of the Lord's Supper, there was a preparatory service in the church. Lent and Passion Week also brought their special services. The poor were sought out in their own houses by a large staff of volunteer district-visitors, each with their special mission. The schools, Day and Sunday, were on a very large scale, and in a high state of efficiency. A striking feature in the latter was the number of grown-up persons, often married men and women, who regularly took their place among the scholars. Then there was an Adult Sunday School, in which some of the pupils were past the three score years and ten, Ragged Schools, and a Refuge for the fallen. The teachers of these schools, and the district visitors, met their pastor once a month for counsel and advice; while every Saturday evening

[117] H. McNeile, *The manifested oneness of the Church of Christ: with some reasons for not joining the proposed Evangelical Alliance* (London 1846), pp. 58-9.
[118] J. B. Marsden, op. cit., pp. 47-8.

Rector and Curates met for prayer and reading the word. There were Libraries too, and a Mutual Improvement Society, and Clothing Clubs, and other minor institutions of a like sort; and all these required and received his continual supervision. The preparation of young persons as candidates for Confirmation was a work upon which Mr. Stowell bestowed much time and pains, meeting them in classes weekly for many months previously, and afterwards having a private interview with each of the candidates, often numbering nearly two hundred. . . . Afterwards Mr Stowell added to these a monthly address to his large adult class. He threw it into the form of a catechetical lecture. It was a singular instance of the influence he then gained over the working classes.

Here the parish structure was adapted almost out of recognition; laymen were given a substantial share of an otherwise insupportable burden of pastoral oversight, there was some organized effort to meet the social needs of the district, and the incumbent still took a notable part in the politics of the town.

By the 'fifties, however, Lord Ashley and others felt they must break through the parish system altogether, and hold services in unconsecrated premises or in the open air. The practical difficulty for the Church was that under the Toleration Act of 1812 it was illegal for more than twenty persons to meet for religious worship in any building but a consecrated church or a licensed Dissenting chapel. This imposed very little restriction upon Dissenters, but was a serious drawback for the Church. Services out of church had long enjoyed the connivance of certain bishops[119] but they had never been safe, and with the Tractarian revival prosecutions were renewed. Despite the unanimous opposition of high-churchmen who could see the authority of the parson swept away by the uncontrolled operation of the evangelical machine, Shaftesbury obtained some legislative concessions, and a celebrated series of evangelistic services began in Exeter Hall. The vicar of the parish, to the chagrin of the bishop, nevertheless managed to secure an inhibition against the continuance of the services, with the result that they were immediately

[119] e.g., C. P. Fendall & E. A. Crutchley (eds), op. cit., pp. 213–14.

resumed by a young unknown, the Baptist orator to end all orators, C. H. Spurgeon; he speedily gathered the congregation which in 1861 opened the Metropolitan Tabernacle for him. The Exeter Hall pioneers moved off into low theatres elsewhere in London, and with the support of local incumbents managed to defeat the legal proceedings taken by the English Church Union. Other new ventures, of which the best-known perhaps was the Children's Special Service Mission, were also undertaken.

The evangelicals had therefore some intelligible answer to the predicament of the Church, which amounted to exploiting the advantages of the establishment and at the same time minimizing the disadvantages of the parish system. The question now was whether the merits of their party were not outweighed by its drawbacks. The great machine which Wilberforce had contrived in order to apply pressure at crucial points in the national life, had inevitably bred a great body of machine politicians to run it, and in the generation which followed his death there was a great chorus of complaints that evangelicals were not what they were. Shaftesbury himself

> ever maintained that the Evangelicals of his day had deteriorated, on the ground that they were not as clear in their views, as distinctive in their principles, or as thorough in their dogmatic teaching, as of old. [120]

It was true that a section of the party reached some very strange conclusions by a technical development of the characteristic evangelical doctrines. Many evangelicals were intensely preoccupied with death-bed scenes, perhaps because they had transformed the doctrine of justification by faith into a ritual repetition of approved formulae, which were indispensable *in extremis*. The doctrine of predestination, as currently taught, raised difficulties over baptism in which virtually the whole community then shared, and over the universal promises of the gospel. *The Edinburgh Review* may not have been altogether apocryphal in reporting that a

[120] E. Hodder, op. cit., iii, 4.

Leicestershire clergyman used to alter his lessons to read, 'God so loved the elect', 'I came not to judge the elect, but to save the elect';[121] and by transforming the authority of the Bible into verbal inspiration evangelicals could proclaim that

> the Bible has not a single scientific error in it; . . . its slightest intimations of scientific principles or natural phenomena have in every instance been demonstrated to be exactly and strictly true, . . . How is it that Moses, with no greater education than the Hindoo or the ancient philosopher, has written his book, touching science at a thousand points, so accurately, that scientific research has discovered no flaws in it . . .?[122]

But not all evangelicals were as foolish as this; they were right in thinking that the difficulties of the Church were not primarily intellectual, and the chief intellectual battle they entered, which culminated in the Gorham judgment, they won.

Moreover, the numbers of the evangelical clergy seem to have grown continuously in the first half of the century and in 1853 were reckoned by the *Edinburgh Review* at (the surely excessive proportion of) one-third of the entire Church. The problem was precisely how to keep such a large body in line, particularly a body created in the first instance as a pressure group. The uses of the machine in the second generation were exemplified in Liverpool where McNeile overawed the corporation and got rid of undenominational schools,[123] and in Manchester by Stowell's ubiquitous Orange organizations. There were other sectional causes, and at the back of them all was Alexander Haldane's *Record*, salvaged from financial collapse by its readiness to purvey the sensational to an emotionally overcharged generation, and alert to destroy the character of any who resisted the dictates of the evangelical wild men. Even if the protests of respectabilities such as

---

[121] *The Edinburgh Review*, xcviii, no. 200 (October 1853), 286n.

[122] This was Dr John Cumming, an evangelical best-selling minister of the Scottish Church, Crown Court, Covent Garden, an example of the unhappy Scots leaven poured into English evangelicalism, quoted in *The Westminster Review*, new ser., viii (1 October 1855), 450.

[123] This process is described in J. Murphy, *The Religious Problem in English Education: The Crucial Experiment* (Liverpool 1959).

John Venn, Archbishop Sumner and the *Christian Observer*[124] are discounted, Shaftesbury's pathetic letter to Haldane in 1856 is a cruel commentary.[125]

> This [the leadership of the Evangelical party] is a position too perilous, too uncertain, and too useless for any one to accept. No one can be an effective leader unless those who follow him are prepared to repose confidence in his judgment and guidance, not during smooth and easy times alone, but in times of doubt and perplexity. No one in these days has such a sentiment. All confidence has ceased; and people, from a variety of causes, take up their opinions, and let them fall, entirely in reference to themselves or their particular sections. A man that aspires to be a leader, or rather to assume the importance of one, must now either drive or be driven. The first is impossible in the state of men's minds; the second is disgraceful.
>
> Besides, though there are very many points, indeed most points, in which I concur theologically with the Evangelical party, there are some in which, as friends or counsellors, &c., &c., I think several of them very far from charity or justice. Let them catch me tripping (and who can always walk upright?) and there would be as much real spite (though veiled under regret) and pleasure, as among the editors of newspapers or the congregation of Puseyism.

This sorry confession from a servant of the cause as single-hearted as Shaftesbury sufficiently illustrates the degeneration of evangelical pressure politics and its inability to redeem the age.

The high-church party also had its machine, and its organ, the *British Critic*, and there was a comic episode in 1823–4 when the rival bodies went into action against each other in the cause of different pundits from the American Episcopal Church who were here on begging errands.[126] But from the time of Catholic Emancipation onwards it became clear to many of the younger men that some different form of organization would have to be thought up, and moreover that the

---

[124] Quoted in G. R. Balleine, *A History of the Evangelical Party in the Church of England* (London 1951), p. 163n.

[125] E. Hodder, op. cit., iii, 3.

[126] G. F. A. Best, 'Church Parties and Charities: The Experiences of Three American Visitors to England, 1823–1824', in *The English Historical Review*, lxxviii, no. 307 (April 1963), 243–62.

high-church gospel itself had become 'dry' and needed fresh presentation. It was the Oxford University by-election for 1829 in which Peel, the new-found friend of Emancipation, was defeated by Sir Robert Inglis, which divided Oriel College against itself, and brought Keble together with the younger men in the College against Copleston, Hawkins, and the leaders of its politics for a generation past; it gave Newman his first experience of public agitation, and threw up the slogans about the march of mind which were to do yeoman service in the 'thirties; and it began the displacement of the Clapton Sect in high-church leadership. This was rapidly completed when the Whig government undertook to reform the Irish Church in 1833, and in 1838 the *British Critic* itself fell into Newman's hands.

Of a subtler kind were the changes which went on in the high-church intellectual atmosphere. After the Reform Bill the Apostolic Succession was more than ever necessary to them as a device for unchurching Dissenters and for giving the Church some standing ground less precarious than its present constitutional status. As such it was carefully restated in 1838 by William Palmer, fellow of Worcester College, Oxford. But Newman regarded Palmer, who had been educated at Trinity College, Dublin, as something of a foreigner to the Oxford spirit and the two soon fell foul of one another. The younger men responded much more readily than their elders to the emotional pressure of the age. Ultimately their great impact upon the Church was in their influence upon the religious life, in both the technical and the untechnical senses of the term; from the beginning they prized 'heart-work' as much as the crudest Primitive Methodist, and set high store upon dogma and tradition and ministry as means by which men could appropriate the riches of the Christian heritage. They were romantics, even enthusiasts, and in their reaction against the dry intellectualism of the old high-church school and the brash rationalism of the Benthamites, they set themselves the problem of the relations of faith and reason in a very acute form. Partly because the Oxford men began with vehement denials of the religious significance of independent reason, they never cleared up this issue explicitly. All agreed that there was a moral basis to faith, and that the great safeguard of faith was a right state of heart; but these were positions capable of very various development. Newman later accepted much modern thought on the ground that, unlike a scientific theory, faith as an act of will was not vulnerable to any predictable accumulation of awkward evidence, while Pusey rejected liberal biblical criticism on the ground that it could only be the fruit of corrupt motives.

The new high-churchmanship did nothing at first to help the Church solve the social problems with which it was faced, problems which the Tractarians understood little, despite their romantic preoccupation with 'Christ's poor'. Keble provided them with a moral ideal of pastoral care, but in its practical bearings it was out of date even in its own day. To Keble's expostulation that he could not know what was happening in the minds of his parishioners at Hursley without hearing confessions, his friend and patron Sir William Heathcote perforce replied that if he did not know a parish of 400 souls without hearing confessions he would never know it. In any case there would never be enough clergy to confess the entire English nation, and although the efforts of the high-churchmen to establish a hall in Oxford for the cheap education of more clergy received influential backing in the later 'forties, they proved altogether abortive. After the middle of the century Anglo-Catholic advance began in parishes in the East End of London and other urban areas, but their chief essay in the urban pastorate before that date, St Saviour's, Leeds, had already suffered calamitously. The church was built by the private generosity of Pusey to assist Dr W. F. Hook, the sympathetic vicar of Leeds, in dividing his unmanageable parish; and it was to provide a new approach to the pastoral problem by enabling a number of clergy to live in common. Unfortunately, everything went wrong with the scheme from the beginning; in 1847 and 1851 there were secessions from St Saviour's to Rome, and Dr Hook became extremely embittered towards Pusey and his friends.

In two respects, however, the party had begun to leave its mark even before the middle of the century. The first lies outside the scope of this essay but requires mention, namely, the great extension of the colonial episcopate. The evangelicals had been first in this field, as in so many others, with the establishment of the see of Calcutta in 1814, and in Charles Perry, who became Bishop of Melbourne in 1847, they still had distinguished representation. But high-church influence lay behind the rapid extension of the colonial episcopate in the 'forties, and reinforced it by the work of the S.P.G. and by Beresford-Hope's gift of St Augustine's College, Canterbury, for the training of missionary clergy. The appearance of high-churchmen in authority in many colonial places introduced a new stiffness in the relations between Church and Dissent, and lashed Dissenters at home to fury.[127] But in other respects it proved a good advertisement for episcopacy in an episcopal system, for the total number of colonial clergy rapidly doubled, and a new vigour came into the Church overseas as a whole.

At home high-churchmen had made a beginning with the restoration of the corporate religious life. The early communities of men established by Newman at Littlemore and Faber in his parish in Rutland were terminated by secessions to Rome before they could accomplish anything tangible. Nor was the first community for women established at Park Village West, near Regent's Park, much more successful. But in the 'twenties and 'thirties the idea of the religious life was very much in the air, and there was a special leaning towards communities of women. Practical men valued the services they might render in visiting the poor or nursing the sick; high-church politicians took note that some outlet was needed for the piety of middle-class spinsters whose discomfort with their lot might otherwise drive them to Rome; Pusey asked nothing more than to give his daughter to the religious life. The Park Village community suffered from an unsuitable superior, and also from the fact that the direction was divided between Pusey and Dodsworth, the parish priest. The conclusion which Pusey drew from this enterprise was that in future an order must wait until it had an able superior, and that there must be no supervision by the parish

[127] The Christian Witness and Church Member's Magazine, iv (1847), 130–1: 'State Churchism: the blade, the ear, and the full corn in the ear'.

priest. Nor was the rule itself altogether satisfactory. The next community was established in Devonport in 1848 under Miss Sellon, a superior with perhaps an excess of talent, and in the same year the Community of St Mary the Virgin began its existence at Wantage, to assist the parish priest. This community was almost extinguished by the secessions occasioned by the Gorham Judgment, but proved in the end to be more durable than anything before it. The religious life had taken root, and was to blossom surprisingly in the next half-century, particularly amongst women. And although, as the Park Village enterprise had suggested, the attempt to promote the religious life with a view to fostering pastoral visiting or sick-nursing would not work, when once the religious life had taken root for its own sake, the Church was to have a valuable addition to its pastoral machinery.

The high-church revival of this period has lately been acutely, and rightly, defended from the charge of having originated in a political crisis,[128] but the political circumstances of its origin were to leave a deep mark upon its history. The power of the Oxford men, and their ability to defend some very reactionary causes in the early days, grew from the sense that they were the dedicated defenders of a persecuted Church, and their ability to manoeuvre a heterogeneous coalition of conservative inclinations dissolved rapidly after 1837 with the dissolution of the main threat to the Church. From then onwards other church parties and many of the non-partisan clergy were to find one aspect or another of the Tractarian position deeply distasteful, and many of the high-churchmen began to lose confidence in a Church which did not conform to their image. As we have seen already, high-church enterprises were over and over again to be injured by high-churchmen's own fears and suspicions of Rome and of what constituted Romanizing in the English Church. The lack of confidence among sections of the party, of which Shaftesbury had complained among the evangelicals, was bitterly reproduced by this issue amongst the high-churchmen.

Nor were these the sole consequences of the crumbling of the coalition which the Tractarians had led in the later

[128] In O. Chadwick, *The Mind of the Oxford Movement* (London 1960), p. 14,

'thirties. High-churchmen found themselves condemned to perpetual opposition in both Church and State, and willy-nilly began to form links with other opposition groups.[129] Nowhere was the change more striking than in Oxford. A party which had begun by defending the constitution of the university against outside critics and even against reforms promoted by the Hebdomadal Board, became convinced that that very constitution was being twisted against them and finally that the whole academic order was illegal. This pressure in the direction of liberal reform was strengthened by Peel's efforts to use every engine of patronage against the party, and by the influence of Gladstone after he had been elected to Parliament for the university in 1847. The next twenty years saw the party constantly torn between its conservative origins and its opposition interests, between its high hopes for the Church and the realities of a plural society; a section of the party in the end began to justify not only Liberal politics but even progressive intellect upon Catholic grounds. The split which became open with the publication of *Lux Mundi* in 1889 had in fact existed for a generation, and Pusey's painful tossing from side to side witnessed graphically to the distresses of sectarianism among the apostles of Catholicity. The appointment of Frederick Temple to the see of Exeter in 1869 finally fixed Pusey to the conservative side, but the agony continued in his favourite son, H. P. Liddon. Anglo-Catholicism deeply marked the religion not only of the Anglican but of other Churches, but it had not the power to keep the post-Tractarian party together, let alone change the basic situation of religion in England. Anglo-Catholic Progress became a term of art for a larger slice of a diminishing cake.

The liberals, who formed the third of the great church parties, had less organization than any of the others, and their friends were tempted (as is the way with historians of party) to say that they were not a party at all.[130] There were, however, two recognizable groups among them. One group originated at Oriel and included Copleston, Whately, Hampden, Baden

---

[129] This theme is more fully worked out in my article on 'Oxford and the Origins of Liberal Catholicism in the Church of England', in C. W. Dugmore & Charles Duggan (eds), *Studies in Church History*, i (London 1964), 233–52.

[130] *The Edinburgh Review*, xcviii, 334.

Powell, and Dr Arnold; in the next generation Rugby was something of a Mecca to a group largely composed of Arnold's colleagues, successors and pupils, with some of their friends such as Jowett of Balliol. The other group stemmed from Coleridge, and included Julius Hare, John Sterling, Frederick Denison Maurice and Charles Kingsley, and had Cambridge associations. The Oxford school had a platonic cast and exalted intuitive perception of the truth. Both of them were favourable towards the progress of science and Biblical criticism, but the Oxford school looked to historical criticism, while the Cambridge men went in for a philosophical pursuit of unity. Both of them (like the other parties) bore the marks of the 'romantic' period, and both of them reacted against the rationalism of the previous century, which (like the other parties) they thought of as 'shallow'.

In the pursuit of social unity no cause seemed more sacred than that of education, and the liberals were above all a party of educationists. Thomas Arnold, Bonamy Price, G. G. Bradley, Prince Lee, A. C. Tait and Temple at the public schools, Tait, Temple, Stanley, Jowett and Lake among the college tutors, exemplified the call; Maurice with his London Working Men's College and Queen's College, Temple at Kneller Hall, Richard Dawes with his model lower-class school at King's Somborne, W. C. Lake with the College of Science at Newcastle, were each seeking to plug the gaps in the national provision of education. National education was gospel, not heresy, to the liberals. The romantic outlook upon history, its perception of childhood and manhood phases in the life of the nation, disposed of the great religious difficulty to national education. The Bible was a book for mature minds only; for children the great need was for the scripture anthologies employed in the Irish national system or for a time in Liverpool, the 'agreed syllabuses' of the period. It was the same with the Church. The mission of the Church, according to Arnold, was to Christianize the nation; to this end the establishment was an incalculable advantage and it was worth sacrificing every inessential in order to secure it on the most comprehensive basis.

The liberals protested against the crude versions of the

doctrine of progress put about by the rationalists of the Enlightenment, yet their doctrine disposed them to optimism. The story is related that the young William Temple approached his father with the question 'Why do not philosophers rule the world, Father? Would it not be a good thing if they did?' and received the characteristic answer, 'They do rule it, silly, five hundred years after they are dead.'[131] The liberal Anglicans left a deep mark upon English education, and had the world been capable of being saved by philosophical pedagogues, they would doubtless have saved it, and ruled, if not in their lifetime, at least through posterity. But history offers immense resistance to schoolmasters and dons, and in many ways the influence of the party waned after the 1850s. Positivism, which the early liberals had combated, began to take possession of the field again among liberals as among others. Liberal reform in the universities proved to be the high-water mark rather than the beginning of liberal theological influence; liberals who in the 'forties and 'fifties had earnestly championed the establishment of a school of theology in Oxford confessed defeat by opposing it with equal earnestness when proposed and carried by Pusey in 1868. Already liberal reconstruction in theology had proved a damp squib, and Jowett had gone on to Plato. The tragic sense of loss which Arnold's early death inflicted on his pupils was a measure of their own lack of constructive power, and in the next generation there was an unhappy record of personal venom among the members of the party. Though liberalism of a kind continued in the English Churches and not least in the Church of England, the liberals of the mid-century were a party of coming men who never quite came.

To conclude this discussion of the predicament of the establishment in mid-century, it is well to say something of Gladstone, so much of whose life was devoted to its problems. As a young man, Gladstone believed that the state had a conscience which required it to make a judgment of Christian truth and to propagate it to the best of its ability. It was not just the Maynooth grant which upset this view; though

[131] F. A. Iremonger, *William Temple, Archbishop of Canterbury: His Life and Letters* (London 1948), pp. 18–19.

Gladstone was not a Tractarian party man and claimed never to have read the Tracts, he had a great deal of sympathy with the men who wrote them, and was grievously distressed by the unrelenting support which Peel gave their enemies.[132] The Gorham Judgment was another blow. While Gladstone was thus becoming more and more convinced that the Church could not fulfil its mission without greater freedom than it at present possessed, he was also learning that many of the outworks of the ascendancy could not be safely defended in Parliament. The loss of the university test by a majority of 90 in 1854 was a spectacular case in point, and a portent, in Gladstone's view, of what was to be expected. The moral was that the Church should shorten its front, defend no more than was absolutely defensible and at the same time support the claims of the underprivileged to liberty with a view to claiming liberty for herself. It was Gladstone's tragedy (particularly at Oxford) that he could never persuade churchmen of the consequences of living in a plural society, and it was a tragedy for the Church that the policy he recommended came to be carried through in a groping and half-hearted way. Gladstone insisted time and again that

> the Church of England as an Establishment is now paying the penalty of the mistakes and misdeeds of her children; that liberty is not to be had without paying for it; that the bulk of her members, clerical and lay, are not willing to pay, and it is vain for the minority to say, Give us liberty, while the majority refuse to pay the price.[133]

Of course it was always possible to challenge Gladstone's generally pessimistic judgment as to what positions could be held and what could not, but after a century of frittering away the resources of the Church in the support of the establishment at least some Anglicans have come to the point of asking for the same liberty as is enjoyed by the Church of Scotland, still perhaps hoping that the price will be a low one.

In the 'fifties the prescription for reviving synodical action

[132] D. C. Lathbury (ed.), *Correspondence on Church and Religion of William Ewart Gladstone* (London 1910), i, 342–7.
[133] ibid., i, 127.

and liberty in the Church was to restore Convocation's powers to do business; in this body the clergy were inadequately represented, and the laity not represented at all. The revival of Convocation was symptomatic of a gradual and perhaps inevitable change in the public standing of the establishment. The great recipe for reform in the case of the East India Company, the Civil Service, and the universities in turn, had been to take them out of politics and leave them to be managed by their own professionals. Now it was the turn of the Church. The professionals in this case were the clergy, and to the normal disadvantages of church government by clergy were now added all those arising from the refusal of the clergy to accept their new role on the only terms on which it could be effectively carried out. In the early days of Blomfield's influence the laity organized in Parliament had a work to do for the Church; by the time of his death in 1857 the Church had taken some stumbling steps towards independence while the state had begun to disclaim responsibility for its welfare. The establishment had been preserved, and with it a Church whose reshaping was the business of no one in particular.

II

Methodist Religion 1791–1849

—————⊃•◉•⊂—————

J. M. TURNER

THE years between 1791 and 1850 have been called the 'Victorian Prelude', years in which there was a 'revolution in manners'[1] providing the transition between the century of Gin Lane and Beer Street and the age of Queen Victoria. The Methodism (and evangelicalism) of the period needs sympathetic understanding rather than the iconoclastic approach of the Lytton Strachey era. Dr Kitson Clark reminds us that

> it is very important to put back religion, particularly popular religion, into the picture of nineteenth-century England. . . . Investigation will admittedly not be easy, partly because it is not clear what evidence should be used; but there is one very large mass of evidence available throughout the nineteenth century which may help. It is the popular literature of the period, the drama, the songs and above all the novels and magazine stories. This will not appeal through its good sense or its truth to life, on the contrary the wildness and absurdity and tastelessness of a great deal of it can hardly be exaggerated. These are certainly wildly distorting mirrors, but they reflect something, they reflect the mind of the people who liked to look into them. The generalizations men accept about life, the morality which commends itself to them, are in some way reflected in the plays they see, in the songs they sing, in the stories they enjoy; and it is our duty as historians to try to understand that reflection. . . .
>
> Much that men relished in the middle of the nineteenth century

[1] M. J. Quinlan, *Victorian Prelude: A History of English Manners 1700–1830* (New York 1941), p. 3: cf. M. Jaeger, *Before Victoria* (London 1956); F. K. Brown, *Fathers of the Victorians: The Age of Wilberforce* (Cambridge 1961); H. Perkin, *The Origins of Modern English Society 1780–1880* (London 1969), pp. 271 ff.

will seem [to the historian] to be tasteless, often mawkish, sometimes meaningless, normally absurd, but this must not lead him to
believe that it was unimportant if it meant something that was
of vital significance to contemporary men and women.[2]

We shall investigate briefly the place of tracts, magazines,
books and other literature in the Methodism of the early
nineteenth century. The role of the Sunday School, of the
'revival' and of the home as features in a pattern of life and
evangelism will then be outlined.

John Wesley maintained that 'the work of grace would die
out in one generation if the Methodists were not a reading
people'.[3] Literature to him and to his followers was 'a weapon,
a tool' of the Gospel[4] – art for art's sake was an impossible
concept for them. The early preachers were expected to be
disseminators of literature, a matter which each of the branches
of Methodism regarded with great seriousness. Each Church
had its connexional magazine[5] of which the *Arminian* (later
Methodist and *Wesleyan-Methodist*) *Magazine*, may be taken as
the pattern. Wesley's original intention was that 'this work
will contain no news, no politics, no personal invectives,
nothing offensive either to religion, decency, good nature, or
good manners', in contrast to those organs of Calvinism
which, he said, 'defended their dear decrees, with arguments
worthy of Bedlam, and with language worthy of Billingsgate'.[6]
The magazine broadened from Wesley's rubrics, but sermons,
matters of personal faith, letters and memoirs of devout
Methodists and extraordinary visitations of Providence largely
filled its pages – the first major incursion into politics was in
1811 when Lord Sidmouth's bill threatened the extinction of
much Methodist lay preaching. The apparent preoccupation
with death-bed scenes is a reflection of the fact that early
nineteenth-century and Victorian England

---

[2] G. Kitson Clark, *The Making of Victorian England* (London 1962), pp. 25–6, 179.
[3] *Letters*, I, xv.
[4] F. H. Cumbers, *The Book Room: The Story of the Methodist Publishing House and Epworth Press* (London 1956), pp. 5–10.
[5] ibid., pp. 144–9: a complete list.
[6] L. Tyerman, *The Life and Times of the Rev. John Wesley, M.A.* (London 1871), iii, 281.

still had a high child mortality rate and that the experience of a large number of deaths within a family was a chastening and disturbing experience. Christians like Charles Kingsley, who believed in a vigorous 'muscular' religion, were numbed by bereavement; vague Christian sympathizers like Dickens wallowed in death-bed sentimentality.[7]

The Methodist Magazines with their large circulation were read outside Methodism as well as within – Charlotte Brontë called them 'mad Methodist magazines full of miracles and apparitions and preternatural warnings, ominous dreams, and frenzied fanaticisms'.[8] The impact of Methodism on the learned Reviews was no less repellent – thus the Whig *Edinburgh Review* in 1808[9] had an article by R. A. Ingram criticizing obsession with particular interventions of Providence.

The Methodists hate pleasure and amusements; no theatre, no cards, no dancing, no punchinello, no dancing dogs, no blind fiddlers; . . . to the learning, the moderation, and the rational piety of the Establishment we most earnestly wish a decided victory over the nonsense, the melancholy, and the madness of the tabernacle.

The Tory *Quarterly Review* in November 1810 joined in the attack with an article which may be attributed to Robert Southey:

Go into the collieries, or to the manufactories of Birmingham and Sheffield, and inquire what are the practical consequences of methodism wherever it has spread among the poor; – industry and sobriety, quiet and orderly habits, and the comfort which results from them will be found its fruits.

But he pours scorn on Methodist pleasures or lack of them and asserts that

in fact, the Methodists already form a distinct people in the

---

[7] Asa Briggs, *The Age of Improvement* (London 1959), p. 463.
[8] H. F. Mathews, *Methodism and the Education of the People 1791–1851* (London 1949), p. 173.
[9] R. A. Ingram, 'Causes of the Increase of Methodism, and Dissension', in *The Edinburgh Review*, xi, no. 22 (January 1808), pp. 357, 362.

state, and the main object of their rulers is to keep up and strengthen the distinction. . . . on those who love poetry it acts upon them as a mildewing superstition, blasting all genius in the bud, and withering every flower of loveliness and of innocent enjoyment.[10]

Much of the pamphlet and periodical attack on Methodism is perverse, but it is true, as we shall see, that Methodists were tending to fall into a narrow groove of activities geared around the chapel and often made 'monasteries for the mind', as a shrewd woman of the time observed. Nevertheless the volume and quality of Methodist literature needs to be seen against the background of widespread illiteracy. In Lancashire and Cheshire in the years 1839–41 'forty per cent of the men and sixty-eight per cent of the women married or witnessing marriages were unable to sign their own names'.[11] The scales also were weighted against cheap literature through the so-called taxes on knowledge.[12] In 1836 the stamp duty was reduced from 4d. to 1d., finally being abolished in 1861. Between 1836 and 1855 no London daily paper was sold at less than 5d. The First Report of the Poor Law Commissioners (1834) contained the following:

> The dearness of newspapers in this country is an insurmountable obstacle to the education of the poor. I could name twenty villages within a circuit of a few miles in which a newspaper is never seen from one year's end to the other.[13]

All the more significant, then, is the use of the religious tract in this period. Methodism was in the forefront of this activity, using the tract before Hannah More's 'cheap Repository Tracts' appeared in 1794 or the Religious Tract Society began in 1799. The Wesleyan Tract Society was re-formed in 1828 by Conference direction and between 1825 and 1838 36,787,111 tracts were published: 'in a typical year like 1841,

[10] The Quarterly Review, iv, no. 8 (November 1810), pp. 491, 505, 507.
[11] H. F. Mathews, op. cit., p. 71.
[12] E. E. Kellett, 'The Press', in G. M. Young, Early Victorian England 1830–1865 (London 1934), ii, 7–10; J. W. Adamson, English Education 1789–1902 (Cambridge 1930), pp. 41–2.
[13] F. Hill, National Education: Its Present State and Prospects (London 1836), i, 110.

the total was 1,326,049.'[14] The Religious Tract Society issued 14,339,197 tracts in 1834 and over 18 million in 1838.[15] Though it may be true that in the more sophisticated towns the tracts were treated with contempt by the working classes as a whole, the success of the most notable tract of the time, Legh Richmond's *The Dairyman's Daughter* (1809), is phenomenal. In the first eighteen years of publication over two million copies were sold and it continued to be in demand until well after 1850.[16] Another well-known tract, *The Sinner's Friend*, had three million copies printed.[17] The simple evangelical piety of these tracts was a notable factor in the creation of Victorian moralism.

The Sunday School movement grew greatly during this period. In many ways there is a close similarity between the Sunday School movement at the end of the eighteenth century and the Charity School movement at its beginning. Both were voluntary movements largely financed by the middle classes, designed to save the souls of the poor and to fit them for their proper station in life.

An organisation which would sweep the children off the lanes and streets into school was welcomed by the rural and urban middle-class adults with enthusiasm. . . . Methodists, Evangelicals and Dissenters were all at one here and they all sought to instill social discipline . . . without upsetting the social order of things it allowed a combination of the discipline of labour on weekdays with the discipline of religion on the Sabbath. It satisfied the demands of Godly piety and Godly discipline.[18]

[14] F. H. Cumbers, op. cit., pp. 49ff.

[15] L. James, *Fiction for the Working Man 1830–1850* (London 1963), p. 118.

[16] ibid., p. 121; *The Dairyman's Daughter* has recently been republished by the Evangelical Society; R. K. Webb, *The British Working Class Reader 1790–1848* (London 1955).

[17] A. Cruse, *The Englishman and His Books in the Early Nineteenth Century* (London 1930), pp. 66–9.

[18] M. G. Jones, *The Charity School Movement* (London 1938), p. 146; but cf. T. W. Laqueur, *Religion and Respectability: Sunday Schools and Working Class Culture 1780–1850* (Yale 1976); W. R. Ward, *Religion and Society 1790–1850* (London 1972), pp. 12–16, 135–41. Laqueur indicates the vital role of the working class in the organization and teaching of the Sunday Schools; Ward demonstrates the radical impulses at work in the early undenominational schools and in the battles they waged against domination by the ordained ministry. English popular religion can hardly be understood unless due note is taken of the part played in it by the Sunday School.

These early Sunday Schools were often 'schools' in the sense that reading writing and reckoning were taught as well as instruction in the Bible, though the Wesleyan Conference in 1814, 1823 and 1837 inveighed against the teaching of writing on Sunday. In Nottingham[19] in 1793

> the children are taught to read, write and cast accompts, and the principles of Christianity. . . . The times of attendance are from half past 8 o'clock to twelve, and from half past one to four. . . . If any scholar be convicted of swearing, lying, Sabbath breaking, or any other capital misdemeanor, his punishment is to wear the Cap of Reproach, and to sit on the Stool of Disgrace for a certain time; if the fault be very notorious, he must wear a badge with the nature of his crime written upon it, be led through the several classes of children, and exposed to public view – If he continues refractory, for the third offence he is excluded.

In 1805 Richard Treffry, senior, organized a Sunday School at Camelford and the hours there were 8–10.30 a.m. with an hour or two in the afternoon.[20] Treffry's purpose was 'to teach the children to read, to train them in the principles of religion and pray with and for them and labour to train them up for heaven'. The long hours were quite normal – in 1835 the *Sunday-school Teachers' Magazine*, reporting a typical Wesleyan Sunday School, gave its hours as '8.30 to 12 and 1.30 to 4 with no breaks' allowed.[21] The Wesleyan Conference only slowly awakened to the opportunities being presented by the Sunday School for Christian instruction. Not until 1820 did Conference declare that weekly meetings for children should be established in each town. In 1827 a set of rules for management was issued bringing schools into direct affiliation with local societies.

> Schools designed for the religious education of poor children ought to be conducted in distinct and avowed *connexion* with some particular branch of the visible *church* of Christ.[22]

[19] Rowland C. Swift, 'Methodist Sunday-schools in Nottingham', in *W.H.S. Proc.*, xxxiii (March 1961), 19.
[20] Thomas Shaw, 'Richard Treffry, Senior and Junior', in *W.H.S. Proc.*, xxxii (December 1959), 68.
[21] H. F. Mathews, op. cit., p. 55; *Sunday-school Teachers' Magazine*, vi (1835).
[22] *Minutes of Wesleyan Conference*, vi (1827), 284.

The Minute went on to say:

> The children of members, and those even of constant hearers in the congregation, are, in an important sense, *the children of the church*, . . . Many of them have been by holy baptism solemnly recognised as among the objects of pastoral charge, and as entitled to the care and spiritual assistance of Christian people.

Where schools were set up the superintendent Minister was responsible and the Sunday School hymnal and Wesleyan Catechism were to be used. In 1838 Conference decreed that each chapel should have its own school.[23] It is probable that in this period the Sunday School was thought of primarily as a means of religious and educational philanthropy for 'poor children' (a significant phrase in a Wesleyan Minute) outside the immediate family of society members rather than as a means of instructing the children of members, for this was the task of the Christian parent.

The other Methodist Connexions sought similar control over their schools. The New Connexion introduced a Catechism for its children in 1827,[24] and the Primitive Methodists sought to set up a Sunday School Union in 1832, though this proved abortive.[25] Teaching methods were often of the most elementary 'monitorial' kind with stress on rote learning, and the inculcation of the fear of hell and death was common.[26] 'The first Sunday-school magazine seems to have been published by William Kent, who was a successful stationer in High Holborn' and a member of the Hinde Street society.[27] In 1817 *Youth's Instructor* was first issued and thirty years later *Early Days* (1846–1916) 'was selling at the rate of 50,000 copies monthly'.[28] *Christian Miscellany* was begun in 1846 as a magazine for readers for whom the *Wesleyan-Methodist Magazine* was too heavy and at the other extreme *The London*

---

[23] *Minutes of Wesleyan Conference*, viii (1838), 355.

[24] G. Packer (ed.), *The Centenary of the Methodist New Connexion 1797–1897* (London 1897), p. 94.

[25] H. B. Kendall, *History of the Primitive Methodist Church* (London 1919), p. 101.

[26] P. Sangster, *Pity My Simplicity: The Evangelical Revival and the Religious Education of Children 1738–1800* (London 1963), pp. 40ff.

[27] H. F. Mathews, op. cit., p. 50.

[28] ibid., p. 173.

Quarterly, begun in 1853, and edited by Dr J. H. Rigg, was intended to meet the needs of Ministers and intelligent layfolk and represent a considerable widening of horizons. Each of the other Connexions had its full range of Sunday School and general magazines.

The number of scholars in Wesleyan Sunday Schools alone had by 1854 reached 401,763, and one million was exceeded at the time of Victoria's death. Sir James Kay-Shuttleworth 'was rightly to observe that the establishment of Sunday Schools prepared public opinion for a general advance in elementary education',[29] but the Sunday School cannot be seen as a prime factor in the making of Methodist converts. In 1857 the *Sunday School Teachers' Magazine* makes the familiar observation: 'under the most favourable circumstances in the best worked schools not a tenth, scarce a twentieth of the scholars remain till they are of the age to become members of the Church' and the *Watchman* earlier had observed: 'dancing, novel-reading, concerts, bagatelle and other trifling games have broken in wide circles on Wesleyan Methodism and have prevented the conversion of children'.[30] One suspects that reasons more profound are the cause of the leakage such as the perpetual Methodist problem of a Sunday School with little relationship to the worshipping community.

'Our literature' was not as diverse as in the days of Wesley, though the Bible Commentaries of Coke and Benson, Clarke and Sutcliffe circulated widely, as did the *Theological Institutes* of Richard Watson, and under the editorship of Thomas Jackson the *Lives of the Early Methodist Preachers* (1837–8) provided a link with Wesley's Helpers, who first began to make the Methodists a reading people, with their saddlebags filled with Mr Wesley's books. Methodism at this time was theologically self-supporting and inbred, and the general range of literature as a tool of evangelism and cultural edification was severely limited. Jackson himself went so far as to say that the Methodists 'had no time for light literature, and chiefly read the Methodist Hymn-Book and the Bible'.[31] Yet

[29] Asa Briggs, op. cit., p. 17; T. W. Laqueur, op. cit., pp. 42–61.
[30] Maldwyn Edwards, *Methodism and England 1850–1932* (London 1943), pp. 220–1.
[31] ibid., p. 68; quoted in T. Jackson, *Centenary of Wesleyan Methodism* (London 1839).

there is no doubt that the meetings for intimate fellowship such as the cottage meeting and the class meeting were indirectly means of education, and 'reading circles' sometimes were linked with the chapels. Thus Dr J. H. Rigg described one at Mousehole in Cornwall as having 'such a spirit of reading, including a sort of club supply of books, as is seldom found even in fishing villages'.[32] It is easy to criticize the narrowness of chapel culture – and such piety has always had its cultured despisers[33] – but against it must be set the self-education of men like William Lovett and Thomas Cooper, the Chartists, who owed their early training to Methodism.[34] Lord Lawson, speaking of his own experiences and the life of his fellows later in the century, writes:

> The chapel gave them their first music, their first literature and philosophy to meet the harsh life and cruel impact of the crude materialistic age. Here men first found the language and art to express their antagonism to grim conditions and injustice.[35]

The growth of Methodism in its various Connexions was never uniform in the first part of the nineteenth century – the first decline in membership recorded in Wesleyanism was before the Liverpool Minutes' call to evangelism and pastoral care in 1820. Yet these same years marked the height of the great Midlands Revival in Primitive Methodism[36] – in fact in 1819 the membership of the Connexion was only 7,842, by 1824 it had risen to 33,507, a quadrupling of numbers in a comparatively short time, though the impetus was not maintained after 1825. Periodic revivalism was always a feature of nineteenth-century Methodism[37] and its popular, aggressive nature and its use of men of eccentric gifts like Lorenzo Dow,

[32] H. F. Mathews, op. cit., p. 79.
[33] A. Cruse, *The Victorians and Their Books* (London 1962): Chapter IV, 'The Chapel Folks'.
[34] G. D. H. Cole, *Chartist Portraits* (London 1941), pp. 34, 62, 188, 190, 209, 215; *The Life of Thomas Cooper*: written by himself (London 1882).
[35] J. J. Lawson, *A Man's Life* (London 1944), p. 69.
[36] H. B. Kendall, 'The Primitive Methodist Church and the Independent Methodist Churches', in Book III, Chap. II of *N.H.M.*, i, 580: H. B. Kendall, *History of the Primitive Methodist Church*, pp. 33–4.
[37] Gordon S. Wakefield, *Methodist Devotion: The Spiritual Life in the Methodist Tradition 1791–1945* (London 1966), pp. 55ff.

Billy Bray and James Caughey 'often occasioned considerable uneasiness to the Fathers of the Connexion, and to the more intelligent and pious of the junior preachers'.[38] There was the fear of government action against disorderly crowds and it could be said that the underlying cause of the expulsion of men like Hugh Bourne from Wesleyanism was not lack of an evangelistic spirit but fear on the part of the Wesleyan Connexion of disorderly meetings, which would bring upon them the wrath of a government only too eager to smell out Jacobinism and radicalism from the ranks of Dissent.[39]

To the revivalist, church order and regulations were of much less significance than soul-winning. In early Primitive Methodism the inspired missioner like William Clowes[40] or the circuit itself was the unit of evangelism – these were heroic days when Hull had its 'missions' in Kent, when Bolton missioned the Isle of Man (1823) and when in 1829 Hull and Tunstall circuits combined in sending four missionaries to the United States.

> Their equipment included a supply of hand-bills which were to make known to the inhabitants of America the fact and purport of their coming.[41]

The world, too, was the parish of the Bible Christians, who in 1821 set up a society

> for the purpose of sending Missionaries into the dark and destitute parts of the United Kingdom, and other countries as Divine Providence might open the way.[42]

With them the pioneering individual – often a woman like Mary Ann Werrey or Catherine Reed – was the key to revival[43] and expansion.

[38] Quoted from T. P. Bunting, in *N.H.M.*, i, 556.
[39] J. T. Wilkinson, *Hugh Bourne 1772–1852* (London 1952), pp. 55–66; *N.H.M.*, i, 566ff.; W. E. Farndale, *The Secret of Mow Cop: A New Appraisal of the Origins of Primitive Methodism* (London 1950); R. F. Wearmouth, *Methodism and the Working-Class Movements of England 1800–1850* (London 1937), p. 58; but cf. W. R. Ward, op. cit., p. 76.
[40] J. T. Wilkinson, *William Clowes 1780–1851* (London 1951).
[41] H. B. Kendall, *History of the Primitive Methodist Church*, p. 48.
[42] Thomas Shaw, *The Bible Christians 1815–1907* (London 1965), p. 33.
[43] R. Pyke, *The Early Bible Christians* (London 1941), pp. 27–9.

It is tempting to seek economic and social motivation for revival, and indeed there is no doubt that Primitive Methodism and the Bible Christians in particular were peculiarly 'sensitive to cyclical fluctuations and the movements of unemployment, and indeed normally explained any fluctuations in their numbers primarily in economic terms'.[44] Small congregations with the maximum of democracy in the village or semi-village seem to have been the consequence of the pulsating revivals in the early part of the nineteenth century; relatively under-developed industrialism – a pattern of living which tended to disappear as the modern pattern of urbanization and factory industry developed – was the congenial home of the revival. Dr E. J. Hobsbawm has propounded a theory that there is a link between revival and economic conditions.[45] Thus he points out that the most rapid years of Wesleyan expansion were in the Jacobin era (1793–5), the increasingly tense years of the Napoleonic Wars (1805–16, especially 1813–16), the years of the Reform Bill and the Poor Law (1831–4) and two periods when Chartism was active (1838–41 and 1849–50). What is equally significant, the expansion slackened and temporarily ceased for all the Connexions in the first half of the 1850s.[46] The years in this period which showed a notable decline in numbers were the years which saw the decline of Chartism and radicalism, the era recently called the 'Age of Equipoise'.[47] 'It is quite obvious', states Dr Hobsbawm, 'that there was a marked parallelism between the movements of religious, social and political consciousness.' E. P. Thompson in the most recent study of the English working class (notably hostile to Methodism) takes the point further when he suggests the possibility that 'revivalism' took over when political or temporal expectations met with despair. Religious 'pulsations'

[44] ibid., p. 45: E. J. Hobsbawm, *Primitive Rebels: Studies in Archaic Forms of Social Movement in the 19th and 20th Centuries* (Manchester 1959), p. 137.

[45] ibid., pp. 126–49; cf. E. J. Hobsbawm, *Labouring Men* (London 1964), p. 32; I have altered Hobsbawm's dates slightly.

[46] H. B. Kendall, op. cit., p. 88: an explanation of the Primitive Methodist decline in the 1850s; W. R. Ward, op. cit., pp. 273 ff.; cf. A. D. Gilbert, *Religion and Society in Industrial England* (London 1976), pp. 30–2. For a local study, see J. Obelkevich, *Religion and Rural Society: South Lindsey 1825–1875* (London 1976), pp. 248ff.

[47] W. L. Burn, *The Age of Equipoise: a Study of the Mid-Victorian Generation* (London 1964); Asa Briggs (ed.), *Chartist Studies* (London 1959), p. 300.

occur after a spate of political agitation. Much more local research is needed before this thesis can be maintained or rejected; it is certain, however, that Methodism was acted upon greatly by social and economic as well as by spiritual forces in this period, though before the Railway Age made communications easy and rapid any generalizations can be dangerous. Indeed, however much we are driven to find economic causes for events in the religious sphere – why, for instance, did both William Clowes and the Bible Christian women missionaries fail to gain many converts in London?[48] – revival is a religious phenomenon, and we should be foolish if we underestimated the power of the dedicated evangelist in all the branches of Methodism, men and women who above all had that 'tongue of fire' without which no Church can live.[49] Methodism too had complete local freedom to develop in its own flexible way:

> Where the National Church required an Act of Parliament, a grant of money, an educated gentleman and a crop of lawyers, the Methodists required only a friendly barn and a zealous preacher![50]

Zealous preachers with a gay, almost Franciscan, optimism, praying, preaching and singing with equal fervour, could still set villages ablaze with religious enthusiasm, and with a Gospel of forgiveness could reach men and women whom their more sober contemporaries would never reach.

Early nineteenth-century Methodism, looked at from one angle, can seem an affair of narrow horizons – the circuit could so easily become the world.

> The box-like, blackening chapels stood in the industrial districts like great traps for the human psyche. It is the paradox of a 'religion of the heart' that it should be notorious for the inhibition of all spontaneity. Methodism sanctioned 'workings of the heart'

[48] Thomas Shaw, op. cit., p. 58.
[49] cf. William Arthur, *The Tongue of Fire: or, The True Power of Christianity* (London 1856; new edition: London 1956); W. R. Ward, *The Early Correspondence of Jabez Bunting 1820–1829* (London 1972), pp. 61f., for an illustration of Thompson's thesis in Manchester in 1821; J. D. Gay, *The Geography of Religion in England* (London 1971), pp. 153–7.
[50] E. R. Wickham, *Church and People in an Industrial City* (London 1957), p. 80.

only upon the occasions of the Church; Methodists wrote hymns but no secular poetry of note; the idea of a passionate Methodist lover in these years is ludicrous.[51]

Methodism with its stress on the after-life is the 'Chiliasm of the defeated and the hopeless'.[52] This view echoes contemporary critics like William Cobbett, who maintained that the Methodists beguiled men into the belief that

> to secure Heaven hereafter you must be poor, ragged and almost die with hunger; that to be a child of grace you must be an assemblage of skin and bone, distressing to the sight and offensive to the smell.[53]

Thomas Carlyle could not abide Methodist preoccupation with themselves:

> Methodism with its eye forever turned on its own navel; asking itself with torturing anxiety of Hope and Fear, 'Am I right? am I wrong? Shall I be saved? shall I not be damned?' – what is this at bottom but a new phasis of *Egoism*, stretched out into the Infinite; not always the heavenlier for its infinitude![54]

No doubt Carlyle's strictures can describe one type of Methodist. The piety of the age was narrow and G. S. Wakefield is right in stressing that Methodist joy and confidence was based on 'a desperate conscientiousness'.[55] In the mind of many evangelicals a subtle barrier was flung between the life of the soul with God and the life of man with man, between worship and work, between piety and culture. 'The doctrine of total depravity governed their thought, and their idea of God was not rich enough.'[56] This led a man like John Pawson to burn John Wesley's annotated copy of Shakespeare as 'worthless lumber'[57] and led John Styles to write on Shakespeare:

[51] E. P. Thompson, *The Making of the English Working Class* (London 1963), p. 368.
[52] ibid., p. 382; but cf. A. D. Gilbert, op. cit., pp. 82ff.
[53] W. B. Pemberton, *William Cobbett* (Harmondsworth 1949), p. 125.
[54] Thomas Carlyle, *Past and Present* (London 1899), p. 117.
[55] G. S. Wakefield, op. cit., p. 87.
[56] R. Newton Flew, *The Idea of Perfection in Christian Theology* (London 1934), p. 340.
[57] *N.H.M.*, i, 389.

Barefaced obscenities, low vulgarity, and nauseous vice so frequently figure and pollute his pages that we cannot but lament the luckless hour in which he became a writer for the stage.[58]

Such sentiments would attune well with *The Family Shakespeare* of Thomas Bowdler published in 1818 from which 'whatever is unfit to be read by a gentleman in a company of ladies' has been removed and with the expurgations of James Plumptre, one of whose more diverting emendations was to change 'Under the greenwood tree who loves to lie with me' to 'Under the greenwood tree who loves to work with me', thus removing the possible *double entendre* and exalting the virtue of industry.[59] The call of the Methodists of this period was for disciplined, simple, pious lives removed from worldly pleasures and centred on home, chapel and business. The duty of hard work, the evils of luxury and extravagance, the virtues of foresight and thrift, moderation and self-discipline, were instilled into ordinary church members and provided an undergirding to the moral earnestness characteristic of Victorian England. And the key here is undoubtedly the home. Archdeacon Cunningham's[60] dictum, that 'Puritanism was the religion of the state, Wesleyanism the religion of the heart, the Evangelical Movement the religion of the home, and the Oxford Movement the religion of the Church', like most generalizations is a little facile, but there is no doubt that family religion played a tremendous role in Methodist and evangelical piety. There was narrowness, sometimes self-righteousness, a scorn of worldly pursuits that appeared to divide life into water-tight compartments, and a frequent fear of the intellect that often goes alongside the virtues of the evangelical-Methodist way of life, but nevertheless the home[61] was a place where virtues too easily crushed by modern living could be preserved, and even among the Methodist preachers there were passionate lovers! Victorian England owed much

---

[58] M. J. Quinlan, op. cit., p. 226.

[59] ibid., p. 235.

[60] Quoted in Charles H. Smyth, *Simeon & Church Order: A Study of the Origins of the Evangelical Revival in Cambridge in the Eighteenth Century* (Cambridge 1940), p. 13.

[61] W. L. Burn, op. cit., pp. 246–53; W. E. Houghton, *The Victorian Frame of Mind, 1830–1870* (London 1957), pp. 341–8.

domestically to homes like that of the Thornes of Lake Farm, Shebbear, and the Reeds of Holwell[62] and innumerable lesser-known havens of refuge. In even the non-religious home the same ethos prevailed.

> We were a Victorian household, and, in spite of an almost militant agnosticism, attached without the smallest tinge of scepticism or hypocrisy to the ideals of the time: duty, work, abnegation, a stern repression of what was called self-indulgence, a horror and a terror of lapsing from the current code.[63]

Methodism constantly stressed the household and family life as the nursery of the Church more vital certainly to the children of members than the Sunday School. Marriage was to be, if possible, within the ranks of the faithful.

> The Conference deem the marriage of a Preacher with a female not belonging to our society to be an instance of culpable imprudence, perilous to the comfort and usefulness of the preacher himself, and likely if not discountenanced to be greatly injurious to the spiritual interests of our people.[64]

The Bible Christians desired young ministers to find their wives among the women preachers, a fact which contributed to a substantial decline in the number of the latter.[65] Family prayers were assumed to be the norm in Methodist homes and no one has the right to scorn the piety of a man like 'Praying William' who

> once refused a holiday which some friends were willing to provide for him. 'No! No! I cannot go; for if I go, who will pray night and morning with my poor children.'[66]

The Puritan Sunday was the great corner stone of family religion and with all its faults

[62] R. Pyke, op. cit., pp. 19–23.
[63] W. E. Houghton, op, cit., p. 239; quoting 'Olivia', *Olivia* (London 1949), p. 13; N. G. Annan, *Leslie Stephen: His Thought and Character in Relation to His Time* (London 1951).
[64] *Minutes of Wesleyan Conference*, 1823.
[65] R. Pyke, op. cit., p. 29.
[66] G. S. Wakefield, op. cit., p. 74; L. Tyerman, *Praying William* (1857).

among the Methodists of the proletariat, depressed in the middle years, Sunday was a day when the working man was . . . made aware of his dignity as a child of God.[67]

The piety of the early Victorian Methodist was bounded by the class-meeting and Sunday worship (not yet entirely dominated by the sermon), prayers in his own home; his reading was dominated by the Bible and the hymn book, pious magazines and tracts; his prayer was always for the revival of God's work and God's Church, and if his religion led him into radical politics, it was because he had learned the meaning of the priesthood of all believers in chapel and class and because there he had caught a vision of the 'optimism of Grace', God's democracy, in which every man is a sinner who can become a saint.

[67] G. S. Wakefield, op. cit., p. 80; W. L. Burn, op. cit., pp. 278–80.

III

The Methodist People in the Early Victorian Age: Spirituality and Worship

N. P. GOLDHAWK

THE distinctive characteristics in the piety of a particular tradition within the Christian Church should be traceable throughout the history of that tradition, although they may well be altered or modified at different stages in the course of that development. Their external manifestations, as expressed in forms of worship and devotion, are not difficult to recognize, but the inner spirituality may elude the observer and defy description. Words and concepts will be handed down from one generation to another, yet their precise connotation may change or their original spontaneity be lost. The historian of religion is accordingly faced with his greatest problem when he attempts to do justice to the spiritual consciousness of a past age. Faith in God is a living experience, which discloses its quality in the last resort only to those who share in it at a particular time. Nevertheless in spite of the hazards which threaten the investigator it can be claimed that Methodist spirituality consisted of certain well-defined characteristics which were evident originally in the eighteenth century and continued to find expression in varying degrees during the first half-century following.

I

Methodist piety was compounded originally of three main

factors: a strong personal urge towards holiness, an evangelistic missionary impulse, and adherence to a distinctive church
order and discipline. Were a description of Methodism as a
whole being sought, these brief statements would require
considerable expansion. The urge to holiness, for example,
implied, according to John Wesley, the Christian doctrine of
God as set forth in scripture and the creeds of the Church,
and a life of communion with God which is realized through
faith. Nor should any of these factors be isolated from the
others. The urge to holiness was both kindled and nurtured
within the ordered life and discipline of the Christian fellowship, whilst the evangelistic, missionary impulse, expressive of
a universal gospel, was an essential consequent of the other
two elements and itself implied a characteristic intensity which
in turn governed them also. Moreover, each of the three was
a variable constant, so that the emphasis placed upon any one
of them might change at different periods. This certainly
occurred during the period 1791–1850. Accordingly the
Methodist movement presented a very different picture at the
end of this era from its appearance at the beginning. Amongst
the factors which helped to bring this about were the removal
of the guiding hand and comprehensive outlook of John
Wesley, the need for the Connexion, despite its close but
undefined relationship to the established Church, to become
increasingly self-sufficient as a Christian denomination, the
changes in the social structure of the community brought
about in the main by the progress of the Industrial Revolution,
and the growing influence of political and ecclesiastical
radicalism. Structurally Methodism was considerably modified. By 1850 the Societies, originally closely knit together as
a Connexion around the dominant figure of Wesley himself,
had developed into a number of denominations, a process
which brought to clearer expression tendencies already
inherent within the movement at the end of the eighteenth
century. In the opinion of the vocal majority of preachers in
the Wesleyan body, radicalism in politics went with democracy
in church affairs, and they believed that both were destructive
of much they held precious. As a result the element in Methodism subject to the greatest tensions was that of church order.

The non-Wesleyan communities, more obviously influenced by the growing Liberalism, evolved forms of church life and government with some characteristics more closely akin to Dissent than was the paternalism of the old body. Nevertheless adherence to a distinctive Methodist type of church order and discipline still remained a feature of their piety, and at the same time the first secessions, represented by the Methodist New Connexion and above all by the Primitive Methodists, were striking examples of the strength of the evangelistic element. In whatever form Methodism appeared, the basic factors in its piety were evident, although each in differing degrees and in variant relationship to the others. Indeed the history of Methodism during this period can be understood as a working out of the tensions produced by the development and inter-relation of the three elements in its characteristic piety.

The three elements can be clearly discerned in a document which was destined to have considerable influence in later years. In 1820 the Wesleyan Conference, meeting at Liverpool, learned that for the first time since statistics had been recorded the membership of the Connexion showed a decrease. At such a time of stress faith is most likely to be exposed for what it really is. The sobering effect which the report had upon the preachers caused them, under the direction of the President for that year, Jabez Bunting, solemnly to address to themselves a question which, both in the form in which it was expressed, and in the lengthy resolutions with which they answered it, clearly disclosed the main notes of Methodist spirituality. They inquired, 'What measures can we adopt for the increase of spiritual religion among our societies and congregations, and for the extension of the work of God in our native country?' The resolutions which followed illustrated in the first place what they understood by 'spiritual religion'. Reaffirming that the primary calling of the Methodist people, and especially of the preachers, was to spread Scriptural holiness through the land, the 'leading and vital doctrines of the Gospel' were described as

repentance towards God; a present, free, and full salvation from sin; – a salvation flowing from the grace of God alone 'through the redemption that is in Christ Jesus', and apprehended by the simple exercise of faith; – a salvation which begins with the forgiveness of sins (this forgiveness being certified to the penitent believer by the Holy Spirit) and (by means of this witness, but by the power of that Divine Spirit who bears the witness) a change of heart; – a salvation which is itself the only entrance to a course of practical holiness.

It is evident that in spite of an emphatic insistence upon initial repentance and 'conversion', these were thought of as incidental to their fulfilment in holiness. Secondly, the evangelistic missionary impulse not only governed the document as a whole in the concern it showed for the progress of the work of God, but the same impulse found particular expression in various additional resolutions dealing with the extension of Methodism. In the third place, the discipline of regular attendance at worship, Lord's Supper and prayer meeting was stressed, together with the cultivation of family religion, the sanctification of the Sabbath and the instruction of children, the exercise of pastoral oversight, the peculiar Methodist institutions of Society and Class meetings and the exercise of lay spiritual leadership.

The Liverpool Minutes[1] were addressed to the preachers of the Wesleyan Connexion, but in spite of the dominant conservatism and authoritarianism of that body at this time, and the insistence upon the distinctive place and function of the pastorate in the economy of the Church, there was no hint of a double standard for ministers and laymen. All were expected to seek the same gift of holiness. The Minutes did indeed summon the preachers to devote themselves 'wholly' to their office, strictly guarding against all occupations of their time and thoughts which had no direct relation to their great calling, and which would injuriously divert their attention from the momentous task of 'saving them that hear us', and 'taking care of the Church of God'. But the people also were to be guarded against expending all their time and energy on

[1] That they are an important witness to the piety of Methodism during this period is indicated by the fact that they were to be read each year in the May District Meeting and Circuit Preachers' Meeting.

local and subordinate enterprises and even works of charity, to the neglect of attendance at the Sunday and weekday ordinances of the Church. This reflected something of the attitude of non-participation in politics which John Wesley had urged upon the Societies, and this was constantly re-iterated by the Wesleyans during the first half of the nineteenth century, thereby acting as a restraint upon those in Methodism attracted by Liberalism, and helping to range the support of the Connexion behind the conservative forces in the land. Even Dr Beaumont, a precursor of the clerical 'Liberal' in Wesleyan Methodism, was reported as having said at the Conference of 1839:

> Methodism ought to have no political line, Whig or Tory. Our mission is chiefly to the poor. As to politics, no Methodist minister must interfere with, or be interfered with by, any of his brethren. It is so in the Established Church of England and of Scotland; it should be so in our own voluntary Church. I am jealous for the high spiritual character of Methodism. Every step we take towards politics reduces our character for high spirituality; thereby some are alienated from us by our political tone.[2]

Behind this attitude lay a deep concern to preserve the character of Methodism primarily as a society in which men were to be reconciled to God and advanced in holiness. This concern might be compromised by too deep an involvement in contemporary politics. No doubt these fathers of Methodism were blind to some of the aspects of 'Christian truth in democratic liberalism and radical reform',[3] but they were not alone in this. In their eyes political action meant political agitation.[4] Methodism must be kept free to promote the object for which they believed it had been raised up.

Nevertheless it may well be doubted whether Methodist piety realized the implications of its doctrine of holiness. The

---

[2] B. Gregory, *Side Lights on the Conflicts of Methodism during the Second Quarter of the Nineteenth Century 1827-1852*, p. 265. The plea was at the same time a defence of the right to hold liberal opinions.

[3] cf. E. G. Rupp, *Thomas Jackson: Methodist Patriarch* (London 1954), pp. 42-3.

[4] It is significant that even the author of *Methodism in 1879*, writing in that year, could devote the whole of the chapter on the relation of Methodism to political movements to the question of the disestablishment of the Church of England.

guidance of John Wesley was no longer available. In spite of his political Toryism, Wesley had been a man of large sympathies, quick to seize opportunities presented by new situations and to appreciate the bearing of the Gospel upon them. The Wesleyanism of the generation after his death was no longer a new and still elastic creation but an organism with a tradition to be guarded. The very rapidity of its growth meant that the energies of its leaders were largely devoted to preserving the 'methodistic' character of the body and to establishing its position in the country as a permanent and respectable institution. For these reasons Conference constantly asserted its loyalty to the Throne, and the great majority of the preachers held aloof from the riots provoked by the general distress or from any direct activity for political reform.

> Their attitude to patriotism was one of scrupulous rectitude, and by it, if they forfeited the respect of the Chartist workingmen, they gained freedom from persecution for the development of the young Church.[5]

The Methodists of the early part of the nineteenth century were keenly aware of the fact that as Christians they had been called out of an unbelieving world; they still kept before themselves Wesley's *Rules for the Methodist Societies*, which, in spite of strong insistence upon the positive duties of Christians, left no room for doubt that many features in the social life of the day were to be avoided. The theatre and fashionable amusements in general, dancing and gambling, the use of spirituous liquor,[6] and showy clothes,[7] were forbidden. Nor was the Methodists' taste in literature very wide, being confined in the main to religious writings,[8] although it should be remembered that the majority of members was drawn from

---

[5] E. R. Taylor, *Methodism & Politics 1791–1851* (Cambridge 1935), p. 113.

[6] But teetotalism was not encouraged in this period.

[7] Even so Conference in 1802 complained of the extravagant dress of some of the preachers' wives and of their irregularity at worship.

[8] cf. Maldwyn Edwards, *After Wesley: A Study of the Social and Political Influence of Methodism in the Middle Period (1791–1849)* (London 1935), pp. 130–1; *Methodism and England: A Study of Methodism in its Social and Political Aspects during the Period 1850–1932* (London 1943), Chapter V: 'Currents in Methodist Literature'.

sections of the population which were not highly educated. Moreover, it was a time when religious works were widely read. When Thomas Jackson, who himself got together a great library of theological works, wrote in 1838 in his *Centenary of Wesleyan Methodism* about Methodist families who had little acquaintance with light and amusing literature, although they had the Bible, 'the incomparable hymns of the Wesleys, with a few other well-read books of spiritual instruction', he was of course referring expressly to poor folk who knew nothing of the 'elegances and refinements' of life. To be sure, the sobriety and frugality of many members brought them increasing prosperity, a fact which Methodist literature at the time regarded as fraught with spiritual danger. And whilst the strength of Methodism during the first part of the nineteenth century was found chiefly in the industrial areas of the North, not many of its members could be said to have come from the lower working classes proper, although the Primitive Methodists were the most successful in gaining adherents among these and the very poor members of the community. In 1838 Thomas Jackson, then President of the Wesleyan Conference, could say that some of the most substantial and honourable men of business in England had become members of the Wesleyan community, and that their success in life hinged entirely upon those qualities which their religion supplied. Most Methodists in fact divided their time and energies between their work, their homes and their chapels, and so achieved what has been called bourgeois respectability. Yet their religion did generate amongst them a genuine humanitarianism which, in spite of its limitations, was both powerful and compassionate. Jabez Bunting and Richard Watson, for example, were active supporters of the Anti-slavery Society.

> In 1830 the Conference guided by Watson decided to depart from its usual policy of abstaining from politics. Methodists were urged to use the election franchise to bring the system of negro slavery to an end.[9]

[9] M. Edwards, *After Wesley*, p. 72.

It should also be remembered that a vital feature of this Methodist piety was a missionary outlook which helped to create a concern for the world at large. If the articles in the *Methodist Magazine* during the first part of the nineteenth century may be said to have been confined to a narrow range of specifically religious contributions, it was not long before news from the Mission field became a regular feature.[10] In 1818 the missionary work of the Church was brought under the general care of the newly-constituted Wesleyan Methodist Missionary Society. In 1821 the Conference Pastoral Address referred to the growth of the work in the various overseas stations, and continued:

> We give thanks to God on this account, and for the opportunities still opening before us for preaching to a greater extent the knowledge of Christ among the heathen. Methodism was from the first thus connected in its hopes and energies with the salvation of the whole world. This object inspired the effort of our venerable Founder; it glows in the hymns which the consecrated genius of his brother furnished for our religious services.

It became the responsibility of the preachers to lay the missionary cause upon the hearts of the Methodist people. The measure of their success in the decade following 1815 was such that missionary giving 'rapidly grew into a denominational habit'.[11]

In spite of all this, the dominant feature in the piety of Methodism remained the urge after personal holiness. That a great many failed to pursue the quest, or became preoccupied with too limited and individualistic an understanding of what holiness involved, or even that the quest for holiness produced in many a preoccupation with self from which true faith ought to set a man free – all this may be admitted. Nevertheless the impressive fact remains that a *desire* for holiness and a love of the good was kindled in a great many rather ordinary folk,

[10] A widening of interest also became apparent in other spheres. After the second decade of the century, regular book reviews were printed. Reports of what was happening in the Connexion increased and there were fewer reproductions of older material. In due course the Tractarian Movement called forth a constant anti-Catholic polemic.

[11] Abel Stevens, *The History of the Religious Movement of the Eighteenth Century, called Methodism* (New York 1861), iii, 277.

many of whom gave evidence in their characters of a real approximation to the ideal. That the urge was so strongly aroused is as significant as the measure in which the goal was attained. The literature of the period bears a constant witness to the strength of this search after holiness. Holiness was conceived of as a divine work in the soul, and the urge for it was essentially a desire for deeper communion with Christ. It was nourished by the continued use of the Wesley hymns, and such works as the *Experience* and the *Spiritual Letters* of Hester Ann Rogers, which were frequently re-issued, illustrate how the search after the gift of holiness covered the whole range of the soul's dealing with God, from its initial 'awakening' and the conviction of sin, through the experience of justifying faith and leading on to sanctification. All was so often laid bare in the literature with simplicity and directness that, in spite of what might be called a formal pattern of the experience of salvation, much of the writing bears the unmistakable mark of reality.

At the time a soul is pardoned, sanctification only begins. Indeed, a babe in Christ has the same kind of faith, love, and knowledge of God, as an adult christian; they only differ in the degree. Here begins that purity of heart, the source of true Holiness, and we must not stop till the soul is perfected in Love. And since God has been pleased to invite, and even court us to love him, with all the powers, vigour, and faculties of our souls, let us neither despise his grace, nor be wiser than his methods; but with arms, as open to take, as his are to give, let us embrace, and hold fast, all the great and precious Promises of Holiness, of complete Holiness, his Blood has purchased for us.[12]

The strong urging which those promises induced in many can be seen in the *Letters of Entire Sanctification*, which the pioneer missionary John Hunt wrote to his friend and fellow-worker, James Calvert, in Fiji, whither they had gone together in 1838. When these were published Calvert wrote of their author in the Preface:

Entire sanctification in experience and practice he earnestly

[12] *Arminian Magazine*, xviii (1793), 438.

pursued. The subject early became of paramount importance to him, and continued to be so to the last moment of his existence. It occupied his best and longest-continued thoughts, and was the subject of his best sermons, and the theme on which he delighted to converse.

One who heard the original lectures in Fiji on which the letters were based commented: 'When he wrote his letters on Christian perfection, so widely known and so highly valued, he wrote his own life.'[13]

Every great spiritual tradition can easily be distorted. Undoubtedly the emotional excitement and depth of feeling, often characteristic of Methodism at this time, were in themselves understood by many to indicate the inspiration of the Holy Spirit, and self-complacency could be mistaken for the peace which comes by believing. Yet there is evidence enough from the sources that in describing the process of salvation not all were deceived. Samuel Drew (1765–1855), a local preacher who refused a university chair in philosophy, wrote in reply to the question about how we are to know when we are saved:

I admit . . . that the common answer, 'By the witness of the Spirit', is vague and indefinite; and perhaps a particular definition is impossible. There are, however, certain characteristic marks which are properly descriptive, although they convey no definition of the thing. First: The soul that experiences the salvation of God feels gratitude towards him for every spiritual blessing. Secondly: This gratitude is accompanied with a degree of love towards him – and we love him because he first loved us. Thirdly: Gratitude implies confidence in his mercies; and this confidence is faith, whether prospectively or retrospectively exercised. Fourthly: This gratitude leads to obedience, not from a dread of punishment, but from a sense of duty and obligation. Fifthly: This gratitude is accompanied with internal peace; and peace presupposes a removal of condemnation. These are marks of a spiritual salvation. But in what degree these *must* be experienced, so as to form a distinguishing criterion, perhaps none but God can discern. If we feel these marks in any degree, let us be thank-

[13] cf. Allen Birtwhistle, *In His Armour: The Life of John Hunt of Fiji* (London 1954), Chapter XIV: 'The Gift of God', pp. 168, 170.

ful; and, through the exercise of thankfulness for past mercies, we shall assuredly have more.[14]

The language here is more sober and analytical than was normal in most cases, yet the authentic notes of the best type of Methodist piety are sounded: gratitude, joy, confidence, love, peace, and expectation. As in the previous century, these qualities were strikingly evident, in particular during the last hours of many of the people. The experiences which were recorded can still make a powerful impression upon the reader. Thus from the 1830s there come the death-bed testimonies of some of the preachers, all of whom had laboured long in the Gospel, and none of whom was afraid when meeting the last enemy. They could cry, 'All is well'; 'Glory, glory! Victory, victory!'; 'I stand upon the rock!'; 'Happy! happy! happy! though I die I shall live!' The Cornish class-leader, William Carvosso, after years of outstanding witness and service, made his greatest confession during the desperate pain of his last hours, causing one to write:

O it was good to be there! . . . Never, since the commencement of his affliction, have I seen him so exceedingly far lifted above himself. At times, for hours together, he is sustained in the highest Christian triumph; when no language of sacred poetry, or of the Scriptures, appears too strong to afford expression to the vivid feelings of his full heart.

Certainly no account of the religion of the Methodists in this period would be complete without reference to such events.

II

Consideration of the ordinary non-eucharistic services of Methodism leads to the conclusion that it is a great deal easier to ask questions about their precise character than to give confident answers. Two traditions were combined in the Wesleyan Connexion: that which kept close to Anglican

[14] *The Life, Character, and Literary Labours of Samuel Drew, A.M.,* by his eldest son (London 1834), Appendix, p. 517.

models and that which was free of prescribed forms of prayer and orders of service. The former, when observed at Sunday worship, was in any case normally followed by services later in the afternoon or evening, is some cases both, at which free forms were used. This practice was confined almost exclusively to some of the town chapels. Even so, there was a tendency for the free form of service to supplant the other, although this must not be taken to imply that there was not in many places a persistent and powerful tradition which retained liturgical forms.[15] Exact statistics cannot be given, although a few facts are indicative of the general state of affairs. In 1795 Conference laid down in the Plan of Pacification that

> wherever Divine service is performed in England on the Lord's Day in Church-hours the officiating preacher shall read either the service of the Established Church, our venerable father's abridgement, or, at least, the lessons appointed by the Calendar. But we recommend either the full service, or the abridgement.

That Conference re-affirmed these words in 1805 and again in 1815 suggests that not all preachers were observing the regulations of 1795. On the other hand, Thomas Jackson could write in 1839:

> The incomparable Liturgy of the established Church is regularly used in many of the Wesleyan chapels in England, and in all the Mission chapels in the West Indies. Translations of it have been made by Wesleyan Missionaries into various languages, for the use of their congregations, especially in the East.[16]

Yet an anonymous writer, referring to a great centre of provincial Methodism, could say in 1841:

> In Leeds we have hitherto been compelled to dispense with the Liturgy. Why, I humbly ask, not allow its introduction into one, say, for example, Brunswick Chapel? Would not the respectability, reputation and size of our Congregation be thereby greatly increased? Have not many of its former esteemed worshippers

[15] In the literature of the time the 'Liturgy' always means the form used at non-sacramental services.

[16] T. Jackson, *Centenary of Wesleyan Methodism* (London 1839), p. 280.

embraced other communions simply because of *their* adoption and use of the National Liturgy?[17]

In what form was the 'Liturgy' used in Wesleyan Methodism? It can be safely assumed that until 1839 Methodists used either the service from the Book of Common Prayer itself or 'Mr Wesley's Abridgement', as it was found in the volume which bore the title *The Sunday Service of the Methodists.* Although this had been drawn up by Wesley in 1784 for the American Societies,

> the fourth edition of 1792 . . . was the first edition to be printed solely for use in this country, and, presumably, also for the English-speaking West Indies, and all subsequent editions follow its main outline.[18]

This book was

> bound with the 1791 edition of the *Psalms and Hymns*, and is the edition of 'our venerable Father's Abridgement' which was authorized for use by Article 10 of the Plan of Pacification of 1795.[19]

This was re-issued by order of the Conference in 1816, and between that date and 1849 it came out at least a dozen times. There are also in existence two copies, dated 1838 and 1842, of *Selections from the Sunday Service of the Methodists; designed for the use of Sunday Scholars on the Morning of the Lord's Day*, which contain only Morning Prayer, the Litany, the Collects, the Holy Communion up to and including the Collect for the Queen, and Select Psalms; but no information as to the extent of its use is available. That the Order of Morning Prayer, together with certain other sections from the Book of Common Prayer which appeared in Wesley's abridgement, hardly maintained their position in the Connexion up to 1850, is

---

[17] *Objections to the Introduction of the Liturgy of the Established Church into Wesleyan Methodist Chapels, considered and refuted*, by 'An Occasional Hearer' (Leeds 1841), p. 17; quoted from a most informative article by Wesley F. Swift, 'The Sunday Service of the Methodists', in *W.H.S. Proc.*, xxxi (December 1957), 112ff., 133ff., 142.

[18] *W.H.S. Proc.*, xxxi, 116.

[19] *W.H.S. Proc.*, xxix (March 1953), 20.

suggested by the fact that in 1839 the Conference ordered the publication of a new book, *Order of Administration of the Lord's Supper and Baptism*, although subsequent editions were to include also forms of service for Matrimony, Burial and Ordination. Thus Wesleyan Methodism was given a Book of Offices without the Orders of Morning and Evening Prayer, although it must be remembered that the *Sunday Service* continued to be re-issued alongside the new volume.

Yet it would seem that in Wesleyan Methodism up to 1850 the Book of Common Prayer itself was more generally used than either of the two Methodist publications. A great many Methodists were deeply attached to the full services and preferred to use them rather than abridged versions. Jabez Bunting, for instance, loved the Liturgy and believed that the close co-operation of the congregation with the minister which it required helped to dispel any sacerdotal conception of the ministerial office. Best of all he preferred a form of worship which combined prescribed and extemporaneous prayers. He was opposed to any attempt at enforcing the use of the service of Morning Prayer upon Methodist congregations.

> When any large proportion of a congregation, deprived of what it considered a privilege, was eager to obtain it, it was his practice to recommend them to wait until the erection of some new Chapel might enable them to gratify their desire, without introducing an innovation, and arousing the spirit of strife.[20]

It is obvious that many Methodists did not like the use of Morning Prayer, and the rise of the Tractarian Movement made many increasingly suspicious of the Prayer Book as a whole.

The non-Wesleyan Methodist movements had little or nothing directly to do with the Prayer Book services, although the first Bible Christians were urged to attend the church in addition to their own gatherings. And within the old body itself many of the services of course had no parallels in the Anglican book; this applied to much of the Sunday worship and nearly all the weekday devotional activities of Methodism.

[20] T. P. Bunting, *The Life of Jabez Bunting, D.D.* (London 1859), i, 385.

The fact that early Methodism owed so much to field preaching, and that it emphasized experimental religion, must have
exercised a conscious or unconscious influence upon its
worship, the quality of which tended to be judged by its
immediate effect upon the worshippers. And although
Methodists felt no direct responsibility to conform to any
older non-Anglican tradition of worship, such as that which
lay behind the Nonconformity of the time, they could hardly
escape the influence of the pattern of worship found in the
Dissenting chapels. Yet perhaps the most powerful influences
which helped to mould Methodist worship were that something of the intimacy and directness of the small fellowship
meetings should be reproduced in the larger preaching
services, and at the same time that the evangelistic mission to
the unconverted should find expression in the services. These
and other factors, such as the growth in importance of the
function of the local preacher during the first half of the
nineteenth century, combined to encourage the development
of free and rather distinctive forms of Methodist services.
These had of course existed from the beginning, although
they were at first intended to supplement the statutory services
of the parish church rather than to supply in themselves the
full diet of Christian worship. It is probable that John Wesley
had been influenced by the model of the University sermon:
two hymns were accordingly deemed sufficient.[21] But forces
were soon at work to modify this. Thomas Wride, who
itinerated from 1768 to 1807, had written a characteristically
querulous letter to John Wesley in 1785 from Norwich,
complaining that two of his younger colleagues allowed more
than two hymns in a service, adding that the people desired
this. Moreover, it is apparent that the practice of introducing
musical items more elaborate than those prescribed by Wesley
was growing, and in 1805 the Conference protested against
this tendency. The preacher was affirmed to be 'accountable
to God' for everything that is done in the chapel while he is
in the pulpit.

Let no Preacher, therefore, suffer his right to conduct every part

[21] cf. H.M.G.B., i, 270.

of the worship of Almighty God to be infringed on, either by singers or others, but let him sacredly preserve and calmly maintain his authority, as he who sacrifices this sacrifices not only Methodism, but the spirit and design of Christianity.[22]

Behind such a protest can be discerned popular pressure to induce services to find their own forms, unrestrained by traditional patterns.

In the earlier part at least of the period under review the order of these services was simple enough: hymn, extempore prayer by the preacher, hymn, sermon, hymn, prayer and benediction.[23] A description[24] of these services written in 1796 draws particular attention to the important role of prayer as 'the life and soul of religion', which 'opens a door of communication betwixt God and man, and is the means we are required to make use of to obtain any promised blessing'. Perhaps the writer, who clearly shows his obligation to Isaac Watts's *Guide to Prayer*, gives a description of the prayers which is more comprehensive than was always the case. At all events he says that the general subjects of the Methodists' petitions were the same as 'in the service of the Church', although they were offered *ex tempore*. They prayed for pardon and true repentance, for grace to overcome spiritual enemies and un-Christian sentiments, for increase of faith and fellowship, that God would 'sanctify us unto himself a peculiar people zealous of good works'. Intercessions were made for all men, the King and all in authority, for the spread of Divine knowledge, and for 'the alleviation of human misery'. Finally 'knowing that the first step towards repentance is a conviction of sin, we pray to God to awaken every sleeping conscience', and for themselves above all things the inspiration of the Holy Spirit. In 1802, Conference complained that too many people sat or stood at prayer instead of kneeling, yet it may be doubted whether kneeling was ever general at the main services.[25] On the whole the seats in most Methodist chapels

[22] *Minutes of Wesleyan Conference*, ii (1805), 291.
[23] In the Methodist New Connexion a fourth hymn was not allowed until the middle of the nineteenth century.
[24] *Arminian Magazine*, xix (1796), 319ff.
[25] It seems to have been common in the smaller fellowship meetings, etc.

were too close to encourage this posture, although it was known for people to turn and kneel against the benches.

Normally the services lasted about an hour in the morning and about ninety minutes later in the day. This meant that they were generally simpler and shorter than most Nonconformist services at the time, although an observer writing in 1807 remarked that this depended much upon the prudence, zeal, modesty, or loquacity of the preacher! At this date apparently Scripture lections were not included – a defect which must certainly soon have been remedied. A writer in *The Wesleyan-Methodist Magazine* in 1831 commented on the changes which had come over Methodist services, which, he claimed, ought no longer merely to be regarded as 'appendages and auxiliaries to worship'. Through the Divine Will, Methodists were now 'a distinct body, enjoying all the privileges of a Christian Church'. Even so, he complained that an attitude deriving from the former situation still continued, too much being attributed to preaching and too little to worship, whereas Christian obligation should bind them to both.

All through this period preaching, both by the circuit preachers and special visitors, held a prominent place in Methodist services. Among the chief publications in the Wesleyan Connexion were four large biblical commentaries, those by Coke, Benson, Clarke and Sutcliffe, written to assist the preachers. Leaders in the affairs of Methodism, such as Watson, Bunting and Newton, were also eminent in the pulpit. No doubt many of the circuit itinerants were but average performers, and some of the local preachers must have been crude enough. Methodism was pilloried too often for one to escape this conclusion, which in any case is only what might have been expected. Yet it was some of these simple or eccentric characters who could speak straight to the hearts of the people. Joseph Nightingale[26] informs us that the morning sermons, often excellent of their kind, were usually intended for the members of the Society, and were generally about some moral or religious duty, whereas the evening sermons

---

[26] His *A Portraiture of Methodism* (London 1807), despite his critical attitude, is valuable for what he discloses.

were either controversial, inviting, awakening or alarming.[27]
On these occasions the preaching was directed at producing
results, and it often succeeded in doing so.[28] During the earlier
part of this period in particular, revivals of religion were
experienced in a number of areas in Methodism, and such
movements were constantly looked for. Extravagances
obviously occurred, but results often justified the unusual
phenomena. Towards the end of the period a more artificial
revivalism seems to have influenced the Wesleyan Connexion,
and a conversation in Conference in 1837 brought forth
expressions of opinion for and against revivals which have
often been heard on similar occasions since.[29]

The hymn-books used were those which had been given to
the Methodists by Wesley himself. The principal collection
was *Hymns for the use of the People called Methodists*, originally
issued in 1780. In 1800 a small supplement of thirty-five hymns
was added, seven of these being hymns on the Lord's Supper,
thereby supplying what was lacking in the 1780 collection,
which was never intended to include all the hymns to be used
by Methodists. No doubt in Wesley's time others also were
sung, such as those in Wesley's own collections of hymns for
the Festivals, Sacraments and Funerals. In addition Wesley
had himself issued in 1741 *A Collection of Psalms and Hymns*,
which consisted largely of psalm paraphrases and hymns from
Isaac Watts. It was this volume which eventually was bound
with the *Sunday Service of the Methodists* and issued in 1792. It
was also known as *The Morning Hymn-Book*, since its hymns
were considered more suitable for the full worship of the
congregation than the experimental type of hymns found in
Hymns for the use of the People called Methodists. In 1816,
Conference recommended an enlarged edition of *Psalms and
Hymns*, 'for use in Methodist congregations in the forenoon'.
Although this continued to be used in some chapels, as were

---

[27] The word 'controversial' must here refer to theological disputes, such as the
points at issue between Methodists and Calvinists or Socinians. Political subjects would
generally be excluded. It has been pointed out that the published sermons of the best-
known Wesleyan preachers during this period were almost without exception concerned
with the Christian's private life.
[28] The Sermon was not an ordinary address. 'In the former part of our public service
we speak to God; in the latter, *He* speaks to us' (*Methodist Magazine*, 3rd ser., x, 1831, 24).
[29] B. Gregory, op. cit., p. 246.

some other collections, it was the 1780 book in its various editions which became by far the most widely used book in Methodism. In 1831 further changes were made in it and another Supplement was added. From that time this became the Methodist Hymn Book proper. Even so it is likely that in some chapels other collections were sometimes used, perhaps in some cases including hymns of a popular type, like those which brought forth caustic comments from John Wesley in 1787.

The music sung in Methodism consisted of tunes inherited from eighteenth-century Methodism, together with others composed during the early part of the nineteenth century. John Wesley had endeavoured to regulate Methodist singing by publishing four tune-books, which contained psalm tunes, adapted German chorals, tunes derived from eighteenth-century songs, and hymn-tunes proper written in his own time, amounting to about 120 tunes in all. A number of editions of these were issued during Wesley's lifetime, and it cannot be affirmed with certainty when the last, entitled *Sacred Harmony*, was first published. These, and in particular the 102 items printed in the *Sacred Melody* of 1761, were the tunes *in common use* among the Societies. Generally speaking, the older tunes included in the collections were stately and measured in character, but some composed during the eighteenth century introduced a new style in psalmody, in which the old form of one syllable of the words being sung generally to one note of the music was giving way to a freer measure in which groups of notes were sometimes given to one syllable. Although this was better suited to the jubilant character of many of Charles Wesley's hymns it could easily be carried to excess. The evidence goes to show that this in fact occurred at the beginning of the nineteenth century, although there are fine examples of early nineteenth-century tunes which became popular among the Methodists. The introduction of new tunes was made easier, since no authorized tune-book existed in Wesleyan Methodism during the first half of the century.[30] Various collections of course were published and were widely

---

[30] In 1876, Conference first authorized the publication of a tune-book, and this 'fixed' tunes and words, although custom had certainly done this in many instances long before.

used, but some indication of the state of affairs may be gathered from one such collection, *David's Harp*, published in 1805, by W. E. Miller, himself a Methodist preacher, who in the preface condemned the frivolity and indecency of much recent Methodist music. In the same year Conference drew up a number of regulations about singing in public worship.

> All instruments of music were prohibited, except a bass viol, which was permitted when the principal singer required it. No hymn-books were allowed to be used but those published at the Book Room. All *pieces* in which *recitatives, solos, fuguing,* are introduced, were positively prohibited. The original grave, simple, and devotional style of music was enjoined to be carefully preserved, which is stated to be admirably adapted to draw off the attention from the singing and the singers, and 'to raise the soul to God only'. Musical festivals were entirely forbidden.[31]

Hymns held a correspondingly prominent place in the early non-Wesleyan Methodist movements. The worship of the Methodist New Connexion has been described as simple and homely.[32] At the Conference which saw the formation of 'The New Itinerancy' in 1797 an issue of Wesley's hymns was authorized, with the addition of hymns for the sacraments and festivals. This book was never produced, but in 1800 *A Collection of Hymns for the Use of the Methodist New Connexion; from various authors; designed as an Appendix to the Large Hymn Book* was published at Leeds to be sold by ministers of the New Connexion.[33] Significantly the *Minutes* of the Conference of that year pointed out that in the book would be found a variety of hymns, adapted to the different parts of Public Worship, 'a deficiency in the Large Hymn Book which has often been lamented'.

Primitive Methodism, whose origin owed much to the revivalism which was a feature of the early years of the nineteenth century, no doubt took over some hymns and tunes used in the older Methodist Societies; yet it was particularly attached to popular tunes of the day. In its early days

[31] George Smith, *History of Wesleyan Methodism* (London 1865), ii, 415.
[32] *N.H.M.*, i, 501.
[33] W. Bainbridge, 'The First Hymn Book of the Methodist New Connexion', in *W.H.S. Proc.*, xiv (March 1923), 21ff.

the Connexion owed much to the literary efforts of Hugh Bourne in the field of hymnody. In 1809 Bourne produced a *General Collection of Hymns and Spiritual Songs for Camp Meetings*, which relied largely on American sources. In 1819 this was enlarged to include sixty-three hymns, and again in 1821 there followed another collection of 154 hymns, which were almost entirely of a mission character, vivid and direct, and this was eventually known as *The Small Hymn Book*. In 1824 Bourne produced yet another book, the *Large Hymn Book for the use of the Primitive Methodists*, and this contained 536 hymns.[34] A considerable number were hymns of John and Charles Wesley, Samuel Wesley, Watts, Doddridge and Cowper, and 20 were written by Bourne himself; a further group were by William Sanders, and had been commissioned by Bourne.[35] No further collections were issued during this period.

The first Bible Christian hymn-book was compiled by William O'Bryan and published in 1824. Its full title was *A Collection of Hymns for the Use of the People called Arminian Bible Christians*, although it was apparently known as *O'Bryan's Hymns*. In general the book followed the selection of hymns in John Wesley's 1780 book, with a few extra hymns inserted at various points. A slightly enlarged edition appeared in 1838. Both books contained supplementary Miscellaneous Hymns, which were virtually the same in either case.[36]

Apart from an occasional stringed instrument and one or two organs, the Methodists sang their hymns unaccompanied until the early part of the nineteenth century, although there were in some congregations 'leading voices' or a 'principal singer'. In the Preface which he wrote for the 1824 *Large Book* for the Primitive Methodists, Bourne referred to the 'leaders of sacred song' who were 'appointed of the Lord'. He held

[34] John T. Wilkinson, 'Hugh Bourne, 1772–1852: A Centenary Tribute', in *W.H.S. Proc.*, xxviii (September 1952), 129.

[35] W. E. Farndale, 'Hugh Bourne and the "Spiritual Manifestation"', in *W.H.S. Proc.*, xxviii, 134–5.

[36] Accounts of the two books appear in Morgan Slade, 'The First Bible Christian Hymn-Book', in *W.H.S. Proc.*, xxx (December 1956), 179ff., and Oliver A. Beckerlegge, 'The First Bible Christian Hymn Book' in *W.H.S. Proc.*, xxxiv (Part 2, June 1963), 34–6. Slade considered that some of the hymns peculiar to this collection were of inferior poetic quality, 'but easy to sing and useful in teaching doctrine', whereas Dr Beckerlegge noted that they were evidence of 'the close connexion between the Bible Christian and the Primitive Methodist movements'.

that 'none should be permitted to take any part in leading the singing service but such as can "sing with grace in their hearts unto the Lord" '. In 1796 it was enacted that no organ should be introduced into any Wesleyan chapel until proposed by the Conference, but in 1808 Conference decided that it was expedient to refuse 'after this present year, their sanction or consent to the erection of any organ in any of our chapels'. In 1820 this injunction was modified. It was then considered expedient to allow organs to be placed in some of the larger chapels to guide the congregational singing, although the sanction of the District Committee and of the Conference had first to be obtained, whilst any restrictions which Conference might consider proper had also to be observed. It is evident that organs were regarded with considerable suspicion, and it was this which lay behind the opposition to the introduction of the instrument in the notorious Leeds Brunswick Organ controversy in 1827. Some believed that organs would mar 'the purity of divine worship', whilst others maintained that the organ would soon be followed by the Liturgy of the church service. But the progress of the organ in Methodism was not to be halted: indeed, the Protestant Methodists who seceded in 1827 were soon to use one in a chapel near Leeds, as well as the Liturgy in their chapel in London.

III

From the first the Methodist people held that the Sacraments of Baptism and the Lord's Supper should be observed by Christians. As is well known, the form and manner in which they were to be retained in the Societies after the death of Wesley proved to be one of the most serious problems facing the Connexion. It was the Lord's Supper which raised issues in their acutest forms. So far as the consideration of Methodist piety is concerned, it is important to note that the Societies, having been nurtured in a rich sacramental tradition, were anxious above all that they should continue to share the benefits of sacramental services. Differences arose over the question as to how this might be achieved. At the time of Wesley's death Methodists in England were accustomed to receive the sacrament either at a regular service in a parish church or in a Methodist building where the officiant was either a sympathetic Anglican clergyman or one of the Methodist preachers ordained by John Wesley.[37] At the Conference of 1791, the first to be held after Wesley died, the preachers engaged themselves 'to follow strictly the plan which Mr Wesley left us at his death', but straightway the ambiguity of this resolution became evident, for very different interpretations could be given of what the plan in fact was. In spite of much discussion nothing definite was done to settle the issue until the Conference of 1795 agreed to 'The Plan of Pacification'. This decreed that

> the Lord's Supper shall not be administered in any chapel except the majority of the trustees of the chapel on the one hand and the majority of the stewards and leaders belonging to that chapel (as best qualified to give the sense of the people) on the other hand, allow it. Nevertheless, in all cases, the consent of the Conference shall be obtained, before the Lord's Supper be administered.

Further regulations required that the sacrament should only be administered by those who were authorized by Conference; and that it should only be held on Sunday evenings,

> except where the majority of the stewards and leaders desire it in Church-hours, or where it has already been administered in those hours. Nevertheless it shall never be administered on those Sundays on which it is administered in the parochial church.

Moreover, in England the form of the established Church was always to be used, although the administrant would have 'full liberty to give out hymns, and to use exhortation and extemporary prayer'. The *Minutes of Conference* furthermore record that

> the Lord's Supper shall be administered by the superintendent only, or such of his helpers as are in full connexion, as he shall appoint; provided no preacher be required to give it against his

---

[37] Between 1785 and 1789 John Wesley carried out 27 ordinations.

approbation; and should it be granted to any place, where the preachers on the circuit are all unwilling to give it, the superintendent shall in that case invite a neighbouring preacher, who is properly qualified, to administer it.

The settlement achieved by this plan was generally acceptable and was as good an arrangement as was possible in the circumstances. Not all Methodist Societies immediately availed themselves of its provisions: in a few chapels the sacrament was not administered at all, in some others only by Anglican clergymen. All the Societies eventually accepted the situation, and 'it was only a matter of time before the Lord's Supper became an integral part of Methodist worship'.[38] Although some Methodists were strongly opposed to the administration of the sacrament by Methodist preachers, desiring above all to retain the close connection with the Church of England, the solution of the problem was a striking indication of the desire of the majority of Methodists to have the sacrament and to receive it from the hands of their own pastors. Nevertheless something was undoubtedly lost, owing in part to the prohibition against celebrating the Eucharist in the four years following the death of Wesley and the introduction of Sunday evening Communion Services brought about by the Plan of Pacification, as a result of which

> there came into Methodism something that was quite unknown in Wesley's time. One result of this was that the glorious Sunday morning celebrations of the early days died out.[39]

During the first thirty years of the nineteenth century the Wesleyan Conference addressed itself at fairly regular intervals to various shortcomings in the practice of the people or to irregularities in the administration of the sacrament. The people were frequently exhorted to be constant in their attendance at the Lord's Table, 'at least once in every month, either in their own chapels or elsewhere, and to make a point

---

[38] J. C. Bowmer, *The Lord's Supper in Methodism 1791–1960* (London 1961), p. 22. This book, together with the same author's *The Sacrament of the Lord's Supper in Early Methodism* (London 1951), is basic for the whole subject.
[39] J. C. Bowmer, *The Lord's Supper in Methodism 1791–1960*, loc. cit.

of staying until the whole service be concluded' (1806). No unauthorized persons were to administer the sacrament, and preachers were to see that only members of society or those with a note of admission from the superintendent be allowed to partake of the Supper of the Lord (1805 and 1813). At the same time the frequency of such discussions in the Conference is an indication of the deep concern felt for sacramental practice and discipline in the Connexion. This anxiety extended also to the form in which the sacrament was administered, which, Conference laid down, should be that of the established Church.[40] Accordingly the Wesleyans used either the service as found in the Prayer Book itself or the revision of it in Wesley's abridgement as it appeared in *The Sunday Service of the Methodists*. This book was re-issued regularly during the first half of the nineteenth century, and the Communion Office also appeared in the *Order of Administration of the Lord's Supper and Baptism*, which was first published in 1839. The changes made in Wesley's revision in these various editions up to 1849 were insignificant, although W. F. Swift was of the opinion that the *Book of Common Prayer* itself was more generally used in Wesleyan Methodism during these years than either of the other books.[41] The chief differences Wesley introduced into the Prayer Book version of the Communion Office were in rubrics concerned with administration within a Methodist chapel rather than a parish church of the Anglican Communion, the substitution of the word 'elder' for 'priest', the omission of the Nicene Creed, and the supplicatory form of the Absolution in place of the declaratory. Rubrics concerning the manual acts and the standing of the people for the reading of the Gospel were retained by Wesley.[42] The normal custom in Wesleyan Methodism was for the communicants to receive the elements from the minister as they knelt in groups at the Communion rail. The wine was of course taken from a chalice.

[40] In Scotland Methodists were permitted to celebrate the sacrament of the Lord's Supper according to the Presbyterian pattern.
[41] Wesley F. Swift, 'The Sunday Service of the Methodists', in *W.H.S. Proc.*, xxxi (June 1958), 142.
[42] For details, see J. C. Bowmer, *The Sacrament of the Lord's Supper in Early Methodism*, pp. 207ff.

The non-Wesleyan Methodist Connexions each observed the Sacrament of the Lord's Supper in ways which eventually marked them as distinct from the parent body. A strong motive at work amongst them was the desire to make their celebrations conform closely to the procedure at the institution of the Supper in the Upper Room. For this reason sitting in the seats to receive the elements was the posture usually adopted, although kneeling was not forbidden. The conduct of the sacramental services was not necessarily restricted to the itinerant ministers, nor was any prescribed order of service followed. Normally, participation in the service was confined to those persons who could show a membership or sacramental ticket. Although the Primitive Methodists were slower than the others to institute a regular sacramental ordinance, there is every reason to conclude that after about 1821 the observance of the sacrament became general throughout the Connexion.

In this way all established branches of Methodism in this period developed a sacramental practice, devotion and discipline; yet it cannot be claimed that the Wesleys' eucharistic doctrine was either retained or explored in its fullness. In particular the rise of the Tractarian Movement and the fear of Roman Catholic aggression, which began to show itself afresh towards the middle of the century, prevented Methodists from appreciating certain facets of the Wesleys' teaching, particularly perhaps on the sacrificial aspect of the sacrament.

The Methodists of this period observed the Sacrament of Baptism, but it is hardly possible to give a satisfactory account of all that was involved or implied in their practices.[43] *The Sunday Service of the Methodists* contained Wesley's revisions of the Baptismal Services for Infants and for those of Riper Years. In all the editions published between 1792 and 1842 the two services remained unaltered, but during the last years of his life John Wesley had made a number of changes in the services, the significance of which is not easy to assess. Yet it may be concluded that during the first half of the century the opinion grew that, in spite of the modifications in Wesley's final revision of the Prayer Book service, too much emphasis

[43] cf. *H.M.G.B.*, i, 159-61.

still remained upon what could be interpreted as baptismal regeneration. The results of this can be seen when it is realized that, although the Infant Baptismal Office in the 1846 edition of *The Sunday Service* was made to approximate in some measure more closely to Wesley's original revision, 'the references to the "mystical washing away of sin" were not restored, nor was the signing with the cross'.[44] This is apparently another instance of that reaction against the Catholic Movement in England which became evident in the Methodism of the time. From about 1837 onwards varieties of opinion on the significance of baptism showed themselves in the discussions of the Conference. Nevertheless W. F. Swift concluded from his investigation of the various editions that, while it is not surprising to discover the alterations which were made in the baptismal offices in 1846 and later years, what does occasion some surprise is the lack of consistency between the emendations made in the service for infants and the service for adults.[45] Indeed it can hardly be claimed that Methodism evolved a consistent or uniform doctrine of baptism, or that the emphasis upon the ordinance in the life of the Societies was as strong as that placed upon the Sacrament of the Lord's Supper. The main point in the discussion on baptism in Richard Watson's *Institutes*, the only major theological publication in Methodism during this period, was that baptism is the initiatory sign and seal of the covenant of grace in its new and perfect form, as circumcision was of the old. This was followed by a defence of paedobaptism and an argument against the necessity of baptism by immersion. In this way infant baptism was linked in the Societies with the training of children in the home.

During the early part of this period Methodists often took their children to the parish church for baptism. Nevertheless the Conference of 1794 pointed out that many of the preachers, long before the death of Wesley, and with his consent, had performed baptisms as well as burying the dead.[46] The Plan of Pacification stated that the administration of baptism should

[44] Wesley F. Swift, 'The Sunday Service of the Methodists', in *W.H.S. Proc.*, xxxi (June 1958), 136.
[45] *W.H.S. Proc.*, xxxi, 138.
[46] *Minutes of Wesleyan Conference*, i (1794), 299.

be determined by the same regulations as those governing the administration of the Lord's Supper and, like the Lord's Supper, was intended only for the members of the Methodist Society. Thus gradually it became normal for Methodist preachers to baptize. In 1815 the Wesleyan Methodists established a Metropolitan Office in London for the registration of births and baptisms. On 12 June 1837, for instance, it is recorded that as many as 44 baptisms took place in Gold Street Chapel, Northampton. Opposition to the practice was sometimes expressed by Church of England clergymen. In 1842 the Rev. T. S. Escott, vicar of Gedney, refused burial to a child who had been baptized by a Wesleyan Methodist minister, and denied that itinerant preachers were ministers of the Gospel. The Committee of Privileges took the case to the Court of Arches, which decided that baptism by Wesleyan Methodists was valid by ecclesiastical and civil law, a judgment which was confirmed by the Privy Council. The importance of the decision lay in the fact that the majority of burials of Methodist members were still performed by Church of England clergymen in churchyards: had the judgment been otherwise, 'the administration of the Sacrament of Baptism by Wesleyan Methodist ministers must have ceased'.[47] The non-Wesleyan Connexions generally saw no reason why baptism should be administered only by their regular itinerants.

IV

The particular devotional meetings, which so far as Britain was concerned were largely peculiar to Wesleyan Methodism during the eighteenth century, continued to be a feature of Methodism during the first half of the nineteenth. Writers in this period referred to the Class-Meeting as one of the institutions through which a devotional discipline was exercised and growth in sanctification promoted.[48] Belonging to a class was regarded as the only door of entry into membership of the Wesleyan Connexion; attempts to relax this rule were always successfully resisted. The Circuit preachers met

[47] N.H.M., i, 403.
[48] cf. Arminian Magazine, xix (1796), 314–19.

the members of the classes quarterly for tickets, when their task was to talk with each member about the state of his religious life. Yet evidently the proper practices of the class-meeting system were not easy to sustain; in 1832 Adam Clarke remarked in Conference that he had heard people complain that instead of the old-fashioned personal advices they had 'just a little sermon'. The preachers obviously did their best to secure regular weekly attendance at class, yet from the time of Wesley onwards this often left much to be desired. In 1826 the minister at City Road indicated that of the fifty members of his class perhaps not more than thirty met at one time, and even so this was better than was general in London. Similarly the smaller Band Meetings proved too intimate for them to continue long to any considerable extent. As early as 1812 Conference drew up regulations for *reviving* and extending them. On the other hand Society Meetings, at which all members could be present together, apparently continued to be held with fair regularity. These gave the minister the opportunity not only to exhort the members but also to bring to their notice news of Christian work elsewhere. In the smaller chapels they were often held on Sunday afternoons or evenings, following the preaching service.

Love-feasts continued to exert a powerful influence and indeed were so popular with some types of people that regulations were drawn up to restrict attendance to holders of Society Tickets or notes of admission. Nevertheless a considerable number of non-members who did come were induced subsequently to meet in class. Quarterly love-feasts were marked on many Circuit Plans, but by 1850 it was the annual love-feast which was becoming increasingly the norm. Sunday afternoon was a popular time for holding them during the early part of the period; later, after evening service became more usual. The Primitive Methodists in particular were attached to the love-feast.[49] At the beginning of the nineteenth century watch-night services were frequently held, not merely on New Year's Eve, but also on the eve of the other quarter-days, before the Quarterly Meetings. The Covenant Service,

[49] On this whole subject, see Frank Baker, *Methodism and the Love-Feast* (London 1957).

which was held on the first Sunday in the year in most of the larger chapels, was always a most solemn and searching occasion.

Finally prayer-meetings performed a distinctive function in the economy of Methodism. They were not restricted to members of the Societies, and were held on a weekday, under the direction of a prayer-leader, who would provide anyone who wished with the opportunity to pray. During the first half of the nineteenth century the custom grew of holding revival prayer-meetings following the evening services. Their aim was to bring individuals to the point of decision or assurance through the agency of 'social prayer', which was directed specifically to the needs of the persons present. Penitents were invited to come forward and kneel at the Communion Rail,[50] and it was common in these gatherings for the message of the evening sermon to be enforced and applied to particular individuals.

[50] cf. R. Young, *The Importance of Prayer-Meetings, in promoting the Revival of Religion* (London 1841).

IV

Ordination

A. RAYMOND GEORGE

THE ordinations which Wesley conducted towards the close of his life raise several difficult questions.[1] His first ordinations were in 1784, the year of the Deed of Declaration, and of Coke's first journey to America. Yet, decisive as that year was, its actions were a consequence of actions taken and opinions formed long before. The decisive step was taken over forty years earlier; it was the decision to allow lay preachers. Soon after that Wesley's attitude passed

[1] See especially J. L. Nuelsen, *Die Ordination im Methodismus* (Bremen 1935); A. Raymond George, in *L.Q.H.R.*, April 1951, pp. 156–9: 'Ordination in Methodism'; Edgar W. Thompson, in *L.Q.H.R.*, April 1956, pp. 113–17: 'Episcopacy: John Wesley's View'; October 1959, pp. 325–30: 'John Wesley, Superintendent'; *Wesley: Apostolic Man. Some Reflections on Wesley's Consecration of Dr Thomas Coke* (London 1957); Colin W. Williams, *John Wesley's Theology Today* (London 1960), pp. 207–42: Appendix: 'The Unresolved Tension; Truth and Unity: Wesley's Doctrine of the Church and Ministry as seen in the history of his relation to the Church of England'; Reginald Kissack, in *L.Q.H.R.*, January 1961, pp. 57–60: 'Wesley's Concept of his own Ecclesiastical Position'; *Church or No Church? A study of the development of the concept of Church in British Methodism* (London 1964), pp. 44–67; Albert B. Lawson, *John Wesley and the Christian Ministry: The Sources and Development of His Opinions and Practice* (London 1963); Gerald F. Moede, *The Office of Bishop in Methodism: Its History and Development* (Zurich 1964); John Kent, *The Age of Disunity* (London 1966), pp. 44–85; Chapter 2; 'The Doctrine of the Ministry in Early Nineteenth-century Methodism'; John Walsh, in *H.M.G.B.*, I, chapter ix, 'Methodism at the end of the Eighteenth Century', pp. 280–2; J. A. Vickers, *Thomas Coke: Apostle of Methodism* (London 1969), pp. 68–78, 87–90, 200–2, 367–9, 372–3; Frank Baker, *John Wesley and the Church of England* (London 1970), especially Chapter 15: '1784 – III: "Ordination is Separation"'; John C. Bowmer, *Pastor and People: A Study of Church and Ministry in Wesleyan Methodism from the Death of John Wesley (1791) to the Death of Jabez Bunting (1858)* (London 1975); W. R. Ward, 'The Legacy of John Wesley: The Pastoral Office in Britain and America', in Anne Whiteman, J. S. Bromley & P. G. M. Dickson (eds), *Statesmen, Scholars and Merchants* (Oxford 1973), pp. 323–50; and writers in *W.H.S. Proc.*, xxx, 72, 162–70, 188; xxxi, 18–19, 21–4, 27–31, 65–70 ,102–3, 147–8; xxxii, 63, 86–7, 169, 190–2; xxxiii, 118–21, 178; xxxiv, 99, 141–7, 167–9; xxxv, 78–9, 88–93, 125; xxxvi, 36–40, 111–14, 159; xxxviii, 81–7, 97–102; xxxix, 121–7, 153–7; xl, 91.

from grudging tolerance to an eager use of this new method. Soon the preachers were organized into a definite body. The annual Conference, with only a very small nucleus of clergymen, the circuits, the division into itinerant and local preachers, the use of some as Assistants and others as Helpers, the status of 'full connexion' after a period 'on Trial'; all this meant that men who were technically laymen were being organized into a kind of supplementary ministry. Their work, like that of some other successful missionary enterprises in the Church, disregarded parish boundaries.

It is therefore not surprising that Wesley at certain periods of his life was involved in controversy, not only about their status, but also about the questions of the relation of Methodism to the Church of England and about the whole structure of the Christian ministry. Wesley never wavered in his view that these preachers were laymen and that laymen had no right to administer the Lord's Supper; the famous 'Korah' Sermon on The Ministerial Office, dated 4 May, 1789,[2] showed that he still held these views at the end of his life. Yet he also took a positive view of their status, as is shown by the vivid phrases of the Minutes of 1746:[3]

> Q. In what view are we and our helpers to be considered?
> A. Perhaps as extraordinary messengers, designed of God to provoke the others to jealousy.

Wesley had some difficulty in controlling them, just as he had some difficulty in persuading the members of his societies to attend the parish churches; and it was inevitable that eventually the members of the societies should desire to receive the sacraments from the hands of their own preachers.

Not only had his earlier actions prepared the way for his ordinations, but also a sudden change in his views in 1746 made possible the action which he did not take till 1784. In 1746 he read what he called, somewhat shortening the title, 'Lord King's *Account of the Primitive Church*', from which, he

---

[2] Sermon CXV (*Works*, vii, 273–81).
[3] *Publications of the Wesley Historical Society*, No. I (1896), p. 34; also accessible in *Minutes of Conference*, 1862 edn, i (1746), 30.

said, 'it would follow that bishops and presbyters are (essentially) of one order'.[4] Bishop Stillingfleet's *Irenicum* confirmed the view.[5]

Wesley was, however, reluctant to use the authority which he judged himself to possess, rightly thinking that by ordaining he would widen the growing gulf between his Connexion and the Church of England. Thus he caused Thomas Maxfield, one of his preachers, to be recommended for ordination to the Bishop of Londonderry, and he obtained ordination for John Jones from Erasmus, whom he believed to be a Greek bishop. Wesley was probably right in this belief, though it has been questioned.[6] But a good deal of trouble arose when other preachers secured ordination from Erasmus without Wesley's consent, and this policy was quickly abandoned.

What led Wesley to his decisive act in 1784 was the need of the people of North America. Here there were about 15,000 members in the Methodist societies; none of the Methodist preachers was ordained; it was useless to urge the people to attend the Anglican churches; there were not very many such churches, and as a result of the War of Independence there were very few Anglican priests. There was no Anglican episcopate there which could ordain priests: America had been regarded as part of the diocese of London. Some of the Methodist preachers had begun to administer the sacraments, though others were loyal to Wesley's views; the societies were in danger of splitting on this issue. Therefore in 1780 Wesley had appealed to Dr Lowth, the bishop of London, to ordain a man for America. The bishop refused.[7] It was not till after Wesley's act of September 1784 that Seabury was consecrated in Aberdeen to be the first Anglican bishop in America.

In 1784 Wesley discussed the matter with Coke and with some of the preachers, and on 1 September at 5 a.m. in a private house in Bristol, Wesley, assisted by Coke and

[4] *Journal*, iii, 232; the full title of Baron Peter King's work is *An Inquiry into the Constitutions, Discipline, Unity and Worship of the Primitive Church* (London 1691).
[5] *Letters*, iii, 135, 182; iv, 150; vii, 20-1.
[6] cf. G. Tsoumas, *The Greek Orthodox Theological Review*, II, No. 2 (Christmas 1956), 62-73; Colin W. Williams, op. cit., pp. 223-5; *Letters*, iv, 287-9; A. Barrett Sackett, *John Jones – First after the Wesleys?* (*Publications of the Wesley Historical Society*, No. 7, 1972), pp. 26-9.
[7] *Letters*, vii, 30-1.

Creighton, who were Anglican priests, ordained Whatcoat and Vasey as deacons. On 2 September he ordained them presbyters, and at the same time ordained Coke as Superintendent. The word 'ordained' is from the private Diary; it does not appear in the printed *Journal*.[8]

Coke then sailed for America, taking with him three documents, all of which deserve careful study. The first was a certificate.[9] After some account of the circumstances Wesley speaks of himself as 'providentially called at this time to set apart some persons for the work of the ministry in America'. He does not use the word 'ordained' or 'consecrated'; the vital words are: 'I have this day set apart as a Superintendent, by the imposition of my hands and prayer (being assisted by other ordained Ministers),[10] Thomas Coke, Doctor of Civil Law, a Presbyter of the Church of England'. The second document was a letter to the Brethren in North America, dated '10th September, 1784', giving a defence and explanation of his action.[11] Here, after explaining why his scruples are at an end, he goes on: 'I have accordingly appointed Dr Coke and Mr Francis Asbury to be Joint Superintendents over our brethren in North America.' He goes on to refer to Whatcoat and Vasey and to the Liturgy which he was sending. The third document was this Liturgy, namely *The Sunday Service of the Methodists in North America. With other Occasional Services*, commonly called the *Sunday Service* of 1784.[12] This book contains 'The Form and Manner of Making and Ordaining of Superintendants,[13] Elders, and Deacons'. The three services which come under this heading resemble closely, apart from the alterations of the names, those for bishops, priests and deacons in *The Book of Common Prayer*, 1662.

These documents show clearly that Wesley's purpose was to

[8] *Journal*, vii, 15–17. The contents of the private shorthand diary, which were not included in the editions of the *Journal* published by Wesley, are now transliterated and published in the modern edition of the *Journal*; cf. *W.H.S. Proc.*, vii, 8–11.

[9] Printed in full in J. A. Vickers, op. cit., p. 367.

[10] Unless some person unknown to us was present, Creighton's assistance must have been supplemented by that of Whatcoat and Vasey, who had been ordained presbyters in that same service.

[11] *Letters*, vii, 238–9.

[12] cf. A. Raymond George, in *H.M.G.B.*, I, chapter viii, 'The People called Methodists: 4 – The Means of Grace', pp. 260–1.

[13] The word was thus spelt in *The Sunday Service* of 1784, but not normally elsewhere.

fill the ecclesiastical vacuum in America by using Coke to organize a Church there. This Coke proceeded to do; shortly after his arrival in America he ordained Asbury on successive days as Deacon, Elder, and Superintendent. Asbury, who had been nominated by Wesley as joint Superintendent with Coke, took this office only when he was approved by his brethren. The subsequent history of the Methodist Episcopal Church in America concerns the present matter only indirectly.

Controversy has continued ever since about the precise significance of Wesley's action in thus setting apart Coke. We had better begin with the question what significance Wesley himself intended it to have. Two extreme views may be at once dismissed. One is that Wesley's appointment of Coke was little more than an administrative act, and that the service was a kind of missionary valedictory service, not intended to raise any ecclesiastical problems at all. This is sufficiently disproved both by the terms used at the time, for example the use of 'ordained' in the Diary, and by the terms in which the preceding discussion and the subsequent controversy were conducted, both by Wesley and others. Clearly something of ecclesiastical importance was at stake. The other mistaken view is to attribute to Wesley episcopalian views of the most rigid type, whereby presbyters and bishops are utterly distinct. We know that Wesley had abandoned that view on reading King in 1746, and clearly, if he had still held it, he could not as a presbyter have ordained Coke at all, or, for that matter, Whatcoat and Vasey. We also notice his subsequent rebuke to Asbury for using the title 'Bishop'.[14]

The view which Wesley himself put forward had two aspects. The first is expressed in these two sentences: 'I firmly believe I am a scriptural ἐπίσκοπος as much as any man in England or in Europe; for the *uninterrupted succession* I know to be a fable, which no man ever did or can prove';[15] and 'I know myself to be as real a Christian bishop as the Archbishop of Canterbury.'[16]

The other aspect of his view is his use of King, Stillingfleet,

[14] *Letters*, viii, 91.
[15] ibid., vii, 284.
[16] ibid., vii, 262.

and the precedent afforded by the Church of Alexandria, where it is supposed that in early times the presbyters consecrated a new bishop when the see was vacant. We may take as typical his statement that King had convinced him 'that bishops and presbyters are the same order, and consequently have the same right to ordain'.[17] The sentence is similar to that in which he wrote of the same subject in 1746,[18] but a little stronger. Actually King had maintained that presbyters were in the early centuries different from bishops in degree, but equal to them in order; a presbyter was a Person in Holy Orders having an inherent right to perform the office of a bishop, but not actually discharging it without a bishop's permission. Stillingfleet had spoken similarly of a power residing intrinsically in the presbyters, but he had thought it could be exercised in case of necessity, and Wesley had good grounds for thinking that America was such a case.

How are the two aspects of this defence related to each other? If somehow he was a bishop, why did he need to defend the rights of presbyters? Presumably because his status as a bishop rested on his status as a presbyter. Are we then to say that his claim to be a bishop was not a claim to be of King's superior grade, but a claim that in his capacity as presbyter he had an 'inherent' right to act as a bishop? If he had ordained only deacons and elders (presbyters), all could be explained in that way. But the case of Coke is more difficult. To what did Wesley set him apart? Not, obviously, to a superior order, for, as a follower of King, Wesley did not believe in that, but to the superior grade, which he called 'Superintendent', a word not previously used in Methodism. How did Wesley have the power to confer that grade? Either he claimed that he had that power through his status as a presbyter or he claimed to be of the higher grade himself. The use of the Alexandrian precedent favours the former view; once one is emancipated from the rigid separation of bishops and presbyters as being of different orders, there is nothing inherently absurd in the idea that one of inferior grade should set someone apart for the superior grade. It could be argued that in

17 ibid., vii, 238.
18 cf. above, p. 145.

England no Superintendent was necessary, for Methodism did not constitute an independent branch of the Church, whereas in America a new Church was to be inaugurated. But this view hardly corresponds to the facts. Wesley was himself virtually the Superintendent of the whole Methodist people, both in England and in America. His action in setting apart Coke 'to preside over the Flock of Christ', as the certificate said, was a delegation of his own power. Wesley was no ordinary presbyter, and Coke was in America to have the same status as Wesley. Coke had indeed, in a letter to Wesley in the discussions that preceded the event, referred to his need of 'the power of ordaining others'.[19] On the Stillingfleet or Alexandrian theory he could already, as presbyter, ordain in an emergency or other such circumstances, but he wanted more than that; he wanted authority to preside over the Church and ordain in the normal course of events. Similarly if Wesley had merely performed occasional ordinations, he might have thought he was acting simply in virtue of his power as a presbyter to cope with an emergency or a vacancy, but in fact there is surely an implicit claim to be more than a presbyter; and this is quite compatible with his explicit claim to be as real a Christian bishop as the Archbishop of Canterbury. Thus his claim to be an ἐπίσκοπος was not based simply or solely on his status as a presbyter, but on his superintendency of the Methodist people.

How, then, had he himself acquired a position as ἐπίσκοπος which could be conferred on Coke only by an ecclesiastical act? In the course of his life it had come to him naturally or rather supernaturally; he had been providentially guided and commissioned; he was an 'Apostolic Man'.[20] Nearly thirty years before, when he had hesitated to ordain, he wrote:

It is not clear to us that presbyters so circumstanced as we are may *appoint* or *ordain* others, but it is that we may *direct* as well as *suffer* them to do what we conceive they are *moved to by the Holy Ghost*. It is true that in *ordinary* cases both an *inward* and an *outward* call are

---

[19] John Whitehead, *The Life of the Rev. John Wesley*, ii (1796), 415–17.
[20] Edgar W. Thompson, op. cit., in both the title and the argument of his book.

requisite. But we apprehend there is something far from *ordinary* in the present case.[21]

By a kind of curious irony the words that he thus used to defend his unordained preachers may equally well be used to defend his own status as an unconsecrated ἐπίσκοπος. He had received an inward call to preside over the whole Methodist flock; this call had not been confirmed by any outward ecclesiastical ceremony, but such a confirmation was not requisite as the circumstances were far from ordinary. He had become ἐπίσκοπος by an extraordinary process.

Coke, however, had not attained any such position, and therefore he had to be formally appointed to it. But that ordination (to use the word which Wesley used at the time)[22] was not a conferment of, or appointment to, a higher order of the ministry; it was a conferment of another grade or an appointment to a special function. There could be no order higher than the ministry of Word and Sacraments, but there were grades within it.

Thus Wesley did not altogether need King's defence of the inherent rights of presbyters. Probably he had for many years nursed the idea that that argument would justify him in ordaining presbyters for England if necessary, but now his thinking had developed to the point that there was a position of ἐπίσκοπος to be claimed and one of Superintendent to be conferred; he continued now to phrase his use of King in the old way, but he could have put it rather differently. The value of King was simply that he broke down that rigid notion of three orders which would have made all such developments impossible. If bishops and presbyters were of one order, then it was reasonable to suppose further that a presbyter could be thrust by providence into the higher grade, as Wesley was.

Thus the appointment of Coke to the higher grade was no mere administrative appointment; it was done by a solemn ecclesiastical act. We have seen that Wesley used 'ordain' in the Diary, but 'set apart' on the certificate. There was a similar feature in Coke's dealings with Asbury. The certificate

---

[21] *Letters*, iii, 150.
[22] 'ordained' in the Diary.

said 'set apart', using the phrase three times, of the successive
stages of deacon, elder, and superintendent.[23] Had it been
intended to distinguish them sharply, the word 'ordain' would
have been used of the first two and 'set apart' of the third.
Coke's sermon at the third of these stages was published, and
its title included the words 'the Ordination of the Rev. Francis
Asbury to the office of Superintendent'.[24] And Asbury wrote:
'my ordination followed, after being previously ordained
deacon and elder'.[25] And all this was quite consistent with the
triple use of Ordination in *The Sunday Service* of 1784. 'The
Form of Ordaining of a Superintendant' uses the word 'ordain'
consistently throughout. This was a departure by Wesley from
The Book of Common Prayer of 1662, which had 'The Form of
Ordaining or Consecrating of an Archbishop or Bishop'; in
the service the candidate is presented 'to be Ordained and
Consecrated Bishop'. Wesley's motive for the omission of any
reference to 'consecration' is obscure, but it emphasizes the
fact that he had no objection to the use of 'ordination' in this
connection. As a matter of general church history, it is not
possible to determine a Church's attitude to episcopacy by
asking which of these terms it uses; it is one of the ironies of
history that in recent times the American Methodists, in their
zeal to assert that the bishops are not another order of the
ministry, have tried to avoid the word 'ordain' and use only
'consecrate', thus reversing Wesley's alteration and going back
to the linguistic usage of *The Book of Common Prayer*.

We may then safely infer that Wesley believed presbyters
and bishops to be of the same order, but that he saw no
inconsistency in ordaining presbyters to a higher grade; for
this higher grade he preferred the name 'Superintendent',
presumably because he wished to avoid some of the associations which had come to be attached to the word 'bishop'.
The system he advocated was certainly not presbyterian,

[23] E. T. Clark, J. M. Potts & J. S. Payton (eds), *The Journal and Letters of Francis Asbury* (London 1958), i, 474.

[24] Extracts accessible in L. Tyerman, *The Life and Times of the Rev. John Wesley, M.A., Founder of the Methodists*, iii (London 1871), 436-7. It is interesting that he connects Wesley's right to ordain with his being 'chief pastor', and uses the precedent of Alexandria to show, not that presbyters may ordain, but that bishops may be elected by the suffrages of other ministers, 'assembled in general conference'.

[25] Clark, Potts & Payton, loc. cit.

though it had some presbyterian features, nor was it altogether episcopalian in the sense which that word had come to bear. Nothing is gained by giving it any such label.

The story of the rest of Wesley's ordinations is somewhat simpler. He ordained on several subsequent occasions, and eventually at least twenty-seven people were so ordained. In 1785 he ordained for Scotland, and, mindful no doubt of the controversy which the ordinations of 1784 had aroused, including the strong opposition of his brother, he was careful to publish a defence of this action. It was not, he contended, separation from the Church, for with the Church of Scotland they were never connected, and the Church of England was not concerned with the steps that had been taken. He characteristically added: 'I dare not omit doing what good I can while I live, for fear of evils that may follow when I am dead'.[26] He disapproved when these brethren began to perform ministerial functions in England. In 1786 occurred the first ordinations for a mission field other than North America.

Ordinations continued, but no new principle was involved till 1788; in that year the ordination of Mather was remarkable in two ways. It was the first ordination for England, and probably Mather was ordained as Superintendent.[27] Wesley possibly intended to make arrangements in this way for the continuance of ordinations for England. He had at various times entertained various ideas as to who should succeed him, and finally decided that the Conference should do so, as in fact it did. But he may have thought that the question of ordination needed some other solution; if so, he did not pursue this with enough vigour to impress it on the minds of the majority of the preachers.

In 1789 Wesley ordained Rankin and Moore for England; the word 'presbyter' now replaces 'elder' on the certificate;[28] that of Moore contains the words 'to administer the Sacra-

[26] *Minutes of Conference*, 1862 edn, i (1786), 193.

[27] This rests on a letter of Pawson, given by G. Smith, *History of Wesleyan Methodism*, ii (London 1872), 98, relating what Mather said to the Conference of 1791.

[28] There had previously been one isolated case, that of Johnson, who was ordained for Scotland in 1786. The certificate, containing the word 'presbyter', is not in Wesley's writing, but it bears his signature.

ments of baptism and the Lord's Supper according to the usage of the Church of England'.[29]

After Wesley's death there were some ordinations at District Meetings, but ordinations without the consent of the Conference were forbidden by the Conference of 1792. In 1793 it was decided that the distinction between ordained and unordained preachers should be dropped; no notice was taken of the implicit claims of Coke and Mather to perpetuate the succession; and the Lichfield plan, which would have made British Methodism episcopal, was rejected by the Conference of 1794 'as tending to create invidious and unhallowed distinctions among brethren'.[30] The main question in the controversies of those years was not whether the preachers should be ordained but whether they should administer the Lord's Supper. In 1795 the Plan of Pacification laid it down that where it was desired, with the consent of the Conference, the Lord's Supper might be administered by persons authorized by the Conference; by which was meant the Travelling Preachers in full connexion.

Wesleyan Methodism never formally separated from the Church of England, but this was a decisive step in the process which resulted in their complete separation. In course of time all the circuits availed themselves of this provision. The preachers had become *de facto* Ministers of Christian congregations and thus naturally fulfilled all the normal duties of Ministers. The idea had arisen that they were virtually ordained by reception into full connexion without the imposition of hands. One result of this was that reception into full connexion was made into a more impressive ceremony.

Even during this period of controversy, however, as well as after it, Coke was in the habit of ordaining with the imposition of hands men who were going overseas. This was done at times and places other than the Conference, and regardless of whether or not the men concerned were in full connexion. He sometimes ordained men who were not going overseas,

[29] Facsimile at *Journal*, vii, 505.
[30] G. Smith, op. cit., ii, 101.

among them John Pawson as bishop.[31] It seems to have become the general custom for men going overseas.[32]

In 1836 the Wesleyan Conference debated the question, as it had done several times in the previous twenty years. The President, Bunting, said that he was 'in essence' ordained himself, and this theory that the Ministers were virtually ordained was unchallenged in the debate; the imposition of hands was but a circumstance of ordination, but it was scriptural and ancient, and thus it was better not to omit it. Accordingly the motion that the Preachers to be publicly admitted into full connexion should be ordained by imposition of hands was carried with only two dissentients.[33] So a service was held which was called 'Ordination or Admission to Full Connexion', and this was carefully distinguished from the formal reception into full connexion of previously ordained missionaries. But at a later date the reception into full connexion and the ordination of Ministers for the home work became distinguishable: first a preacher was received into full connexion; then, normally only a few hours later, he was ordained by the imposition of hands. This clearly could give rise to various questions about the respective effects of these two rites, rather like the controversies which surround the respective effects of baptism and the other rites which immediately followed it in the early Church. As in the parallel case, the question becomes more acute if the rites are considerably separated in time. But whereas baptism and confirmation came to be normally separated in the Western Church, it was only in a few instances that reception into full connexion came to be separated by more than a few hours from ordination by imposition of hands. Overseas missionaries were still ordained when they went overseas, and this might often be at the beginning of their probation rather than at the end of it;

[31] *W.H.S. Proc.*, xxxvi, 36–40; J. A. Vickers, op. cit., pp. 201–2. Shaw, who was ordained in 1819, was President of Conference in 1865, and thus preserved a sort of succession, derived from Wesley through Atmore.

[32] cf. *Wesleyan-Methodist Magazine*, 1836, p. 689 (misprinted as 698): 'This has long been the mode of ordaining the Wesleyan Missionaries.'

[33] *Watchman*, 1836, pp. 251ff.; B. Gregory, *Side Lights on the Conflicts of Methodism*, p. 220; J. Kent, op. cit., p. 50; *Minutes of Conference*, 1841 edn, viii (1836), 85. It is interesting that the resolution said: 'by [not 'with'] imposition of hands'.

and thus they were ordained long before they were in full connexion. This later applied also to probationers who became chaplains to the Forces; and ordinations at the Welsh Assembly preceded by some weeks reception into full connexion at the Conference. And whereas no one but the Conference ever had the power to receive into full connexion, these exceptional ordinations seem not to have required its authority. Presumably the President performed them on his own authority, just as Wesley ordained in 1784 without regard to the Conference of that year. Thus something of the pre-1836 atmosphere lingered on: those who before 1836 had quite logically maintained that reception into full connexion was virtually ordination sometimes continued to say this after 1836 and even after the subsequent separation of the two rites; it was asserted by some that the real Methodist equivalent of the hands laid on in other Churches in ordination is the hand raised to vote the brethren into full connexion, and this continued to be said even when the reception was done by a standing vote. The fact that hardly any of the non-Wesleyan Methodist Churches[34] used the imposition of hands naturally contributed to this interpretation, though in some of them the separation even by a few hours of the Ordination Service from the vote of the Conference or District Meeting, even though the service lacked the imposition of hands, raised fundamentally the same problem. But it is clear that, wherever the main emphasis lay, the total result of this whole process, itself to be seen in the context of all those procedures of selecting, training and testing that preceded it, was that those whom the Church believed to be called of God became both Travelling Preachers in the Wesleyan Methodist Connexion and Ministers of the Word and Sacraments in the Church of God. The same could be said, *mutatis mutandis*, of the other branches of Methodism.

As the Travelling Preachers had for the most part not begun to exercise all the duties of the Christian ministry till near the close of the eighteenth century, 1795 being the most decisive date, it was natural that the nineteenth century should

[34] The history of ordination in these Churches, being less complex than of that in the Wesleyan Church, is not treated here.

see much discussion about the nature of the pastoral office; the claims which many Wesleyans made for it may be studied in the pamphlets, sermons, monographs, and theological systems of the period. The claim that certain functions in respect of church discipline belonged exclusively to the Ministers and not to the leaders was not universally accepted, and it was disputes on issues of this kind that led to some of the divisions of Methodism. But the 'pastoral office' rather than the 'ordained ministry' was the central theme of these discussions, which thus do not directly bear on our theme. Methodism had many such issues to face in its transition from being a Connexion of societies to being a Christian Church.

Similarly various views were held of the superintendency. In Wesley's lifetime the first preachers in the circuits were called 'Assistants', for they assisted Wesley. The word 'Superintendent' makes its first appearance in 1784, and then only in connection with America. The Americans soon gave the name 'Bishops' to Coke and Asbury, their first Superintendents, one of the arguments being that 'Superintendent' is but a Latin version of the Greek ἐπίσκοπος; but eventually they distinguished Bishops or General Superintendents on the one hand from District Superintendents on the other. In England after Wesley's death it was slowly realized that the first preachers were not assisting anyone but were in fact superintending the affairs of the circuits, and so the word 'Superintendent' came into use in the Minutes of 1796. There was never thereafter any serious suggestion that they should be ordained or consecrated to this office, though in England as in America it was maintained by some theologians that to be a superintendent was to be a bishop. The idea that the chairman of the district in some way resembles a bishop was not characteristic of this period. But many of the powers associated in some periods with episcopacy, such as that of admitting Ministers and exercising discipline over them, were exercised by the Conference, and it could be maintained, at any rate of Wesleyan Methodism, that episcopacy resided in the Conference.

But if we go to the New Testament itself we find another sense of the word 'bishop'. At first the words ἐπίσκοπος and πρεσβύτερος were used absolutely synonymously and interchangeably; or, at least, if one term was used to call attention to one aspect of the office and the other term to another, yet they were used of exactly the same persons. It is easy to see how the state of affairs described by King grew out of this, but it is to be distinguished from it. This New Testament episcopacy, which all the presbyters possessed, was the pastoral care of the flock; they exercised it jointly like a committee; and the presbytery, that is, the presbyters acting together, must have exercised discipline and oversight over the individual presbyters, though no doubt apostles also exercised some supervision in some cases. Thus, when the term ἐπίσκοπος came to be confined to the president of the presbyters, King's higher grade, it was possible to draw a distinction between the oversight of the flock, still exercised by all the presbyters, and the 'higher' oversight of the flock and of the Ministers, episcopal powers in the later sense, exercised mostly only by the bishop, but felt to be still latent in some sense in the presbyters. These facts were known to the Methodist theologians of the eighteenth century, Richard Watson for instance,[35] but they gained more widespread acceptance in England when Bishop Lightfoot of Durham expounded them, not hesitating to use the word 'synonymes' (*sic*) in speaking of the words 'bishop' and 'presbyter'.[36] Thus when we speak of the Superintendent or possibly the Conference as exercising episcopacy in the sense of the care and discipline of the flock and of the Ministers, we do not exclude the other truth that every presbyter or pastor and therefore every Methodist Minister has episcopacy in the New Testament sense, that is, the care and discipline of the flock.

To this truth expression was given in the form of service adopted by the Wesleyans in 1846. Until that year the numerous editions of *The Sunday Service*, with a few exceptions, had included the three ordination services, though presumably the forms for Deacons and Superintendents were never used in England after Wesley's death. But in 1846 these three forms were replaced by a single service called 'Form for Ordaining

[35] *Institutes*, iii (1829), 344–57, esp. 354.
[36] J. B. Lightfoot, *St Paul's Epistle to the Philippians* (Cambridge 1868), p. 93.

Candidates for the Ministry in the Wesleyan-Methodist Connexion'.[37] The basis of this service was, as we should expect, the old form for ordaining Elders, but the portions of scripture appointed included some of those previously appointed as Epistles and Gospels for the ordination of Deacons and all of those appointed for that of Superintendents as well as those appointed for that of Elders; and to this service were added exhortations which, both in *The Book of Common Prayer* of 1662 and in *The Sunday Service* of 1784, had been used only for Bishops or Superintendents.[38]

In the Wesleyan Connexion it was for long the rule that the Sacraments should be administered only by Travelling Preachers in full connexion; in 1829 it was decided that Preachers on Trial might in certain very special circumstances be permitted by their Superintendents to administer the sacrament of baptism. Towards the end of the century it was felt right to allow some Preachers on Trial (i.e. Probationers) to administer the Lord's Supper, and in 1892 a procedure was laid down whereby a dispensation to a Probationer to administer the sacraments[39] might be obtained from the President. In 1902 the method of obtaining these was modified by bringing the Stationing Committee into the procedure. In the other branches of Methodism the administration of the sacraments had never been confined to the Travelling Preachers, though there was some variety: sometimes each society was free to make its own arrangements, and little was made of the distinction between Travelling Preachers and others; sometimes there was a greater desire to control the administration of the

[37] Wesley F. Swift, in *W.H.S. Proc.*, xxxi, 112–18; John C. Bowmer, in *W.H.S. Proc.*, xxxix, 153–7.

[38] In the drastic alterations which culminated in *The Book of Public Prayers and Services* of 1882 the ordination was almost unchanged.

[39] The use of the plural presumably implies that this regulation, primarily concerned with the Lord's Supper, was intended to cover baptism also. The idea sometimes expressed that a Church ought never to seek to prohibit lay baptism arises from the traditional view that a layman may and indeed ought to baptize an unbaptized child who is in danger of death. But those who hold that view do not usually hold that it justifies lay baptism in other circumstances, though they would add that, if baptism has, whether rightly or wrongly, been administered even by a layman, it has been 'validly' performed and should not be done again. But this whole notion found no place in Wesleyan legislation, though it may have lain behind the very limited exception made for preachers on trial in 1829.

sacraments accompanied by the occasional authorization within a circuit of those who were not Travelling Preachers or even preachers at all.[40] These departures from Wesley's principles somewhat weakened the significance of Reception into Full Connexion and, in the Wesleyan Church, of ordination by the imposition of hands. But the principle was preserved that the sacraments are the sacraments of Christ in His Church, so that a man ought not to take it upon himself to administer them but ought to do so only when authorized thereto by the appropriate officer or court of the Church.

Wesley's decision in 1784 to ordain had thus far-reaching results: indeed by far the larger number of the ordinations which sprang from this have taken place in America, and this story we have not traced, save in so far as it throws light on events in England. And Wesley's action was in many ways characteristic of his whole outlook: it was his zeal for order and regularity, his desire to do everything in accordance with correct primitive precedent, that led him to ordain rather than to secure the administration of the sacraments in some other way. This outlook he had learnt from the Church of England, and he wished even after 1784 to be regarded as a loyal member of that Church. Loyal to its highest interests he may have been but he disobeyed its normal rules; and this action led in the direction of that final breach which cannot be said to have occurred till after his death. Yet by the institution of a preaching order, albeit an extraordinary one, and of preaching services, albeit supplementary ones, he had long before taken the steps which made his ordinations an almost inevitable development, leading in turn to a more complete separation. For he was not simply an Anglican or a traditionalist. He set loyalty to the scripture and the salvation of men above all these things. The care he took to defend his action in 1784 shows that it is untrue to say that he would have had no patience with our modern discussions on the validity of orders; but he was far more deeply concerned with the inward

---

[40] cf. Norman W. Mumford, in *L.Q.H.R.*, April 1947, pp. 113–19; January 1951, pp. 61–70. The word 'ordination' does not seem to have been used of deaconesses in the Wesleyan Church. In the non-Wesleyan Churches the recognition of local preachers was probably sometimes called 'ordination' in popular usage.

call and with the purpose of all ministry.[41] His comment on certain clergymen in America 'who knew something of Greek and Latin, but who knew no more of saving souls than of catching whales'[42] shows where his emphasis lay. The primary task of this apostolic man was to save souls himself, and to send others to share in this God-given work.

[41] F. Hildebrandt, in G. O. McCulloh (ed.), *The Ministry in the Methodist Heritage* (Nashville, Tenn. 1960), pp. 67–100, especially p. 74.
[42] *Letters*, vii, 31.

V

The Mid-Nineteenth-Century Background

⟶∘◉∘⟵

T. E. JESSOP

THE middle of the century cannot, of course, be here taken as a year or a line but as a belt, narrowing or widening according to the particular interest that happens to be in view. Our concern is with the jerky movement of events, moods and ideas, in which Methodism and Methodists lived.

I: POLITICAL REFORM AND INDUSTRIAL EXPANSION

The legal emancipation of Nonconformists. In 1801 the population of England and Wales was nearly nine million, in 1851 eighteen (in 1901 thirty-two). Such a growth was demanded and made possible by advances in government and industry, the first stages of the changes that shaped present-day Britain. Perhaps the most decisive internal political event of the century was the Reform Act of 1832. It ended the system of government that had operated since the final fall of the Stuarts, and started the process of widening popular participation that reached its logical end in universal adult suffrage. Before the Act the House of Commons was stocked with men put there by a small body of electors, who in turn were controlled by a smaller body mostly in the House of Lords. There were members for boroughs that had scarcely any inhabitants, and large centres of population that had few electors. The system, then, was only feebly representative. The Act adjusted the boundaries of the constituencies to the changed distribution of the population, and reduced the property qualifications for electoral rights, bringing in even the more modest part of the middle class, the 'ten-pound householders'. The electorate was thereby increased by about a half, even so being only one-sixth of the total population.

A large number of Nonconformists thus became legally able to do something about who should rule and how. True, so also did more Anglicans, but these had always been overwhelmingly represented in the Commons, as also in the Lords; the special interests of Nonconformists now got a fair expression for the first time. Three years later the municipal vote was given to every ratepayer; and by executive action the Whig government procured the appointment of representatives of the middle class, including Nonconformists, to the urban magistracy. The liberation to franchise and office was restricted to the towns. The rural areas were still under the sway of aristocrat, squire and parish priest, this last also sitting usually with the other two as a magistrate. The distinction was loosened in 1867, when the municipal vote was given to all male town householders, and so far to the industrial workers, nearly doubling the electorate, yet was still withheld from rural workers, i.e. from miners as well as farm-labourers. In picturing the human scene before this year we have not only to see the distinction of rich and poor, but also to recognize that the distinction of town and country meant, besides the natural contrast of industrial and commercial interests with the agricultural, the politically devised contrast of the voting and the voteless, the partners in government and the mere subjects.

The forces that bent the old ruling classes to accept the initial reform of 1832 were partly secular, e.g. the Benthamites. Some were religious. The Industrial Revolution had produced a sizeable class of fairly well-to-do millowners, and increased the number of similarly circumstanced tradesmen and of the humbler tradesmen and artisans ranked next below them. Of all these Nonconformity had at least its proportional share, so that the immediate enfranchisement of some and the later enfranchisement of the rest constitute the external explanation of the power which they came to exercise. They used the power, naturally, to remove their special grievances. Outside this area they did not think alike. The Wesleyan Church, with

its Anglican memories and its governing body wholly ministerial and not elected even by the ministers under it, was
strongly Tory; but what proportion of its rank-and-file
ministers and its laymen was of the same mind cannot now be
determined (five of the six Tolpuddle martyrs were Wesleyans).
The various groups that by 1850 had broken away from the
Wesleyan Church were in general not of that mind, for they
had recoiled from its authoritarian constitution and practice.
It is well known that the Primitive Methodist Church in
particular produced political radicals, though the Conference
and officers steadily refrained from adopting any one political
attitude. The older Nonconformist bodies had a strong
middle-class core; but Toryism was too closely bound up
with the State Church to win the support of the Baptists and
Congregationalists, firmly opposed to the very idea of a
Church established by law, tied by law to one set of liturgical
forms and subject in the appointment of its highest spiritual
officers to the Crown through the Prime Minister. Nonconformists provided much of the strength of the political party
that was soon to call itself Liberal.

As Dissenting religious bodies, the Nonconformists had
been freed before 1832, either by clement usage or by law,
though open-air preachers continued, fitfully, to be summoned
before the magistrates (as late as 1854 the *Primitive Methodist
Magazine* was reporting instances). The Corporation Act of
1661, requiring all members of corporations to receive
Communion according to the Anglican rite, had been a dead
letter almost from the start, and the Test Act of 1673, making
such reception a condition of admission to any office under
the Crown, eventually became nearly as dead. The latter Act
was witheringly characterized by the Anglican Evangelical
William Cowper:

> Hast thou by statute shov'd from its design
> The Saviour's feast, his own blest bread and wine,
> And made the symbols of atoning grace
> An office-key, a pick-lock to a place.[1]

Both Acts were repealed in 1828. Some religious grievances,

[1] *Expostulation*, 376-9.

however, remained. (*a*) Sore to principle and pocket was a law that laid on the inhabitants of each parish the duty of maintaining its church, and empowered the parish to levy a rate for that purpose. The widespread refusal of Nonconformists, who were bearing the full cost of their own chapels, to pay this rate resulted in occasional instances of distraint and even of imprisonment, and led everywhere to persistent unpleasantness in the local communities. The Nonconformists organized their discontent in a Church Rate Abolition Society (1836), but had to wait until 1853 for the rate to be made voluntary, and until 1868 for the law to be annulled. (*b*) Touching sentiment more acutely was a law of 1753 requiring all marriages except those of Quakers and Jews to be solemnized in the parish church. It was repealed in 1836; but, touching grief at its sorest, burials in public cemeteries had still to be performed with Anglican rites and by Anglican clergy until 1880. (*c*) A third disability was something approaching exclusion from the two ancient universities. From 1772 Cambridge had admitted non-Anglicans, but no one could proceed to a degree without subscription to the Thirty-nine Articles. Oxford demanded subscription as a condition of both admission and receiving a degree, but by an Act of 1854 restricted the test to reception of the Master's degree and of Fellowships. The discrimination was an injury as well as an irritant, since without a degree men were debarred from certain professions; and it kept open a very effective status-gap between Anglicans and Dissenters, despite the learning which some of the latter acquired either by strenuous self-teaching, or by going to the universities of Scotland or Germany, or, from 1828, to the new and strictly secular University College of London, or, from 1851, to Owen's College, Manchester, which trained for London degrees. Opposition to the removal of the discrimination in the two universities themselves and in the House of Lords delayed the legal removal of the tests until 1871.

The Industrial Revolution on the move. By the middle of the century the making of commodities by power-driven machinery had succeeded sufficiently to attract investment, which was soon to be legally encouraged by the Companies Act of 1862, setting limits to the risks of shareholders. The sense of achievement displayed itself, like a peacock raising and spreading its gorgeous tail, in the Great Exhibition of 1851, in the specially-built Crystal Palace (the first wonder of what is now called functional architecture), kept open for four astonishing months – the earliest mammoth trade-fair. It looked like a pompous celebration of material prosperity, a ceremonious idolatry of the machine, and a shout of worldly optimism; and so it was, except that it was also an expression of pride in human inventiveness, so that its proclamation of progress, unlike the armchair dogma of the eighteenth-century rationalists, was exhibiting its proving evidence; and it was saved from mere materialism by a contemporary upswing of moral and religious sensibility.

The industrialists' necessary zeal for efficiency was one ground, alongside a settled love of liberty, of their opposition to State interference, for the methods of State action were leisurely, cumbrous and archaic, being still in the hands of civil servants neither selected nor trained for relevant competence. Self-interest was another ground, but many of them were convinced of the practical rightness of unrestricted trade as taught by the economists who followed in the steps of Adam Smith. This line was championed by Richard Cobden and the Quaker John Bright, who, besides being men of unimpeachable integrity, knew industry from the inside. The Anti-Corn Law League was formed in 1839, and eventually triumphed. The repeal of the Navigation Acts in 1849 and 1854, ending the monopoly of shipping between British (home and colonial) ports, and the abolition of import duties in 1853 and 1860, helped the surge of foreign trade that carried the country to unparalleled prosperity, and also, by throwing the colonial territories open to the traders of all countries, took the sour edge off foreign jealousy of the Empire. Free trade had already been secured in agriculture by a campaign against the protective Corn Laws, begun during the Chartist period. The controversy was not between the rich and the poor but between the industrial and the agricultural interests, the former wanting cheap bread to keep wages low, the latter wanting to maintain the price of corn. The former, organized as the Anti-Corn Law League under Cobden and Bright, represented not only the middle-class factory employers but also many of their employees. The strength of Nonconformists in the industrial areas was recognized by the calling of a conference of about 700 of them in Manchester, at which Cobden tried to induce them to pronounce the Corn Laws to be un-Christian. The failure of the home crops together with the Irish potato famine of 1845–6 forced Peel to urgent action: the disputed laws were repealed in 1846. The results were that the price of bread, though only slightly lowered, was stabilized; that agriculture was not hurt by the easier entry of foreign corn until the American prairies began to unload their vast produce in the middle of the 'seventies; and that the imported corn, needed by a growing population, became a very convenient exchange for our industrial exports. In short, prosperity rose without a check for about thirty years. Peel's action had an important political consequence: it split the Tory party, Disraeli heading the affronted agriculturists, and Gladstone going over to the Liberals, who governed for nearly thirty years.

One prior condition of the prosperity, the improvement of internal communications, had been attended to: about 5,000 miles of our main railway lines had already been constructed. Besides opening up new areas for factories and mines and linking these to one another, and greatly easing the mobility of workers and businessmen, the railway system also brought about a social revolution, making possible more, and more diverse, holiday-making, the expansion of the old public schools and the springing up of new ones to provide for the sons of the rising industrialists, and enabling national bodies, among them the Churches, to maintain quicker and closer contact with their members. As for the movement of goods and travellers overseas, there had been a big advance since the first ocean-going steamer of 1813: the Cunard Company had four steamers on the American route in 1840, and 1858 saw the launching of an iron monster, the *Great Eastern*, with a displacement of 32,000 tons. Emigration was able to expand from streams into floods: in the first twenty-nine years of

Victoria's reign three million people left this island for America and Canada (another two million from Ireland), and the discovery of gold in Australia in 1851 drew nearly fifty thousand persons a year from our two islands during that decade. Another boon in communications for industry and commerce, for governmental relations as well as for the spreading of news, was the swift transmission of messages: telegrams were introduced in 1846, and in 1866 the *Great Eastern* was laying a cable across the Atlantic. The shrinking of the globe had started, so providing more occasions for hand-clasps, and more for fighting.

This picture of a growing prosperity, despite its fragmentariness, explains the material basis of the remarkable volume of church-building by all the Churches at mid-century; that is why, when the growth and redistribution of the population required more churches and chapels, they could be built.

The Lot of the Workers. The patient poverty of ages had one of its bouts of restiveness at the end of the previous century, showing itself in an impulse to 'combine'. Pitt's Combination Acts of 1799 and 1800, making trade unions illegal, were prompted by the belief, with the French Revolution in mind, that such combinations were bound to be conspiratorial and insurrectionary. Although the Acts were repealed in 1824, combinations remained suspect, especially in the rural South, still under the sway of squires and parson-magistrates. The Tolpuddle martyrs, six Dorset farm-labourers, transported in irons to Australia in 1834, had to be convicted, not for having formed a local union, but on the feigned charge that they had administered an oath to a 'seditious' society. A wave of moral disgust rolled over the country, and in 1836 got the sentence washed out, with a free pardon from the King. In the less feudal industrial North the employers regarded a union rather as obstructive and premature than as politically rebellious, for they believed that in those days of small factories wages had to be kept low because most of the profits were needed to build up the capital required for expansion.

Chartism was outside the trade-union path. The People's

Charter presented to Parliament in 1839 consisted of political, not economic, demands, such as universal suffrage, voting by ballot, and equal electoral constituencies. The Reform Act of 1832 had raised the hope of a much wider enfranchisement, and it had become evident that no such step was in view. The disappointment had been exacerbated by a Poor Law of 1834, which restricted outdoor relief to the sick and the aged, providing for the remaining poor nothing but the work-house.[2] The Chartists' petition having received no response, sporadic rioting broke out in the 'hungry 'forties'; yet in 1848, the year of revolutions on the Continent, the movement quietly collapsed. Violence in England seems to infect few, and even then to falter in action.

The dreadful conditions in the factories cannot here be described, but only the first main measures for their improve-ment. The Report of an Anglican Commission in 1833 stabbed the conscience of the nation, and Shaftesbury, an Evangelical, who sat in the Commons from 1826 to 1851, moved into his great role there as promoter of reform, besides leading the Ragged Schools Union for nearly thirty years. A Mines Act of 1842 forbade the employment underground of women and of children under ten, and a Mines Inspection Act of 1850 en-forced certain safety regulations. In 1831 a Bill for a working day of ten hours had been introduced (by a Tory Wesleyan, with another Wesleyan pressing the cause in the country, and a Bible Christian editing *The Ten Hours Advocate*); but not until 1847 did the Ten Hours Act come, a provision for women and children in factories but in effect applying to the many men who could not work without having them alongside as helpers. The Bill had a difficult passage. Some of the mis-givings had been anticipated by a manufacturer quoted in the Commission's Report of 1833:

'First, I read in the New Testament that there are twelve hours in the day in which men ought to work; secondly, by making fewer hours it would tend to demoralize the people; being loose, they would assemble and commit serious depredations; besides,

---

[2] One is described by Dickens in *Oliver Twist* (1838); Carlyle attacked the Act in his *Chartism* (London 1839).

our manufactories would cost more than other States, and we should not be able to meet them in the market.'

A law of 1850 decreed that women and young people should stop work on Saturdays at 2 p.m. in the textile factories, and the rule was gradually extended during the next fifteen years. Thus began the English Saturday, itself a social revolution. These State measures worked imperfectly until an inspectorate was formed large enough to ensure their enforcement. In reform, as in industrial advance, the more spectacular second half of the century was but carrying further what had been basically determined in the first.

For the toilers the middle of the century was a turning-point. The unquiet mood of the previous decades, with its occasional and local explosions of disorder, passed away. In 1848, the year of the last Chartist demonstrations, a large body of the workers offered to the Queen a gold medal as a sign of their gratitude for the Ten Hours Act. Political radicalism lost ground. Trade unions grew, locally more than nationally, being valued as much for fellowship and benefits of the Friendly Societies kind as for defence against employers. The will to work was there, the temper being one of self-help, which Samuel Smiles's book under that title (1859) did not originate, but articulated, illustrated and encouraged. The spirit of reform in higher quarters had shown itself after all to be genuine, and mounting industrial production had begun to increase wages in amount or purchasing power or both. The old squalor, sullenness, and almost animal degradation (though humanity did break through), had begun to contract. The mass at the bottom end was now differentiating itself into ascending degrees of sobriety, skill and status. There had always been artisans, but more and more were being called for by the technological progress, and more workers fitted themselves to step up to meet the need and earn their reward.

Behind the political, social and industrial behaviour of the reforming mid-century was a widening strain of moral aspiration and moral scruple. This was evident in public discourse and public action. It is fair to connect this spreading moralism with the contemporary absorption of more of the nation into the churches and chapels. The population had doubled between 1801 and 1851; more importantly, interest in them and activities within them had increased. Religion was taken seriously. Churchgoing, which for very many had long been largely a convention, and was to become so again (though at a better level), came to be accompanied more broadly by the realization that religion is not simply a set of good usages which the State, or the traditional organization of society, finds convenient to encourage, but a personal commitment and an inner as well as an outer discipline. Some change of character and conduct was a natural as well as a supernatural consequence. More masters and men saw one another on Sundays. In the chapels they also met more closely at week-evening meetings; and the place there given to the laity, by practical necessity as well as on principle, in the fellowship of office, gave working men opportunities that unleashed and exercised unsuspected powers, and brought them a sense of social usefulness and authentic self-fulfilment. Many such men became leaders, major or minor, in working-class movements, and their influence was one of the factors that kept the British trade unions from the wholly secular, often aggressively atheistic, policies and methods of the Continental radicals. The stratification of ability among the unprivileged was being discovered and encouraged in the chapels before a public educational system arose to detect it early and help it to develop as far as it could go.

There were, of course, still dregs of filth and crime in London and the larger towns, pockets of artisans who swore by Thomas Paine, and simple drudges who just responded to each situation as it came, gladly or sadly or dully, with no large hope and even with no large conscious despair, but finding life a little more tolerable than it had been. The first of these three classes disgusted the eyes and noses of the religious until the Salvation Army (1865), followed by the Church Army (1882), showed the Churches how far Christian love should go; the third class, too unimaginative or weak-willed to do anything but drift, have been the despair of evangelizers ever since the Church lost the power to compel them to come in, if only for confession and discipline.

II. THE ECCLESIASTICAL SITUATION

It would be rash to call the eighteenth century a predominantly religious one, even counting the influence of Whitefield, Wesley, and the Anglican Evangelicals. These touched only the minority, not yet enough to alter the look and feel of our national life: there was much indifference, and a strong current of rationalism. The national Church had retained its political and social primacy, but its colouring of public life had become religiously pale. By contrast, in the course of the nineteenth century we became unmistakably a religious nation: religion in some quarters helped the reforming turn in politics; public speakers used its language freely, literature reflected it without apology, social codes adjusted themselves to it, and behind closed doors it was acknowledged with grace at meat and family prayers. This was the period when church-going became more general and Sabbath observance more strict, when preachers gripped large congregations, and when, after a very long lapse, the English became musical again, making the land ring with hymns, oratorios and sacred cantatas, and, in consequence, with non-religious music too. Religion established itself as social orthodoxy: we were consciously a national stronghold of the Christian faith and way. Not everything in all this that appears in retrospect to be faulty can be dismissed as rant and cant and hypocrisy. Lamps were lit that still guide us, fires kindled that still warm us, and decencies stamped on public life that continue to be our standards, or are mouthed as such, even when our practice has fallen greatly below them.

The religious upswing was part of a general mental quickening, in politics, literature, science and technology. How far it was due to that general awakening, and how far to an inner maturing of its own, is too big a question to be pursued, but anyhow the life of a nation is not a line of causes but a web of them in mutual interaction. Our concern in this section is simply to describe the religious scene as that of a variety of Churches.

The Roman Catholics. The most dramatic ecclesiastical event was the re-emergence on the public stage, after centuries of seclusion, of the Roman Catholics. The Catholic Emancipation Act of 1829 removed their disqualification for membership of either of the two Houses of Parliament and for civic office. Its purpose was political, to appease unquiet Ireland. Deep divisions of opinion cut across the distinctions of party and of Protestant denomination. Most of the Anglican bishops stood firmly against the Bill. The project had been mooted for some time, with solid Nonconformist opposition on the ground that such an Act would give Romanists a more privileged position than their own. This ground was taken away in 1828 with the repeal of the Test Acts. In 1848 the further step was taken of recognizing the temporal status of the Pope as a sovereign by establishing diplomatic relations with the Vatican. In 1850 the climax was reached, but not now by an act of State. Without notifying the Government, the Pope re-instituted the diocesan system here. All of a sudden this very Protestant country found itself with Roman Catholic bishops equipped with territorial titles and jurisdiction, under Wiseman as Metropolitan, created Archbishop of Westminster and Cardinal as well. The steps of 1829 and 1848 had stirred the old anti-papal embers into flames again. The daring move of 1850 added a chill of fear to the heat of anger: the secrecy of the planning, the thoroughness of it, and the suddenness and rudeness of its execution, confirmed afresh the historical distrust which the expanding liberalism of the next half-century would otherwise probably have weakened. The talk was of the 'Papal Aggression'. A Bill was quickly passed through Parliament with a massive vote and massive support in the country, forbidding the Roman Catholic bishops, under a heavy penalty, to use their territorial titles. The bishops took no notice; no prosecutions were made; the Act was put on the shelf, and repealed in 1871.

The national Census of 1851 gave the Roman Catholic population of England and Wales as 679,000. There had been a rapid increase by immigration from Ireland. The rise was embarrassing; only a powerfully organized Church could overcome the practical difficulties it brought. The 826 priests were inadequate for the scattered flocks and isolated families:

the training of more priests, and the building of churches, were matters of urgency. Elementary education for the children had to be provided, also higher education for the sons of the English Catholic families of long standing, belonging almost entirely to the aristocracy and landed gentry, to whom our public schools and universities were closed. These native Catholics having lived, like generations of their forebears, remote from regular Vatican control, did not like the prospect of it, nor did their traditional clergy, used to the same freedom. Wiseman's policy (and Manning's after him) emphatically aimed at ensuring an Ultramontane position. Before long Wiseman had to cope also with a group of intellectuals, among whom the historian Lord Acton took a bold place. These urged the benefits of free inquiry, and of encouraging priests and laity to adjust themselves to the coming age of natural science, dispassionate historical research, industrialism and democracy. They were authoritatively quietened by papal discipline after the Vatican Council of 1870. In this year Rome was annexed to the new Italian kingdom. The Pope's refusal to negotiate with the King over this loss of temporal authority became another ground of disagreement among the English Catholics. In the meantime the former Oxford Tractarian, Henry Manning, had become Archbishop of Westminster (1865). In the later period of his leadership he showed a strong Christian concern about social ills. His personal and successful intervention in the London Dock Strike of 1889 was a novel event in our ecclesiastical history.

The Anglicans. The rejection of the Reform Bill in the House of Lords would not have happened without the votes of most of the bishops. Popular anger vented itself in some acts of violence – one or two assaults on bishops, and the burning down of the palace at Bristol. This is mentioned to indicate that the Church approached mid-century with an unpopularity which it wanted to and did overcome by several internal reforms. Talk of disestablishment petered out because there was no general desire among the public to see the House of Lords without bishops, or the nation without the Queen as guardian of its religion. The membership of the Church had grown, and many churches had been built. The number of attendants on the day of the Census of 1851 was nearly four million. The clergy, and through them many of the laity, fell into three groups, which must be described.

(1) The warm response of some Anglican clergy to the work of Wesley and Whitefield eventually produced within the Church an Evangelical movement, which by the 1830s had become a party, with a large and active body of laity, mostly of the well-to-do and – this is usually overlooked – a fair proportion of aristocrats. They were spiritually in the line of the early Puritans who had not left the national Church. They put the Bible, held to be verbally inspired, above tradition, and stood firmly for the Reformed elements (a moderate Calvinism) in the Anglican formularies; they recoiled from a 'churchy' piety, in particular taking a 'low' view of the Sacraments, rejecting baptismal regeneration and the Eucharist as a sacrifice; and, while taking the authority of bishops for granted, they had little or no desire to sanctify it by claiming it to be apostolic. The pulpit counted more than the altar, which, following the Prayer Book, they preferred to call 'the Lord's Table', and they regarded the Church not as a repository of grace mediated through priests but as a fellowship of ministers and laity, and a voice calling on individuals to come face to face with God. On the whole they were narrow in their intellectual interests, and consequently unable to appreciate positively the new stirrings of biblical scholarship, theology and science; the pursuit of truth for its own sake, or spending long hours in strenuous study, seemed to many of the clergy both a desertion of parish duties and a highway to the sin of intellectual pride. Their strength lay in the parishes, until Charles Simeon of Cambridge won over that University, Oxford soon following. After his death (1836) a trust set up under his will for purchasing the right of presentation to benefices enabled the Evangelicals (as a reaction against the Oxford Movement) to perpetuate their hold on some parishes and to acquire it in others. They had few representatives in high places (not a single bishop until 1815). It was they who re-opened their parish churches for weekday worship.

It was they who put the singing of hymns round the liturgy of the Prayer Book, even before the century opened. The *Olney Hymns* of John Newton and William Cowper, two devout Anglicans, provided them with congenial examples. The practice was frowned on by the bishops, by some on the ground that subjectivism is avoided when only scriptural or ancient canticles are sung in a service of public worship, by others because the collections at first used had no relation to the Church's calendar. This second objection fell when Bishop Heber's collection appeared (1827), 'adapted', runs the title, 'to the weekly services of the year'. By the middle of the century all Anglicans were singing like the Evangelicals. After a sequence of collections, *Hymns Ancient and Modern* came forth (1861). The inclusion in this of versified translations of ancient and mediaeval hymns was the fruit of Tractarian influence.

A distinctive mark of the Evangelicals was their preoccupation with philanthropy. Among their laymen, Wilberforce and Shaftesbury were conspicuous examples; and numberless women busied themselves with charitable work. Zeal for foreign missions was a parallel expression of their philanthropy, organized by the founding of the Church Missionary Society (1799). Their evangelistic zeal made them pioneers among the Anglicans in interdenominational collaboration: they were involved in the founding of the London Missionary Society (1795), the Religious Tract Society (1799), and the British and Foreign Bible Society (1804; its first meeting was in the home of a Methodist layman).

(2) The High Churchmen, perhaps less numerous, were much more powerful in the first third of the century, having a virtual monopoly of the episcopal bench. They were the heirs of those conservatives of the sixteenth and seventeenth centuries who stood for making only minimal concessions to the vigorously Protestant Puritans in the Church's new formularies of doctrine and order. The line weakened during the eighteenth century, but became firmer when the Evangelicals came to make themselves felt. High Churchmen held that the Church of England did not begin in the reign of Henry VIII: the old Church of this land had only thrown off

the yoke of the Bishop of Rome, and discarded the purely Romish discipline of celibacy and the imprisonment of Bible and liturgy in the Latin tongue. Put positively, it remained, they claimed, a Catholic Church, maintaining the essential doctrines of the early Fathers, with an episcopate in the apostolic succession and a priesthood ordained and disciplined accordingly, and therefore with full Catholic authority to mediate the divine grace through its Sacraments, the grace of incorporation and regeneration in Baptism, the grace of the Real Presence in the Eucharist, and the grace of Absolution to penitent sinners. It was as Catholic as the Roman Church, indeed more so because it honoured more the contribution of the Greek Fathers to the undivided Church, and purer because it omitted some of the Roman deviations. Moreover, secular sovereignty being an ordinance of God, Sovereign and Church are close partners in the government of the people, whose allegiance can therefore be demanded by each to the other. Such were their claims.

All this is rather too explicit and precise to be attributable to every high-church priest and layman. In some it operated practically as a mood or attitude, e.g. as primary devotion to the Sacraments, as respect for God's ministers, as a high warrant for loyalty to the national Church, or as a religious warrant for Toryism. The high-churchmen were indeed Tories, and, until the Bills for the emancipation of non-Anglicans were passed, they asserted and guarded the prerogatives of Anglicans. But we should get the picture awry if we omitted the parsonage where the incumbent pored over his Hooker or Pearson, and knelt with Andrewes's *Preces privatae* to guide him. It was in such a parsonage that the good Keble was reared. All adhered rigidly to the liturgy of the Prayer Book, deploring the free handling of it by the Evangelicals. To all of them Nonconformists were regrettable, to most of them they were outside the Body of Christ and not capable of being brought into the Church of England except at the price of an unprincipled latitudinarianism.

This was the old high-church party of the first third of the century. It was soon to be drawn into the Oxford Movement,[3]

[3] See below, Sect. IV.

to suffer the agony of losing good men to Rome, to be itself suspected of being Romish, but recovering its standing; and in its Tractarianized form it helped to bring more dignity and colour into every parish church in the land.

(3) The term 'Broad Church' was in use by 1850. It stood not for a common set of doctrines or a common sort of devotion but for a modernity of outlook. The Broad Churchmen found the life of the Church, both High and Evangelical, stuffy, its thought conservative and even petrified, too 'churchy', rarely straying beyond ecclesiastical interests either to the active intellectual searchings of the Continent or to the new political reformism and industrial expansion. The poet Coleridge, born in a vicarage but from his student days literally and meta-phorically a wanderer (with a Unitarian phase), was one of the first Englishmen to draw in the breath of the recent German literature and philosophy, which kept religion linked with the other activities of the human spirit. This wider perspective, together with his own fresh return to the Anglican fold, came as a relief and a release to a handful of Oxford scholar-clergymen in the 'twenties, and so also did the fitful news of the new biblical scholarship that was being pursued in Germany. These clerics pleaded, from their somewhat isolated standpoint, for frankness and modernity in the study of the Bible, for a lighter load of dogma and a less rigid and finical theology, and for a closer fellowship of all the Christians of England, if possible within the Anglican Church. These attitudes found their first collective expression in the *Essays and Reviews* of 1860. There were some Broad high-churchmen, some Broad evangelicals, and some who would call themselves just Broad.

The older Nonconformists. In the first half of the century the Nonconformists were not the solid body of partners which they became during the second half. They fell into two groups, the old Dissenters, descending from the sixteenth and seventeenth centuries (Presbyterians, Congregationalists, Baptists, Unitarians, and the Society of Friends), and the Methodists, themselves divided. Within the first group the denominations had begun to settle each in its own life, with not very much fellowship except an awareness of their common freedom from the State and of the civic disabilities which this freedom cost them. Wesley's Church was regarded by them, and regarded itself, as not on all fours with them. To make those divisions intelligible, a few selective characterizations and historical notes are necessary.

During the Commonwealth a minister could get a charge in a parish church whatever his denomination – even an Anglican, if he would drop his royalism and his Book of Common Prayer; the old Dissenting chapels continued; so that in effect English Christianity was a very loose association of congregations of diverse types, the type in many cases depending on the minister for the time being. The Restoration returned the parish churches to the Establishment, thereby reviving the distinction of Anglicans and Dissenters. It left among some of the latter a strong desire for inclusion in the restored Church of England, which, although it had vocal Latitudinarians, was unable to concede their stipulations. Among most of the Dissenters there was a renewed awareness of their separatist convictions.

The *Presbyterians*, finally disappointed of their hope (going back to the sixteenth century) of being part of the national Church, dwindled. Comprising wealthy merchants and men of good education, they felt the impress of the rationalizing movements of the eighteenth century, with the result that many of them lost both their Calvinism and their Trinitarianism, thus passing into Unitarianism. In the first half of the next century the continuing Presbyterians existed only in few and small congregations, except in Wales, where they had been revitalized and somewhat Arminianized by Welshmen influenced by the early Methodism. The congregations, except those linked with the Scottish Presbyterians, united as the Presbyterian Church of England in 1844. The *Congregationalists* – the old name 'Independents' was usual until well after 1800 – were also Calvinists, of varying shades because of their local autonomy. They too had many educated members, but succumbed far less than the old Presbyterians to the currents of thought that led to Unitarianism. They had responded to the stimulus of the Methodist revival on its

Whitefield side (losing some members to the Wesleyans), acquiring the evangelistic impulse that led them during the nineteenth century to extend their membership to the folk who earlier had been too poor to share in the support of a wholly independent congregation. They founded the London Missionary Society jointly with some Anglicans, Presbyterians and Methodists in 1795, later supporting it alone, and in 1832 formed themselves into the Congregational Union. The *Baptists* had been riven since the seventeenth century into the 'General', who were Arminian, the 'Particular', who were Calvinist, and the 'Strict', an offshoot of the 'Particular' marked by the exclusion of the unbaptized from the Communion Table. They too had a strong middle-class element, with some passing of members to and from the Congregationalists. An open and lasting linkage of the oldest stream of the General Baptists with the Unitarians took place at the end of the eighteenth century. The Baptist Missionary Society was formed in 1792 (sending the great William Carey to India in 1793), and in 1813 the Baptist General Union, which only very slowly realized the aim of an all-inclusive assembly. The *Unitarians* were the result of a Socinianizing tendency in several of the Churches. It was an Anglican clergyman, Theophilus Lindsey, who opened the first overtly Unitarian chapel (1774, London), and a Presbyterian minister, the scientist Joseph Priestley, was defending the position at the same time. The stability of the congregations warranted the formation of the Unitarian Society in 1791; and by the Nonconformist Chapels Act of 1844 those congregations that held chapels which had previously belonged to one of the older Dissenting denominations were legally vested with them if they could prove continuous usage for 25 years. Their intellectual leader in the later decades of the nineteenth century was James Martineau, whose writings on ethics and the philosophy of religion, as well as his personality, were admired in all religious circles. The *Society of Friends*, organized in 1668, were a remarkable proof of the ability of a Christian body to go on maintaining order without Orders, and spiritual continuity without the imposition of a particularized creed. They, again, were largely of the middle class, able as well as eager to work philanthropically: within our period they took a leading part in the abolition of slavery (1807 and 1833), the humane treatment of the insane (The Retreat at York, 1792), the exposure of the horrors of our prisons (Elizabeth Fry, *d.* 1845), and the institution of Adult Schools (1845). Being by conviction a Society, not a Church, they kept apart from the disputes of the Churches.

The Methodists. These being the subject of these volumes, we need only consider their peculiar position as, during the first two-thirds or so of the century, standing apart from the older Nonconformists. Their formal secession from the Church of England, besides being recent, had had different reasons from the older bodies – not overt dissent in doctrine, or disavowal of the whole Book of Common Prayer, or rejection of the principle of a Church integrated with the State, but by differences of emphasis, scope and method, e.g. by a strong emphasis on the sermon and demand for the freedom of extempore prayer and of song, but above all by claiming the right, as the correlate of a paramount duty, to evangelize those whom the Church had neglected, and to do so by itinerant preachers, indeed even by lay preachers, across all parochial and diocesan boundaries. In some of these respects resembling the old Dissenters, they differed outwardly in being strongly centralized under a national annual Conference, doctrinally in being the only Church, apart from a small section of the Baptists, that was unanimously and emphatically Arminian. Indeed, as most of the Anglican Evangelicals were in the Puritan line, it is only a slight exaggeration to say that the Methodists were an Arminian enclave in a country of Calvinists. This is a most important part of their isolation. Another was that although the continuing Wesleyan Methodists had become almost as 'respectable' as the other Dissenters, in political alignment these were on the whole Whigs, while the former, in their ruling section, were Tories. Yet another dividing feature was that the Wesleyans had a decidedly Anglican colouring. They revered the Anglicanism of their founder, and many of them continued the pre-secession practice, enjoined by Wesley, of going to the parish church for Communion. Dean Inge has recorded that when he was a boy – he was born in 1860 – in his grandfather's Yorkshire parish 'there was a small Wesleyan chapel in the village, but half the Methodists came to church once on Sundays'. The Wesleyans were thus conformist as well as nonconformist, not wholly in either camp. To the Anglicans they were recent runaways, and, like the old Nonconformists, claimed to ordain without bishops. To the old Dissenters they were half-Anglican, a hybrid sect, and politically too conservative. What has here been said does not apply to its offshoot Churches, of which there were eight between 1797 and 1849, in reaction against the constitution and practice of the Wesleyan Church, in which authority was legally vested in a self-perpetuating and wholly ministerial body, another feature that put that Church apart from the old Nonconformists. Some of the offshoots, e.g. the Primitive Methodists, were as unacceptable to the old Nonconformists as they were to the Wesleyans, because they would not confine public worship to decorum; shouts of joy broke out, and in penitence they wept.

How and why all the Methodists came to be fully assimilated to Nonconformity in the last third of the century will doubt-less emerge from the other chapters in this volume. One relevant fact in the period covered by this chapter is their common recoil from the growing influence within the Church of England of the loyal Tractarians led by Pusey.

Statistics. From the Census (England & Wales) of 1851. Total population is given as 17,927,609. Only the Churches mentioned in this chapter have been abstracted.

	Places of worship	Attendants on day of census (estimated)
Church of England	14,077	3,773,474
Presbyterian:		
Presb. Ch. of England	76	28,212
Scottish	84	31,919
Independents	3,244	793,142
Baptists	2,769	587,978
Isolated congregations	539	63,572

	Places of worship	Attendants on day of census (estimated)
Methodist:		
Wesleyan	6,579	907,313
New Connexion	296	61,319
Primitive	2,871	266,555
Bible Christian	482	38,612
Wes. Meth. Asscn.	419	56,430
Wes. Reformers	339	53,494
Independent	20	1,659
Calvinistic Methodist:		
Welsh Calv. Meth.	828	151,046
Lady Huntingdon's Conn.	109	29,679
Unitarian	229	37,156
Society of Friends	371	18,172
Roman Catholic	570	305,393

The number of all places of worship was 34,467, those not of the established Church being 20,390. The Report accompanying the Census estimates that, in all, 7,261,032 individuals attended once or more on the Census Sunday, and that the total population 'able to attend' (i.e. omitting children, sick etc.) was 12,549,326.

III: THE NEW BIBLICAL SCHOLARSHIP

The story here is how the Churches came, very slowly, to move from a literal understanding of the Bible as a single and wholly consistent book and therefore of equal authority throughout. Of course, sheer spiritual insight had kept breaking through, but the older approach was usual and official. The change of approach was due partly to moral shock at some of the actions attributed to God in the Old Testament. Of the external factors two of the chief were the legacy of Graeco-Latin scholarship, and the sense of historical distances and differences which, after the vague romantic stimulus, began to assume a critical form in the work of foreign secular historians.

The dons at Oxford and Cambridge were aware that the texts of the ancient pagan writers they worked on were usually constructed from several manuscripts not agreeing at all points. The biblical scholars among them must have known the *Novum Testamentum* of 1707, in which John Mills, printing the old Greek text of Stephanus, collected variant readings from 78 Greek MSS. and other ancient sources. This cost him thirty years of close labour; it had curiously little effect in England (it was reprinted on the Continent in 1710 and 1723). Further, the structure of the books of the Bible was scarcely studied, and interpretation went on in its old way. The break-away was made in Germany, and one important study, *Introduction to the New Testament* by J. D. Michaelis, was made available by H. Marsh (1793–1801, 4 vols.), who appended a dissertation of his own, 'On the origin and composition of our three first canonical gospels'. This had no perceptible effect, and of his lectures at Cambridge the same has to be said. The first open call for a move forward came from a small group of Fellows of Oriel College, Oxford, 'the Noetics', chief of whom were Thomas Arnold, R. D. Hampden and Richard Whateley. Was it not time, Arnold asked, to have, for instance, a History of the nation of the Old Testament comparable with Niebuhr's *Roman History* (1st German edition 1811–12; scarcely noticed until the next, 1827), that is, a critically dated and causally explanatory account of their public life? The call was answered in 1830 with Milman's *History of the Jews*. The novelty of its outlook brought more disparagement than appreciation. The long-standing habit of isolating 'sacred history' was distressed when God's people was put plainly in its secular setting, seen as flesh and blood (e.g. Abraham as a nomadic sheikh), and when relations with neighbouring states were described and elucidated in political terms. This was taken by the conservative to mean that the role of God in human affairs, at any rate in the long Jewish drama, was being denied. Nor were the English Churches ready for a questioning of the assumption that the printed order of the Old Testament books, and of the contents of each, expresses the temporal order of the chosen people's religious career. In the first decades of the century German scholars, on whose work Milman had partly drawn, had made prescient advances in the detection of various layers of tradition in the

Pentateuch, and by 1853 had both distinguished those denoted as 'J', 'E', 'D' and 'P' respectively and arranged them in that temporal order. One of our few scholars who were interested, Samuel Davidson, of the Lancashire Independent College, was thought to be too liberal for a seminary, and had to resign (1857). During the years 1862–79 Colenso, Bishop of Natal, published a book on the Pentateuch and Joshua, in which he followed the Germans in querying the Mosaic (and substituting a mosaic) composition of the Pentateuch, and also examined the Old Testament use of very large numbers, to see whether they were reliable or exaggerated (a caution usual in handling pagan Greek and Latin writings). In both respects he was deemed impious. His metropolitan (of Cape Town) declared him deposed and, when overruled by the Judicial Committee of the Privy Council, excommunicated him; Charles Kingsley preached a series of sermons against him; but Colenso kept his diocese, which stood by him. Stanley, then Dean of Westminster and a leading liberal, defended him. Stanley was at this time producing his *Lectures on the History of the Jewish Church* (1863, 1865), with the benefit of German researches since Milman. At this point Matthew Arnold juts in, to say much the same as his father had been saying some thirty years before. In an essay on Stanley's *History*, referring to the hostile reception of Colenso's book, he rebukes the lack of all sense of religious proportion in both the attackers and some of the defenders, as alike obscuring 'the real essence of the Bible'. His comment must be given in his own words:

> ... as this world has for years been prone to say, 'We are the salt of the earth, because we believe that every syllable and letter of the Bible is the direct utterance of the Most High', so it would naturally, after imbibing the Bishop of Natal's influence, be inclined to say, 'We are the salt of the earth, because we believe that the Pentateuch is unhistorical.' Whether they believe the one or the other, what they should learn to say is: 'We are unprofitable servants; the religious life is beyond.' ... And you are masters in Israel, and know not these things; and you require a voice from the world of literature to tell them to you![4]

[4] Matthew Arnold, 'Dr. Stanley's Lectures on the Jewish Church', in *Macmillan's Magazine*, vii (Cambridge 1863), 333, 336.

Before the century opened, these analytic and genetic methods had been applied in Germany to the New Testament also. Coleridge had learned them there, and commended them at home: he had found it good to read the Bible 'as I should any other work', not as 'a hollow passage for a voice' but as a richly varied literature from many centuries, for then the developing message found *him*. The most recent practitioners of the methods were D. F. Strauss and his first teacher F. C. Baur, both then at Tübingen. The pupil caught the public eye the earlier with his *Das Leben Jesu* (1835, translated by George Eliot in 1846). There was an uproar, for the book denied that the Gospels are reliable records: following the analogy of many folk-legends, Strauss regarded them as memories embroidered and enhanced by excited and devout imagination. There was a Jesus, the witnesses were not consciously falsifying; but their overlaying was so permeating that the facts about him were irrecoverable. This contention was more radical than the simple exclusion of everything supernatural in H. E. G. Paulus' *Das Leben Jesu* (1828). That the Gospels include interpretation was not a wholly new idea, but Strauss applied it so indiscriminately that, had he widened his field, he could have turned nearly all ancient history into legend. He worked with analogies and hypotheses, i.e. mere possibilities, imposing them on the records, not checking them by these, and did not face the question what there must have been in Jesus to explain why His early followers gave Him such total adoration. Yet his intention was not to dismiss the deposit of Christian faith, but to expose unencumbered its core of eternal truth. Here he leapt away from his documents to the Hegelian philosophy (dominant in Germany), which for him meant that spiritual truth is apprehended by reason, that it is as much obscured as suggested by passing happenings, and that the Spirit creatively and directively at work in the universe only comes to perfection at the end of the process, not in the brief span of one man's years in ancient Palestine. Hegelianism had not yet come to England, so that Christian believers saw only his negations and were outraged. We have today a parallel to Strauss's combination of extreme historical scepticism with a spiritual escape to a philosophy, with the difference that his philosophy was an objective one, claiming to vindicate eternal truths, whereas Bultmann's is highly subjective and individualistic.

Baur gathered the results of his prolonged research into his *Paulus*.[5] He applied the methods of 'higher criticism' to the entire New Testament, with the distressing conclusions that the only epistles rightly attributable to St Paul are Romans, Galatians, and 1 and 2 Corinthians, and that every other writing except Revelation is later than A.D. 70, most of them belonging to the second century, the Fourth Gospel to a date near its end. The English reception was incredulous, though it was recognized that here was something weightier in scholarship and reasoning than Strauss's book. Baur, scrutinizing minutely, looked for statements and emphases that could be related to known situations or to natural tendencies: e.g. the Fourth Gospel reflects such deep meditation that it must be late, its doctrine of the incarnate Logos must be a counter-blast to the second-century Gnostics, and the ecclesiastical organization evident in the Pastoral Epistles is too developed to be assignable to the days of St Paul. Like Strauss, Baur was an Hegelian, which in his case showed itself in a fondness for 'dialectical' thinking: e.g. first there were the Judaizing Christians, then Paul's universalism, countering their legalism and ritualism, and finally the Church's synthesis of law with grace and of priests with 'prophets'.

For a while the work of the Tübingen critics seemed to have met with nothing but unreasoning repugnance. Some intellectual consciences, however, had been made uneasy. Two problems had been set – how to continue in a positive way the quest for 'the Jesus of history'[6] and how to take up the 'higher criticism' of the whole of the New Testament, again more positively, and base on it a new kind of exegesis.

On the first problem mention must be made of Renan's *Vie de Jésus* (1863), for although this was not in the line of Strauss, not resting on any systematically critical study of the Gospels, it was new in a non-German way, and romped round Europe, in the original and in various translations, including an

---

[5] 1845; translated into English in 1873, but known earlier.
[6] This expression is found in the title of a later book by D. F. Strauss (1865).

English one of 1864. It was fairly brief, fresh, humane, lit up with imagination and warmed with sentiment, full of the local colour of the Palestine from which Renan had just returned, and in its original tongue delicately written – in short, light-weight, temptingly readable. But the Jesus found in it is no more than an attractive personality, so that orthodoxy every-where hurled broadsides at it. A fully English book came next, J. R. Seeley's *Ecce Homo* (1865), which ran into six editions in a year and thereafter was steadily reprinted. What it presents is not primarily a Life but, within an undated framework of the public ministry, a most sympathetic and penetrating account of the moral and social teaching of Jesus, with no inquiry into its religious grounds or implications. At the end Seeley speaks of the teaching as a divine revelation, and of the Church, the guardian of it, as a divine marvel, but his silence about Christological dogma and his frank criticism of the contemporary claim that man needs only that revelation and not also the power to control the physical conditions of living in the light of science, which was 'dispersing every day some noxious superstition, some cowardice of the human spirit' – all this blinded many clerics and laymen to the excellence and practical concern of the exposition. Among those who condemned it was Pusey. The most graceless judge-ment was Shaftesbury's: 'the most pestilential volume ever vomited forth from the jaws of hell'. The demand for an orthodox popular *Life* was met by Farrar in 1874, and for a more scholarly orthodox one by Cunningham Geikie in 1877. To venture only one step further, Edersheim's *Life* (1883), by a Jew who had taken orders in the Church of England, was pre-critical in the technical sense, but was long valued by scholars for its wealth of material from rabbinical lore. In the meantime the genetic analysis of the Gospels was continuing in Germany, and more than one learned *Life* was written there which English scholars studied but did not emulate, being less prone to jump at hypotheses accoutred with impressive but not always judicious erudition.

The second problem, the handling of the whole of the New Testament with something like Baur's methods but without his pioneering rashness, was taken up with distinction. Stanley produced a fresh and vivid picture of the religious life of the first Christian communities in his *Sermons and Essays on the Apostolical Age* (1847). Alford's commentary on the Greek New Testament (1849–61), covering both textual and 'higher' criticism, was learned, fresh, and acute, the first bold and weighty English commentary of the modern kind of that scope. Bishop Christopher Wordsworth's (1856–60) was as competent philologically but less modern, its outstanding merits being its rich array of patristic quotations and the spirituality of its expository notes. While Alford's work was proceeding, two shorter commentaries of the new kind were issued in 1855, on 1 and 2 Corinthians by A. P. Stanley, and on Romans, Galatians and Thessalonians by B. Jowett, the latter too liberal for many people's liking. Then came the remarkable and still admired volumes of Lightfoot on Galatians (1865), Philippians (1868), and Colossians and Philemon (1875), the ones in a series planned by him and his friend Westcott and Hort in 1860 to cover modernly the entire New Testament. Even earlier, Westcott and Hort had launched themselves on their basic work of preparing a new critical text of the Greek New Testament, which did not appear until 1881. This labour of thirty years in the austerest branch of biblical erudition took rank as a classic.

English New Testament scholarship, then, had moved so far from the backward state complained of by the Oriel group in the 'thirties as to stand alongside the German, except in the field of the grammar and vocabulary of New Testament Greek. W. F. Moulton, one of the Revisers of the New Testament, translated in 1870 the then standard German *Grammar* of Winer, and gave us later, in collaboration with another Wesleyan, A. S. Geden, the still indispensable *Concordance to the Greek Testament* (1897). The brilliant work of his son, J. H. Moulton, in the same field, falls in our own century. Old Testament scholarship had made its new start, and was soon to advance under the two Scots, W. Robertson Smith and G. Adam Smith, and the Anglican S. R. Driver. In this survey of the earlier period the only non-Anglican scholar that had to be mentioned was Samuel Davidson. The day of distinguished Nonconformist participation on a large scale was to come in the later period.

Only a cursory notice can be given of the state of the direct knowledge of Palestine (omitting Egypt and Mesopotamia) in our period. After travellers' accounts for centuries, skilful exploration of the surface began about 1800. The most extensive survey was made by two Americans, Edward Robinson and Eli Smith, whose joint *Biblical Researches in Palestine* was published in London in 1841 (3 vols). Excavation started about 1850, though a valuable dating of strata, by pottery, was not hit on until 1890, by Flinders Petrie. Dean Stanley recorded a wide tour in his *Sinai and Palestine in connection with their History* (1856). A special interest in geology, fauna and flora marks Canon Tristram's *The Land of Israel* (1865). To glance ahead, in 1880 the Palestine Exploration Society (founded 1865) issued a map of Western Palestine, an inch to a mile, drawn from a survey made by C. R. Conder and the future Field-Marshal Kitchener. Outside Palestine the itineraries of St Paul were followed step by step by Sir William Ramsay from 1880 onwards.

IV: THEOLOGICAL CURRENTS

The first phase of liberalism. Until after 1850 theology, like biblical research, so far as it was moving, was almost entirely an Anglican affair. The Church of England had most of the scholars; these, whether at Oxford or Cambridge or elsewhere, had usually more means and leisure than Nonconformist ministers; and they usually commanded a wider range of readers. Its theology had had a long sleep since the deistic and Arian controversies of the first half of the eighteenth century, settling into an orthodoxy with a High character in some quarters and a Calvinistic one in others, so that Wesley's outburst of practical Arminianism had to spend itself outside.

The orthodoxy was first challenged from within by the Oxford Noetics. They demanded, besides a new approach to the Bible, a change in theology, as required by the awakening intellectuality and moral practicality of their day. They were stimulated in part by Coleridge. That inconstant genius, for ever bubbling with ideas, had come back from Germany with his lungs full of its metaphysical air, which he panted out in the close atmosphere of England. The voice of the group most widely heard was that of Thomas Arnold, a man of strong scruples, who had had to hammer out his faith before daring to be ordained. What impressed him in Coleridge was not his speculative flights but his conception of the religious as not wholly a supernatural layer but also a flowering of man's created spiritual nature, and his seeing, in his *On the Constitution of the Church and State* (1830), the Church as a necessary instrument in the education of an organized national society. Arnold was interested in theology so far as it was relevant to keeping the religious and moral life well poised. For him it was therefore not a wire-drawing of the metaphysical attributes of God, but Christocentric, seeing God as revealed in Christ, as the only mediator, thus leaving no room for sacerdotalism. The Church is charged to realize the Kingdom of God not only in worship inside its walls but also in the varied life outside. Hence it should make a larger use of the laity; and as it is for the whole nation, it should be a single national Church, open therefore to the Dissenters with freedom to worship in their own way in the parish church at different hours. The divine requirement, then, is not a single creed and a single ritual, but a sound inner and outer life in individual and nation. These views, expressed partly from time to time, were gathered up in Arnold's *Principles of Church Reform* (1833). Those who later were to be called Broad Churchmen did not subscribe to all those views, but in general openness of mind he was their pioneer. His influence might have been swifter and larger if in the very year 1833 the Church had not been thrown into the storm of the Oxford Movement, and if he had not died in 1842 in his own forties.

Carlyle has to be set alongside Coleridge as a breaker of the theological dike from the side of literature, letting in the waves of Germany's literary and philosophical high tide. Living until he was nearly ninety, he had a longer spell of productivity and a much wider area of readers. He ceased to be a Christian, but his Scottish puritanism, shed only intellectually, thrust him to prophetic heights. He climbed to his rostrum in *Sartor Resartus* (1834), and from then onwards forced the English public to listen to him, not only because the thunder of the Everlasting Yea came through the heavy tread of his Teutonic prose, but also because of his terrible sincerity, his hammerlike moral absolutes, his grand conviction of God. Intolerant of humbug, he made many wince at their own, and many enjoyed what they took to be the exposure of others'. From his Sinaitic heights he proclaimed religion as a body of ultimate commands to be obeyed in bravely honest living, not a cobweb of finely spun doctrine, not a pageant of ritual, not a deposit which only a Church could receive, guard and dispense. His affirmations were magnificent, his negations sometimes inhuman, but the two together prodded many on the fringe of the Churches not to let the new industrial materialism drive religion out, and many inside the Churches to see the need for sorting out their priorities, in this respect assisting liberalism of the Arnoldian kind.

The Oxford Movement. Shortly before Carlyle became a prophet, the Tractarians began their agonizing upheaval of the Church of England. The Movement was a halt to look backwards, far back, not to the Reformation, not to the Middle Ages, but to the fourth century, when there was but one Church in the one Empire that stretched from the headwaters of the Tigris to Britain; and the interest was not in the Christology of that age but in a theology of the Church. It had three present targets, the State, Popery, and Dissent.

The precipitating event, Keble's sermon on 'National Apostasy' in July 1833, was provoked by the Church Temporalities Act of that year, suppressing twelve of the twenty-two Irish bishoprics. There were certainly too many of these, but Keble's point was that the spiritual autonomy of the nation's Church had been undermined by a secular legislature of a very mixed kind, as though that Church really belonged to the nation, not to God. In that consisted the 'National Apostasy'. Very soon after the sermon the *Tracts for the Times* began to appear, running to ninety (1833–41), and going well beyond protest against the current Anglican

Erastianism. Newman, who had written the first, wrote the last, Tract 90, which brought to a head a growing suspicion and hostility. It claimed to show that the Tractarian doctrine of the Sacraments was not inconsistent with the Thirty-nine Articles, for the Articles, historically interpreted, were worded to exclude not the doctrinal system of the Roman Church, as they appeared to be, but only wrong theories and practices that had crept in during the Middle Ages. At last, exclaimed a shocked public, the general purport of the Tracts was plain: all along they had been advocating Romanism, for anyone who belittles the break of the Reformation must be a papist. The posthumous publication of R. H. Froude's *Remains* (1838–9) had already been thought to betray that trend, and W. G. Ward's *Ideal of a Christian Church* (1844) was to show it frankly and without apology. The emphasis on Apostolic Succession in Tract 1 need have troubled only the Evangelical and have done no more than irritate the Nonconformist; but the further unfolding, devaluing the Reformation, stung them both, and with them some of the old high-churchmen, and, of course, the non-religious Englishman, for whom the sight of anything like Romanism in the State Church was politically intolerable. Within Oxford, reaction was swift. Tract 90 was condemned within a few weeks by the Heads of the Colleges, and Newman's bishop instructed him to issue no more. Seeing his power of public influence destroyed, Newman withdrew from the city in 1842, went into retreat, re-examined his thwarted plan for Anglicanism as a *via media*, neither Romanist nor Protestant, and in October 1845 passed into the Roman Church, perhaps more driven than drawn. Ward had preceded him in September, Faber followed in November, and other clergymen seceded from time to time in the ensuing years.

The splitting of the Church into two continuing parties brought with it a permanent enrichment of scholarship, for both of them took in hand the documenting of their respective antecedents: in 1841 the Evangelicals began the publication of the Parker Society's 53 volumes of the Anglican Reformers, completed in 1853, which were counterbalanced by the 'Library of Anglo-Catholic Theology', also begun in 1841, an even larger collection, containing the writings of the High divines of the seventeenth century.

In the year of his secession Newman issued an *Essay on the Development of Christian Doctrine*, worked out in his retreat. He there faced the problem set by the large difference between the simple teaching of the first Apostles and the elaborate doctrinal system of the Roman Church, and explained it by the principle of divinely guided development. The principle was not new, having been operative, even when not formulated, in all the major Churches. Differences have arisen over which developed doctrines, i.e. what content, could rightly be brought under it. Newman's interest was characteristically in a quite different question, namely, what sort of Church has the authority to develop doctrines beyond Scripture, the rightness of these being for him determined by the title-deeds. His Tractarian view had been that the authority lay with the Church before it was divided into the Church of the East and that of the West. In the *Essay* he concludes that that Catholic character has passed to the Roman Church: the divine source of dogma is infallible, and of God's infallibility there must be a continuing earthly expression. Newman's hunger for an infallible institutional guarantee of dogma insulated him from both the biblicism of the Evangelicals and the problems and searchings of the liberals. After the *Essay* he disappeared for a while from the public scene. His lovely and moving *Apologia* of 1864 can only be mentioned in passing. In 1870 he came forward as half-psychologist and half-philosopher with his *Essay in Aid of a Grammar of Assent*, a perceptive study of the inner factors that lead to religious belief, written to expose the inadequacy of the customary abstract metaphysical demonstrations. Without denying that reason and faith should stand together, he would not reduce all reasoning to logic-chopping, nor would he admit that every belief, aspiration, scruple, cry and song of the religious soul was unjustified if it lacked the sanction of icy logic. Here he stood above confessional distinctions, and was widely read.

Keble and Pusey remained to pursue the original purpose of internal reform. Keble, reared in a high-church vicarage, having always seen and felt his Church as a part of the Church

Catholic, was serenely stable, unlike Newman who, coming from an Evangelical background, caught that idea as a somewhat late revelation, and was swept off his feet by it. With Keble's full support the leadership of the movement after the first secessions passed to Pusey, under whom it became a party, with an influence out of all proportion to its numbers. It was in this second stage, the distinctive doctrinal position having been clarified by him, that the strong interest in ritual began, a care for ceremonial with attendant symbols and furnishings, taken from mediaeval usage. This care was sometimes pushed to the point of challenging and incurring episcopal censure and discipline (the 'ritual controversy'), with a few cases of imprisonment under a Public Worship Regulation Act of 1874, which was soon allowed to fall into desuetude. There was, however, a wider consequence: the concern of the Puseyites (a contemporary term) for external proprieties of worship spread to the whole Church of England, resulting in cleaner and tidier churches, the setting of cross and candles on the altar, and the restoration of the white surplice in place of the black Genevan gown. As services had become irregular and slipshod, some reform was overdue.

These external changes widened the gulf between Anglicans and Nonconformists. So also did a deeper change, due to the Puseyites, a spreading awareness within the Anglican Church of this as not merely the 'Church as by law established' but as also the national representative of the one true Church. For many more Anglicans than before, Nonconformity now meant being outside the true Church, as well as – old charges – having ugly chapels and plain worship and being given to individualism and 'enthusiasm', in the sense either of claim to personal inspiration or of indecorum. This attitude made the Nonconformists all the more aware of what they took to be their distinctive function within the divine economy, and helped to edge the Wesleyans into full fellowship with them.

That the original anti-Erastian note of the Tractarians found a response outside their own party is illustrated by the noise raised by the 'Gorham case' of 1849–50. The Rev. George

Gorham, nominated to a living in the diocese of Exeter, was refused institution by the bishop on the ground that his view of baptism was un-Anglican, and an ecclesiastical court confirmed the bishop's action. Gorham appealed to the Judicial Committee of the Privy Council and won his case. His contention had been that baptismal regeneration was conditional on fit reception, and that therefore any benefit accruing to an infant must be due to some other form of grace; but what came uppermost in the ensuing storm was not doctrine but the fact that a committee of State had presumed to decide on such a matter – although its decision was not that Gorham's interpretation was the right one but only that it was compatible with the formularies. The conviction that doctrinal matters should be discussed and settled within the Church and by its clergy was heightened, and linked itself with an already growing dissatisfaction with the long abeyance of the Convocations. The result of the uproar was that the Convocation of the Province of Canterbury was revived in 1852 (that of the Province of York in 1861). In 1851 Manning and some other Tractarians were so disgusted with the alleged judicial presumption of the State that they seceded to Rome.

An independent theologian: F. D. Maurice. While the tensions set up by the Oxford Movement were in their early stage, F. D. Maurice was also grappling with the idea of the Church Catholic, not however as an institutional locus of divine authority on earth but as a conception implied in a general theology. The son of a Unitarian minister, he had to leave Cambridge without taking a degree (although he won a First), because he could not in conscience make the requisite subscription to the Articles. Before long he felt drawn to the Anglican Church, went to Oxford, took his degree, and was ordained in 1834. Only four years later he published what has been called his 'most enduring book', *The Kingdom of Christ*, which procured him a Chair at King's College, London. One influence behind it was Coleridge's twinning of intellectual freedom with religious insight and loyalty. Negatively the book was a recoil from the Calvinism of the Evangelicals and older Dissenters -- God as wrathful, even as fore-ordaining some souls to damnation, and man as starting life with an entail of sin so heavy that it virtually blots out God's image. Positively it was a theology of love. God's love, manifest in Jesus, operates also in Christ the Logos, the source in every man of his life and light – in *every* man, so that nobody is by nature cut off from God. We are God's children not by a particular act of grace but by His general grace in our created nature. The fathering deed of God is done in all of us. What needs to be done is our becoming aware of it, believing it and living accordingly. Maurice thus excludes the idea of salvation as the undoing of a primal Fall, also the idea of baptismal regeneration as the receiving of a new nature (he speaks instead of an individual 'taking up his pardon by baptism'). As for the Church, it is one and therefore Catholic, but it need not be a single institution: it is the family of all who recognize their oneness in Christ (as Coleridge had said), and under the pressure of this are ready to abandon some of their denominational tenets. This contention was heavily criticized; Tractarians, Evangelicals and Nonconformists inferred that they would have to give up what for them was essential. Maurice was not an easy-going Latitudinarian, he was arguing theologically; but he did not come to grips with the human difficulties. Some of his readers, defeated by his often obscure style, dismissed it all as mysticism, which at that time usually meant mistyism. Benjamin Jowett had this in mind in his remark on a sermon preached by Maurice at Oxford: 'All I could make out was that today was yesterday, and this world the same as the next.'

Maurice's *Theological Essays* of 1853 brought down on him in the same year dismissal from King's College, chiefly because of the last essay, on Eternity. His maintaining that this was not temporal, not a serial quantity but a divine quality, could scarcely of itself have been judged heretical, for it had recurred in Platonizing theologians through many centuries; but when he dismissed 'eternal death' the fat was in the earthly fire, for he was not tilting at the crude use of a term but asserting that the very idea of such a finality is incompatible with any idea of God in which love is central. It was very hard in his day for the ministers of all denominations to manage the care of souls without warning of the risk of ultimate unending punishment; it could not be replaced with what Maurice explicitly called 'universal redemption'. In 1857 the Wesleyan divine, J. H. Rigg, dealt severely with him in his *Modern Anglican Theology*. In 1866 Cambridge elected Maurice to the Chair of Moral Philosophy, and there he found rest and peace. There is no space to dilate on his pioneering work with Charles Kingsley and a few others, known as Christian Socialism – oddly, for it was not connected with any economic or political theory but followed simply from his doctrine of love and his loving heart.

Essays and Reviews. The secular Victorian optimism was not being reflected in religious circles. The alleged Romishness of the Tractarians, and the 'Papal Aggression', had raised fears in all the Churches. The few published signs of theological unorthodoxy – ethical criticisms such as Maurice's rejection of hell, questioning whether God in His favouring of the Jews had really hidden himself from the teeming millions of the Far East, and J. McLeod Campbell's dissatisfaction with the penal theory of the Atonement (*The Nature of the Atonement*, 1856), and some botherment about miracles – were symptomatic of a wider disquiet. Some intellectuals, able to appreciate the principles of German biblical criticism and of the developing natural sciences, and sensitive to the possible materialism of the new industrial order, were anxious, depressed or pessimistic; they were caught in a trial of faith, and slipped into varying degrees of unbelief, e.g. J. A. Froude, A. H. Clough, Matthew Arnold, and Tennyson in his *In Memoriam* (1850). Against such mental unsettlement official Anglicanism and the bulk of Nonconformity seemed to have put on a protective armour.

It was to speak to this situation that seven Anglican scholars published in 1860 the instantly notorious *Essays and Reviews*, which reached a ninth edition in 1861. It was the first collective pronouncement from the forward-looking side. The aim is put in the brief foreword as

a free handling, in a becoming spirit, of subjects peculiarly liable to suffer by the repetition of conventional language, and from traditional methods of treatment.[7]

Jowett put it more bluntly in a letter to Stanley:

We are determined not to submit to this abominable system of terrorism, which prevents the statement of the plainest facts, and makes true theology or theological explanation impossible.

The strength of the orthodox pressure on teaching at Oxford, and on writing and preaching everywhere, advertised itself in the vehemence of the reaction to the volume. Someone, adapting Aeschylus, spoke of 'the Seven against Christ'; Pusey said, donnishly, that the book 'participated in the ruin of countless souls'; Bishop Wilberforce attacked it vigorously in The Quarterly Review; the Primate issued a declaration against it, signed by twenty-four bishops; a bishop and a clergyman secured the condemnation of two of the essayists in the Consistory Court of the Southern Province; the annulment of this verdict on appeal to the Judicial Committee of the Privy Council provoked a protest, organized by Wilberforce and Pusey, from 11,000 clergy, and another from 137,000 laymen; finally, the Southern Convocation pronounced a synodical condemnation on the volume. These events ran from the beginning of 1861 to October 1864, with Colenso's book of 1862 adding fuel to the fire.

Although the essays are clear and firm, they are almost consistently restrained and equable; but the religious atmosphere was highly inflammable. The learning was up-to-date and handled with ease, tedious at times to a present-day reader only because addressed to a desperately conservative mentality. To give these general comments a little content, some samples of the points put forward must be produced. The two essayists prosecuted were Williams and Wilson. The former, a distinguished Hebraist, starts from the position that 'we cannot encourage a remorseless criticism of Gentile histories and escape its contagion when we approach Hebrew annals'.[8] He summarizes the reasons for supposing that the Pentateuch is not of one hand or period, and for taking

[7] J. Parker (ed.), Essays and Reviews (London 1860), 'To the Reader'.
[8] ibid., p. 51.

prophecy not as foretelling but as proclamation of spiritual truth. Towards the end he passes to a few sensitive points of theology: justifying faith is 'opposed, not to the good deeds which conscience requires, but to works of appeasement by ritual';[9] on baptism, 'the first Christians held that the heart was purified by faith; the accompanying symbol, water, became by degrees the instrument of purification';[10] and when the priestly consecration of bread and wine set in, 'salvation from evil through sharing the Saviour's spirit was shifted into a notion of purchase from God through the price of his bodily pangs. . . . a commercial transfer, and this effected by a form of ritual'.[11] Wilson, a former Bampton Lecturer, claims to be speaking for many in asking whether the enormous mass of pagans are to be represented as outside the Saviour's reach, under the curse on Adam,[12] and expresses the hope of a final redemption for all.[13] He would not have the Thirty-nine Articles altered, but subscription abolished, for 'no promise can reach fluctuations of opinion and personal conviction';[14] but he would leave standing the canons forbidding public teaching contrary to them. He also asks for no needless barriers excluding Dissenters 'from the communion or the ministry of the national Church', though the hope of entire inclusion would be utopian.[15] Baden Powell, Savilian Professor of Geometry at Oxford, would probably have been prosecuted had he not died shortly after the *Essays* appeared. He denied the possibility of a physical event contrary to natural law: facts unexplained must for science be in principle explicable, so that what is at issue is not the evidence for such facts but the kind of explanation to be sought.[16] Goodwin, the only layman, insists that the account in Genesis 1 must be taken to mean what it says:

> It bears on its face no trace of mystical or symbolical meaning. Things are called by their right names . . . different from the imaginative cosmogonies of the Greeks, in which the powers and phenomena of nature are invested with personality.[17]

[9] ibid., pp. 80–1. [10] ibid., p. 86.
[11] ibid., p. 87. [12] ibid., pp. 153–4.
[13] ibid., p. 206. [14] ibid., p. 189.
[15] ibid., p. 198. [16] ibid., p. 141.
[17] ibid., pp. 222–3.

So understood, it is no longer tenable; attempts to harmonize it with modern science merely twist its plain words and plain intention and thereby destroy its simple grandeur.[18] Benjamin Jowett's essay, twice as long as any other, running to 104 pages, is still worth reading by non-specialists. His general thesis, very like one of Coleridge's, is that the primary duty of the exegete is 'to read Scripture like any other book'.[19] The phrase, torn out of its context, stung, and raised a howl. He meant that we must begin by recovering the original meaning. He had said on the previous page that 'no one who has a Christian feeling would place classical on a level with sacred literature', and later says, 'When interpreted like any other book, by the same rules of evidence and the same canons of criticism, the Bible will still remain unlike any other book'.[20] The two other essays are by Frederick Temple (the future Primate) and Mark Pattison, the former a balance of learning and spirituality, the latter a history of English religious thought from 1688 to 1750.

The *Essays* mark a turning-point. From the 'seventies onwards theology as well as biblical scholarship sprang into life, soon with full and able Nonconformist participation. The *Lux Mundi* volume (1889), edited by C. Gore, was the first expression of Anglo-Catholic modernism. After the early founding of such bodies as the British and Foreign Bible Society, it was the religious scholarship of the last quarter of the century that first crossed and recrossed the ecclesiastical boundaries, despite high walls and barbed wire. That was the proper and lovely fruit of the marriage of piety and intellect. A less happy consequence, more evident, however, today than then, was that sometimes the doctrines of God and man presented could appeal to intellectuals only, whereas the picture-thinking and practical absolutes without which simpler minds cannot manage were left unassimilated to the doctrines. Perhaps the most general question of theology is whether God is for everybody. If He is not, if He cannot be preached without grave distortion except to intellectuals, can

[18] ibid., pp. 249–50.
[19] ibid., p. 338.
[20] ibid., p. 375.

there be a Christian theology? If we believe that He is, we are making the one Christianly necessary *sacrificium intellectus*, which means, not that we are to put God-given brains to sleep, but that the proud distinction of the learned from the unlearned is religiously trivial.

V: THE STATE OF SCIENCE AND PHILOSOPHY

The impact of science. In the first half of the century there was much interest in the results, little in the spirit, of science: 'natural history' was the hobby of many clergy and layfolk, and knowledgeable articles were frequent in religious magazines, both to satisfy curiosity and to illustrate the wonders of God's creation. The attitude was friendly. The Copernican theory, as developed by Galileo and Newton, reducing man's earth to a very little machine speeding round one of innumerable suns, had become familiar by habit, the early fears of deism and determinism having been removed psychologically rather than logically, though they were soon to be revived. There could be pride in the refounding of chemistry by Dalton (1805) and in Faraday's advance in the study of electricity (from 1831), for these were men of indubitable piety, their theories did not obviously clash with Scripture or doctrine, and their results were of practical use.

The waters were not troubled until Lyell produced his *Principles of Geology* (1830). Hitherto, major changes in the earth's crust, such as the formation of the great mountain ranges, had been attributed to sudden catastrophic action. Lyell argued, from the basic methods and criteria of the sciences, that even such changes should be referred to forces now known to be steadily at work, e.g. pressures within or below the crust. With that book geology was reformed. One result was that geological time was stretched much further backwards than had ever been imagined. On how old the earth is Lyell was reticent, the facts needed to give an answer not being yet available; but the theory required it to be very old. Troubled layfolk had to be reminded that 'B.C. 4004' in the margin of Genesis 1 had been inserted in editions of the Authorized Version from 1701 and was simply the result of a calculation made by Archbishop Ussher about 1650. Soon one divine after another claimed to show that the stages of creation in Genesis 1, whatever their duration might be, follow the sequence given by modern geology. The efforts involved much arbitrary exegesis (e.g. the usual Hebrew word for 'day' could only mean an epoch), but as that sort of exegesis was then common, clergy and layfolk seem to have been reassured.

Such fear as remained that science was moving against the Bible came out on the appearance of Robert Chambers's *Vestiges of the Natural History of Creation* (1844), which reached an eighth edition by 1850. He believed in the sovereignty of God, but because he affirmed that besides the earth the living things on it were not created in their present form but developed from simpler forms, he was hotly attacked. Disraeli's novel *Tancred* (1847) reflects some of the drawing-room chatter about the book, e.g. 'I do not believe I ever was a fish'. 'Oh! but it is all proved: . . . We are a link in a chain. . . . This is development. We had fins – we may have wings'.[21] Many were disturbed by the theory of evolution sketched amateurishly by Chambers. Before long they were to see it stated with precision and with a vast array of evidence by a scientist of the first order.

Evolution as a form of the world-process had been an old idea in philosophy. As a theory of change in animal species it had been current among zoologists in the latter half of the eighteenth century, which explains its presence in the *Zoonomia* (1794) of Erasmus Darwin, Charles's grandfather. To take it out of guesswork and give it a scientific shape, two things were necessary: to collect the data and to formulate the causal law or laws of the process. On the latter point, Lamarck (*Philosophie zoologique*, 1809) concluded, too firmly for other zoologists' liking, that the origin of change was a new need in a species (e.g. because of a change in the environment), with consequent attempts to satisfy it, and a development of the organs thus brought most into play; and that the change in the organs became hereditary. What Darwin did, starting from the fact of a general struggle for existence (for

[21] (ed. 1847), p. 226.

the number of animals of one kind remains roughly constant despite their fertility), was to collect instances of changes with unprecedented thoroughness, and to frame his law of 'natural selection', i.e. 'random' changes occur in some of the young of a given species, some of the changes turn out to be more suited to survival and vigour in the given environment, and those animals that have them thus tend to live longer and reproduce more than the rest, which latter sooner or later become extinct. The time required for an old species to fade away and a modified one to establish itself was bound to be considerable, but the lengthening of the earth's time-scale by Lyell had removed any difficulty on that score. Darwin's theory of evolution by natural selection was new because it postulated not a novel urge or initiative on the part of individual animals, but a winnowing on the part of the environment of the individuals lacking the favourable variants. He did not claim to account for the appearance of the variants, though in calling these 'random' or 'chance' he did not mean that they were inexplicable but only as yet unexplained.

The theory was first presented in a paper to the Linnaean Society in July 1858 by Darwin and Wallace jointly, only a few weeks after they had discovered that they had arrived independently at the same conclusions. Darwin's full material, however, was nearly ready. His *On the Origin of Species by Means of Natural Selection* appeared on 24 November 1859 and sold out on the same day; there were three more editions in the first half of 1860, a fifth not until 1869. As the five editions together amounted to only 7,500 copies, the uproar it caused must have been based largely on second-hand knowledge. *The Times* perceptively chose T. H. Huxley to review it. Some scientists criticized it sharply, including the geologist Sedgwick of Cambridge; Canon H. B. Tristram, a naturalist, was one of the few clergy who openly welcomed it; the contributors to the *Essays and Reviews* of 1860 wrote just too early to be able to consider it.[22]

[22] The articles in the English newspapers and magazines between 1859 and 1872 are systematically listed and summarized in Alvar Ellegård, *Darwin and the General Reader* (Göteborg 1958; Stockholm 1959), both an English and a Swedish edition.

The overwhelming majority of the members of the Churches, clerical and lay, unable to judge Darwin's work on its scientific merits, naturally saw only its apparent bearing on the Bible and doctrine. They supposed that the Bible taught the fixity of species, so that all known animals must have originated from their like. As for man, although not considered in the *Origin of Species* – Darwin's *Descent of Man* did not come out until 1871 – the apparent implications of the new theory were clear and at once seized on: that the race had sprung from a lower species, that it probably did not begin in one place from one pair of parents, that a primeval state of perfection and a Fall were excluded, that with these disappeared the ground usually given for the need of a Saviour and for the Church's rite of baptism, that a being descended from an animal remains one, sharing the animal's lot, and therefore has no supernatural destiny, and that Paley's argument from design to a divine designer was undermined. The Bible was disproved, theology annulled, and man's peculiar prerogative denied. These certainly were the apparent bearings. Whether all were really so, or whether some of them might be no more than a tearing away of old trimmings from Christian belief, was scarcely examined. Instead, the mistake was made of looking for a hole in the theory – e.g. the 'missing link' between the first men and the subhuman species they allegedly sprang from not having been found, it was declared (begging the question) that it never would or could be found – so that the directly creative hand of God may be put into that hole. People innocent of the outlook, tasks and methods of the natural sciences could not fairly be expected to avoid those misunderstandings, or to see the sheer magnificence of a theory that brought into its sweep all animals from the earliest fossil ones to the present very different ones, and turned the agglomeration of the artificial classes of the text-books into a system of genealogical trees. But that most religious scholars could assume that nothing more was at stake than the total preservation of a traditional way of interpreting the Bible, and that therefore they themselves had no rethinking to do, proves how far the world of learning of the mid-century was from that of its close. Too much of the controversy was between extremes, those who cried, 'The Bible, therefore no evolution', and the atheists asserting that 'biology, like physics, does not need to bring in a God, therefore there is no God'. The unlovely sight and sound turned many away from the Churches, not always to atheism but often to a private moral and religious faith. Huxley kept both his head and his heart: as a biologist the most formidable of the Darwinians, as a leading educationist (which he was) he urged the educative value of Bible-reading in the schools, though defining his own faith (for he had one) as agnosticism.

Darwin's book shook not only the religious but many who nevertheless still believed in the dignity of human nature, with the result that they concluded not, 'Let us eat, drink and be merry, for tomorrow we die' but, 'Let us improve this short life, and the social conditions for those who are to follow us'. As for the notion of evolution, it was brought into almost every subject, losing its precise biological sense, becoming a cliché for a supposedly inherent law of racial advance. From this muddled identification of evolutionary process with progress Huxley was free. He saw, and emphatically said, that biological evolution gives no moral guidance: the 'nature red in tooth and claw' (the phrase comes from Tennyson's *In Memoriam* of 1850) is the very nature which man has to fight, the law of his distinctive nature, set in his unique sort of mind, being benevolence and co-operation.

The developments in the natural sciences after the 'sixties were too rich to be summarizable, and anyhow, though technically exciting, had no specially pointed bearing on religion. They won acceptance by their obvious success. Then, as now, they had practitioners who knew how to write for the general public, chiefly Huxley himself, Clifford of Cambridge, who popularized science brilliantly but rambled in his theory of a 'mind-stuff', and the physicist Tyndall, the two latter virtually materialists. Some of their addresses and essays were sold in paperback editions (as low as 6*d*.), and had a wide circulation among artisan radicals. This current of artisan unbelief, which had fed since the early years of the century, and continued to do so after the end of it, on Tom Paine's deistic *Rights of Man* (1791) and *The Age of Reason* (1794), has to be noted alongside the rather highbrow currents to which this section has had to be confined. It was among them chiefly that the cheap editions of *The Riddle of the Universe* by the German biologist Ernst Haeckel (Engl. trans. 1900), expounding an evolutionist materialism, circulated as the final word on the subject.

The extension of the scientific outlook and methods beyond the physical and biological spheres to the study of man in his humanity was one of the features of the second half of the century. Anthropology, in the sense of the study of the customs and ideas of primitive peoples, had E. B. Tylor as its English pioneer, publishing his first work in 1865 and his well-known *Primitive Culture* in 1871, in which, of course, the question was raised of how and in what form religion began. For some decades the subject suffered from a shortage of critically observed facts and a surfeit of hasty theorizing. Occasionally a divine took umbrage at some of the anthropologists' definitions of religion and at the tendency of some to link this closely with magic and thereby with superstition, but no shattering controversies resulted. In the 'seventies psychology began to break loose from philosophy, but not until the present century did it begin to clash with Christian convictions, e.g. in the Freudian theory of sexuality as man's fundamental drive and religion as a sort of neurosis, and in a theory inferred from Baudouin that prayer is simply a form of autosuggestion. A third extension of scientific method, new in its sharpness, was into human history, with H. T. Buckle's provocative *History of Civilization in England* (1857, 1861), which emphasized statistics as the objective data on which the historian should as far as possible work, though the contention sprang partly from an anti-religious, indeed a frankly materialistic, bias. It roused considerable interest, passing into a fifth edition in the 'sixties, but the public interest soon passed, and the professional historians moved away from all general theorizing to the critical establishment and chronological and causal ordering of particular facts.

The rift between the Churches and philosophy. In the first half of the century religion and philosophy did not stand near to one another. Few minds that worked in the one worked also in the other. One reason is that in neither outlook nor content had philosophy anything to attract those whose main concern was religious. Such philosophy as there was was mainly a hangover from the second half of the previous century, carried on rather than developed or re-examined. It was an empirical study of the mind, most of it really psychology. It pulled the mind to bits, and claimed that our experience is built up chiefly by the simple process of association: if A occurs several times with B, then, when either recurs thereafter the other tends to recur with it, whether A and B be sensations, emotions or desires. Knowledge and morality were 'explained' in this simplifying quasi-mechanistic way. Even the much more philosophically minded Scots were still defending common sense against Hume, who in fact had plenty of it himself. The physical universe was left to the scientists, for whom it was a mechanical system. Coleridge, poetical and religious, and Carlyle, passionately moral and powerfully imaginative, schooled in those analytic and mechanistic systems, came from them bored and hungry, and turned to the literary and philosophical explosion in Germany for a wider vision, for the stimulation of the whole mind, intellectual, aesthetic, moral and religious. In demanding this they were exceptional in this island. Not until the last third of the century did the demand for width, depth and height, for large themes, come into our strictly philosophical circles.

In ecclesiastical circles only two men of technically philosophical competence appeared before Maurice and Mansel. The first was Whately of Oxford, later Archbishop of Dublin. His *Historic Doubts Relative to Napoleon Buonaparte* (1819) was a *reductio ad absurdum* of the scepticism avowed by Hume in matters of human evidence in his notorious essay on miracles. His *Elements of Logic* (1826) brought some life into the subject without advancing it. The second was William Whewell, the outstanding intellectual who was Master of Trinity College, Cambridge, an able scientist with a philosophical grasp of the principles of all natural science, worked out in his *Philosophy of the Inductive Sciences* (2 vols., 1840), in preparation for which he had written an erudite *History of the Inductive Sciences* (3 vols., 1837, very soon translated into German), both of them read by Mill when preparing his own *System of Logic*. There is no obvious evidence of his having stamped his large outlook on his fellow-clergy.

The most respected professional philosopher was Sir William Hamilton, professor at Edinburgh from 1836 onwards. With him German philosophy first came into ours. He was impressed by Kant's scepticism of speculative metaphysics: we are bound, he argued, to postulate an Absolute or Unconditioned, but we can never know it in itself, because our modes of knowing enter into every object we know ('to think is to condition'). It follows that no rational theology is possible. This conclusion, with Hamilton's reason for it, was taken over by the High cleric and Oxford don H. L. Mansel, and expounded in his Bampton Lectures, *The Limits of Religious Thought Examined* (1858), and in his *Philosophy of the Conditioned* (1866). The only escape, he urged, from the relativity of knowledge to our faculties is through revelation, which reason can neither prove nor disprove. The winds of criticism blew hard on him, not only from Mill and Huxley but even from some theologians, e.g. Maurice, who shrank from protecting revelation at the cost of declaring the impotence of reason beyond common experience. The acutest criticism of the contention that to think the Infinite would be to destroy the very idea (on the ground that to think is to relate and limit) was made in an immediate review of *The Limits* by James Martineau. This able and sensitive religious philosopher (Unitarian) did not systematize his views until the 'eighties, but that review and several others (collected in vol. 3 of his *Essays, Reviews and Addresses*, 1891) reveal him as a critical observer of the philosophy and theology of the earlier decades. The controversy was aggravated by Spencer's borrowing of Hamilton's Unknowable (*First Principles*, 1862). Spencer was more usually thought of for his propagation of evolution as an utterly general cosmic law; but by 'evolution' he meant increasing differentiation or individualization, the passage from the simple to the complex, not, what Darwin meant, a process by which in a given environment a new species of living organism appears and an old one disappears. He was not thought well of in this country by either scientists or philosophers. Spencer's Unknowable, apprehended by an 'indefinite consciousness', was caustically described by the Oxford philosopher Bradley as 'a proposal to take something for God simply because we do not know what the devil it can be'.

Known to a far wider body of readers than Hamilton, whose light soon went out, was J. S. Mill, who, indeed, in his *Examination of Sir William Hamilton's Philosophy* (1865), helped to quench it. He moved into the public eye with his articles in the *Westminster Review*, which from 1837 to 1840 he controlled. His *System of Logic* (1843) and *Principles of Political Economy* (1848) became standard works. The former is of interest here because it got a review of nearly a hundred hostile pages from W. G. Ward in the Tractarian *British Critic*. A sequence of books made Mill's moral and political philosophy known to almost all educated people, because of the straightforwardness of his thinking, the simplicity of his style, and his transparent integrity ('the saint of rationalism', said the high-churchman Gladstone). Philosophically he stood always for the eighteenth-century kind of empiricism: what is given to us is not a great physical world but a series of sensations, emotions and desires; these are all that reason has to operate on; and the principles of reason have themselves been formed in the course of experience, are not born in us as an endowment. Here was a thoroughgoing naturalism, which made him sympathetic to Comte's Positivism, until Comte transmogrified it into a religion. In his ethics he developed Bentham's Utilitarianism, basing morality on desire for happiness, with 'the greatest happiness of the greatest number' as the criterion of it, of law, and of political policy. It was enough for religious readers that he had rooted our highest acquisitions and demands in nothing but human nature: his secularism repelled them as atheism, which it was.

Only after his death in 1873 did religious judgment on the man become generally more kindly. His posthumously published *Autobiography* (London 1873) of the same year was a winsomely honest self-disclosure of a rare type of mind.

After telling how his father had reared him he mentions the intended and actualized consequence: 'I am thus one of the very few examples, in this country, of one who has, not thrown off religious belief, but never had it.'[23] After that simple explanation, only brutes could have stuck daggers into him. In 1874 his *Nature, the Utility of Religion, and Theism,* three essays hitherto not known of, startled everybody, shocking, however, not the Christians but that school of Utilitarians whose chief spokesman he had been for nearly half a century. The logician, empiricist and secularist had unexpectedly let his heart come through. The Coleridge and Wordsworth who long ago had moved him for a short time had presumably remained in the depths and at the end resurfaced. The third essay turned on the problem of evil: the ultimate Power, if there be but one, may be conceived either as perfect or as omnipotent, but not both – which had been said by others before, the novelty being that he thought the matter worthy of discussion, that he treated it with evident seriousness, and that he seemed to be groping for a religious faith.

In the meantime, Positivism had come from France to England, and became one of the new forms of unbelief. Rejecting all theological and metaphysical interpretations of the universe as outmoded by science, it reduced philosophy to the synthesis of the results of the physical, biological and social sciences. In general, Mill had approved of it, and had corresponded with Comte in the 'forties. G. H. Lewes, the intimate friend of George Eliot, in his widely read *Biographical History of Philosophy* (1845–6), treated it as the culmination of the age-long philosophical quest. Comte's six-volume work was condensed into English by Harriet Martineau (sister of James), who had jettisoned religion. Beginning as anti-religious, Positivism ended as a religion, for the worship of Humanity: the London Positivist Society, founded in 1867, turned its headquarters into a temple, with images of great men, and services with a liturgy, hymns and sermons. To the claim of one of its leaders that Positivism was 'Catholicism plus science' Huxley, not liking either its dogmatic atheism or its sentimental worship of Man, retorted that it was 'Catho-

[23] p. 43.

licism minus Christianity'. The movement remained a coterie, which someone dubbed 'three persons and no God'. Frederic Harrison alone represented it, brilliantly, in the literary world, which responded to its humanism and could follow its general science and thin philosophy without needing any technical knowledge.

From the two preceding sections it should be evident that around the middle of the century there was an extensive spiritual *malaise*. There was a materialistic atheism suggested by science, and a non-materialistic one exemplified in the subjective empiricism of Mill; an agnosticism based on the supposition that the only knowledge we can have is scientific; a philosophical agnosticism that regarded even science as infected with elements injected by the mind itself; and a deistic tendency among those who accepted from science the universality of natural law, yet wanted to reserve a place for God at the beginning of it all. There were intellectuals inside the Churches, on the fringes, and outside, who on ethical grounds had lost respect for the presentation of God in biblical literalism, in the penal doctrine of the Atonement, and in the renewed emphasis on what seemed to be an exclusively ecclesiastical and sacramental mediation of salvation. The Churches, apart from a few voices that were still being shouted down, had not begun to face the spiritual distress or dis-illusionment with a clear, ordered and evidenced statement of the relation of Christian doctrine to the kind of thinking that was overflowing from the natural sciences, to the critical methods and evaluations of the new historians of life and of literature, and to the expanding sympathies of poets, novelists and essayists. In other words, the Churches had no compre-hensive philosophy. The native empiricist philosophy was too superficial to suggest one, and had turned religious and poetical minds not only from it but (excepting Coleridge and Carlyle) from philosophy as such. The long divorce between theology and philosophy had in effect prevented the emergence within the Churches of anyone with the kind of mind and training required to provide a comprehensive philosophy whether originally or by adaptation.

Philosophy itself was to rise up from the 'seventies onwards against its two hundred years of subjectivist, empiricist and unspeculative thinking in this island. It caught up the daring Objective Idealism of Hegel. This took mind or spirit as both the primary fact of experience and the ultimate fact in reality, discarded the overworn emphasis on sensation, substituted a versatile reason for the narrow and rigid reason of the logic-books, and traced its shaping work not only in the individual mind but also in its objective products such as the political organization of society and the cultural marvels of art, morality, religion and science; and in all these, and in the physical universe itself, saw a cosmic Spirit evolving into a fuller awareness of itself through a growing actualization of its rational creativeness. This philosophy was directed against subjectivism, scepticism, Positivism and materialism. It was at once staggeringly wide and sternly intellectual. It was taught at Oxford by T. H. Green, F. H. Bradley and Edward Caird, and carried by the last to Glasgow. At length our island had a philosophy big enough to cover the whole range of man's spiritual activities, so that those who followed it could converse intelligently with scientists and theologians, historians, anthropologists and sociologists. The response of the clerical intellectuals in the Churches to this Objective Idealism was small, if judged by the number of those who openly espoused it, e.g. the Scottish Presbyterian John Caird (brother of Edward) and the Anglican J. R. Illingworth (of the *Lux Mundi* group), small partly because the system had a pantheistic look; but the barrier between philosophers and theologians was broken, and remained so until the twenties of the present century, when changes on both sides again put them apart.

VI

The Wesleyan Methodists to 1849

JOHN KENT

IT might have been expected that after 1797 Wesleyan
Methodism would continue to progress peacefully as a
new religious body. The formation of the Methodist New
Connexion did not check the growth of the Wesleyans themselves, but apparently drew off the more insistent democrats,
so that a generation passed before fresh demands for reform
were raised, once again in north and north-western England.
Nevertheless, the years between 1797 and 1857 did not
entirely fulfil the promise of the eighteenth century. They
were tragic years for anyone who believed that it was the
business of the Methodist societies to spread Christian
Holiness throughout Britain, for in them the religious
potential of Wesleyan Methodism was greatly reduced by
internal dissension about the nature of the Church, and by
actual secession. The major withdrawals, involving thousands
of people, were those of the Leeds Protestant Methodists
(1827–8), the Wesleyan Methodist Association (1834–7), and
the secession which began in 1849 and led to the formation of
the United Methodist Free Churches in 1857. There also took
place a series of smaller withdrawals, such as those of the
Unitarian Cookites (1808), the Tent Methodists (1825), and
the little band of devoted followers who followed Joseph
Rayner Stephens when he pressed the case for Anglican disestablishment too fiercely in 1834. The effect of these controversies on the growth of Wesleyan Methodism is difficult
to assess. Primitive Methodism, which suffered no major
secessions in the nineteenth century, reached its growth peak

between 1861 and 1881, and the evidence suggests that if the Fly Sheets agitation (1849–57) had not taken place Wesleyanism would have reached its limit of statistical expansion at about the same time. If the figures for Wesleyan Methodist membership are related to the growth in population one finds that the position of the denomination was declining in the second half of the nineteenth century.[1] Much more important, however, was that the possibility of a single, major Methodist challenge to the traditional ecclesiastical structures of the country vanished, the disarray of the movement being emphasized by the emergence of two new Methodist bodies, the Primitive Methodists and the Bible Christians, formed between 1800 and 1820, not so much by secession from Wesleyanism as by spontaneous generation in the rural working class, to which the older forms of Methodism had not successfully adapted themselves.

This complicated pattern of conflict could hardly have been anticipated in 1800. The events of 1795–7 had introduced constitutional limits to the power of the Wesleyan Ministry; for the moment, the laity seemed satisfied that they had a guaranteed share in the government of the Connexion. What this constitution amounted to was another question, however, and agreement was made continually more difficult by the changing composition of the laity and the developing self-consciousness of the itinerancy. By 1834, the leaders of the reforming party argued that the regulations of 1795–7 denoted a surrender of power on the part of the pastorate and the grant of co-pastoral status to the laity. More moderate Wesleyan opinion held that the regulations had been intended to place just so much restriction on the power of the ministry as would protect the laity from irresponsible government. Once the Leeds Organ affair had started (1827), Jabez Bunting took the view that the ministry had an authority somewhat akin to the royal prerogative claimed by the Stuart monarchy; the phrase 'pastoral prerogative' came into fashion, and Bunting believed that this inherent, divinely ordained ministerial authority could not be overridden by an appeal to

[1] There is some discussion of nineteenth-century Methodist statistics in Robert Currie, *Methodism Divided: A Study in the Sociology of Ecumenicalism* (London 1968).

Conference legislation or to Congregationalist theories of the relationship between the laity and the ministry. In an essay published in 1829 John Beecham[2] asserted that

> in 1795 and 1797 the power of the Pastor was not taken away from him, and given to others, or even shared with them; . . . all the privileges then conceded by the Conference were only so many fences and guards thrown around the Pastor, to prevent him from using his power injuriously, . . . the final decision of extraordinary questions is not with the people, but is what it ought to be – it is pastoral.[3]

A more conciliatory figure, the theologian, Richard Watson,[4] still held the same view, saying that the minister must have the last word in disciplinary matters, and that the ministry assembled in the Annual Conference must have sole legislative power.[5] In effect, a constitution existed only in the sense that the regulations existed to be appealed to, but there was no agreed interpretation of them; the more extreme supporters of ministerial authority were prepared to say that if the regulations appeared to give the reformers something of what they wanted then this could not have been the intention of those who framed them. In fact, by the end of the 1820s both groups wanted to alter the existing situation: the eighteenth-century rules were not democratic enough for the radical reformers, some of whom wanted to transform Wesleyanism

---

[2] John Beecham (1787–1856) was secretary of the Wesleyan Missionary Society from 1831 to 1855; President of Conference 1850.

[3] *An Essay on the Constitution of Wesleyan Methodism* (London 1829), p. 111.

[4] Richard Watson (1781–1833) was a Missionary Society secretary in 1821–6, 1832–3; he was President of Conference in 1826. His reply to Adam Clarke's unsound speculation on the doctrine of the Eternal Sonship of Jesus Christ (1818) played a part in later controversies, for James Everett did not forget the attack on his hero. Watson's *Theological Institutes: or, A View of the Evidences, Doctrines, Morals, and Institutions of Christianity*, 3 vols (London 1829), formed the Wesleyan theological mind until W. B. Pope's *Compendium* replaced them in the 1870s.

[5] *The Works of Richard Watson* (London 1835), vii, 98: 'Certain powers are inseparable from the duties of the ministry, and cannot be transferred or put into commission with those who have not this calling.' Obviously, the English reformers could draw on a long indigenous tradition, but it is interesting to note that during the eighteenth century similar ideas about the rights of the laity penetrated French and thus European Jansenism through the influence of Pierre Quesnel (1634–1719), and that the Wesleyan insistence on pastoral prerogative coincided with the collapse of Jansenism in the wake of the failure of the French Revolution.

into a loose federation of Independent chapels; the upholders of pastoral prerogative, on the other hand, felt that the Conferences of the 1790s had not understood clearly enough, at any rate in writing, the nature of the Christian ministry.

Nevertheless, externally the position of the Connexion grew stronger throughout the period. Between 1800 and 1815 Wesleyanism was already wearing down the suspicion in government circles that Methodist chapels were really Jacobin sanctuaries for the worship of the Supreme Being and the advancement of Parliamentary Reform. Lord Sidmouth's clumsy attempt in 1811 to tighten the official licensing of non-Anglican preachers served to show that a new generation of Wesleyan leaders, among them Jabez Bunting[6] and Richard Watson, was now emerging, and that such men, while not prepared to identify themselves with Dissent, inasmuch as they did not object theoretically to the establishment of the Church of England, had abandoned the notion that Wesleyanism could somehow become a permitted society within the framework of the Anglican Church, an idea which still lingered in the minds of older men like Thomas Coke, and probably in that of Adam Clarke. Bunting had been offered Anglican ordination in 1801 and had refused on the ground, as he said in 1844, that he 'could not conscientiously subscribe all its Articles, nor even read all its offices'.[7] This was a considered statement, for he made it in an ordination charge; the words must be taken at their full value: he did not simply equate Wesleyan and Anglican ritual and dogma. He did not belong to the late eighteenth-century generation of Wesleyans, some of whom still regarded themselves as members of the established Church; he belonged to a generation which preferred to insist that it did not count itself among the Dissenters, and which was to be stimulated in this attitude in the 1840s by the rise of the Anglo-Catholic party. As for the relationship

---

[6] Jabez Bunting (1779–1858) was elected President of Conference 1820, 1828, 1836, 1844; he played a large part in organizing the Missionary Society, and was President of the Theological Institution from 1834 to 1857. For the problems of his career, see John Kent, *The Age of Disunity* (London 1966), Chapter 4: 'Historians and Jabez Bunting'.

[7] B. Gregory, *Side Lights on the Conflicts of Methodism during the Second Quarter of the Nineteenth Century 1827–1852*, p. 361.

between the Church of England and Wesleyanism, Bunting said:

> When Mr. Wesley was alive something ought to have been done; but not now. We must now maintain a separate and distinct position, and yet hope that the time may come for a more formal union to be effected. But we must look toward the millennium. At present it is not practicable nor, in our circumstances, desirable.[8]

This was in 1841.

The change in the attitude of many Wesleyans towards the Church of England which was implied in their successful resistance to Lord Sidmouth reflected both the increasing denominational self-consciousness of the Wesleyans and the hardening of Anglican, and especially of Anglican Evangelical, suspicion towards what now seemed, from the point of view of the Establishment, to be a powerful reinforcement to Dissent. Loyalty to the parochial system remained a fundamental element of Anglican Evangelicalism: the Evangelical incumbent saw no good reason why the Wesleyans should set up a separate centre of worship in his parish. The gulf widened still further in the 1830s when Anglo-Catholicism challenged the accepted understanding of the Anglican tradition; the abolition of Negro slavery did not usher in a new era of Evangelical triumph, but was the last episode of what the American scholar Ford K. Brown has called, with some exaggeration, 'the Age of Wilberforce'.[9] Jabez Bunting put the Wesleyan point of view of the 1840s when he expressed surprise that Evangelical and moderate Anglican opinion did not combine to discipline the Anglo-Catholic leaders on doctrinal grounds. This was what would have happened in the Wesleyan Connexion, and the Anglican failure to take decisive action, the *de facto* tolerance accorded to Pusey and his friends after Newman's secession in 1845, seemed to the

---

[8] ibid., p. 317.
[9] Ford K. Brown, *Fathers of the Victorians: The Age of Wilberforce* (Cambridge 1961). For comment on Brown's devaluation of John Wesley and over-valuation of William Wilberforce, see D. Newsome, *The Parting of Friends: A Study of the Wilberforces and Henry Manning* (London 1966).

Wesleyan leaders evidence of weakness in the structure of the Establishment.

> Unless the Church of England will protest against Puseyism in some intelligible form [said Bunting in 1841], it will be the duty of the Methodists to protest against the Church of England.[10]

In the first half of the nineteenth century Wesleyans shared with most Evangelical opinion a total failure to appreciate the origins of the Anglo-Catholic movement. In 1858, for example, *The Wesleyan-Methodist Magazine* was still prepared to print (and the official Book Room to reprint, in 1860) an article by J. C. Leppington[11] in which the author deliberately rejected the suggestion that Tractarianism sprang from a renewed 'earnestness' in the Church of England.

> To us it has ever appeared [Leppington wrote] that the Tractarian movement was the result of a deliberate attack by the Papacy on the Church of England; and the progressive development of that movement to the present time has done nothing but confirm that opinion. Oxford was chosen as the basis of the operation. To indoctrinate and warp by degrees the great body of the English Clergy, and through them to reach the people (especially the educated and wealthy classes), was the object. How the aggressors began, it is difficult to say; but *Jesuits* would be the men employed.[12]

And he traced the roots of the disaster back to the removal of Roman Catholic disabilities in 1829.

Such views were widespread, and the problem of the neo-Anglican revival, in its various forms and stages under Newman, Pusey, Liddon and Gore, was to dominate Anglicanism down to the close of the century. Wesleyan Methodism, which had begun to forget its ill-treatment at the hands of some Anglicans in the eighteenth century, found itself once again on the defensive as the theory of episcopal ordination,

---

[10] B. Gregory, op. cit., p. 317.
[11] Leppington entered the Wesleyan ministry in 1832, and died in 1859.
[12] J. C. Leppington, *The Confessional in the Church of England* (London 1860), p. 17; he said firmly: 'We do not disapprove of an Established Church, as such' (p. 1).

which Newman had devised in the first of the Oxford Tracts (1834) for the defence of the ministry of the Church of England, was used by others to question the validity of the orders of other ministries. There were Wesleyan, as well as Oxford, 'Tracts for the Times', for Wesleyanism had gained sufficient confidence by the 1840s to be willing to defend its denominational identity, ordained ministry and theology. Ten of these tracts were published in 1839. Among the titles were (1) *Why Don't You Come to Church?*, (4) *Wesleyan Ministers True Ministers of Christ*, (5) *Modern Methodism Wesleyan Methodism*, (7) *Lyra Apostolica an Impious Misnomer*, (8) *Baptism not Regeneration*, (9) *Wesleyans have the True Christian Sacraments*, and (10) *A Letter to a Country Curate. A Defence of the Wesleyan Tracts for the Times*, written by Robert Jackson,[13] was also published in 1839, at Macclesfield. The aim of all these works was to defend the orthodoxy and ecclesiastical integrity of the Connexion against the new exclusiveness of the Tractarians. The *Lyra Apostolica*, to which a whole tract was devoted, was a book of Tractarian verse, the better part of it written by J. H. Newman, published in book form in 1836 (though the poems had already appeared in the *British Magazine*): the Oxford Tracts for the Times treated the theological, these poems rather the ethical, aspects of Christianity.

The exchange continued, reaching a new peak of intensity when Pusey, who was to lead the Tractarians after the withdrawal of Newman, publicly dismissed Wesleyan theology as 'degenerating into developed heresy'. Pusey said that Methodism taught 'Justification by feelings', that a man's persuasion that he would be saved – this was Pusey's version of the doctrine of assurance – was made 'virtually the *only* condition of his salvation', and that 'permanent repentance and anxiety and grief for sin are accounted contrary to the Gospel'. These heretical tendencies had been held in check as long as the Wesleyans remained in association with the Church of England and its sacraments, but were developing rapidly as Wesleyanism moved into isolation.[14] Pusey did not claim to

[13] Robert Jackson entered the Wesleyan ministry in 1823, and died in 1881.

[14] E. B. Pusey, *A Letter to His Grace the Archbishop of Canterbury, on Some Circumstances Connected with the Present Crisis in the English Church* (Oxford 1842): the passage summarized above occurs in the 3rd edition, pp. 159–63.

be expounding John Wesley, or later Wesleyan writers; on justification, he seemed to equate Wesleyan teaching with popular revivalism; in 1859-60 Anglican Evangelicals of the stricter school made similar criticisms of revivalist practice, and said that the need for repentance was being ignored. This first Tractarian generation shared the belief that evangelicalism in general relied on a doctrine of assurance which meant that the believer treated sins committed after 'conversion' as of no vital importance. Applied to Wesleyanism, however, this offered an odd comment on John Wesley's doctrine of Christian holiness, which was deeply concerned with the possibility of eliminating sin after justification.

Thomas Jackson[15] published a semi-official reply to Pusey's sweeping condemnation; his answer perhaps marked the deepest point of alienation of Wesleyanism from the Church of England in the course of the nineteenth century. In his *Letter to the Rev. Edward B. Pusey* (London 1842) Jackson said that Pusey's own doctrine of justification was nothing more than that of the Council of Trent, 'and therefore at variance with the [Anglican] Articles and Homilies'. *Tract Ninety* (which Newman had published only a short time before) was designed, Jackson said, to show that although the Thirty-nine Articles were apparently opposed to the tenets of Rome, they might nevertheless be construed 'so as not very materially to differ from the Papal creed'. It was all very well for Pusey to accuse the Wesleyans of antinomianism, Jackson said, but the Puseyites' continuance in a Protestant Church while they propagated the doctrines of Papal Rome was at variance with every principle of justice, truth and honour, while 'their spirit of bitter exclusiveness is perfectly alien from the charity of the Gospel'.[16]

Jackson, who in 1842 was one of the leading ministers of the Connexion, replied to Pusey because he had shown his willingness to defend the Church of England in 1834 by writing another semi-official pamphlet, *The Church and the Methodists*, to vindicate the refusal of the Wesleyan Conference to allow

[15] cf. E. G. Rupp, *Thomas Jackson: Methodist Patriarch* (London 1954). Thomas Jackson (1783-1873) was President of Conference in 1838 and 1849, and served as Connexional Editor and as a Tutor at Richmond Theological College.
[16] Jackson, *Recollections of My Own Life and Times* (London 1873), pp. 100-3.

the Rev. Rayner Stephens to agitate for disestablishment as a member of the itinerancy.[17] Jackson, that is, could not be accused of prejudice against the Church of England. In 1834 some Wesleyan leaders had hoped that a 'kindlier understanding' might be established between Wesleyans and Anglicans, but this possibility had disappeared as the Anglo-Catholics began to set the pace in the Church of England.[18] An assault like Pusey's suggested that even after a hundred years Wesleyan Methodism was still not altogether accepted as part of British society. Even as late as 1849 it can hardly have surprised the ministerial leadership that they had to face in the course of the Fly Sheets controversy not only renewed demands for change from within but also attacks from outside, from the Free Churches and even from the *Times* newspaper, whose qualifications to interpret Wesleyanism must have been rather limited. Perhaps the ruthlessness with which so many circuit superintendents expelled reformers between 1825 and 1850 may be partly explained by their sense of being surrounded on all sides by hostile forces: the feeling that there were hostile groups outside the Connexion added to the anxiety about the reformers inside and helped to stimulate vigorous action. That the action was vigorous is certain:

On 17th October 1834, twenty-seven laymen of the North and South [Liverpool] Circuits addressed a letter to the already notorious Dr. Samuel Warren, stating that they had long groaned under a load of accumulated grievances which were now insupportable, and that they would submit to irresponsible authority no longer. Nor had they to endure their sufferings much further, for during the following three weeks all found themselves expelled – some *instanter* by the fiery, swarthy Samuel Jackson,

[17] cf. M. S. Edwards, 'The Resignation of Joseph Rayner Stephens', in *W.H.S. Proc.*, xxxvi (February 1967), 16. I agree with him that Stephens was censured because he advocated disestablishment, not because he was suspect on other political grounds; in fact, Stephens took up the Factory Question after he had left the Wesleyan ministry.

[18] Jackson, op. cit., p. 271. Jackson would have known also of the activities of the strongly pro-Anglican itinerant, James Kendall, between 1834 and 1836; see his *Miscellaneous and Free Strictures on the Practical Position of the Wesleyan Connexion towards the Church of England* (London 1836). Kendall proposed the episcopal ordination of the travelling preachers, and negotiated unsuccessfully with the Bishop of Exeter. Rumours of such private activities helped to make the position of Jabez Bunting intensely difficult: he was constantly suspected of wanting to reach a backstairs agreement with the Bishops.

superintendent of the North circuit, others by the more refined and scholarly George Marsden, of the South circuit, who proceeded with greater reluctance and greater tact, having already had experience of lay rebellion in the Leeds Organ case.[19]

The challenge from inside, the challenge from outside, suggest that one key to the history of early nineteenth-century Methodism was that both ministry and laity still found the nature of Wesleyan Methodism itself a problem. It may be said that they should have been prepared to accept that more than one definition, more than one kind of Wesleyanism, was possible, but that was not a mood characteristic of the early Victorian period. Indeed, one secret of Jabez Bunting's grip on the majority of Wesleyan Methodists between 1815 and 1840 was that he seemed, with his articulated grasp of the structure, the theology, the social and political implications of the movement, capable of imposing a single solution. In the period covered by this chapter, however, the options remained open: was Wesleyanism, for example, a new denomination in the old Dissenting style, or a religious society which ought to exist within the framework of the Church of England, or was it, as Bunting sometimes suggested, an ecclesiastical bridge between Dissent and the Establishment, a bridge whose usefulness was sadly limited because neither Dissent nor Anglicanism at this period wanted to make use of it? Similar problems emerged when one turned to the question of the Wesleyan pastorate: were Wesleyan ministers a special case not to be judged by the models of the past, were they just a fresh variety of Dissenting minister, or were they, as the Anglo-Catholics said in the 1840s, not ministers at all?[20] Wesleyan opinion was itself deeply divided about such matters. Theologically, this was because separation from the Church of England had taken place on a pragmatic, not a theoretical basis, so that once separation was a fact it was still possible to disagree about how

[19] Ian Sellers, 'The Wesleyan Methodist Association in Liverpool, 1834–5', in *W.H.S. Proc.*, xxxv (June 1966), 143; Sellers was an expert on the Victorian religious history of Liverpool. Samuel Warren led the first stages of the 1834 controversy which produced the Wesleyan Methodist Association.

[20] Some Wesleyan reformers really thought that they were not ministers at all, though they did not base this opinion on Anglo-Catholic premisses.

separation should be defended; sociologically, separation had been followed, rather than preceded, by the entry of large numbers of non-Anglicans into the Wesleyan societies. Nor was there now anything like the social homogeneity of a sect in which most of the membership is looking at problems from much the same point of view.

What characterized Wesleyan Methodism in the first half of the nineteenth century, in fact, was that almost any stimulus produced a sharply divided response. To take minor, but not unimportant, examples, there was a mixed reaction to American religious enthusiasms like revivalism and total abstinence, both of which crossed the Atlantic at this period and both of which encountered stiff official opposition in the Wesleyan Conference, despite having much local circuit support.[21] In the case of revivalism, the most important instance was that of the American Methodist professional revivalist James Caughey, who came to England in 1841 and was finally forbidden the use of Wesleyan pulpits and premises in 1847. In general, Wesleyan opinion held that evangelism should take place steadily through the circuit system and distrusted the professional revivalist, then a very new pheno- menon, with his arrival dated in advance and his strong emphasis on his own personality. Caughey divided circuit after circuit, partly by his methods and partly because he became the centre of argument about the nature of Methodism itself. In York, for example, he was supported by James Everett, the apostle of discord, who was probably eager to take the chance of yet another stab at Jabez Bunting, who disapproved of Caughey. Everett also probably believed that Caughey's revivalism came closer to the mood and style of eighteenth-century Wesleyanism than did the middle-class denominationalism into which the movement seemed, to men like Everett, to be developing. Total abstinence was one of Caughey's favourite themes, his advocacy of it one of the means by which he split the circuits he entered. The Wesleyan Conference condemned teetotalism as early as 1841, on the ground that wine (in the common-sense meaning of the word)

[21] cf. F. Thistlethwaite, *The Anglo-American Connection in the Early Nineteenth Century* (Philadelphia, Pa., 1959), pp. 84–96.

must be used for the service of Holy Communion: behind this verdict lay the fact that in this early stage the total abstinence movement represented a kind of social dissidence – it was later than 1850 that middle-class leaders finally tamed teetotalism and made it a servant of political Nonconformity. The decision to silence Caughey in 1847 was certainly seen as a blow against teetotalism as well as against revivalism and provided support for the attack on the Wesleyan Conference in 1849.[22] The decision of 1847, however, involved the assertions that the ministerial Conference had the right to make final judgements of this sort which the laity must accept, and that the Conference had the power to say for what purposes Wesleyan premises could be used: neither of these assertions passed unchallenged by 1847.

Nevertheless, one great achievement of Wesleyan Methodism between 1800 and 1850 was to establish itself as a national denomination. In its earlier stages the movement had seemed to have all the makings of a classic sect, complete with charismatic leader (John Wesley), particular doctrinal emphases – the doctrines of assurance and Christian perfection – and the tendency to grow best among alienated groups on the fringe of eighteenth-century society. In the early nineteenth century, however, Wesleyanism broke out of this pattern of development, expanded on a national scale, survived without any renewal of the charismatic leadership – Jabez Bunting cannot be regarded as a leader of this type – and restated the

[22] The teetotal crisis of 1841 culminated in the withdrawal of R. Tabraham, the minister most passionately dedicated to abstinence. His *Love to Man: An Appeal to the Pious in Favour of Total Abstinence* (Ipswich 1845) used biblical and practical arguments. More influential in the Connexion was W. J. Shrewsbury, who in 1840 published *Alcohol against the Bible, and the Bible against Alcohol*; he was answered by George Osborn in *A Letter to the Rev. W. J. Shrewsbury* (London 1841): Osborn disputed the biblical argument, and denied that abuse of alcohol meant that its use was always sinful; he was defending the Conference decision. Another well-known minister, W. H. Rule, wrote *A Brief Enquiry concerning Wine and Its Use in the Sacrament of the Eucharist* (London 1844), to meet the objections of those who were already abstaining from the Eucharist because of the use of alcoholic wine; the decision of 1841 did not prevent the slow growth of Wesleyan teetotalism. There was nothing approaching unanimity, but it is interesting that Jacob Stanley, a minister who often voted with the minority in the Conference, published in 1841 two pamphlets criticizing teetotalism. At this stage, however, it was still possible to attack the new movement on the ground that many of the supporters of the famous socialist, Robert Owen, were teetotallers, and so to imply that total abstinence and atheism did not lie far apart; cf. J. Caughey, *Letters on Various Subjects*, 5 vols (London 1844–7).

themes of assurance and perfection in more traditional terms. This national, denominational growth produced internal conflict between the older 'sectarian' tendency (which usually thought of itself, nevertheless, as 'reforming') and newer denominational tendencies (which were often represented as 'conservative' even by those who advocated them). Conflict also arose because the vague concept of 'Wesleyanism', which John Wesley himself had done little to clarify at the institutional level, now had to be stretched to cover many different strata of British society: the Connexion could hardly, in the mid-nineteenth century, be described as socially homogeneous.

Transition to a denominational scale was only one of the achievements of Wesleyan Methodism in this period. Despite the inner conflicts, which led directly to some loss of membership, there was a steady increase in membership from about 89,000 in 1801 to about 328,000 in 1841. Such an increase led to the first great chapel-building period, though most of the Wesleyan chapels built in the first half of the century were replaced in its last quarter. The process may be illustrated by the case of Melton Mowbray, in 1800 a very small town famous mostly for fox-hunting. Wesleyan Methodism there had developed slowly; in 1794 there were ten full members, but the enthusiasm of their leader, a chemist called Pearson, led to the erection of a small chapel in 1796. Pearson virtually paid for the building, which remained his personal possession until 1808, when he conveyed it on trust to the Connexion. At that time the Melton society owed him £419, of which £193 was paid when the society took over the chapel, and the remainder in 1823. By 1824, membership had grown to 100, and so it was decided to have a new chapel. This second chapel was opened in 1826; the price was £2,500 and there was seating for 700 people. The second chapel was in debt throughout its existence: only £1,000 had been paid in 1826, £40–50 per annum was paid in interest for the following forty-five years, and in 1868, when a third chapel was projected, £800 had still to be paid of the original price. Thus the second chapel, priced at £2,500, actually cost £4,000–£5,000. Membership had increased to 133 in 1835, but Melton Mowbray suffered from the Schism of 1849 and there were only 114 members in 1863. The figure was rising, however; there were 139 in 1870, and 279 in 1895, so that the price of the third chapel, opened in 1871, was paid off quickly.[23] Here were the classical elements of the chapel-building situation: the anxiety of the smallest societies to have some sort of building; the figure of 100 members, which in Victorian terms was about the number needed to make an urban chapel of any size a feasible proposition; the chapel debt, which was not always settled as easily as it finally was in Melton; and, in details not quoted above, the money-raising efforts and 'Anniversary Sermons' which became part of the accepted rhythm of Wesleyan life. Another good example was at Exeter, where the Wesleyan membership, 70 in 1798, rose to 291 by 1815. The chapel in Musgrave Alley became too small, and so in 1812 the trustees bought the Mint Unitarian Chapel for £720 in order to obtain a new site. The sale of the old Wesleyan Chapel and a subscription list produced £737, and on the strength of this a new building, to hold 700 people, was erected in 1813. This chapel originally cost £3,873, but the premises were not cleared of debt until 1859, by which time another £7,000 had been spent in interest, legal expenses and so forth.[24]

The size of the outstanding debt on local chapels was a constant problem, however, for even in the heyday of Bunting's alleged absolutism nothing the Wesleyan Conference did could prevent local societies from committing themselves to the erection of larger chapels than they could afford. What was called the General Chapel Fund was set up in 1818 in order to collect money from the Connexion as a whole which might be used to help weaker societies meet their obligations. The total amount subscribed to this Fund between 1818 and 1845 was £128,154. When the Centenary

[23] For this information, see John Gill, Jnr, *History of Wesleyan Methodism in Melton Mowbray and Its Vicinity* (Melton Mowbray 1909).

[24] cf. Elijah Chick, *A History of Methodism in Exeter and the Neighbourhood. From the Year 1739 until 1907* (Exeter 1907). For a brief modern discussion of Exeter Methodism, cf. A. Brockett, *Nonconformity in Exeter 1650–1875* (Manchester 1962). At Oxford, New Inn Hall Street Chapel (1818) cost £5,013, of which £4,000 came from loans and annuities; between then and 1869, when the debt was finally extinguished, £3,437 was paid in interest; cf. J. E. Oxley, *Wesley Memorial Church, Oxford, 1818–1968* (Oxford 1968).

Fund was raised in 1840[25] a special grant of £38,000 was made for the same purpose. Between 1818 and 1845 the Chapel Fund granted £128,146 for the liquidation of chapel debts, on condition that the local trustees made special efforts at the same time: the trustees in their turn raised £134,555, so that altogether £262,701 of debt was paid off. In 1940, prior to any war damage, there were 7,597 Wesleyan Methodist chapels still standing, the overwhelming majority of which must have been built before 1914.

One of the achievements of Bunting's generation, then, was to give structure and depth to the idea of Wesleyanism as a national Connexion. The most striking example of this was the Wesleyan Methodist Missionary Society, which the Centenary Committee reckoned to have started life officially in 1803. By 1844, when the Society had 382 missionaries and 102,750 members on foreign stations, it was calculated that the Connexion had raised in Britain £1,784,530 for its support, and the Centenary Fund, itself another considerable financial achievement, made a gift of £70,000 to the Society, part of which was used to build proper offices for the Society in London.[26] The Centenary Fund also provided £71,000 with which to build a northern ministerial training seminary at Didsbury, Manchester, in 1842, and a southern seminary at Richmond, Surrey, in 1843, which could take one hundred students between them. The confidence acquired in this kind of Connexional organization partly explains the ambitious scale of the day-school building programme which was launched at the Conference of 1843,[27] but which was completed largely outside our period. Another indication of this Connexional expansion and consolidation was the rise in the number of active ministers from 442 in 1800 to 1,484 in 1845, a figure which represented a slight fall from 1 minister per 205 members in 1800, to 1 minister per 229 members in 1845.[28]

[25] See below, p. 234, n. 40 for Everett's reaction to the Centenary.
[26] The Wesleyan Conference of 1837 set up a committee to arrange a centenary commemoration of the formation of the first Wesleyan society in 1739; from this grew the idea of a Fund, which was collected over several years and amounted to about £220,000. Apart from the sums mentioned, £16,000 went to pensions and £5,000 to education: *Report of the Wesleyan Centenary Fund* (Leeds 1844).
[27] See below, p. 243.
[28] The 1975 figure for the Methodist Church was about 260 members per minister.

Growth in the size and efficiency of the Connexional machinery was indisputable. When one turns to the spiritual life of the Wesleyan societies, however, one faces the problem of deciding how far eighteenth-century Wesleyan traditions were still shaping a new denomination and how far the eighteenth-century inheritance of Wesleyanism was being modified to suit the needs and aspirations of social groups which all called themselves Wesleyan, but which differed from one another in some ways in different parts of the country.

Thus one of the many threads which led to the catastrophic schism of 1849 was a nagging controversy about the use of 'Morning Prayer' in Wesleyan chapels. No one could say that the use of the Liturgy involved innovation: John Wesley himself had abridged the Anglican Morning Prayer for the use of his societies and certainly expected them to follow it. There is some evidence of a move in the 1830s and 1840s to make Wesley's *Abridgement* the normal morning service in Wesleyan Methodism, but that many of the congregations resisted. This was to some extent a practical question. Joseph Beaumont (1794–1855), for example, a moderate conservative in such matters, thought that the combination of Morning Prayer with further extempore prayer, and a sermon of about an hour in length, was inadvisable. His son and biographer commented that

in many cases where it is used by the Wesleyans the congregations adopt the practice of entering the chapel in the middle of the service when they take the prayers to be over.[29]

It is significant that Richard Watson should have defended the use of the Liturgy and criticized the arguments in favour of purely spontaneous prayer which had already become commonplace in early nineteenth-century Wesleyanism:

If the use of forms of prayer in prose be objected to, their use in

[29] *The Life of the Rev. Joseph Beaumont, M.D., by his son* [Joseph Beaumont] (London 1856). For the older generation of itinerants the use of Morning Prayer, and the wearing of the preaching gown which was sometimes associated with it, symbolized the achievement of denominational identity: they saw this as a Wesleyan, not an Anglican custom. Richard Watson interpreted it in this way. Beaumont entered the Wesleyan ministry in 1813.

verse ought to be rejected on the same principle; and extemporaneous psalms and hymns must, for consistency's sake, be required of a Minister, as well as extemporaneous prayers; or the practice of singing, as a part of God's worship, must be given up. . . . Another objection is that the perpetual repetition of the same form of words produces weariness and inattentiveness in the congregation. There is some truth in this; but it is often carried much too far. A devotional mind will not weary in the repetition of a scriptural and well-arranged Liturgy, if not too long to be sustained by the infirmity of the body. . . . The objection, as far as it has any weight, would be reduced to nothing, were the Liturgy repeated only at one service on the Sabbath, so that at the others the Minister might be left at liberty to pray with more direct reference to the special circumstances of the people, the Church, and the world.[30]

Watson certainly thought of himself as defending the Wesleyan tradition, but he also knew that by the 1830s there were some Wesleyans for whom the introduction of Morning Prayer meant a betrayal of the freedom and spiritual spontaneity which they thought of as integral to the traditions of the movement, and a return to an Anglicanism which had rejected John Wesley, and which ought in its turn, after the Tractarian developments of the 1830s, to be rejected; they also interpreted the use of Morning Prayer as a surrender to the influence of wealthy laymen, whereas Methodism, they said, had been intended by God for the service of the poor.[31] The last point is important, because it is clear from a reading of the tracts written in the Wesleyan schisms which occurred between 1830 and 1857 that a serious social division was taking place within the societies as a result of early Victorian urbanization. A religious body which aspires to hold together a majority of the social groups in a given country can do so successfully only through a very loose system of organization like that of the Church of England, one which does not over-press the demand for uniformity. Attempts to insist on the use of Morning Prayer, attempts which in themselves were meant to assert denominational, not a kind of Anglican, status,

[30] R. Watson, *Theological Institutes*, 3rd edn (London 1832), iii, 259, 262–3.

[31] There is no space here to substantiate these statements, but all of them were frequent themes in the literature of the period.

inevitably met resistance in the new industrial and old rural areas where the Establishment was not popular in the early nineteenth century. The drive to introduce the service was petering out by the 1840s, and by the 1880s the number of Wesleyan chapels which used Morning Prayer was shrinking again. To some extent, of course, Wesleyanism was yielding to the same influences which caused mid-Victorian Free Churches in general to emphasize liturgical spontaneity and pulpit personality. An interesting late example of the process may be found in Stockport, where in 1848 the successful, middle-class Wesleyan society at Tiviot Dale, with a massive chapel building in the classical style put up in the centre of the town in 1818,[32] decided to erect a mission church in the neighbouring industrial suburb of Portwood, where row after row of workingmen's cottages flanked a broad through-road. Tiviot Dale said Morning Prayer, and so the new chapel (built, however, to the now fashionable Early English model which had just been adopted connexionally in place of the allegedly more expensive Greek model) was expected also to say Morning Prayer. The service remained in use at Brunswick, as the mission chapel was somewhat surprisingly called, until the 1880s, when the Leaders' Meeting voted its disuse; at Tiviot Dale the use of Morning Prayer was retained until after the second world war. The example of Portwood Chapel is also significant because the Wesleyans built a day-school on the opposite side of the road to the chapel. This marked one difference between the eighteenth- and nineteenth-century Wesleyans: the eighteenth-century evangelists did not often cross social boundaries, their work was more a matter of organizing the surviving Pietist tradition into non-Anglican forms; but in the early nineteenth century the confidence of the wealthier Wesleyan chapels had increased to the point at which they were willing to try to incorporate other socially inferior groups into their own cultural and religious pattern, a process which could be seen both in the siting of the Portwood Chapel and in the combination there of Morning Prayer and a day-school.

[32] For the architectural background, cf. G. W. Dolbey, *The Architectural Expression of Methodism: The First Hundred Years* (London 1964).

John Wesley had tried to keep a balance between formal prayers, the Eucharist, and preaching understood as an all-out assault on the individual in order to bring him to the experience of justification by faith. In the early nineteenth century this balance was no longer kept. The formal prayers became less common; the Conference recommended that members should communicate at least once a month; the evangelistic sermon took new forms, which included the styles of both the popular preacher and the revivalist.[33] The cult of the popular preacher was as Victorian as the railway lines which made his peripatetic career possible. He was not a Methodist invention, but he flourished in the wide but tightly-knit Wesleyan world. His role was to excite and edify an already existing congregation, to captivate the younger generation. The most important in this period was Robert Newton (1780–1854), the son of a Yorkshire farmer, four times President of the Wesleyan Conference, and its Secretary on nineteen occasions between 1821 and 1847. He was so popular that in his later years he was actually given an assistant minister to care for his circuit work in order that he might give all his energy to speaking on special occasions.[34] At the celebration of the fiftieth anniversary of his marriage Newton said that no unkind word or look had ever passed between him and his wife,

> unless an incident which took place when he was stationed in Leeds might be regarded as an exception. He had, as usual, been from home during the week, and was expected to return on the Saturday evening. In the afternoon of that day, when sailing up

[33] I do not mean that there existed no tradition of sober edification; see, for example, *Sermons by Wesleyan-Methodist Ministers* (London 1850), edited anonymously, but dedicated to the well-known London layman, Thomas Farmer: this included eighteen sermons, one of which, on the Eucharist, said: 'None have a right – that is, a scriptural and spiritual right – to come, but those who are pardoned or panting to be forgiven all trespasses. No power on earth should tyrannically force a minister to give this sacrament to anyone whom he knows to be immoral' (p. 254). It is illustrative of the mood of the period that this contains an advertisement for a version of the first book of Spenser's *Faerie Queene*, issued by the Wesleyan Book Room and called *The Knight of the Red Cross*, which was recommended 'for its adaptation to strengthen in the minds of men a just abhorrence of Popery, and a firm attachment to British Protestant Christianity – it is worthy to be placed by the side of Bunyan's *Pilgrim*'.

[34] For Newton, cf. T. Jackson, *The Life of the Rev. Robert Newton, D.D.* (London 1855); D. T. Young, *Robert Newton, The Eloquent Divine* (London n.d.; c. 1910).

the Humber, the steamer was enveloped in a dense fog; and the Captain, deeming it unsafe to proceed, cast anchor till about four o'clock on the Sunday morning, when the atmosphere became clear. At Selby he met with another interruption, having to wait a considerable time before the train started; so that he did not arrive in Leeds till about eight o'clock, when he had to procure a conveyance to his appointment, which was about eight miles distant. He had therefore scarcely time to inquire after the welfare of his family, who had been kept all night in a state of anxious suspense. As he had to meet some classes after the preaching in the evening, he did not reach home till about ten o'clock. On the Monday morning he rose at an early hour, having a long journey before him, and not expecting to return to his family before the end of the week. Mrs. Newton, according to her usual practice, rose to see him comfortably provided for before his departure; and, at the hour of five o'clock, as she was pouring out a cup of coffee for him, burst into tears, and said, 'This is melancholy work.' He said, 'I left home that morning with a sad heart.' It grieved him to find that his mode of life was a cause of sorrow to one who stood in so near and tender a relation to himself; but that which she for the time being felt to be 'melancholy' was a source of joy and everlasting benefit to thousands.[35]

Thomas Jackson, of course, unhesitatingly approved of Robert Newton, with whom he was associated in the councils of the Connexion for more than thirty years, and in whom he probably saw something of a reflection of the career of John Wesley. As the popular preacher *par excellence* Newton stood for order and edification and the rising sun of Wesleyan Methodism:

From three to four thousand chapels were erected during the period of his extraordinary popularity; and at the opening of the greater part of them he was present, and rendered his efficient aid.[36]

Newton, however, also committed himself entirely to the hierarchical interpretation of Wesleyan Methodism when, as

[35] T. Jackson, op. cit., p. 392; the remainder of Jackson's biography is formal and unrevealing as far as Newton's personality is concerned.
[36] ibid., p. 418.

Chairman of the Manchester District in 1833-4, he took action against Rayner Stephens,[37] who wanted Wesleyanism to support the Dissenting campaign for Anglican disestablishment, and also against Samuel Warren,[38] who tried to raise Manchester Wesleyanism in revolt against the proposal to set up a Wesleyan seminary for the training of the ministry: Warren's followers, who became the Wesleyan Methodist Association in 1837, wanted lay representation in the Conference and self-government for local congregations. When Thomas Jackson called Newton 'conservative of Methodism', he was expressing the conviction, which he shared with Newton, Jabez Bunting and Richard Watson, that the policy which all four advocated was essentially one of conserving the eighteenth-century Wesleyan tradition, of keeping intact the institutions, the methods and the theology which had formed a coherent body of Christians over more than a century. It is difficult to reject this use of the word 'conservative', but if one uses it one has to recognize the extent to which many Wesleyans between 1800 and 1850 found the transition from one period to the other a revolutionary transformation of ethos, so that, although the opposition to the conservative policy were pleased to be described as 'reformers', they also believed that the 'conservatives' were changing the nature of Wesleyan Methodism. Inasmuch as a man like Robert Newton did not want to admit lay representatives to the Wesleyan Conference he was regarded by the 'reformers' as a 'conservative', but when he supported the gradual centralization of Wesleyan decision-making, and approved (in 1834) of the plan for a trained, professional ministry, which the reformers rejected, he did not seem to the opposition to be 'conservative of Methodism' at all. And the reformers attacked him on both

[37] Joseph Rayner Stephens (1805-1879) was the son of John Stephens, himself President of the Wesleyan Conference. He was expelled from the itinerancy in 1834 because he would not give a guarantee not to agitate for disestablishment. He became a Chartist speaker for a time, but after imprisonment in 1839 confined himself to preaching and writing. He was a strong advocate of 'Tory Radicalism'. See G. J. Holyoake, *Life of Joseph Rayner Stephens, Preacher and Political Orator* (London 1881); J. T. Ward, 'Revolutionary Tory', in *Transactions of the Lancashire and Cheshire Antiquarian Society*, lxviii (1958), 93ff.

[38] Samuel Warren (1781-1862) entered the itinerancy in 1802, but was expelled in 1835. In 1838 he received Anglican ordination, becoming rector of All Souls, Manchester, until his death.

counts; he became a principal victim of the Fly Sheets, the fourth of which clamoured against his re-election as President of the Conference in 1848.[39] If, as one is entitled to believe, James Everett[40] either wrote or edited the Fly Sheets, there was a cruel irony in this, for Everett's greatest pleasure was travelling immense distances in order to act the popular preacher himself at week-ends.

Thomas Jackson might praise Newton as a Methodist conservative and the Fly Sheets attack him as a 'Tory', but the emergence of the popular preacher was a response to social change and so was the coming of the professional revivalist, such as the American James Caughey, into whose hands the more individualistic side of the eighteenth-century sermon fell. The third Fly Sheet, distributed in 1847, made an eleven-point comparison between Caughey and Newton, entirely in the American's favour.[41] Those who have relied too much on Benjamin Gregory's famous *Side Lights on the Conflicts within Methodism* for their impressions of the period inevitably underestimate the importance of Caughey's career.[42] He remained a hero in Methodist circles long after his

[39] *Fly Sheets, from the Private Correspondent, Number 4:* By order of the Corresponding Committee for detecting, exposing and correcting abuses. (London, Manchester, Bristol, Liverpool, Birmingham, Hull, Leeds, Glasgow, in the year of grace, 1848). The case for Everett's authorship is chiefly stylistic, but very convincing.

[40] James Everett (1784–1872) entered the itinerancy in 1807; from 1821 to 1834 he was superannuated on grounds of health. His first known anonymous publication was *The Disputants; or, The Arguments in favour of the newly established Theological Institution among the Methodists, Brought to the Test; and the Institution itself proved to be un-Wesleyan, un-Scriptural, un-Necessary, Impolitic, & Dangerous. By a Disciple of the Old School* (London 1835), written to support the reformers in the Warren controversy, in which he attacked Bunting. He wrote a biography of his hero, Adam Clarke, in *Adam Clarke Portrayed*, 2 vols (London 1843, 1849). In 1841 he published anonymously *Wesleyan Takings: or, Centenary Sketches of Ministerial Character, as exhibited in the Wesleyan Connexion, during the First Hundred Years of its Existence,* 2 vols (London 1841, 1851), satirical sketches of about a hundred Wesleyan ministers. When asked by the Conference of 1841 to admit authorship, he refused to answer the question. He was again superannuated in 1842. When accused of writing the Fly Sheets in 1849, he behaved as he had in 1841. Expelled, he became a leader of the United Methodist Free Churches. He maintained his silence about the Fly Sheets until his death.

[41] The third Fly Sheet was distributed in 1847, with the same uncommunicative identification as the others. The essence of the comparison was that Caughey was being censured by the Wesleyan Methodist Conference for working as an itinerant evangelist while Newton was being praised for doing much the same thing.

[42] cf. John Kent, *The Age of Disunity,* for my analysis of the weaknesses of *Side Lights,* especially pp. 109–20. Gregory tended to reduce Wesleyan history to a function of Bunting's character; he has had many imitators.

departure to the United States in 1847; when he came back in 1860 he spent six weeks at Baillie Street Chapel, Rochdale, one of the emotional centres of the United Methodist Free Churches.[43] The following table of his alleged evangelistic success was published in 1847:

Place	Justified	Sanctified
Dublin	700	100
Limerick	130	30
Cork	300	50
Bandon	70	20
Liverpool	1,300	400
Leeds	1,600	1,000
Hull	2,300	900
Sheffield	3,352	1,448
Huddersfield	1,879	755
York	1,314	727
Birmingham	2,800	1,400
Nottingham	1,412	553
Lincoln	368	283
Boston	260	140
Sunderland	711	227
Gateshead	80	46
Scarborough	134	66
Chesterfield	599	137
Doncaster	356	170
Macclesfield	260	140
Wakefield	200	130
Visits to London etc.	1,500	500
	21,625	9,222[44]

Benjamin Gregory implied that these results depended on Caughey's use of tricks such as the false penitent, whose pre-arranged coming forward at the climax of the evangelistic

[43] For Baillie Street, cf. E. C. Cryer, *A Centenary History, 1837–1937* (Rochdale 1937). The Baillie Street mixture of evangelical pietism, radical politics, pacifism and teetotalism owed something to Caughey.

[44] *A Brief Memoir of the Labours and a Vindication of the Character and Call of the Rev. James Caughey. By 'A Wesleyan Methodist'* (London 1847), pp. 40–1.

appeal was intended to stimulate response; and on mysterious suggestions that he had it on divine authority that certain people in his audience would soon die, and would go to Hell unless they were converted. Caughey certainly relied on the use of threats of eternal suffering in Hell, for he defended this approach in his published *Letters*.[45] Other evidence suggests, however, that the secret of the American's successful six-year tour lay in his brand of inflated, romantic rhetoric:

> 'I have hell enough in this life.' – I shall not dispute with you about that; but should not this satisfy you? 'Pant ye after second death?' What is hell upon earth? Is it anything else than a fore-taste of the torments of the damned? What is the 'bottomless pit' mentioned in Revelation? What, but the eternal sinking of the soul from God? Hell, then, most assuredly begins in this world; and the mouth of the pit opens wide in time. Every unconverted sinner is within the circumference of the pit. 'A wicked man', says one, 'is a candidate for nothing but hell'; and, says another, 'Hell is the centre of every sinner's gravity.' These are facts; and there is no standing still. The motions of a sinner downward are as steady as the weights in a clock. Such things go down slowly, but surely, by the ordinary revolutions of the time-piece; – or the cord may break, and they fall at once. . . . There is no law in nature more steady than the progress of a sinner to his horrible centre; but the cord may be severed by an accident, or by the friction of its own workings; or by the stroke of God; . . . and thus you may drop into an *eternal* hell at once.[46]

This was a common preaching style in the 1830–60 period, and once again one notes a gap between generations. Just as Jabez Bunting and Richard Watson found themselves out of sympathy with older men like Thomas Coke and Adam Clarke, so by the 1840s a new style had developed, of which Caughey was one example and William Morley Punshon (1824–81) was to be another.[47] Gregory did not realize that Caughey's extravagant oratory delighted a generation of Wesleyans who had tired of the more formal, classical manner of preachers like Jabez Bunting.

[45] cf. *Letters*, especially vol. ii (London 1845), letter XVIII.
[46] ibid., pp. 200–1; there was attached a description of a descent into Vesuvius, as a further analogy of Hell.
[47] cf. W. M. Punshon, *Lectures* (London 1882; but all written much earlier).

Gregory did not suggest that Caughey was a holiness revivalist at all, but in practice nearly one-third of his converts were sanctified, not justified. His emphasis on sanctification reflected the early stirrings of the American Methodist nineteenth-century holiness movement.[48] The so-called Tuesday Meeting for the Promotion of Holiness had started among New York Methodist women in 1835; Phoebe Palmer, who was herself to visit England as a holiness revivalist in 1859, was 'sanctified' in 1837; the Holiness Meeting which usually met at the Palmers' New York house (Phoebe's husband was a doctor) was thrown open to men in 1839. In American terms, the presentation of sanctification revivalistically as a sudden, revolutionary transformation, developed either as a way of sustaining the flagging appeal of revivalism in the 1830s or as a cautious retreat from the social and political enthusiasms which began to replace revivalism in America by the 1840s.[49] Caughey's holiness meetings in England showed that he was in touch with the latest developments of the American religious scene; they also represented, as did his whole British career, one of the comparatively rare moments when American Methodism was having a direct effect on the English movement.

By the 1840s, however, the doctrine of holiness was dividing the British Methodists just as it was to divide the American Methodists, and the root of the difference may be summed up in a brief comparison between the way in which Adam Clarke and Richard Watson expounded it. Clarke followed the strain in John Wesley's teaching according to which holiness was a gift which God bestowed on a man instantaneously in terms of faith.[50] This approach naturally commended itself to

[48] cf. J. L. Peters, *Christian Perfection and American Methodism* (New York 1956), the chief study of this tradition, which William Warren Sweet, the best-known American historian of Methodism, rather ignored in his books.

[49] Whitney R. Cross, *The Burned-over District: The Social and Intellectual History of Enthusiastic Religion in Western New York, 1800–1850* (Ithaca, N.Y. 1950), is a brilliant study of American revivalism in the first half of the nineteenth century; W. B. McLoughlin, *Modern Revivalism* (New York 1959), showed the appearance of the Holiness motif in non-Methodist denominations, especially Presbyterianism; Perry Miller, *The Life of the Mind in America from the Revolution to the Civil War* (Princeton, N.J. 1968), contains another analysis of revivalism in this period.

[50] Wesley's views are conveniently documented in A. C. Outler, *John Wesley* (New York 1964), an anthology from Wesley's writings which includes a section on holiness

revivalists who found in it authority for their efforts to draw people to a moment of definite personal commitment. The revivalist, however, altered the meaning of the doctrine so that sanctification became not so much the sudden act of God in a faithful man as the expectant act of a faithful man who consecrated himself wholly to God, 'laying his all on the altar', as the phrase was.[51]

Richard Watson did not deny the possibility of this sudden transformation, for to have done so would have meant conflict with John Wesley's own writings; he preferred to say that holiness was a kind of spiritual maturity for which time and gradual development were needed. His view was that of most Wesleyan conservatives, but as the division in the denomination widened after the Leeds (1828) and the Warrenite (1834) secessions, Caughey's emphasis on an American variety of the holiness tradition which claimed John Wesley's authority increased once again the reserve with which the two camps regarded one another. Caughey's nine thousand instances of sanctification are also interesting because they mean that at any rate something approximating to the experience of sanctification which is described in several of the spiritual autobiographies of the eighteenth-century itinerant preachers[52] survived in Wesleyanism into the mid-nineteenth century.

Thus, as far as religious behaviour is concerned, one has to imagine a Wesleyan Methodism torn between the excitements of the past and the prosperity of the present, between revivalism, for instance, and rhetorical popular preaching, between worship as 'common prayer' and worship which resembled more and more closely that of the Dissenting tradition, between holiness as sudden change and holiness as gradual growth. Primitive Methodism and the Bible Christian move-

---

(pp. 251–305). Dr Outler's editorial suggestion of the primary importance of Byzantine sources (especially of Gregory of Nyssa through Macarius the Egyptian) for an understanding of Wesley's doctrine of perfection must, however, be treated with caution; Wesley read voluminously in spiritual literature, but what he made of what he read is another question.

[51] Phoebe Palmer (1807–1874) popularized this language, and through her influence upon the Booths it characterized the early Salvation Army Holiness teaching; but her claim that John Wesley would have approved of her language was not well-founded.

[52] cf. T. Jackson (ed.), *The Lives of Early Methodist Preachers*, 3 vols (London 1836); see especially, i, 367–452: the autobiography of Alexander Mather.

ment (which began in the earlier nineteenth century) absorbed much of the rural working-class element which might otherwise have strengthened the Wesleyan tendency towards revivalism and improvised worship; these other, socially marginal, groups also adopted teetotalism as an official policy more quickly than did the Wesleyans. It is incorrect, however, to imply that the division in Wesleyanism lay between the laity and the ministry. The Wesleyan middle class in the main supported their ministerial leaders in the rejection of teetotalism and 'instantaneous' sanctification; they were rather less enthusiastic about the use of the liturgy; they were troubled by conservative criticisms of revivalism – Jabez Bunting himself became an unsparing critic of Caughey – because they felt that revivalism fitted into the Wesleyan tradition itself. This was a period in which Wesleyanism was concentrated intensely upon itself. The element of withdrawal from the environing society came out strongly in the warnings of the annual Wesleyan Conference against novel-reading, against visiting even pious friends on the Sabbath, against financial speculation and political activity (to be distinguished, perhaps, from holding political opinions), and in general against whatever would bring the society member into tempting contact with people outside the Connexional world. Such warnings rarely sounded as strained as they did among the Anglican Evangelicals; they still contained another note, not the eschatological pessimism so deeply engrained in the sects, but the note of cheerfulness which was the wiser side of John Wesley's doctrine of Christian holiness. It was often those who called themselves 'Wesleyan Reformers', and who liked to think of themselves as on the side of 'progress', who seemed to lose their sense of proportion: Robert Newton was constantly abused for travelling to his Sunday appointments by train; Jabez Bunting was denounced for showing too much interest in politics; and John Scott (1792–1868) was vilified as a traitor to both the Wesleyan and the Dissenting traditions because he accepted in the 1840s that the State must play a large part in a national educational system.

Education, in fact, was yet another subject which split the Old Connexion in these years. This was true just as much of the Sunday School as of the Day School. The Sunday School movement had started as a layman's affair. Some of the schools, like the famous Stockport Sunday School, were as much for adults as for children, but, whatever the age of the students, the early nineteenth-century Sunday School was often as devoted to instruction in reading, writing, and even on occasion arithmetic, as it was to the study of the Bible and Catechisms. An understandable working-class appetite for the rudiments of education clashed with an evangelical vision of the perfect Sunday School which the Wesleyan Conference expressed in these words:

> Let them recollect, that a Sunday-School is strictly and entirely a *religious* institution, whose object is to train up children in the nurture and admonition of the Lord; and that whatever has not a direct tendency towards this end, is equally inconsistent with the principal design of such charities, and with the sanctity of the sacred day in which they are conducted, and that ultimately it will prove subversive of all genuine moral and religious effect. We regard it as essential to the religious character of Sunday-Schools, that the children should be carefully instructed by Catechisms in the doctrines and duties of religion; that they should be accustomed to read the Scriptures, accompanied with the pious advices and explanations of their teachers; that they should on every Sabbath be regularly brought to the public worship of God; ...[53]

In its historical context, this statement was a cautious move towards the prohibition of the teaching of writing in Sunday Schools. This had been on Jabez Bunting's mind ever since he had been on circuit in Sheffield in 1807–9, where the practice was prevalent. He based his case on what he regarded as the moral obligation to keep the Sabbath Day holy:

> Writing is, in all its direct and immediate uses, a secular art. The religious use of it is at best remote, contingent, and indirect. The design of children in learning it, and of masters in teaching it, is chiefly, if they will confess the truth, the temporal advantage of it.[54]

[53] *Minutes of the Wesleyan Methodist Conference*, v (1819), 64: The Annual Address.
[54] T. P. Bunting, *The Life of J. Bunting* (London 1859), p. 322. The quotation is from an unpublished memorandum, but there is no reason to doubt that Bunting broadcast these opinions at the time.

Writing should therefore be taught during the week, and even in industrial areas like Sheffield, Bunting thought, poor children who wanted to learn it could still find time to do so on Saturday evenings in the summer.

It was difficult to enforce such a policy, however, for not all the schools were directly under Connexional control, and the dispute about what ought to be taught made many of the managers cling to their independence. There was no Connexional policy on the subject for many years, and Bunting was not likely to forget that, although he managed to impose a ban on the teaching of writing during the latter part of his time in Sheffield, his ministerial successors reversed his policy after 1809, made peace with the laymen whom he had forced out of the Wesleyan societies, and gave official permission for writing to be taught. A similar struggle between ministers and laity for the control of the local Sunday Schools lay behind the Leeds Organ controversy of 1827: of the leaders of the Protestant Methodists at Leeds, John Barr, Matthew Johnson and John Yewdall had all taught in the schools concerned.[55] It was the Wesleyan Conference of 1827 which decided to assert its authority over Wesleyan Sunday Schools: a set of rules was promulgated, the intention of which was to give local Wesleyan itinerants control over all Sunday Schools which claimed to belong to the body, and to authorize them to prevent writing from being taught. Both ministerial control and the prohibition of the teaching of writing and arithmetic were bitterly resented in areas where the Sunday School movement was at least in part a response to strong working-class demands for some education on the one day of the week which was completely free for such activities, and such feelings played a part in the subsequent divisions in Wesleyanism in 1849. One reason also for the growing unpopularity of the Wesleyan Conference in this period was that a purely ministerial body should, as it seemed to some

---

[55] *Sound Thoughts for Sound People, by Careful Observer* (Leeds 1830). The writer said that most people had expected that when trouble finally came in Leeds, the Schools would be the direct occasion of it. He claimed that the teachers were 'liberals' in politics: 'if a union with Methodism does not operate to alter, or at least greatly to modify, these crude republican sentiments', such people were likely, he thought, to find Methodist institutions 'liable to caustic animadversion'.

laymen, attempt by decree and without any sort of democratic process to determine the nature of an institution which the laymen prided themselves on having created, organized, staffed and financially maintained. As the number of day schools increased, however, the social importance of the Sunday School diminished; the Sunday Schools abandoned 'secular' subjects, and the controversy died out.

The provision of day school education for the children of poorer people proved, however, equally controversial. Here John Scott, who had entered the Wesleyan ministry in 1811, in the long run moulded the official policy. The Wesleyan Conference first approved the establishment of day schools in 1833, the year in which the British government authorized the allocation of public money to the support of day schools run by voluntary religious societies. Very little was done at first, and in 1837 there seem to have been only nine Wesleyan infant schools and twenty-two day schools for older children. In 1838 the Conference rather reluctantly set up a Connexional Education Committee, which in its turn tended to mark time. But in February 1843, Sir James Graham, as Home Secretary of the Conservative government, introduced a Factory Education Bill which provided that children between the ages of eight and thirteen working in the factories were to attend three hours a day at a school supported partly by the State, partly from the local poor rate, and partly from deductions from the children's wages. The teaching was to be essentially Anglican and the children were to attend church; but Nonconformists could contract out and there were to be 'nondenominational' Scripture lessons. The schools were to be managed by seven trustees, the chairman being the local Anglican minister, together with two churchwardens, two masters, and two others chosen by the magistrates. Graham's proposals made allowance for the existence of Dissent (which had not at this stage done very much towards the general education of children in the northern manufacturing districts which were the subject of the Bill), and he was certainly more concerned about the chronic shortage of schools than about strengthening the Church of England. Nevertheless, immense hostility greeted his scheme – more than two million signatures were collected for petitions against the Bill in its original form – and eventually he had to withdraw the Bill altogether. Most of the opposition came from Dissent, and Graham was disappointed in his hope that Wesleyan Methodism would at least preserve what was by now popularly regarded as its 'middle' role between Anglicanism and the Free Churches. The rise of Anglo-Catholicism had frightened the Wesleyans into opposition, however, and Graham was unfairly accused of joining in a Puseyite plot for getting the education of the people into the hands of a 'priestly monopoly'. The enthusiasm with which the Wesleyans campaigned against the Graham Bill was very important: they had never previously committed themselves so whole-heartedly to the anti-Anglican side. It was also the first time that they realized how much political influence they could wield, for many observers thought that their opposition decided the fate of the Bill. The campaign was also important in relation to the Wesleyan schism of 1849, for it was the laity – rather than the ministerial group led by John Scott – which really disliked the idea of the State entering the field of education, so that the apparent Wesleyan unanimity on educational policy collapsed in 1846, when Scott accepted State interference (and inspection) in principle, but did not carry with him the bulk of lay opinion.

It is in the light of the fierce agitation of 1843 that one has to judge Wesleyan education schemes in the succeeding years. The main battle over Graham's plan took place in the March–May period of 1843; Scott brought to the Wesleyan Conference in the summer a plan for the building of 700 Wesleyan day schools in the following seven years (in practice it was to take about twenty-five years to build 670). This programme was a defensive denominational measure on the part of a body which had not invested heavily in popular education since 1800 but which recognized that it could not shrug off the Government's criticisms of the amount of education which the Churches were providing in the industrial areas.[56] The same was true of the decision to found a teachers' training

---

[56] cf. J. T. Ward, *The Factory Movement 1830–1855* (London 1962), for the general context, especially pp. 258–68. The importance of the affair in the history of Wesleyanism has not been generally recognized.

college in London (Westminster College, finally established in 1851 as a mixed college; in 1872 the small group of women became the nucleus of a women's training college, Southlands): John Scott was first Principal until his death in 1868. These new day schools were inevitably regarded as evangelistic instruments as well as social and civilizing agents, but they soon became the means of a kind of temporary territorial establishment of the Wesleyan (and other) Free Churches, at once gathering and consolidating within the borders of the denomination a majority of the children in certain areas, particularly in Lancashire, Yorkshire and the Midlands. These schools formed a completely new organ of denominational policy, and their comparative success was to strengthen Wesleyanism in the later nineteenth century.

To some Wesleyan laymen, however, the events of 1843 seemed to have committed Wesleyanism irretrievably to opposition to a state system of education, and to support for the so-called 'voluntaryist' system. As J. H. Rigg[57] put it, describing this point of view,

> Through fear, on the one hand, of the usurpation by the Established Church of the function of national education, as if this were a right inherent in the Church endowed by the State, neither to be controlled in its exercise by any co-ordination of lay associates, or of political functionaries, nor to be shared with any dissenting Christian communities; and, on the other hand, through jealousy of the theories and projects of secular educationists, who would make the education of the people altogether an affair of the State, and would entirely separate it from religious influences or Church co-operation; a large class of energetic men, belonging chiefly to the Baptist and Independent denominations, but including also a certain proportion (we believe a very small proportion) of Wesleyans, have been led to adopt the principle, that the education of the people is a matter to be left entirely to voluntary exertions, and that 'all Government interference with the education of the people is at variance with sound principle, involving a departure

---

[57] J. H. Rigg (1821–1909) entered the Wesleyan itinerancy in 1845. He was Principal of the Westminster Teachers Training College from 1868 to 1903, and President of Conference in 1878. He published a short study of Jabez Bunting in 1905. He remained all his life on the side of Wesleyanism which drew its inspiration from Anglicanism rather than from Nonconformity.

from the legitimate province of Government' . . . the State can have no authority in such a matter: to claim this for the State would be a treason to parental rights, an invasion of parental responsibilities, an investiture of the State with moral functions, a demand of despotism in which lies concealed, however subtly disguised, all the peril and poison of continental centralisation and imperialism.[58]

More than a small proportion of the Wesleyan laity, however, had invested their emotional capital on this side of the argument in the 1840s, and when John Scott persuaded the Wesleyan Methodist Education Committee in 1847 to accept both government grants for the connexional day schools and the official inspection which inevitably accompanied them, and did this without any large-scale consultation with the Wesleyan laity, he was felt to be proving the case of the reformers that Jabez Bunting and his associates not only wielded absolute power but also used it against Dissent.[59] The pressure for Wesleyanism to declare itself officially on the Dissenting side of the deep gulf which divided British society had been mounting ever since the expulsion of Rayner Stephens in 1834 for advocating disestablishment. What counted in the long run was that Scott's educational policy was the right one for the future; what counted in the short run was that he had alienated a powerful section of Wesleyan opinion. The Wesleyan official abandonment of the voluntaryist system undoubtedly increased the popularity of the reformers' demand for lay representation in the Wesleyan Methodist Conference.

This was all the more true because an earlier educational controversy had emphasized the freedom of the Conference from lay control. Reference has already been made to the struggle which convulsed the Connexion in 1834 over the proposal to set up a seminary for the training of Wesleyan

[58] J. H. Rigg, *Essays for the Times on Ecclesiastical and Social Subjects* (London 1866; but written in 1859), pp. 483–4. Rigg remained faithful in these *Essays* to the Bunting tradition, saying that Wesleyanism did not regard church establishment as wrong in principle, but that the Church of England ought to be so reformed as to work well as a Christian and national institution.

[59] See *The Wesleyan*, the principal newspaper published on 'reforming' principles, between 1844 and 1848. James Everett wrote regularly for it.

ministers. At the simplest level, critics of the process of Wesleyan institutionalization which was taking place believed that in the proposed seminary young men would be taught to demand obedience to the existing Wesleyan constitution (including the all-ministerial Conference), and would be encouraged to use Morning Prayer, to wear preaching gowns and to read their sermons; that the seminary, in other words, would be used to strengthen the hold of the innovating party. (The tradition that Jabez Bunting and his friends were opposed to change and reform in religion and politics is now at once so well established and so seriously misleading that it is worth describing him as an innovator in order to underline what was really happening.) Those who had objected, in 1827–8, to the installation of an organ in Brunswick Chapel, Leeds, on the ground that such music was artificial and that God relished only the sound of the human voice in worship, similarly objected to the 'training' of the ministry in 1834, on the ground that an 'artificial' or 'man-made' preacher had no place in the pulpit, where a man must speak with the inspiration of the Holy Spirit or be silent. The Evangelical Revival had its own tradition of irrationalism, talked much about 'the religion of the heart', and believed – perhaps deriving the idea from Francke and German Pietism – that in the moment of justification a man must crucify his reason, which could only be working against God in that spiritual crisis. Those who minimize this aspect of the Evangelical Revival have obscured the fact that the eighteenth-century conflict between professional, academically trained Anglican priests and untrained, though not necessarily uneducated, but certainly unordained, Wesleyan itinerants was repeated within Wesleyanism itself in the nineteenth century in the form of a conflict between the Wesleyan ministry (as it slowly became between 1791 and, say, 1836, when ordination by the imposition of hands was finally made the normal procedure), and the lay, or local preacher. The local preacher's sense of being reduced to an inferior status often expressed itself with great bitterness between 1800 and 1857, so that one sometimes suspects that some of the Wesleyan Reformers believed that any preacher without ordination could not but be spiritually superior to any preacher with ordination. The following letter could be paralleled from many sources:

'The "ministers", as they now call themselves, look upon Local Preachers as mere laymen – that is, as unordained preachers of the Gospel of Christ; and they would, if possible, have silenced them before now, but for the gold they bring to the coffers. The "ministers" look upon themselves as a separate and more elevated and honourable class of men, and yet they are from the same stock. They were not born sons of Levi: one is the son of a tradesman, another of a mechanic, another of a miner, etc., and the ordination of which they boast is not by the laying on of hands of some prelate, but simply by that of those of each other, so that they themselves create a caste. . . . If paid ministers alone are to be considered pastors, the Apostle Paul was not a pastor, for "he worked with his own hands that he might not be chargeable to any". But if he was a pastor – and who dares to say that he was not? – then Local Preachers have decidedly the advantage over the "ministers", because they, like Paul are "diligent in business" while they are "fervent in spirit", serving the Lord. . . . [Local Preachers] have the privilege of attending, for the most part, Quarterly, as well as Preachers' Meetings – but for what purpose? To assist the itinerants carry out their own projects. The "pastor" who occupies the chair, overrules everything according to his own will, so that the Local Preachers are only there either as silent spectators, obedient serfs, or as the servants of Christ in priestly bondage. . . .'[60]

Significantly, this is not a quotation from the more famous Fly Sheets.[61] Those anonymous attacks on Jabez Bunting and his closest associates expressed only the opinions and grievances of a small group of Wesleyan ministers, centred on James Everett. These men, who originally circulated the Fly Sheets only among the Wesleyan ministers as a body, were largely unconcerned, before 1849, with the position of the laity in the Wesleyan constitution, though they were perhaps genuinely anxious to make the ministerial Conference less of

[60] *The Wesleyan Reformer* (1852), pp. 11, 27: the letter was signed 'Trophimus', and was apparently sent from Newcastle upon Tyne.

[61] There were four Fly Sheets: the first appeared in 1844, the second in 1846, the third in 1847, and the fourth in 1848; a fifth, altogether shorter, was published with the others for the general public in 1849.

an organ of government and more of a theatre of discussion, to make it more an advisory than a legislative body. Everett's own intentions were primarily personal, he wanted to discredit Bunting and Newton in particular; it is unlikely that he foresaw a third and larger secession from Wesleyanism. He did not even employ in the Fly Sheets the slogans calculated to bring out the laity in support of the discontented ministers; he was as 'conservative' as the men whom he hated, but he could not bear them to rule. When the Wesleyan Conference in 1849 expelled William Griffith,[62] Samuel Dunn[63] and James Everett because they refused, as the men most suspected of the authorship of the Fly Sheets, to answer questions about them, it acted without the kind of concrete evidence which convinces public opinion: those who voted in the Conference had many of them known Everett for years and drew their own conclusions; all three of the expelled were known as religious journalists who wrote on the 'reforming' side. (The issue was further complicated by the fact that *Papers on Wesleyan Matters* had been published by the Wesleyan Book Room from January 1849 as a monthly periodical containing articles signed with pseudonyms which hit back at the Fly Sheets in their own style of abuse: the reply was natural, and anonymous publication was far from unusual at the time, but in the eyes of many observers the semi-official nature of the *Papers* weakened the case of authority against Everett's methods.)[64] The expulsions gave the reformers a golden chance to discredit the Conference and to demand lay representation again, but their enthusiasm for reform was not generated by the Fly Sheets. The division of 1849 was caused

[62] William Griffith (1806–1883) was the son of a Wesleyan itinerant; he entered the ministry in 1828. He wrote for the 'reform' paper, the *Wesleyan Times*. In 1855 he settled at Derby as minister of a Wesleyan Reform chapel. He disliked the title 'Reverend', was a republican in politics, and objected to the establishment of the Church of England; cf. R. Chew, *William Griffith: Memorials and Letters* (London 1885).

[63] Samuel Dunn (1797–1882) entered the Wesleyan itinerancy in 1816, was the first Methodist preacher in the Shetland Islands and a friend of Adam Clarke. With William Griffith he edited the *Wesley Banner*, a revivalist journal, to which the 'conservatives' objected, from 1849 to 1854. After 1849 he became a free-lance minister, even working in New York, from 1865 to 1868; cf. J. Dunn, *The Transfiguration, etc., with a biographical sketch* (London 1890).

[64] For a contemporary confirmation, see G. Smith, *History of Wesleyan Methodism*, iii, 462.

by the inner contradictions set up in Wesleyan Methodism by over-rapid growth between 1790 and 1840; all the pressure exerted by a creative tradition with a reputation for success, all the skill of Bunting and his fellow administrators, all the devotion of a remarkable ministry, could not fuse together the varied human material brought in by evangelism, by social expansion and by population increase. The overwhelming majority of ministers remained faithful to the men who had led them for a generation, to Jabez Bunting, Thomas Jackson and Robert Newton. The Wesleyan constitution remained unchanged until the 1870s, when lay representation was at last conceded. But an era had ended, the long bright summer was over, continuity had snapped. The division of 1849 was a religious, not a political, tragedy, the collapse, on the Evangelical side of Protestantism, of a long sustained attempt to maintain, on a denominational and not just on a sectarian or shut-in local scale, something of the full weight of discipline needed to sanctify a community. Such enterprises commonly generate their own destruction, but this is no ground for ignoring the true quality of the aim.

From the contemplation of the tragedy one turns to its interpretation. Since 1909 the understanding of early nineteenth-century Wesleyan history has followed very distinct lines, lines which have repudiated the Wesleyan tradition as it was recorded in the *New History of Methodism* by J. R. Gregory. One reason for this departure is that although twentieth-century historians have frequently invoked Methodism as a factor in their analysis of early Victorian history, they have rarely paid much attention to the internal affairs of Wesleyan Methodism itself: they have looked for links between Wesleyanism and the political and economic issues of the period, but they have not made an equal effort to understand Wesleyan Methodism as a religious phenomenon in its own right. In general, they have assumed that one can interpret the story of Jabez Bunting and of the early nineteenth-century secessions from Wesleyan Methodism in terms of the political and social controversies of the time, so that under Bunting's leadership Wesleyanism is supposed to have passed through the same kind of conservative reaction which took place all over

Europe between 1815 and 1848. The Fly Sheets crisis, which conveniently took place in 1849, offered a tempting parallel to the widespread political revolutions of 1848. The Wesleyan laity, it seemed, oppressed by the dictator Bunting, finally rose against him, demanding a greater share in the government of the denomination, much as the same people, in another capacity, wanted a greater share in the government of the country. A pioneer in this vein was the French historian, E. Halévy, who said in so many words that the formation of the United Methodist Free Churches in 1857 was due 'not to a doctrinal but a political issue'.[65] In his account of 1849 (in which he did not mention the Fly Sheets, whose authorship, after all, was the ground of James Everett's fatal expulsion, and whose contents, exclusively devoted to internal Wesleyan affairs, contradicted his political interpretation) Halévy made the principal issue the freedom of the press. It is true that *The Times* thought that this was what mattered, but the Wesleyans themselves, suffering from an unceasing barrage of books and pamphlets about their denominational troubles, can hardly have thought that press freedom was in danger. Working from the outside, Halévy saw in Wesleyanism an organization to which other historians had paid little attention but which might enable him to explain why British society had apparently remained more stable in the early nineteenth century than French society. He thought that Wesleyanism, socially conservative and deeply opposed to violence, had deprived a potential English revolution of much of its natural leadership and mass support. Exponents of his ideas sometimes speak as though Methodism in the early nineteenth century saved England from revolution.

Halévy also applied political explanations to the internal course of nineteenth-century Methodist history. It was the political conservatism of the Wesleyan leaders, so valuable to society at large, which stirred up a Methodist rebellion in 1849, when the laity applied to Wesleyan institutions the lessons which they had learned in national politics. According to this analysis, the lay opposition to Jabez Bunting, with its

[65] E. Halévy, *A History of the English People in the Nineteenth Century*, IV: *Victorian Years 1841-1895*, Eng. trans. (London 1951), p. 379.

250

claim to representation in the Wesleyan Methodist annual Conference, ought to be described as 'liberal' and 'reformist' (and of course the opposition often called themselves 'Wesleyan Reformers') while Bunting and the 'High Wesleyan' party must be labelled 'Tories'. Such descriptions carried with them approval of the Fly Sheets and disapproval of Bunting, for Halévy was not so enamoured of stability as to approve of what he understood to have been an ecclesiastical dictatorship.

Some caution is nevertheless necessary. That Bunting was normally thought of as a 'Tory' in his own lifetime has seemed to many people to confirm Halévy's analysis. Bunting's political opinions varied, however, as political opinions do: he was not a partisan. The story of how he hurt himself by falling over a bench in the House of Commons has been told almost too often – Dr Currie has revived it in *Methodism Divided*, mentioning it more than once in tones which imply that the accident was subtly disgraceful – but I would suggest that what fascinated Bunting in Westminster was the nature and use of power itself, not the fortunes of the Tory party. Life taught him much about authority, though it is another question whether he ever quite mastered the use of it himself. Thus, he certainly supported Roman Catholic Emancipation in 1828, and gave a moderate welcome to the Reform Act of 1832; he made no effort to rally Wesleyan Methodism in public demonstrations against either. His tacit support of the deportation of the Dorchester labourers, another action often quoted against him, was support of a non-Tory administration. He no doubt welcomed Sir Robert Peel's victory at the polls in 1845, partly because Lord John Russell's activities in the Whig government had alarmed denominational leaders about the State's intentions in the field of education. Yet, though his approval of John Scott's decision in 1847 to abandon the voluntaryist camp in education, as far as day schools were concerned, was neither doctrinaire Toryism nor doctrinaire Free Churchism, this sensible change of policy roused the laity against him far more than his occasional outbursts of Toryism had done. Halévy did not allow for the internal complexities of Wesleyan Methodism, nor realize that much of the opposition to Bunting was 'conservative' rather than 'radical', or that when the struggle rose above the level of personal animosities it was really between two competing conservative groups, who did not agree in their interpretation of the Wesleyan past.

Halévy certainly influenced the two chief studies of early nineteenth-century Methodism written by Methodists in the 1930s. These were *After Wesley*, by Maldwyn Edwards (1935), and *Methodism & Politics 1791–1851*, by E. R. Taylor (1935). Dr Edwards's book was sub-titled 'A Study of the Social and Political Influence of Methodism in the Middle Period (1791–1849)', and as such broke new ground among Methodist writers. He said that between 1800 and 1830 Wesleyan Methodism was predominantly conservative in its social and political ideas: 'the Toryism of Bunting was an accurate repetition of the political opinions of his people.'[66] Between 1830 and 1849 a radical opposition gradually emerged, of which Dr Edwards wrote:

> One cannot separate the Radicalism which split Methodism from manifestations of the same spirit on the continent and in the great Chartist movement of our own country.[67]

After 1850, this Wesleyan Toryism declined:

> The time came when the former close connexion with the Church was forgotten and Methodists regarded themselves as Nonconformists. A Church that drew its members from the new industrial middle classes, and had become allied with Nonconformity, could not remain Tory in politics.[68]

Three comments may be made here. First, it is difficult, and Dr Edwards recognized it as difficult, to generalize about the political stance of Wesleyan Methodism as a whole. If one takes Manchester as an example, Dr David Gowland has recently discovered that, apart from the Wesleyans who seceded with Dr Warren in 1834 and who moved gradually towards a radical Liberalism, there were between 1832 and

[66] *After Wesley*, p. 163.
[67] ibid., loc. cit.
[68] ibid., p. 46.

1857 three strands of Wesleyan political opinion in Manchester.[69] There were strongly pro-Anglican Tories like
James Wood, a manufacturer who opposed the Corn Laws
without becoming a member of the Anti-Corn Law League,
who opposed the ballot and the abolition of Church Rates, and
who attacked R. H. Greg, the Whig candidate in the Manchester by-election of 1839, because he was a Unitarian. There
were more liberal Tories, represented by Holland Hoole, who
joined the Anti-Corn Law League, disliked Anglicanism, and
warned Jabez Bunting's son, William, who was on circuit in
Manchester from 1838 to 1841, that he talked too much about
politics (on the Tory side) in the pulpit. Finally, there were
Whig businessmen like George Chappell, who wanted
immediate repeal of the Corn Laws and shared Hoole's
antipathy towards 'Church and Tory Wesleyans' such as
James Wood.

The difficulty of generalization becomes obvious when Dr
Gowland shows, from an examination of the Manchester
poll-books, not only that in the Manchester election of 1832
an overwhelming number of Wesleyans voted for the Whigs,
but that in the by-election of 1839 the Wesleyans, in many
cases the same persons, gave a similar degree of support to the
Tories. The secession of 1834–5 had helped to discredit
political Liberalism with Wesleyan tradesmen, skilled artisans
and shopkeepers who might otherwise have been expected to
vote for a Whig candidate. Generalizations about Wesleyan
Toryism might lead one to suppose a closed situation at this
point, but in fact Toryism diminished rather than increased in
Manchester Wesleyanism between 1841 and 1847. For this
Dr Gowland suggests two explanations: the Maynooth Bill,
carried in 1845, which gave Maynooth College a permanent
endowment, independent of a vote in Parliament, angered
Manchester Tories, who were normally anti-Roman Catholic,
and the aggressive political preaching of William Bunting and
James Dixon actually thinned the Tory ranks; many Wesleyans
voted for John Bright in 1847, although he was also the

[69] In this account of Manchester Methodist politics I am following Dr Gowland's
unpublished Manchester University thesis, 'Methodist Secessions and Social Conflict
in South Lancashire, 1830–1857' (1966). For a résumé of this part of the argument,
see W.H.S. Proc., xxxvi (February 1968), 93–104.

favoured candidate of the Wesleyan Association. There were two elections in Manchester in the period of the Fly Sheets controversy, in 1852 and 1857; in both the Wesleyan voters moved back to the Tory side, contributing to Bright's defeat in 1857. The explanation of this change of allegiance was that the secession of 1849–57 reduced the number of Wesleyans who usually voted for the Liberal Party, and that the Methodist reformers' demand for change stiffened the Toryism of the remaining Wesleyans.

On the basis of Dr Gowland's evidence it would not mean very much to say that in this period Wesleyanism in Manchester was either Tory or non-Tory. The statement that the secessions from Wesleyanism were produced by the influence of political Liberalism on Wesleyan internal politics has also to be treated with caution, for it is at least as clear that in 1835 and 1849 the secession movements strengthened political Toryism in the Wesleyan societies. In other words, the choice between Bunting and secession did not amount only to a political choice, though it could be expressed in political terms and frequently was, especially in 1848, when it seemed as though all the despotisms of Europe were about to crash to the ground. One has to look more deeply for solutions to the explosion in Wesleyanism in 1849. One vital factor was that the expansion of Wesleyanism after 1791 had transformed its social structure so that institutions and customs formed within a fairly homogeneous social group were exposed to the strains of a much wider section of British society. This did not mean a simple social division. A fair degree of tension built up within the group of businessmen associated with Manchester Wesleyanism, for example; and Dr Gowland makes it clear that in 1839 a considerable number of tradesmen, skilled artisans and shopkeepers followed the lead of the Tory (not even the Whig) manufacturers. Nevertheless, he is probably right in suggesting that when members of this lower social group seceded, as they did in 1835 and 1849, they did so because social status and religious upbringing were frustrating their desire to share in the wider events and experiences of their time. Gowland therefore interprets the setting up of the reformers' Grand Central Association in 1834 as to some extent a playing at politics for lack of more authentic means of action. This seems to me fair, and more percipient than traditional talk about 'political influences': from this point of view Wesleyan Methodism was becoming socially unmanageable as early as the 1790s, but it staved off the main crisis until the 1830s, when a large number of those who found Wesleyan Methodism unresponsive to their social demands broke away. (Given the point in the history of Protestantism at which these events took place, it was not surprising that they set up new denominational structures: by the twentieth century similar problems were solved either by denominational migration or by total withdrawal.) Bunting's policy, which from the Leeds Organ controversy onwards was to strengthen the power of the various Connexional authorities, only increased the impulse to secede; this does not mean that his wish to preserve the Wesleyan system which he had inherited was 'wrong', only that he was fighting against social facts as well as against political and ecclesiastical theories. The situation was further confused because Bunting was not the static Tory that Maldwyn Edwards implies: after 1840 he changed his position, and the Wesleyan Education Committee's decision in 1847 to give up the doctrinaire voluntaryist financial system for day school provision antagonized the Wesleyan Tories just when Bunting was about to need their help.[70]

While I agree thus far with Dr Gowland, I think that there was another, religious element in the situation. This was the widespread early nineteenth-century Methodist idealization of eighteenth-century Wesleyanism as a kind of 'classless society', a period when the ethos of the movement had been, at least internally, egalitarian. This mood was felt by many to lie at the core of the Gospel; it naturally appealed more to the socially weaker groups. In the nineteenth century the idea that the early Wesleyans had been a band of brothers was often invoked against the itinerants, because they seemed to want to distinguish themselves from the people. This mood had long

[70] While it is true that in the later nineteenth century outstanding Wesleyan M.P.s such as Sir Robert Perks stood for the Liberal Party, the extent of the change should not be exaggerated; Perks was on the right wing of the Liberals and followed Lord Rosebery into Liberal Imperialism.

historical roots in Christian history and it continued to affect the relationship between the Wesleyan ministry and laity throughout the century.

E. R. Taylor's *Methodism & Politics 1791–1851* (Cambridge 1935) contained a more elaborate interpretation of Wesleyan history than that suggested by Dr Edwards. On the one hand, he accepted the idea that the crisis of 1849 had political roots: he thought that Wesleyan Methodism ought to have developed politically in a Liberal direction, but that a minority of ministers, Jabez Bunting chief among them, had used the 'no politics' rule to prevent any official expression of Wesleyan sympathy for either Dissent or political Liberalism, while retaining their personal freedom to speak as though the Connexion was permanently and naturally committed to conservatism and Anglicanism. This attempt to dictate political opinion on pseudo-religious grounds led inevitably to the outbreak of lay resentment in 1849. On the other hand, Bunting's errors did not stop at the political. Taylor thought that Methodism also missed its religious way under Bunting's influence. Methodism might, he thought, have united its Catholic elements with the doctrine of the priesthood of all believers, have allowed the lay administration of the sacraments (which was never permitted in nineteenth-century Wesleyan Methodism, though recurrent in the other Methodist bodies), and so have helped to develop what he variously called 'a really Catholic Free Churchmanship' and 'High Protestantism'. Bunting, however, introduced a system of clerical paternalism and thwarted the 'natural' ecclesiastical development of Wesleyanism. The consequent religious disaffection added to the force of the explosion when it came in 1849.

This twofold attempt to represent Bunting as having thwarted the natural Wesleyan line of development is, however, not entirely plausible. Bunting, for instance, could not really prevent Wesleyan laymen from taking the Liberal side in politics; indeed, his special offence in the case of education was to have found, unintentionally, a point at which the Wesleyan administration could actually commit the Connexion to political action of some importance even though many laymen disagreed. Laymen did not in general mind if the Conference silenced 'political preachers' like William Griffith, but this did not mean that they took their own political views from 'a masterful ecclesiastic', as Taylor calls Jabez Bunting. In fact, one of the differences between the first and second halves of the nineteenth century may be found in the freedom and self-importance of the 'political preacher' after about 1870; preachers of this kind, Guinness Rogers and Sylvester Horne, for example, to name only two of the better known, were by no means all Wesleyan Methodists, so that their emergence has to be accounted for in terms of other than Methodist factors. In any case, the opposition to Bunting grew among Tory as well as Liberal itinerants. James Dixon (1788–1871), for example, who became President of the Wesleyan Methodist Conference in 1841, took the Tory side in politics as strongly as Bunting himself, yet was no admirer of Bunting's Methodist policy:

> 'He dreaded centralisation. He watched with apprehension the increase of organism, the multiplication of bureaux and committees. He feared lest the old spirituality and simplicity should be dissipated in the machinery of the system.'[71]

As a Wesleyan, that is, Bunting did not seem Tory enough for Dixon, but Toryism here meant both the old conservative opposition to centralization and bureaucracy, and also the tempting idealization of the eighteenth-century Wesleyan past as an example of spirituality attained through simplicity. In his reflections on the visit which he paid to the United States and Canada in 1848, Dixon openly expressed his nervousness about the Wesleyan future:

> The church has invariably, in all ages, ruined itself. And the ruin has generally approached through an excess of tinkering at its polity. Institutions, in the beginning both Christian and necessary, have become, in the hands of thoughtless, often of designing, occupants, snug, tight, circumscribed things; the centres of power, instead of light; the means of oppression, instead of

---

[71] cf. R. W. Dixon, the later Anglican church historian, in his biography of his father, *The Life of James Dixon, D.D.* (London 1874), p. 313.

blessing; the machinery of *depression*, of *suppression*, and of *immoderate* and *universal control*, instead of expansion and progress.[72]

It was not surprising that the *Wesleyan Times*, the newspaper which supported the Wesleyan reformers, openly called on Dixon to assume leadership of the opposition in 1849; caught in the conflict of two loyalties, to the past and to the future, he tried to solve the problem by rejecting the reformers' overtures but taking a moderate line as Superintendent of the Birmingham West Circuit. He did not repudiate the victory which Bunting's successors temporarily won, 'but he also knew and mourned over the cost at which the victory was won'.[73]

As for Taylor's views on Bunting's religious significance, it certainly seems true that the conflict of 1827–57 had its chief origin in differences of religious style and in disagreements about the nature of Methodism. One must not exaggerate Bunting's originality, however, or imagine that he changed the direction of Wesleyan Methodist history. He saw his own role as that of the guardian of John Wesley's system. It was Wesley, after all, who set up the ministerial Conference as the absolute authority in the Connexion; Wesley who established the Methodist tradition of clerical paternalism – which he did not for that matter invent, but learned as a part of his Anglican education. Wesley certainly disapproved of the lay administration of the sacraments. Even Bunting's political Toryism might be regarded as a moderate expression of the views which John Wesley published in his political writings. Bunting assumed in most of his controversies that continuity with John Wesley was a knock-down argument, but his opponents regarded Methodism as more than the sum of its founder's opinions, as an organism which might change out of all recognition without fundamentally betraying its past. This issue, however firmly fixed by events in the nineteenth century, has often been raised in Christian history. Bunting represented the classical doctrine of obedience to a

[72] James Dixon, *Methodism in America: with the Personal Narrative of the Author, during a Tour through a Part of the United States and Canada* (London 1849), p. 287.

[73] R. W. Dixon, op. cit., p. 321.

living tradition; his serious opponents[74] showed, though without at this stage any great intellectual clarity or distinction, the influence of the eighteenth-century Enlightenment, which regarded dogma and not doubt as the threat to belief and was sceptical about the value of inherited authority. It was hardly an accident, therefore, if both the United Methodist Free Churches, and their successor, the United Methodist Church, distrusted the compulsory use of credal statements.

These Methodist variations on Halévy's theme did not affect secular historical writing as much as did the books of J. L. and B. Hammond, *The Town Labourer 1760–1832*, *The Skilled Labourer 1760–1832*, *The Age of the Chartists*, and *The Bleak Age*. The Hammonds also treated Methodism as a part-explanation of the absence of revolution in Britain between 1815 and 1850, but whereas Halévy thought in institutional and political terms, and said that Wesleyan Methodism not only inculcated an ethic of political acceptance but also directed potentially revolutionary leadership into new, socially more stabilizing, roles, the Hammonds took the religious content of Wesleyanism more seriously, insofar as they understood it, and said that Wesleyanism functioned socially through its capacity to generate what was understood as religious emotion, through the constantly re-enacted drama of sin, repentance and salvation, through language and ritual (here the ritual of revivalism rather than the ritual of Anglo-Catholicism), which transformed the monotony of the tired worker's life, filling it with compensatory religious excitement. One might add that inasmuch as this was true it did not necessarily mean bribing the working classes to accept the miseries of the present with the promise that Heaven would show an improvement, but rewarding faith here and now with the concrete satisfaction of conversion and absorption into the community of the local chapel.

This community was a more positive force than the Hammonds admitted. In Bolton, for example, where Wesleyan

[74] Not, for instance, James Everett, whose life was a kind of avenger's tragedy, an intensely personal pursuit of the downfall of Jabez Bunting, whose destruction gratified Everett's conscious desire to avenge Adam Clarke and his less conscious need to avenge himself.

Methodism had a long history, the Ridgway Gates Sunday School had been started as far back as 1785, and by 1819 had about 2,000 children on its books. The basic intention of these schools was to teach reading and writing as well as religion, and the Bolton school ignored the Wesleyan Conference resolutions of 1814 and 1823, which prohibited the teaching of writing on Sundays. From 1827 onwards the Conference sought to enforce its will, with the result that in July 1834 nearly 200 members and about 1,000 scholars withdrew from the circuit: they called themselves the Wesleyan Refugees; the name-stone of their Hanover Street Chapel was inscribed: 'Wesleyan Refuge'; they remained an independent community until 1870 and had 1,600 children in the Bolton Coronation Procession for Queen Victoria in 1838. The Ridgway Gates school survived the secession, but significantly continued to teach writing until 1843, when as the result of the opening of a Wesleyan day school the Sunday School opened a night school twice weekly in lieu of Sunday tuition in writing.[75] This clash between a central Wesleyan administration which wanted to purify the curriculum of the Sunday Schools in order to make them (as it was hoped) more effective in converting children to Christianity, and a local society which was determined to preserve local control and satisfy local needs, was repeated elsewhere in the new industrial areas and helped to form the discontent which came to a head in 1849.[76]

Since 1945 the historians' view of the early nineteenth century has changed. A longer experience of the process of industrialization has led to a greater degree of acceptance of the process itself, even to a certain complacency about it. Social dislocation, vile overcrowding, poverty, disease and

[75] cf. C. D. Little, *The History and Romance of our Mother Sunday School: 150 Years of Bolton Methodism* (Bolton 1935). The population of Bolton increased from 17,416 in 1801 to 61,172 in 1851. In the 1820s perhaps a quarter of the working children of the town went to the Wesleyan Sunday School at any one time.

[76] For further criticism of the Hammonds' rather negative picture of early nineteenth-century Methodism, cf. R. F. Wearmouth, *Methodism and the Working-Class Movements of England 1800–1850* (London 1937), in which is emphasized the part played by Methodists in radical politics and trade unionism. Wearmouth, however, sometimes attributes too much to a Methodist background and upbringing; he does not allow for the possibility that for some men early contact with Methodism meant only an experience which they rejected.

ignorance, the degradation of men into 'hands' and of labour into 'machine-minding', all this is seen as an historically unavoidable (and therefore not tragic) stage through which British society passed on its way towards a universal transformation of living standards. Post-war historians have also often adopted the 'administrative' point of view, that is, they have sympathized with the troubles of government more than with the trouble of the governed. On this analysis any revolution that might have happened in England between 1815 and 1848 or even 1870 would have had disastrous consequences because it would almost certainly have retarded industrialization and so have prolonged the agony of the working class. Halévy had valued Wesleyan Methodism as an indirect cause of social stability; Maldwyn Edwards, E. R. Taylor, R. F. Wearmouth and the Hammonds all criticized Wesleyanism because its leaders had not championed the working classes. From this changed point of view, however, any moral condemnation of early nineteenth-century Wesleyan social conservatism became an error of judgement: Jabez Bunting may not have entirely understood what was happening – it is unlikely that he did so in the case of what was taught in Wesleyan Sunday Schools, which he saw more as an administrative than a social problem – but his sociopolitical instinct was sound.

In reality, violent revolution was very unlikely, and the statement that 'Methodism saved England from revolution', which has sometimes been made, goes too far. Political revolution from beneath occurs when a long-established social order reaches an unbearable pitch of rigidity and inefficiency. Early nineteenth-century England, however, was changing rapidly. The eighteenth-century social order was collapsing over wide areas of the country; the working classes in places like the South Staffordshire coalfield complained of the desertion of the aristocracy, not of oppression by them. Those who talk about the absence of revolution perhaps ignore too easily the recurrent violence of the period from 1800 to the 1840s. Neither the social stability nor the lack of popular leaders for Chartist meetings or loom-smashing expeditions were so obvious to contemporaries. But this popular violence was repressed successfully; much of it was directed at the new industrial world, not at the vanishing old one. The kind of leadership which the Wesleyan m: ddle class might have given to this popular conservative violence was given instead to the side of change. Mill-owners like the Whitehead brothers in Rossendale, who started from nothing and owned three mills in the valley by 1824, had their power looms broken in 1826 and their boiler plugs hammered home in 1842; their answer was to back the Free Trade agitation vigorously and to build day schools. It was often men of this sort, tough, self-made, intensely local, not inclined to leave the provinces for the sake of the myth of London, used to authority, clear that, taking life as a whole, they had been creative rather than destructive, who grew increasingly irritated at their exclusion from the ministerial Conference, which always seemed prepared to tell them how they should run their local affairs.[77] The Whitehead brothers were uneasy Wesleyans; they opposed the foundation of the Theological Institution in 1834 without joining the side of Dr Warren; there was trouble in the valley when the circuit ministers vetoed an invitation to James Caughey[78] to come and preach. In the wake of the Fly Sheets agitation, but almost certainly not because of what the Fly Sheets said (the issue of 'centralization' perhaps excepted), David and Peter Whitehead at last withdrew. They contributed most of the cost of the erection of a new chapel at Haslingden Road (it cost £10,000), but although they associated this chapel with the United Methodist Free Churches they administered it for several years on Congregational, not Connexional, principles. It was important for any psychological study of their history that when families like the Whiteheads (or the Cozens-Hardy

[77] Local Wesleyan histories constantly illustrate this: cf. C. D. Little, *Our Old Sunday School (and Day School): 150 Years of Wigan Methodism* (Wigan 1933). Not all the successful families revolted. Compare the Meeks of Wigan: there were six brothers, born between 1806 and 1822, sons of a Wesleyan minister. George and Joseph Meek opened a drapery business in Wigan in 1830; John and Robert started a similar business in Macclesfield in 1837; George, Robert and John began a wholesale business in Manchester in 1839. Two other brothers, Benjamin and Thomas, went to Preston in 1844. Joseph, who died in 1885, dominated Wigan Wesleyanism for many years, and was Mayor in 1864. The next generation of the family became lawyers, doctors, and so forth.

[78] See above, p. 223.

family in Norfolk) finally led some kind of insurrection it was the Church, not the State, that they attacked.[79] In *Methodism Divided* Dr R. Currie stressed the conflict between laity and ministers in this period but has not analysed sufficiently the concept of 'laity': the Wesleyan Reform agitation of 1849 differed from the agitations of 1827 and 1834 inasmuch as it was not primarily a lower middle-class movement – what mattered was that in 1849 a large section of the new Wesleyan bourgeoisie led a secession, instead of watching others secede. The next generation of Wesleyan middle-class leadership did not secede, but finally obtained representation in the Wesleyan Conference, in 1878. Jabez Bunting appreciated the importance of this group of men: after the Warren agitation had started he tried to appease them by what was called the 'law of 1835', which was meant to improve communications between the Conference and the circuits by enabling the circuit Quarterly Meetings to send memorials directly to the Conference on subjects which concerned them. This memorializing process only emphasized, however, the absence of lay representation in the Conference itself. Such a concession came too late; by the 1840s what decided the issue at the local level was the behaviour of the circuit ministry.

Despite what has been said, however, some students of early nineteenth-century English history still retain the hypothesis that revolution from below was possible at some time after 1789. The most important recent work of this kind is *The Making of the English Working Class*, by E. P. Thompson. Thompson regarded the British working class as being formed between about 1790 and 1832, and he was convinced that a proletarian revolution could have occurred at certain times during this period:

> 1819 was a rehearsal for 1832. In both years a revolution was possible (and in the second year it was very close).[80]

This revolution was prevented by political repression, by

---

[79] For the Whiteheads, cf. W. Jessop, *An Account of Methodism in Rossendale and the Neighbourhood* (Manchester 1880).

[80] *The Making of the English Working Class* (London 1963), p. 671.

middle-class reformers who persuaded the working classes to follow constitutional methods, and of course by Methodism, which diverted revolutionary impulses into religion.

This was the Halévy–Hammond interpretation in essence, but the approach had now become psychologically based. Behind Thompson's book lay *The Angel-Makers*, by G. R. Taylor,[81] a psycho-analytical study of Christian history in which Methodism was given extended treatment, and *Battle for the Mind*, by W. Sargant,[82] which included an ingenious, but historically irrelevant, description of the nature of Wesleyan religious conversion. Jabez Bunting now ceased to be the political despot and became the mentally twisted head of an organization dedicated to the subversion of the poor.

> In Bunting and his fellows we seem to touch upon a deformity of the sensibility complementary to the deformities of the factory children whose labour they condoned. In all the copious correspondence of his early ministries in the industrial heartlands . . . among endless petty Connexional disputes, moralistic humbug, and prurient enquiries into the private conduct of young women, neither he nor his colleagues appear to have suffered a single qualm as to the consequences of industrialism.[83]

Certainly, his son's biography does not suggest that Bunting doubted the value of the factory system.[84] The period in question was 1805–14, when he was stationed in Manchester, Sheffield, Liverpool, Halifax and Leeds. In 1812 he was at Halifax, where many of the Methodists were poor artisans who suffered from the introduction of new machinery and from the high price of food, so that they were tempted to join the Luddites. If Bunting opposed violence, he also organized relief for his members. If, as his son implies, he succeeded in keeping his poorer members out of trouble, perhaps this was as much as could have been expected in a man who was never as unusual as has sometimes been

[81] Gordon Rattray Taylor, *The Angel-Makers: A Study in the Psychological Origins of Historical Change 1750–1850* (London 1958).
[82] William Sargant, *Battle for the Mind: A Physiology of Conversion and Brainwashing* (London 1957).
[83] E. P. Thompson, op. cit., p. 354.
[84] T. P. Bunting, *The Life of J. Bunting.* Thompson produced no other evidence.

asserted, himself then a young man in a society which had for the moment identified the democratic revolution with anti-Christianity.[85] It is true that Bunting showed no extraordinary sensibility in these affairs; but did this, in 1812, mean a 'deformity of sensibility'? As for the prurient inquiries, it is not clear what Thompson intended, but the correspondence contained in the biography suggests that the young ministers were fond of discussing the suitability of young women as parsons' wives. In these letters, money and religion predominate, and there seems no particular trace of prurience.

According to Thompson, the Methodism which Bunting directed was

a phenomenon almost diabolic in its penetration into the very sources of the human personality, directed towards the repression of emotional and spiritual tendencies.

Thompson did not choose to criticize Methodist conversions in the early nineteenth century (as he might more safely have done) as having become a ritualized form of entry into an inherited society, but described them as 'the psychic ordeal in which the character-structure of the rebellious pre-industrial labourer or artisan was violently recast into that of the submissive industrial worker', a 'ritualised form of psychic masturbation'.[86] Thompson did not discuss the Wesleyan secessions in detail, but on his premises they might be regarded as occurring because the tamed Methodist industrial worker's thwarted revolutionary consciousness finally turned against those who had prevented its open political expression – an explanation which would have similarities with Dr Gowland's

[85] cf. R. R. Palmer, *The Age of the Democratic Revolution: A Political History of Europe and America, 1760–1800: The Struggle* (Princeton, N.J. 1964). The eighteenth-century Evangelical Revival had run against the main current of the century and so had been preserved against certain kinds of corruption; Methodism entered the nineteenth century in the midst of a much more general, more socially corrupted, politically defensive religiosity.

[86] E. P. Thompson, op. cit., pp. 367–8. At some points Thompson was mistaken: to call Wesleyanism the 'chiliasm of despair' misses a major distinction between Wesleyanism and Anglican Evangelicalism at this time; it was Evangelicalism which had a prophetic wing. Thompson's statement that Wesleyanism was obsessed with the sinfulness of sex and the sexual organs required evidence which he did not produce; it seems unlikely that Methodism varied from the nineteenth-century social norm for its class structure in this matter.

suggestion[87] that in the 1830s the Wesleyan radicals in Manchester were substituting ecclesiastical politics for the secular politics from which they felt excluded.

The statement that Wesleyan Methodism was one of the 'psychic components of the counter-revolution' is unconvincing. There is no evidence, for example, that 'conversion' is tied to any particular social behaviour: George Fox was a social radical, John Wesley a social conservative, and Shaftesbury both a critic of child labour in England and a supporter of British rule in India. Moreover, in discussing any religious denomination one must distinguish between the hard core of profoundly religious people and the majority of the membership, whose adherence has social rather than deeply religious roots. One would want evidence that conversion experiences made the minority, supposing them to have been factory workers in the first place, more passively obedient to the demands of their employers and the industrial system.

The statistical problem involved is considerable. E. A. Rose has done work on Droylsden, near Manchester, which changed from a village into a small industrial town in the 1830s when cotton mills were built near the canal. In 1845 the population had become 5,500. The first Anglican rector of an independent parish, the Rev. P. Thompson, inquired of 450 families representing 2,493 people in 1845 as to their religious attendance. He found that there were 38 Wesleyan Methodist families, 30 Anglican, 7 Primitive Methodist, 6 Moravian, 5 Independent, 3 Roman Catholic, 2 Baptist, 2 Methodist New Connexion, 1 Quaker and 1 Unitarian, leaving 355 families which made no religious profession at all. These families included 1,352 children, of whom 260 attended the Wesleyan Sunday School, 180 the Anglican, 68 the Moravian, 65 the New Connexion, 50 the Primitive Methodist and 10 the Roman Catholic. A parish church was built in 1848, after which presumably more Anglicans would have been recorded. Rose stresses the high proportion of those without religious connection:

From the beginning of the time when the urban working class

[87] See above, pp. 253-4.

was first created by the herding together of families from the countryside in the new industrial towns, these people, *as a class*, have been outside the church.[88]

There is no point in generalizing, but here is a specific instance. Were the 38 Wesleyan families fundamental to the development of the factory system in Droylsden? Primitive Methodism, which has sometimes been regarded as typical of working-class religious movements in the nineteenth century, was thin on the ground, though 1810–1850 was its chief period of growth.[89] More significant from the Methodist point of view was the fact that, of the 633 children who attended Sunday Schools, 375 went to the various Methodist bodies; but these infants are not likely to have been converted in Thompson's sense before they left again. The Wesleyan membership in Droylsden was 59 in 1829, when the population was 2,900; 107 in 1866, when the population was about 8,000. A later (and last) generation of Wesleyan mill-owners, the Byrom family, of whom Joseph (1813–1888) was the founder, provided the capital for expansion in the late nineteenth century, when the membership rose to a peak of 411 in 1892, in a population of 9,500.

It is not clear that what W. Sargant and E. P. Thompson meant by 'conversion' ever took place at all. This does not mean that there was no link between religion and the mills. In 1831, for instance, one finds Thomas and David Whitehead writing

of the glorious work of God amongst our work-people in the mill. . . . About 8 or 10 weeks back, Mr. Slack held a prayer meeting after the Sunday evening Service. Ed. Ashworth, watchman, was there, and laboured under very strange convictions, but did not make it known at that time. . . . while on the watch he poured out his soul to God in prayer, and in his deep distress found the Lord to bless and give him peace. . . . Since his conversion, James Cunliffe, weaver, John Lonsdale, Dresser,

---

[88] E. A. Rose, *Methodism in Droylsden 1776–1963* (Manchester 1963), pp. 18–19.
[89] cf. E. R. Wickham, *Church and People in an Industrial City* (London 1957); in fact, Primitive Methodism was not strong among factory workers.

John Collinge, Junr., weaving shop, and Reginald Hargreaves, weaver, all state that they have found peace with God.[90]

One should be cautious, however, of assuming that the weavers were going to be less independent than they had been before. In any case it is not necessary to assume this in order to explain the gradual formation of an orderly race of factory workers. The employers disciplined their 'hands' much as one would have expected. They blacklisted awkward men throughout a locality and resisted the formation of trade unions which would strengthen the men's bargaining power; they used corporal punishment, especially on children at the beginning of the century; they offered incentive payments, made threats of dismissal and levied fines for irregular timekeeping. There was nothing mysterious about all this, nor was there any need to dress it up with labels like 'counterrevolution'. Still less need one be surprised if Bunting and other ministers did not know much about what was going on. Wesleyan Methodism did not play a major role in breaking the spirit of the former rural labourer and turning him into a submissive factory 'hand' – taking the nineteenth century as a whole, it is not so obvious that anyone did. That it was Anglicanism which provided most of the religious energy behind the Factory Movement is undeniable, but when one seeks to explain the much smaller part played by the Wesleyan Methodists one must remember the kind of social philosophy which inspired men like Richard Oastler and William Ferrand. They

> represented an ancient Toryism, local, paternal, and long 'outdated' in 'progressive' circles. They adopted traditional dislike of centralisation against Benthamite social planning, and old doctrines of social cohesion against liberal individualism. They announced no strictly 'new' philosophies, but sought to leaven squirearchic Toryism's defence of Church and State by stressing the social duties of both.[91]

Bunting might sometimes call himself a 'Tory' but he had

[90] E. H. Taylor, *History of Longholme Wesleyan Chapel and Schools* (Rawtenstall 1921), p. 30.
[91] J. T. Ward, *The Factory Movement 1830–1855*, p. 422.

little contact with the social groups which favoured ideas like these. In his own more limited sphere Bunting supported 'centralisation', and exalted the tradition of obedience over that of individualism, but he could not draw on the traditions of the squirearchy for a doctrine of economic responsibility. As in so many other issues at this time, Wesleyanism did not quite know where it stood, and it is significant that it was from the Primitive Methodists, rooted in groups which disliked the Church of England and were instinctively hostile to the urban middle class, that the chief Dissenting support for the Factory Movement came.

The most thoroughgoing attempt to construct a theory of nineteenth-century Methodist history, *Methodism Divided*, by R. Currie, still depends upon a picture of a rather Neronic Bunting, though here the influence was less that of Halévy than of E. R. Taylor, for Dr Currie describes his villain as perverting the 'natural' line of Wesleyan Methodist growth. For Dr Currie the issue is social rather than political. He begins from the thesis that 'the chapel is the central fact of Methodism',[92] and explains the division of 1849 as the outcome of a struggle between the conflicting claims of this essentially lay chapel society on the one hand, and of the Wesleyan ministry on the other. Dr Currie regards Bunting (and not John Wesley) as the creator of this authoritarian caste, which he developed after 1800 when the Connexion seemed to be collapsing into chaos under the weak leadership of Coke.

> Bunting's excesses were so gross that few can have imagined them necessary to rectify the marginal weaknesses of Wesleyan organization misdirected by Coke and his fellow preachers. Nor could they seriously claim that the feebleness of Coke's leadership demanded the vigour of Bunting's tyranny to redress the balance.[93]

He concludes:

> Bunting's rule and doctrine established a Wesleyan priesthood in conflict with the Wesleyan people.[94]

[92] R. Currie, *Methodism Divided*, p. 44.
[93] ibid., p. 37.
[94] ibid., p. 42.

And so the people revolted and set up the United Methodist Free Churches, only, as Dr Currie sees it, to be betrayed once again by ecumenical leaders who persuaded them to return to something like their former servitude.

This is a one-sided argument: some passages in *Methodism Divided* read like a Free Methodist Victorian polemic against the Wesleyan tradition. Dr Currie exaggerates the extent to which Bunting played the tyrant and does not grasp the religious basis of Bunting's attitude, his sense of himself as the conscientious custodian of John Wesley's system. The local chapel was not meant to be the central feature of Wesleyanism by either Wesley or Bunting. Eighteenth-century Wesleyanism developed as a balanced system to which the religious societies (not chapels) and itinerant ministers (deliberately permitted to remain only for short periods at particular places) were equally necessary. Just as nineteenth-century Wesleyan reformers were entitled to argue that Wesleyanism should be 'reformed', so Jabez Bunting was entitled to regard the stress they laid on the autonomy of the local chapel as a departure from the original system which he ought to resist. John Wesley's Methodism was much more unusual than it appears if it is presented as no more than a variation on a standard Nonconformist meeting-house tradition. Wesley's originality for the historian of religion lies in his effort to devise a new model of the Christian life in an eighteenth-century culture which was rapidly divesting itself of the classical Christian assumptions about what constitutes human perfection (the model of the anti-economic man, one might call it). The perfected Wesleyan was to live and work in the ordinary world without allowing his relation to God to be corrupted by civil society; he would attain the goal of Christian holiness within the Wesleyan society but without withdrawing from the world.

The obvious danger in such a method of spiritual culture was complacency, an individual or collective failure in self-criticism. Therefore the itinerant's role was that of pastoral critic of his society's members. This role required authority, the right to expect obedience, and it was natural for John Wesley as an Anglican to see this authority as inherent in the pastoral office, as a power which he could delegate to his itinerants, and which Bunting's ministers could regard as theirs by virtue of their office. Wesley added the claim to direct his followers' political ideas because Christian perfection required total control of one's behaviour, politics included: politics, as the nineteenth-century Wesleyan Conference frequently said in its Annual Address, aroused many undesirable emotions.

Jabez Bunting tried to maintain this system between 1805 and 1845. Perhaps it was inevitable that to the generation of the 1840s his conservatism should seem to the laity more concerned with the authority of the ministry than with the holiness of the laity. Yet one should not think of Bunting primarily in political terms, as a tyrant finally overthrown by liberal reformers. His was a religious tragedy, not a political defeat. It is not even exact to say that his mission was to change Wesleyanism from a 'society' into a 'church': it is not exact because in a sense he was trying to preserve Wesleyanism as a 'society'. He wanted to preserve the balance of forces which seemed to him fundamental to the expansion of the whole.[95] There was a complete contradiction between those who believed that eighteenth-century Wesleyanism had been a band of brothers and those who believed that the key to success had been, not the comparative equality of the laity and the first itinerants, but the tension between the societies and the pastoral absolutism of John Wesley. And one has to remember that for years statistics, in which nineteenth-century Methodists believed very deeply,[96] seemed to tell on Bunting's side. In 1801 the Connexion returned 89,529 members; in 1821, despite troubles ranging from politics to revivalism, the figure had become 200,074; in 1831, despite the Leeds affair and the rapid growth of Primitive Methodism, the total was 249,119; and even in 1841, after the Wesleyan Associationists had seceded, expansion had continued to

[95] cf. the so-called 'Liverpool Resolutions', issued at Bunting's prompting by the Conference of 1820; cf. above, Chap. III, p. 115. These essentially recalled the itinerants to eighteenth-century methods: for example, more open-air preaching; cf. *Minutes of the Wesleyan Conference*, 1820, pp. 148–53.

[96] It was, for example, an article of faith, widely held, that God would grant major membership increases to the denomination which possessed the polity nearest to the Divine mind.

328,792. If one calculates this membership figure as a percentage of population, there was an increase from 0.85 per cent in 1801 to 1.77 per cent in 1841; in 1851, however, when membership had fallen to 302,209, this had become 1.45 per cent, and in fact the ground was never made good, for the membership in 1901 (454,982) represented only 1.23 per cent of the population.[97] Between 1805 and 1845, the years of his effective power, however, Bunting could regard his defence of the traditional order as justified; he, and many others, saw the demands of the reformers as the product of over-abstract, even secular, thinking about church politics. This did not mean that Bunting did not appreciate the reformers' dislike of the authority of the Wesleyan itinerants, but that he interpreted it as wrong-headed, even sinful, as a refusal to accept the need for a divinely appointed spiritual director with power to interfere in one's private and public life on religious grounds. In the checks and balances of John Wesley's system the class leader (a layman) was supposed to keep smooth the relation between itinerant and members; but the heart of the system was the absolute power which Wesley had bequeathed to the pastors, and in the nineteenth century the class leaders – of course, there were individual exceptions – fell into the background. Here Wesley anticipated the Anglo-Catholic movement. If one takes seriously what the Wesleyan ministry was trying to do, the Victorian gibes about 'the hundred Popes of England's Jesuitry' do not seem so wide of the mark: the apparent ruthlessness with which the ministers expelled members in 1849 has to be understood in this religious context.[98] It was inevitable that 'pastoral prerogative' be defended to the last ditch, for without it there might be a sort of Christianity, but there could not be Wesleyanism in the last analysis; Wesleyanism meant not mutual spiritual direction but pastoral direction, and the 'pastorate' could not be reduced to the 'preaching ministry' which was the most that many of the reformers would tolerate. Bunting would have

[97] cf. the figures given in R. Currie, op. cit., pp. 87–90. I agree with Currie that 1800–50 was a 'boom period' in British religion, and that 1850–1900 was a time of decline.

[98] A failure to take seriously the religious context seems to me to explain the weaknesses of many modern books on Methodist early nineteenth-century history.

preferred to see the method vanish before he would agree to change it; he was the 'last Wesleyan' because he was still fighting to preserve the whole system intact, whereas a man like J. H. Rigg, to whom at first sight the description might seem more appropriate, knew that compromise had become inevitable.

In June 1850, Jabez Bunting, ageing and embattled, visited Leeds and spoke at a Public Breakfast given in his honour by Leeds Wesleyan Methodists. His speech summed up his creed. He began by assessing the role of the laity. He believed, he said, in ministers seeking

> the co-operation of our lay brethren. . . . I think we ought to be made one. . . . I think our people ought to have security that they shall not be oppressed by any man. That security I think they have. . . . I am no universal suffrage man. We must not be governed by mere considerations of theory. . . . We are not Independents. We are Wesleyan Presbyterians. It is a peculiar form and organization of presbyterianism, but the presbyterian principle is our principle.[99]

As for changes, there must be evidence of a general desire for change before the constitution is altered.

> Surely, we have better work to do than to squabble about minute points of ecclesiastical order. . . . The result of my observations about this constitution mending is, that it is the idlest work that good men ever go to. Men set about mending the constitution, but do they mend their own tempers by it? Do they add to the comfort of their fellow creatures? I think not.[100]

From the problem of the laity he turned to the problem of the pastoral ministry. He talked of this in terms of what he called the law of purity:

> The Christian Church, though it may not be a perfect body, yet, in a very high and important sense, as far as human regulation and human vigilance can keep it, ought to be a pure body. We must not have unholy men – men notoriously and undeniably

[99] Dr Bunting's Visit to Leeds, June 19th, 1850 (Leeds 1850), p. 23.
[100] ibid., p. 27.

such – within the pale of our Methodism. We must not allow such men, from any fear of Christian discipline, administered affectionately and kindly, to deprive us of our Purity. . . . There must be persons invested with some degree of responsibility and some degree of power. Where there is duty, there must be power to carry that duty into effect; and those should not receive the power who have not the responsibility. I think that this consideration has, in a great measure, been lost sight of. . . . Talk of the power of the preachers! Why, they would be a very odd set of preachers if they had no power. They would not be the preachers of the New Testament. They would not be the order of preachers which the Scriptures recognize, men especially called of God, and then especially set apart by the concurrence of the church – the ministry and the people together – to take charge, as its pastors, of the Purity of the body. If we are to have that charge, we must have power. We may exercise it erroneously in many instances, but that is no argument for abolishing the power. What is there that may not be abused, if men are not so wise and holy as they should be?[101]

Since the above was written, further contributions have been made to the history of Wesleyanism in this period. Among the most original is *The Methodist Revolution* (1974) by the American scholar, Bernard Semmel. Taking up R. R. Palmer's view that the years from 1760 to 1815 were 'an age of democratic revolution' in Europe and America, he suggests that the Wesleyan revival was the English equivalent of this 'democratic revolution', and that its theology, which he thought had been neglected by historians, formed a liberal and progressive ideology, in the sense that it helped to bring forward the change from the *ancien régime* to modern society. A Methodist non-violent revolution saved England from violent secular revolution. At the same time, Semmel describes the Wesleyan leaders as redirecting the evangelistic energies of Wesleyanism into the overseas mission fields as a calculated way of drawing off enthusiasm which might otherwise have threatened domestic stability. It is difficult, however, to see Jabez Bunting as an unconscious 'revolutionary democrat'; the shift from the theological ideas of free will and free grace

---

[101] ibid., pp. 25–6.

to the political ideas of liberty and equality is not as plausible as Semmel makes it seem: Jabez Bunting certainly believed in free grace and as certainly disbelieved in democracy. Nor is there much evidence to sustain the argument that Methodist overseas missions were a kind of imperialist distraction for the Wesleyan masses.

The most useful new work is Professor W. R. Ward's edition of Jabez Bunting's surviving correspondence. In 1972 he edited *The Early Correspondence of Jabez Bunting 1820–1829* (Camden Fourth Series, Volume 11); and in 1976 he completed the task in *Early Victorian Methodism: The Correspondence of Jabez Bunting 1830–1858*. These books have deepened our knowledge of how the Wesleyan Connexion worked, while confirming the view that Bunting's own stature has been exaggerated, especially through the influence of Benjamin Gregory's *Side Lights on the Conflicts of Methodism*.

VII

The Rise of Other Methodist Traditions

———◦⊖◦———

JOHN T. WILKINSON

FOLLOWING the death of Wesley a Connexional crisis in Methodism was inevitable, and Wesley himself had anticipated in some measure this possibility. As far back as 1766 he knew of a demand for

> a free Conference; that is, a meeting of all the Preachers, wherein all things shall be determined by most votes. . . . It is possible, after my death, something of this kind may take place. But not while I live. To *me* the Preachers have engaged themselves to submit, to 'serve me as *sons in the gospel*'. . . . To *me* the people in general will submit. But they will not yet submit to any other.[1]

Three years later Wesley ventured the suggestion that there would be a break in unity, and that the Connexion would fall into three groups: some, 'perhaps a fourth of the whole number' would seek to 'procure preferment in the Church'; others would 'turn Independents and get separate congregations'; the main portion would 'preserve a firm union . . . to preach the *old Methodist doctrines* and . . . observe and enforce the whole *Methodist discipline*'.[2] In 1784 Wesley crystallized his desires for the future structure of Methodism by the Deed of Declaration, appointing a 'Conference' consisting of one hundred preachers and setting forth their duties in detail for the government of the Connexion. Wesley envisaged as little change as possible: doctrine must remain unaltered and the

---

[1] *Minutes of Wesleyan Conference*, 1812 edn, i (1766), 60.
[2] *Minutes*, 1812 edn, i (1769), 88–9 from a Paper read by John Wesley to the Conference, 4 August.

itinerancy must be upheld. The Conference was to assume his place, and as he had brought the preachers into consultation, so this 'Legal Hundred' was to act in a similar way. This concern of Wesley was reinforced by a letter which he wrote from Chester on 7 April 1785:

> I beseech you, by the mercies of God, that you never avail yourselves of the Deed of Declaration, to assume any superiority over your Brethren; but let all things go on . . . exactly in the same manner as when I was with you, so far as circumstances will permit. . . . do all things with a single eye, as I have done from the beginning. . . . without prejudice or partiality.[3]

Thus

> the autocracy of the Hundred was to be equal to Wesley's own, and was to be wielded with the same kindliness and supreme regard for the work of God as he had manifested.[4]

Whilst the Deed of Declaration secured the permanence of the societies as a 'Connexion', certain matters remained untouched. The document was 'as eloquent in its silence as in its speech'. The government was to be exclusively in the hands of the preachers, yet whilst this had been the case in Wesley's lifetime, the transference of authority to a corporate body involved a new situation in terms of new relationships. The preachers who had been regarded by Wesley as his 'assistants' would now assume a different status. It would seem that Wesley did not realize both how far he himself had gone towards constituting a separate Church and how far this demand on the part of the people for their own Church had developed. The Deed of Declaration was a far-sighted proposal, but it did not go far enough. In the structure of the Connexion, the laity were completely ignored in matters of administration.

Wesley died on 2 March 1791. Four weeks later, on 30 March, nine preachers met at Halifax, and issued a circular letter addressed 'To the METHODIST-PREACHERS in general, and to

---

[3] *Minutes*, 1812 edn, i (1791), 234; *Letters*, vii, 266.
[4] *N.H.M.*, i, 382.

the *Conference* and *Assistants*, in particular'.[5] The following is an extract:

> There appears [*sic*] to us but two ways: either to appoint another King in Israel; or to be governed by the Conference Plan, by forming ourselves into Committees. If you adopt the first, who is the Man? What Power is he to be invested with? . . . But *this is incompatible* with the *Conference Deed*. If the latter, we take the Liberty to offer our Thoughts upon that Subject.

To prevent this, the writers urged that a President and Secretary of the Conference should be elected annually; District Committees should act during intervals between Conferences, each to have its own President to be appointed annually. It soon became known that the majority of the preachers approved the Halifax proposals. This was the initial step in facing the fundamental problems which confronted Methodism after the death of Wesley. It was the problem of leadership. The Rubicon had now been crossed, and henceforth Methodism was to be established 'on a system of government broadly conciliar rather than monarchical'.[6]

In facing the issues of 'our future plan of economy' the Conference of 1791 had declared its intention: 'We engage to follow strictly the plan which Mr. Wesley left us at his death.'[7] This assertion, however, involved some ambiguity, particularly in one respect, namely its relation to the established Church. This matter remained undetermined, but also presented a further problem. On the one hand there were the 'Church Methodists' who followed Wesley in asserting that any separation was undesirable, despite the fact that 'Methodist places of worship were licensed under the Toleration Act, as Dissenting conventicles, many Methodist preachers as Dissenting preachers'. On the other hand, there were those who, whilst not desiring a formal break with the Church, yet realized that Methodism was 'a growing, a developing organism' and, also following Wesley, wished to continue his

[5] George Smith, *History of Wesleyan Methodism*, ii, Appendix E; Victor E. Vine, "Episcope" in Methodism', in *W.H.S. Proc.*, xxx (December 1956), 165.
[6] J. D. Walsh, in *H.M.G.B.*, i, 279.
[7] *Minutes*, 1812 edn, i (1791), 246.

'pragmatic tradition' of experimentation in the interests of an expanding evangelism.[8] This problem focused itself upon the question of the administration of the sacraments. Was such administration to be restricted to those preachers who were Methodist clergymen and preachers ordained by Wesley, or was it to 'follow the openings of divine providence'? It was abundantly clear that there was a growing demand for administration by the itinerant preachers as a whole.

At the Conference of 1792 this crucial issue was decided by lot, which fell out on the negative side.[9] For the next two years, with some reluctance, greater liberty was allowed. The position was further complicated by the question as to whether services should be allowed in church hours and also as to the degree in which Quarterly Meetings and Trustees should have any power of decision in the matter. Throughout the Connexion there was growing ferment in disputation. In 1795 the Plan of Pacification[10] brought decision, by throwing the responsibility on the societies themselves. It was agreed that the sacraments could be administered by persons authorized by the Conference, and each society must make its own choice. This decision was crucial: through it Methodism and the established Church became separate. The right to hold services in church hours and to administer the sacraments being thus determined, the serious crisis threatening a deep fissure in Methodism was past.

The most difficult problem facing the Conference of 1791, however, still remained. It was that of the relation of the layman to the administration of the Church. In June 1791, a company of about fifty laymen at Redruth, in Cornwall, issued a manifesto in which they formulated principles of church government which involved radical change. The 'members constituting every class . . . shall choose their Leader'; and the 'people in every society' shall choose the Society Stewards; . . . no preacher shall admit into, or expel from the society any member without the consent of a majority of such society; no person should be 'recommended

[8] H.M.G.B., i, 286.
[9] Minutes, 1812 edn, i (1792), 260, 262–3.
[10] Minutes, 1812 edn, i (1795), 322–6.

to Conference (or sent out) as a travelling preacher, without a certificate from the Stewards assembled at the quarterly meeting'. In addition, disapproval was expressed 'of the proposal for dividing the kingdom into districts'. They claimed the right to receive the ordinances at the hands of their own ministers and also freedom to worship at convenient hours; in church courts laymen should be allowed to co-operate with the preachers in matters of administration.[11] Such a position was not only in grave contrast to the pro-posals of the Halifax circular, but in direct opposition to that affirmed by Wesley himself on the question of lay representation.[12]

Another aspect of the problem was presented by the sacramental controversy which arose in Bristol in 1792, when Henry Moore, who had administered the sacrament, was in consequence prevented from preaching in two other chapels by the trustees who were 'Church Methodists'. The real issue was whether trustees had the right to prohibit a preacher who was ordained by Conference, for to admit such right con-stituted a dangerous precedent. The important issue of lay control was at stake.[13]

This question of the relation between the preachers and the laity was to precipitate 'the grand crisis of Methodism',[14] and this was to remain the major problem for the next half-century and beyond.

To the issues which arose in the first half of the nineteenth century we now turn, and in this period we shall be largely concerned with origins and early developments.

I

The first challenge to this growing situation of tension in the

[11] G. Smith, op. cit., ii, 85–7; J. Blackwell, *Life of the Rev. Alexander Kilham, formerly a preacher under the Rev. J. Wesley; and one of the founders of the Methodist New Connexion in the year 1797. Including a full account of the disputes which occasioned the separation* (London 1838), p. 137; *W.H.S. Proc.*, xxx, 165.

[12] *Letters*, viii, 196: 'As long as I live the people shall have no share in choosing either stewards or leaders among the Methodists. We have not and never had any such custom. We are no republicans, and never intend to be. It would be better for those that are so minded to go quietly away.'

[13] cf. *H.M.G.B.*, i, 283–4.

[14] Jonathan Crowther, *A True and Complete Portraiture of Methodism* (1811), p. 133.

Connexion focused itself in the person of Alexander Kilham (1762–98),[15] who at the death of Wesley was an itinerant preacher of six years' standing. Born in Epworth, he had been accepted by Wesley in 1785 as one of his preachers, and it was very early in his ministry that he found himself facing the issue of church government. Licensed under the Toleration Act as a Dissenting minister, he encountered a personal problem regarding the baptism of his second child, for he objected on principle to the proposal that the rite should be administered by a clergyman. Kilham's antipathy to the established Church became stronger and he came to affirm his conviction in no uncertain terms. 'Our being so closely connected with the church cannot be looked on in any other light than as a species of trimming between God and the world.'[16]

He was first led to take up his pen following the issue of a letter sent by the trustees in Hull to the stewards of the Connexion on 4 May 1791, the object of which was three-fold: to prevail upon the Methodists not to profess themselves Dissenters, nor to establish worship in church hours, but to repair to the parish church for the purpose of receiving the sacrament. Kilham's reply to 'the signal gun' fired from Hull was in the form of an anonymous circular, which, to conceal its authorship, was posted at York, and was sent to Newcastle upon Tyne, so that the friends there, having already received the Hull letter, would answer as they deemed best. Kilham's letter was adopted, with trifling alterations, and became extensively circulated as an antidote to the Hull communication. It was moderate in tone and judicious in statement and expressed affection for Wesley, but Kilham indicated that many Methodists never took the sacrament of the Lord's Supper because they could not conscientiously receive it from ungodly ministers and with manifestly unworthy communicants at the parish church; some preferred to take it with Dissenting congregations and some preachers even ceased to insist on the ordinance as an obligation for the same reason.

[15] J. Blackwell, op. cit.; W. J. Townsend, *Alexander Kilham, the First Methodist Reformer* (London 1889).
[16] J. Blackwell, op. cit., p. 162.

He argued that in fact Methodists were *de facto* Dissenters, and that consistency demanded that they should accept the fact and recognize that their own preachers possessed all qualifications necessary to enable them to administer the ordinance. The circular was accompanied by a prayer marked by true charity:

> If it be for Thy glory that we should separate from the Established Church in these lands, dispose the hearts of the people to submit cheerfully to it; if it be most for Thy glory to continue as we are, reconcile all our minds to it.[17]

By the Conference of 1791 Kilham was appointed to the Newcastle upon Tyne circuit. The supernumerary preacher, Joseph Cownley, one of Wesley's ordained preachers, had consented to administer the sacrament, in consequence of which certain members had severed themselves from the society, and one, Robert Grey, wrote a letter of severe reprimand, which he eventually published. Kilham was aroused by this injustice and published a pamphlet: 'An Address to the Members and Friends of the Newcastle Society'. This attracted great attention and brought expressions of approval from many quarters.[18] At the following Conference Kilham was heavily censured and his pamphlet condemned. Stressing the view that in these pages Kilham had written injuriously of Wesley, Dr Coke moved for expulsion, but this was not entertained.[19]

In 1792 Kilham was appointed to Aberdeen, which proved to be a congenial situation; there was no problem in regard to the administration of the sacrament, as this was generally observed in the chapels in Scotland. Further he observed the operation of the presbyterian system of church government in which the ministry and the laity were co-ordinated. From now onwards he became increasingly absorbed concerning the extension to the laity of the governing power of the Church. It was under these strong convictions that in 1791 he published a letter signed 'Trueman and Freeman', which he sent

[17] ibid., p. 136; W. J. Townsend, op. cit., pp. 28–9.
[18] J. Blackwell, op. cit., pp. 150–1.
[19] ibid., pp. 157–70.

to leading preachers and laymen throughout the Connexion. In this letter he indicated that numerous petitions and addresses sent to the last two Conferences both by societies and by private persons had been left unexamined. These had been concerned with matters of administration. He dealt with the question of the appointment of leaders, stewards and local preachers, the recommendation of men for the ministry, and the management of finances, and further suggested that these issues should be decided by meetings composed of both preachers and laymen. He went even further by raising the question: 'Would it not be proper for every circuit or every district to be represented in Conference by a delegate of its own choosing?' This letter, received with approval by the Newcastle society, was reprinted and widely circulated.

The situation became intensified for Kilham when the famous 'Lichfield Plan'[20] became known. Several preachers, meeting secretly, had decided to recommend to the Conference that a number of 'bishops', under the name of 'superintendents' and with powers to ordain, should be appointed. The proposal was promptly vetoed by the Conference of 1794, but early in 1795 it formed the subject of a pamphlet from Kilham's pen, urged to the conflict by his friends who were against the 'Bishops Plan'. It was written with severity and sent forth over the signature of 'Martin Luther'.

The controversy at Bristol in 1794, in which the main issue was whether the trustees had the right to interfere with ministerial appointments or to forbid the administration of the sacrament where a society desired it, brought a further pamphlet from Kilham, signed 'Aquila and Priscilla', in which he clearly expounded the principles involved in the quarrel.[21]

To the 1795 Conference at Manchester Kilham took a manuscript which he had written, and signed 'Paul and Silas', and which he printed there for circulation amongst the preachers. He sought to show that, although Wesley's plan of organization should not be regarded as final, its implications were progressive. Many things done by the preachers since Wesley's death would not have been viewed by him with

[20] ibid., pp. 188–9; cf. H.M.G.B., i, 280.
[21] ibid., pp. 195–204.

approval, but in matters of administration the Scriptures formed the basis of authority. Kilham concluded by suggesting methods of procedure which would increase efficiency.

Although the Plan of Pacification was accepted by the majority at the Conference of 1795, an influential minority remained dissatisfied. Kilham drew up an address, signed by fifty-eight preachers, in which he asked for the explanation of ambiguous phrases, while at the same time approving the plan as an instalment. He was disappointed that no reform was suggested of the constitution of Conference by the inclusion of lay representatives, but he was pleased at the proposal concerning the administration of the sacrament. In his manuscript diary of the Conference proceedings he declared:

> 1. We have gained a great deal more than we expected. 2. Our people are not prepared for more at present. 3. In two or three years we shall have all that we wish. These are the sentiments of many of us.[22]

He was disturbed, however, to note that the preachers still retained ultimate authority; they could withdraw the rights they had granted.

By the time of this Conference Kilham was stationed at Alnwick, and his return to English Methodism convinced him more deeply that, the measure of reform notwithstanding, matters should be pressed still further. He therefore prepared an account of the various steps taken by Methodism since the death of Wesley and added an outline of such constitution as on a scriptural basis he believed to be necessary: this document, *The Progress of Liberty, amongst the People called Methodists. To which is added the Out-lines of a Constitution. Humbly recommended to the serious consideration of the Preachers and People, late in connection with Mr. Wesley*, proved to be his most important writing. He urged that, despite the concessions already announced, something was needed 'to prevent any preacher from acting contrary to the interests of the society as well as to make the preachers act in concert with each other'; furthermore, that the consent of members should be obtained for the

[22] ibid., p. 225.

admission and expulsion of members, and for the appointment of class-leaders; that lay preachers should be examined and be approved by leaders' and circuit meetings; that any preacher proposed for the itinerancy should be approved by the circuit meeting; that lay delegates should be appointed by circuits to district meetings and by district meetings to the Conference of Preachers 'to transact the affairs both spiritual and temporal' along with them. The document was a moving plea for liberty in matters of religion.

> Liberty of conscience is one of the most valuable blessings which a people can enjoy. It leaves every person perfectly free to examine all the doctrines and discipline of the different national churches and dissenting congregations, . . . Every thing is rejected that does not agree with the word of God: which is the only and sufficient rule, both of our faith and practice. . . . In these nations we have a very great portion of liberty of conscience. Our excellent laws allow us to prove all things in religion, and to hold fast that which is good. . . . Is it not amazingly strange that any sect or party should refuse to give to their brethren what the laws of our country so cheerfully allow?[23]

The Progress of Liberty brought to a crisis the widespread opposition to Kilham. At the instigation of certain London ministers[24] he was summoned to appear before the Newcastle District Meeting for trial, from which the matter was deferred until the Conference should meet.[25] In a pamphlet he strongly protested the sincerity of his intentions towards the Connexion. As the Conference drew near he found that the determined attitude of the London preachers had caused some of his friends to waver in their support; nevertheless, the opinion that representatives from the societies might reasonably be admitted to the Conference was gaining ground amongst the preachers as well as the people. Undaunted, Kilham prepared for the final issue.

[23] Kilham, *The Progress of Liberty amongst the People called Methodists* (Alnwick 1795), pp. 18–19.
[24] *The London Methodistical Bull*, 5 December 1795; J. Blackwell, op. cit., pp. 243–4; A. Kilham, *A Candid Examination of the London Methodistical Bull* (1796).
[25] A. Kilham, *A Short Account of the Trial of Alex. Kilham, Methodist Minister, at a special District Meeting held at Newcastle, On the 18th, 19th, and 20th, of February, 1796* (Alnwick 1796).

The trial took place at the 1796 Conference in Wesley's Chapel, City Road, London. Kilham's works were examined and passages considered to be abusive were named. His request that he should be given a copy of the charges laid against him was not allowed; it would certainly have been reasonable to grant it. The Conference considered the answers which he gave to be 'insufficient' and protested that his writings had exercised a wide and disturbing influence; he was expelled on 28 July 1796.[26]

Six days after his expulsion Kilham wrote a moving letter[27] to the President of the Conference, pleading that he might still be allowed to preach the gospel, if only as a layman. He received a curt reply:

> We consider your sufferings as the effect of your imprudence. If you wished your letter to be understood as an acknowledgment of your fault . . . a few of the preachers shall be authorised to meet and converse with you.[28]

The meeting took place, and it was demanded that Kilham should bind himself to the Plan of Pacification, taken in its literal sense that he thereby indicated his recantation, and it was further demanded that he should desist from any criticism. These demands Kilham could not accept and the parting became final.

It should be noted that no charge was made against Kilham's character, teaching or abilities, and, recognizing the nature of the court – which was part of the system he condemned – he acknowledged his trial as fair. The door remained open for his return, but he was not prepared to pay the price of submission and silence.

It cannot be denied that Kilham was an intrepid reformer, whose sole concern was for the welfare of the Church, which he deeply loved, and for the progress of the gospel. The numerous prayers scattered throughout his diary and else-

[26] *Minutes*, 1812 edn, i (1796), 347; J. Blackwell, op. cit., pp. 262–89; A. Kilham, *An Account of the Trial of Alexander Kilham, Methodist Preacher, before the General Conference in London: On the 26th, 27th, and 28th July, 1796* (Nottingham 1796); *A Defence of the Account* . . . (Leeds 1796); *Minutes of the Examination of Mr Alexander Kilham before the General Conference in London . . . 1795*.

[27] J. Blackwell, op. cit., pp. 285–6.

[28] W. J. Townsend, op. cit., p. 72.

where bear witness to the quality of this concern. His zeal sometimes led him into undue warmth of utterance and his writings are at times marked by biting sarcasm,[29] for which he later expressed his regrets; but these were days when plain speaking was not unusual. To some measure he suffered undoubted injustice at the hands of his accusers and was at times in the wilderness through the disloyalty of his friends. The flame of zeal which burned within him led to impatience on his part with the situation as he found it, but greater insight upon the part of those who arraigned him would have prevented his expulsion; a deeper understanding could have prevented a final break. It is difficult to dismiss the judgment of W. J. Townsend:

> Looking at the whole procedure apart from the dust and din of the distant controversy, it is impossible not to conclude that the sentence of expulsion was unmerited, and that he was not treated with either charity or justice by the Conference. The die, however, was now cast, and he had perforce to go out. . . ., not knowing whither he went.[30]

The fact that the far-sighted suggestions opened up by Kilham's numerous writings were later largely adopted in Methodism is the true vindication of the soundness of his demands.

Kilham continued after his expulsion to touch the Methodist societies by the publication, in October 1796, of *The Methodist Monitor*, which was continued monthly until January 1798. Although he found growing sympathy with his proposals for reform, he had still to face calumny from some quarters. At this time any challenge to authority was suspected of being infected with the principles of the French Revolution, and it was proclaimed that Kilham was a Jacobin and a follower of Thomas Paine. Sadly enough there were those who in print threw aspersions upon his character and career as a minister.[31] Clearly feeling ran high on both sides.

[29] Kilham's pamphlet, *The London Methodistical Bull*, bore a crude woodcut representing a mad bull belching forth flame and smoke.

[30] *Alexander Kilham*, p. 77.

[31] J. Pawson & A. Mather, *An Affectionate Address to the Members of the Methodist Society, in Leeds, and Elsewhere; Respecting the Late Transactions at Bristol; by Onesimus* (Leeds 1794), p. 8.

At many centres committees were now formed and circulars were issued pressing for the reforms outlined in Kilham's *Constitution*, in particular that lay representatives should be appointed to assemble at the next Conference, to be held in 1797. In view of this a large delegation of trustees, together with other delegates from the circuits, gathered at Leeds. Negotiations between the Conference and these groups were conducted and some concessions were added to the Plan of Pacification. Most of the trustees seemed satisfied, but others from the circuits pressed for the further reforms outlined by Kilham. The Conference rejected the proposed admission of lay representatives into District Meetings. A further proposal that lay representatives should attend but meet apart from the preachers, and that no new legislation should be passed without their concurrence, was also refused. The concessions in the revised Plan of Pacification were 'improvements of considerable importance' and probably represented the degree of advance acceptable to the majority of Methodists, but they left the right of all nominations with the preacher, and forbade any meetings without his presence, and, above all, failed 'to bring together preachers and duly appointed representatives in the courts of the church'.[32]

Eventually the 'delegates of the people' believed that the final answer of the Conference left no alternative to separation. They were convinced that co-operation between preacher and people on a legalized basis was essential for the peace of the Church. On 9 August 1797 three preachers – William Thom, Stephen Eversfield and Alexander Cummin – left the Conference and met Kilham in Ebenezer Chapel, Leeds, and together they formed 'The New Itinerancy', later to be called 'The Methodist New Connexion'. In this there was to be close co-operation between preachers and laymen, and societies were to be formed wherever there were those in agreement. It was a separation 'with great reluctance' and the spirit of the assembled delegates was manifest in the following observation:

[32] *Minutes*, 1812 edn, i (1797), 360–3, 374–8: 'To the Methodist Societies August 7, 1797'.

Notwithstanding we are constrained to separate from our brethen, we hope we shall ever be ready to give them the right hand of fellowship: therefore members of the Old Connexion will be admitted at love-feasts and sacraments.

William Thom was chosen as President of the first Conference and Alexander Kilham as Secretary.[33]

From centres far and wide[34] people came forth, in all about five thousand, and this figure shows that five per cent of the Methodists carried their reforming zeal to the point of secession. For the immediate future the preaching ministry of the new denomination was held together by local preachers who rendered exceptional service, and the incessant labours of Kilham journeying far and wide in these early and difficult days brought encouragement and cohesion.[35]

At the second Conference, held in Sheffield, there were sixteen preachers and seventeen lay representatives from ten circuits. A constitution was adopted and presented to the circuits by Kilham and Thom. A general declaration of principles was set forth:

It was not from an affectation of singularity that determined us to proceed in supporting the rights and liberties of the people. . . . It was a conviction arising from Scripture that all the members of Christ's body are one; and that the various officers of it should act by the general approbation and appointment of the people.[36]

Kilham was stationed at Nottingham, but it was little more than a centre for his wide travels. His unremitting labours had taken toll of his health; though a sick man, he set off towards

[33] *Minutes of Conversations between Travelling Preachers and Delegates of the People late in Connexion with the Rev. Mr Wesley, held in Ebenezer Chapel, Leeds, in August 1797.*

[34] ibid., p. 8: Sheffield, Nottingham, Banbury, Burslem, Macclesfield, Chester, Liverpool, Wigan, Bolton, Blackburn, Manchester, Oldham, Huddersfield, Leeds, Epworth, Otley, Ripon, Newcastle, Alnwick, etc.

[35] The following give detailed accounts of the rise of the denomination: *A Brief Statement of the Dispute and Causes of the Division amongst the Methodists at Nottingham, Sheffield, Leeds, Manchester and many other places in the Kingdom* (Nottingham), September 14, 1797; *A Plain Account of the Methodist New Itinerancy* . . . by J. Grundell & W. Thom (Leeds 1797); *An Apology for the Methodists of the New Connexion* . . . (Hanley 1815) by A Trustee and Layman; *A Catechism of the Methodist New Connexion* . . . by D. Barton (London 1834).

[36] *Minutes* (Methodist New Connexion), (1798), p. 10.

the end of the year on a journey through Wales, where he suffered a serious collapse. Completing his journey, he returned home, and on 20 December 1798 he died at the age of thirty-six. He was buried at Hockley Chapel, Nottingham. Kilham's work as a reformer should not be allowed to obscure his main object, of evangelism; the spread of the gospel was his chief concern. As a reformer he was in advance of his time.

William Thom (1751–1811) succeeded Kilham as the leader of the New Connexion. Possessing a well-trained mind, 'he was the Melanchthon, as Kilham was the Luther, of reformed Methodism. . . '. He was six times President, and throughout the New Connexion was deferred to as a father.

> His constructive statesmanship equipped it with the necessary departments and funds; his calm, steady character consolidated its fellowship; his discourses, addressed rather to the understanding than to the emotions, his orderliness and culture, laid the lines of development which the Connexion never left. For a century afterwards its ministry more frequently resembled that of Thom than the burning evangelism of Kilham.[37]

During the first years of the New Connexion, various causes prevented its rapid progress.[38] At the end of ten years the membership had reached only 7,202, with less than 200 societies and 38 ministers. There were only 84 chapels. Some deserted when they found that the real freedom which the Connexion provided did not permit insubordination; others from worthier motives returned to the parent Connexion. Because the most populous parts were largely occupied by the parent Churches, the New Connexion sought to labour in other regions; in consequence its adherents became widely scattered, and the smallness of population in some areas prevented it taking root, sometimes because financial assistance was not available. There was also great difficulty in finding preachers; preachers' allowances were sadly insufficient,[39] and the burden of the work was often beyond their strength, so

[37] *N.H.M.*, i, 498–9.
[38] *An Apology for the Methodists of the New Connexion*, pp. 34–8.
[39] *Minutes* (Methodist New Connexion), (1798), p. 6.

that some gave up.[40] The early years proved 'a season of darkness and dismay'. A most difficult and distressing problem was that of obtaining chapels or meeting places, and not seldom the place of assembly was the home of some accommodating layman. In these early years there were cases involving unpleasant litigation, for it was found that trust deeds did not allow the transfer of chapels to the New Connexion, as the Wesleyan Connexion possessed legal right, even if the majority of the trustees preferred the new order.[41]

A further impediment to the spread of the community was the want of a legal foundation.[42] It was not until 1846 that a Deed Poll was adopted, defining the constitution of the Conference and its relation to the several parts of the Connexion, and legalizing the community in the persons of twenty-four – twelve ministers and twelve laymen – as 'guardian representatives'.[43] In the same year a Model Deed for trust property was approved.

As with Kilham, so with his followers: the failure of many both in the Old Connexion and outside it to understand the principles of liberty which marked the new community brought accusations upon its members of being Jacobins, Rebels, Levellers or Painite revolutionaries.

Despite these innumerable difficulties of the early years when the numbers 'diminished to a few', the loyalty of those who persisted was unmistakable and was recognized:

> To this faithful few, who safely steered our little vessel with its precious treasure into its desired haven, with delight do we revert; we record their character, their zeal and unabated fortitude.[44]

In 1817, Conference resolved to introduce the Connexion further afield. A Home Mission was established and the

[40] 'Of eighty-four preachers admitted in the first seventeen years, almost half the number resigned after an average service of six years' (N.H.M., i, 501).

[41] Minutes (Methodist New Connexion), (1813), p. 22: for example, Hockley Chapel, Nottingham.

[42] An Apology for the Methodists of the New Connexion, p. 35.

[43] The Deed Poll was enrolled in Chancery September 1846. There had been reluctance to enter into legal arrangements, and even as late as 1819 the Conference had rejected a Deed of Settlement.

[44] Minutes (Methodist New Connexion), (1809), p. 31.

Connexion was divided into ten Districts.[45] Missionaries were sent to Ireland[46] and to Scotland. In 1824 the Irish Mission became firmly established, William Cooke becoming its General Superintendent in 1836. In the same year, 'firmly believing it to be our duty to take a part in the great cause of Foreign Missions' the Liverpool Conference decided to send a missionary, John Addyman, to Upper Canada – the first venture in overseas enterprise.[47]

During the first half-century, in addition to its founders, Alexander Kilham and William Thom, the New Connexion produced men within its ministerial ranks who were marked by exemplary faithfulness and zeal. Amongst these the following may be named: John Grundell (1761–1815),[48] the blind preacher who edited a *Life* of Kilham, and was the first lay Secretary of the Conference; William Driver (1764–1831),[49] formerly a coal-miner, who became President on three occasions; Richard Watson,[50] who in 1811, after eight years of service, resigned the ministry with the New Connexion and returned to the Wesleyan Connexion, which he had left because of unjust imputations of heresy. Possessing great talent as a preacher and administrator, he might have become the leader of the denomination, but the New Connexion did not give him the opportunity for the development of his exceptional gifts. It was with mutual good will that he returned to the parent body and there won distinction as author of a *Life of Wesley*, *A Biblical and Theological Dictionary* and his famous *Theological Institutes*.

Certain laymen were outstanding as leaders in this period. William Smith (1763–1798),[51] of Hanley, took an important part in the early struggle for religious freedom by presenting the first petition to the Conference of the parent body, and

[45] ibid. (1818), p. 39.
[46] ibid. (1799), p. 16. In 1798 thirty-two stewards or leaders of the Lisburn Church had appealed to the Irish Conference in Dublin to admit lay representatives to the District Meetings and to Conference, but the appeal had been rejected; in 1799 they became part of the 'New Itinerancy'.
[47] ibid. (1836), p. 46.
[48] G. Packer (ed.), *The Centenary of the Methodist New Connexion 1797-1897* (London 1897), pp. 89–90.
[49] ibid., pp. 99–101.
[50] ibid., pp. 86–7; N.H.M., i, 501.
[51] ibid., p. 81.

his own home later became the place of assembly for the society; Robert Hall (d. 1827),[52] of Nottingham, a friend of Wesley, was twice elected Conference Secretary and by his wealth assisted the cause (he introduced Kilham to the Nottingham reformers in 1796); Samuel Heginbotham (1756–1829),[53] of Ashton-under-Lyne, was the outstanding financial administrator of the new community, and the architect of its funds for the care of disabled ministers and their widows, and for the support and education of ministers' children; William Black (1745–1835)[54] was a stalwart of the cause in Ireland from its beginning.

Another name must be noted for a very different reason. At the Halifax Conference of 1841, Joseph Barker was expelled from the Connexion on grounds of doctrinal unsoundness. He had published a pamphlet against creeds and formularies of every kind, and had instituted a periodical in which he denied the divine authority of baptism and so refused to administer the rite; he also denied any permanent obligation to observe the Lord's Supper. After his dismissal he did his utmost to divide the societies; chapels were wrested from the Connexion and were restored only after expensive litigation. The main area affected was Newcastle upon Tyne. To counteract the movement William Cooke was sent to the region, and on 9 August 1845 he successfully engaged Barker in public debate. The people at Newcastle presented Cooke with a copy of the *Encyclopaedia Britannica* in acknowledgment of his victory. Barker left for America where he lectured in support of infidelity, but later he regained his faith. Through this declension the Connexion suffered the loss of twenty-nine societies and 4,348 members, yet under the crisis its solidarity became strengthened.

In the Jubilee year of the Methodist New Connexion (1847) a Fund to raise £20,000 was proposed for the purpose of relieving distressed chapels, of establishing a ministerial training institute and supporting missionary operations both at home and overseas. The amount eventually raised, however,

[52] ibid., pp. 94–6.
[53] ibid., pp. 97–8.
[54] ibid., pp. 102–3.

was only £7,721. In this year the numbers of the Connexion were as follows: 19,289 members of society (including 3,201 in the Canadian Mission); 126 travelling preachers and missionaries; 776 local preachers; 579 societies and 327 chapels.

By this time, through many tribulations, reproaches and persecutions, the Methodist New Connexion had thoroughly established itself and proved its pioneering ability and its doggedness in the cause of religious liberty, a position from which it never swerved.

II

The Bible Christians[55] had their beginning as a denomination in a small group of farmhouses on the northern border of Devon and Cornwall, and arose out of the labours of a Methodist local preacher, William O'Bryan, from Luxulyan, in mid-Cornwall, who visited the area. It emerged as an evangelistic enterprise outside the control of the parent Methodism.

In seeking a true assessment two factors are important. First, it should be remembered that Methodism had been firmly established in Cornwall by Wesley himself; in the west country there were important centres at strategic points such as Taunton, Plymouth Dock and Exeter, from which special mission areas were planned following the Conference of 1805. It was within this context that the Bible Christian movement emerged. Secondly, it is important to possess a right estimate of the condition of the Church of England in this region. Earlier historians of the movement tend to leave the impression that the area was without any effective parish ministries. That there were cases of pluralism

[55] The following are the primary sources: William O'Bryan, *The Rise and Progress of the Connexion of People called Arminian Bible Christians* (1823); J. Thorne, *A Jubilee Memorial of Incidents in the Rise and Progress of the Bible Christian Connexion* (Newton Abbot 1865); F. W. Bourne, *The Bible Christians: Their Origin and History* (London 1905); Richard Pyke, *The Early Bible Christians* (London 1941); Thomas Shaw, *The Bible Christians 1815–1907* (London 1965). See also *Minutes of Conference* and *Bible Christian Magazine*; Oliver A. Beckerlegge, 'The Bibliography of the Bible Christians', in *W.H.S. Proc.*, xxxv, 45–50 (June 1965), 74–76 (September 1965), 100–4 (December 1965), 128–9 (March 1966).

and indeed of gross neglect cannot be denied, but the popular notion that the region was a spiritual wilderness is an exaggeration of the facts; this is made clear in the writings of more recent historians.[56]

William O'Bryan,[57] born on 6 February 1778 at Gunwen Farm in the parish of Luxulyan, was a man of restless temperament and wide interests. In his youth he experienced a spiritual crisis and made early efforts at personal evangelism. Beginning to preach, he received the 'impression', which was accentuated during a severe illness, that he must give himself wholly to the work. Despite discouragements in 1810 he presented himself as a candidate for the ministry but was not accepted.

The fact, however, that he had supplied appointments during the absence of an itinerant preacher deepened his conviction and afterwards, hearing that there was no Methodist preaching at Newquay, he went there and eventually founded a society. At his own expense he built a chapel, from which he was later, in 1810, to suffer expulsion on the ground of indiscipline.[58] A portion of the society also suffered expulsion along with him, and his followers then met at his house and elsewhere. Thus a small unnamed Methodist group had come into being, a group which may be designated 'Mr O'Bryan's people'.[59]

Leaving Newquay, O'Bryan began to open fresh work on the edge of Bodmin Moor with considerable success, and in the work he enlisted women as assistant preachers. These societies became incorporated into the Methodist circuits. The success of these labours renewed in O'Bryan, now once more a Methodist, the urge to enter the itinerant ministry and

[56] T. Shaw, op. cit., pp. 36–7; J. H. B. Andrewes, in two articles, 'The Rise of the Bible Christians', in *Transactions of the Devonshire Association*, xcvi, 147ff. and *The Preacher's Quarterly*, ii (1965), 51–8; G. C. B. Davies, *The Early Cornish Evangelicals: 1735–60* (London 1951). Yet we may note the view of E. W. Benson, Bishop of Truro: 'He always recognised quite frankly that Methodism had kept religion alive in Cornwall when the Church had almost lost the sacred flame' (A. C. Benson, *Life of E. W. Benson*, London 1899, i, 430).

[57] In the early records the family name is spelt variously: 'Bryan', 'Brian', 'Bryant'; but on account of a supposed, though probably doubtful, Irish ancestry, William adopted the form 'O'Bryan'; see S. L. Thorne, *William O'Bryan* (Bradford 1878).

[58] See O'Bryan's account in *The Rules of the Society* (Launceston 1818), preface, pp. i–xvi.

[59] T. Shaw, op. cit., p. 7.

he embarked upon a further enterprise, this time along the north Devon and Cornwall border amongst the new societies of the Stratton Mission which was an out-thrust of the Launceston circuit. He discovered that along the river Tamar there were some twenty parishes without any Methodist preaching, and he made this area the place for his new labours, which, although welcomed at first, became regarded as irregular. Meanwhile his ticket of membership in the St Austell circuit had been withdrawn by the superintendent on the ground that he had not attended class for three weeks. Thus for the second time O'Bryan found himself expelled from the Methodist society. The new superintendent who had the oversight of the Stratton Mission soon manifested his disapproval of O'Bryan's enterprise and ruthlessly opposed him, though some of the circuit officers – in particular, the circuit steward, Robert Spettigue – and the societies openly supported O'Bryan's ministry. On 22 September 1815, Spettigue and others met O'Bryan at Poundstock and decided to make a final appeal to the Quarterly Meeting; they resolved, if it failed, to proceed to separation, and in view of this possibility they prepared a fortnight's plan of appointments. At the Quarterly Meeting Spettigue suggested a compromise which would discipline O'Bryan to preaching on Sundays according to the circuit plan, but would allow his itinerant labours during the week. This implied a measure of independence of the superintendent, which the latter found unacceptable. Informed of the decision, O'Bryan at once put into operation the plan prepared at Poundstock:

> On Saturday, the 30th I came to Bridgerule, and found out how the affair stood, and the next day, October 1st, 1818 entered on my circuit at Mary-Wee and Hex.[60]

Thus the new Connexion, though as yet unnamed, was born. There is no evidence that O'Bryan sought to attract the friends from their Methodist loyalty, but they expressed their determined support of him when the superintendent visited the society and in their presence tore up the membership roll.

A further development took place when O'Bryan visited the

[60] ibid., p. 12.

home of John and Mary Thorne at Lake Farm, Shebbear, and after a preaching-service twenty-two people were enrolled as class-members. This was a crucial event and was the real foundation of the Bible Christian Connexion. It should be noted that the Rev. Daniel Evans,[61] the curate at Shebbear, was an earnest evangelical preacher and, despite the recognized unpopularity of the act, had allowed Mary Thorne to bear public testimony to her spiritual experience at the close of a Communion service in the parish church. He visited and took part in the new class-meeting at Lake shortly after its formation, declaring himself as one who had prepared the way for O'Bryan's ministry.[62]

At the first Quarterly Meeting on 1 January 1816 eleven societies and 237 members were recorded. Some of these who came over from the Methodists were preachers and leaders and therefore naturally gave similar help in the new denomination. Early in the year O'Bryan chose James Thorne,[63] the son of John Thorne, of Lake Farm, to be a regular helper. The Connexion had now two itinerant ministers, and together they began to construct the constitution according to the Methodist pattern. New societies came into being over a wide area, sometimes independent of and sometimes alongside those of the Methodists. In some places the Methodists certainly suffered loss[64] in consequence, though in reply to the accusation that O'Bryan had 'stolen our people' he was prepared to allow that they might have come voluntarily 'seeking for a little better pasture'.[65] It is certain, however, that the Methodist advance, particularly in Devon, was retarded by the Bible Christian development.

The first time we meet with any reference to the name of the denomination is in August 1816. In some places they were

[61] F. W. Bourne, op. cit., pp. 9–13, 25–6.
[62] In the adjacent parish of Hatherleigh, the Rev. Craddock Glascott, one of the Countess of Huntingdon's itinerants, was also an ardent evangelical and Calvinistic clergyman who preached at Shebbear (Bourne, op. cit., p. 7).
[63] John Thorne, *James Thorne of Shebbear* (London 1873).
[64] T. Shaw (op. cit., pp. 38–41) suggests that on a conservative estimate 30 per cent of the first recorded Bible Christian membership was formerly Methodist, and a considerable percentage was from the Church of England. Probably only 30 per cent had been gathered from outside the Churches.
[65] O'Bryan, *The Rules of the Society*, preface.

still called by the term 'Methodists', but on the way to an appointment O'Bryan was informed that the name 'Bible Christians' was being used; this he willingly accepted,[66] and prefixed 'Arminian' to it as expressive of his theological viewpoint.

By the end of 1816 the membership had reached nearly 600 and the denomination had assumed the usual pattern of Methodist institutions, though as yet there was no annual conference, the whole Connexion consisting of one local circuit. In 1817 *The Rules of Society, or a Guide to Conduct for those who desire to be Arminian Bible Christians* was drawn up – 'as close as possible to Mr Wesley's *Rules*' – by O'Bryan and Thorne and was published in the following year with a 'Preface' explaining the causes of separation. In 1817 the wide circuit was divided and new fields were opened up. An independent circuit in the area of Truro, built up by a former Methodist itinerant preacher, John Boyle, requested admission to the denomination and an effective union was created.[67]

The first Conference of the Connexion was held in 1819 at O'Bryan's own house named Baddash, in Launceston. Sixteen male and fourteen female itinerants were recorded, including O'Bryan as President, listed as 'General Superintendent', and James Thorne as Secretary. The *Minutes* were printed in the town but the term 'Bible Christian' is nowhere mentioned, the description on the title-page being: *Minutes of the First Conference of the Preachers in Connexion with William O'Bryan.* Twelve circuits are shown, and although there is no statement of membership it amounted to something over two thousand, for by this time the Connexion had extended far into Cornwall. The *Minutes* record a long discussion on the subject of a female ministry, and such appointments were unanimously approved. For some years to come this was to remain a feature of the Bible Christian Connexion.[68]

[66] Other local designations were also given: 'Free Willers', 'Shining Lights', 'Ranters', 'Bryanites' and 'Thornites'; the term 'Bryanite' was widely used for half a century.

[67] This small group was known as the 'Boylites'.

[68] Although the number of female itinerants steadily declined, their labours in the early years were a valuable element in the progress of the Connexion: see W. F. Swift, 'The Women Itinerant Preachers of Early Methodism', in *W.H.S. Proc.*, xxix (December 1953), 76–8.

The year 1820 brought a new development in extension of territory. Two years earlier a society had been formed at Plymouth Dock, and one of the members had removed to the dockyard at Chatham, in Kent, taking with him a copy of the 1818 *Rules*, with the result that a letter was sent back requesting preachers. Two were chosen, and the new Kent mission field was opened up in an area which was already a strong Methodist region. The two preachers endured much privation and also suspicion from the Methodist authorities, but the work grew, and two other preachers, female itinerants, were sent. In 1822 new ground was opened in London where the work first took root in the area around City Road. While preaching in the open air in Southwark, one preacher, Henry Freeman, was arrested, tried and imprisoned, though after a fortnight he was released with something like an apology.

Despite many difficulties the work progressed, spreading into Somerset at the end of 1820, to the Scilly Isles in 1821, to Monmouthshire and the Channel Islands in 1823, and to the Isle of Wight in 1824. In 1824 also a mission was opened in Northumberland under the spiritual concern of Mary Werrey, an itinerant preacher.

The early preachers were full of evangelical labours and received little remuneration.[69] Strictness of discipline was enforced, particularly regarding general appearance and dress, it being desired that 'a primitive simplicity' should be maintained – a reflection of the formative Quaker influence upon O'Bryan in his early days. It was also suggested that itinerants who intended to marry should choose partners from the female travelling preachers.

The growing demands of the work resulted in the dividing of the Connexion into Districts in 1828, and an important step was taken in 1825 by the formation of a Chapel Fund to control building enterprises. A Trust Deed was adopted which placed chapels under 'William O'Bryan during his natural life . . . to have and enjoy the said premises'.[70]

A contact between the Bible Christians and Primitive Methodism is revealed by a brief correspondence between

[69] *Minutes* (Bible Christians), (1820), p. 7.
[70] ibid. (1825), pp. 12–14.

O'Bryan and Hugh Bourne.[71] It embodied the notion of some form of co-operation, but no joint action resulted, save for a brief contact of preachers of the two denominations in London in 1822, when two Primitive Methodists were temporarily engaged by the Bible Christians, one in London and the other in Kent.

The year 1821 saw a significant change in the title-page of the *Minutes*. At the Conference at Lake it was decided to drop the word 'Arminian' and reference was no longer made to 'William O'Bryan and the People in connexion with him', the wording being changed to 'the Ministers and Representatives of the People denominated Bible Christians'. This was significant because it indicated the feeling of dissatisfaction against O'Bryan on the part of the preachers which had been steadily mounting, and was to reach its climax in 1829.

For some time O'Bryan and Thorne had differed in their views regarding the government of the Connexion, and O'Bryan's introduction in 1825 of the Deed which invested the chapel property in himself occasioned surprise on the part of the preachers, who had agreed to it only reluctantly. At the Conference of 1826 they requested an amendment; O'Bryan accepted this hesitatingly, insisting that in all matters his single vote should be determinative. This led at once to open conflict. In 1827 the preachers prepared a draft of the constitution they desired: Conference was to be the focus of government, and O'Bryan should be prepared to take a circuit, though he should be allowed to make his choice. The preachers were also concerned at the growing debts on Connexional funds, and they questioned O'Bryan's own personal expenses.

In 1828, at the Conference at Ebenezer Chapel, Lake, O'Bryan relinquished the chair, and William Mason was elected as President. For the first time the name of O'Bryan appeared in the list of approved preachers.[72] Agitation con-

[71] The letters are printed in the *Primitive Methodist Magazine* (1821).

[72] During the year O'Bryan had issued a pamphlet complaining of the treatment he had received from the Financial Committee, and a reply had been issued: *A Vindication of the Acting Members of the Financial Committee*; see *Minutes* (Methodist New Connexion), (1829), p. 17. The tension of the situation is shown clearly in recently discovered original letters now printed in Oliver A. Beckerlegge, 'The Rule of William O'Bryan', in *W.H.S. Proc.*, xxxiii, 30–5; cf. T. Shaw, op. cit., pp. 42–8.

tinued to increase and before the next Conference, also held at Lake, a preliminary meeting-extraordinary was held on 23 July 1829, the decision of which went against O'Bryan. He declared: 'I will do no more business with you; I adjourn this Conference to Liskeard next Monday', and then left the meeting. By this action he separated himself from the Connexion.

O'Bryan now found himself at the head of a small group of supporters who resumed the old name 'Arminian Bible Christians', but since he himself was away in America for three years, the leadership of the group during the six years of its existence was uncertain. No records are available, but a small circuit in Cornwall was established with seven itinerant preachers and seven hundred members. O'Bryan eventually decided upon permanent residence in America and the small group chose to seek reunion with the Bible Christians. A deputation attended the Conference in 1835 and after long discussion an agreement was concluded by which they were to declare O'Bryan's faults, and he was to renounce all claims upon the Connexion, and sign over the copyright of the Hymn-book, being recompensed by a payment of £85. On account of debts incurred only unmarried preachers received admission; members numbering 543 were reunited.[73] It is good to record that in the ensuing years the Conference afforded generous treatment for O'Bryan, and he received an annual gift of £20. He frequently visited the homeland and was welcomed. He died in New York on 8 January 1868, at the age of ninety.

William O'Bryan stands out as a strange figure and his character has been excellently summarized by the most recent historian of the Connexion:[74]

> by birth an Anglican, by inheritance a Quaker and by choice and temperament a Methodist. And yet an unsatisfactory Methodist, for his allegiance was only to its doctrines and not to its discipline. He claimed a roving commission subject to no ecclesiastical superior, the privileges of a new Wesley, a law giver but not a law abider. . . . he was a wandering evangelist and popular

[73] *Minutes* (Bible Christians), (1835), pp. 11–13.
[74] T. Shaw, op. cit., pp. 16–17.

preacher, whose character was beyond reproach, but who was constitutionally unable to work in harness with other people either as a colleague or leader.

The effect of the disruption and the reunion which followed was small. In 1829 the recorded membership was 7,599 and by 1836 it had reached 10,786, and in addition adherents to the societies were numerous.

From now onwards the task of leadership fell mainly upon James Thorne. A fervent evangelist, he was also a tireless organizer and a capable administrator, who had the complete confidence of the preachers. Intellectually well-endowed, 'he knew how to shape policies and deal with people', and for more than thirty years was the chief architect of the denomination.

On O'Bryan's departure steps were taken to secure a legal settlement of the Connexion, and a Deed Poll was enrolled in Chancery in 1831. This provided for lay representation in the Conference and for an equal number of ministers and laymen at every fifth Conference from 1830 onwards. The constitution bears remarkable similarity to that of the Methodist New Connexion.

In 1838 the Conference published a *Digest of the Rules and Regulations of the People denominated Bible Christians*, and two changes are interesting. The term 'Methodist Superintendent' gave place to 'Circuit Pastor', the title 'Superintendent' being reserved for the Chairman of a District; the 'Leaders' Meeting' was altered to the 'Elders' Meeting'. Further the long-continued principle of 'no fixed quarterage' which had been superimposed by O'Bryan was replaced by the suggestion that each member should subscribe at the rate of one penny per week.

The growth of the denomination was materially assisted by its publishing department (under the care of Samuel Thorne, who had married O'Bryan's daughter, Mary, an itinerant preacher), which was eventually placed at Shebbear. Samuel Thorne was also the pioneer of the educational work of the denomination, for as early as 1820 he projected the idea of a school at Shebbear. It was not until 1829 that the project found fulfilment, when a school with about twenty scholars was opened. Thirteen years later the Connexion assumed responsibility and in future years it was to have an important influence on the life of the denomination.

Two developments remain to be noted in this period. The first was the opening up of overseas enterprise in response to an invitation from the many Cornish emigrants who had gone over to America.[75] In 1831 two preachers were sent out – John Glass to Upper Canada and Francis Metherall[76] to Prince Edward Island. Within two years the latter had established thirty-six preaching places, and a further preacher sent to Canada built up a circuit nearly two hundred miles in length. Beginning with a first recorded membership of 77, by the end of our period it had reached the number of 1,473.

The second development was the rise of the Temperance Movement within the denomination in the 1830s, with the formation of a Total Abstinence Society in 1837. The movement spread widely, but for a considerable time there was a mood of caution amongst the leaders of the denomination as to its possible divisive effects owing to ill-judged criticism of those unable to commit themselves.[77] Though the movement achieved great strength, total abstinence was never imposed as a condition of membership, and it was not until 1882 that the Conference officially established the 'Bible Christian Temperance Society'.

During the later years of the period we are reviewing, the growth of the Connexion went forward steadily under increasingly efficient organization on the part of those who as young men had begun the work with O'Bryan, but the real secret of its advance lay in the unflagging labours of its faithful preachers, among whom in the earlier days the female itinerants fulfilled a remarkable and powerful ministry. In 1850 there was an overall total membership of 15,267; travelling preachers numbered 134 and local preachers 1,153. There were 415 chapels.

[75] It is interesting to note that from 1832 the Connexional statistics state annually the number of emigrants.
[76] See J. Harris, *Life of Francis Metherall* . . . (1883).
[77] *Minutes* (Bible Christians), (1838), p. 14.

III

The place of origin of Primitive Methodism[78] was the borders of Cheshire and Staffordshire gathered around the rugged eminence of Mow Cop. It was an expression of the revivalism which marked the opening of the nineteenth century, and its beginnings were associated with the establishment of camp meetings, a modification of the old field-preaching through American example and influence. These camp meetings symbolized the claim of evangelism to freedom of method and experiment.

The two founders of Primitive Methodism, Hugh Bourne (1772–1852), a moorland carpenter, and William Clowes (1780–1851), a potter, would doubtless have remained devoted members of the parent Methodist Church if they had not been expelled on account of their participation in the camp meeting movement. Primitive Methodism was therefore the result of an expulsion and must not be regarded as a secession.

Born in 1772, at Fordhays Farm, in the parish of Stoke-on-Trent, in Staffordshire, Hugh Bourne[79] came to an experience of conversion after twenty years of 'seeking the light', aided by his reading. Shortly afterwards he joined the Methodist society near Bemersley. In disposition he was shy, even dour, yet courageous and persistent. For purposes of his occupation he was fixed for a time in that part of Staffordshire under the shadow of Mow Cop. His significance for the history of Primitive Methodism began when, on Christmas Day, 1800, he broke through his reserve sufficiently to talk with his cousin, Daniel Shubotham, an irreligious and dissipated collier, concerning spiritual matters, and in parting put into his hands a written account of his own conversion. As a result Shubotham, and later another collier, Matthias Bayley,

---

[78] The following are the primary sources: MS. Journal of Hugh Bourne; *The Journals of William Clowes* (London 1844); Hugh Bourne, *History of the Primitive Methodists ... to the Year 1823* (Bemersley 1823); and later histories: John Petty, *The History of the Primitive Methodist Connexion from Its Origin to the Conference of 1859* (London 1860; revised and enlarged 1880); H. B. Kendall, *The Origin and History of the Primitive Methodist Church*, 2 vols (1905; revised and enlarged 1919).

[79] John Walford, *Memoirs of the Life and Labours of the Late Venerable Hugh Bourne*, 2 vols (London 1855, 1857); William Antliff, *The Life of the Venerable Hugh Bourne* (London 1872); John T. Wilkinson, *Hugh Bourne 1772–1852* (London 1952).

were converted, and under the influence of these three men a revival of religion broke out in the village of Harriseahead, chiefly through 'conversation preaching' – the speaking of man to man on spiritual concerns – and through cottage prayer-meetings. At the close of one of these meetings, which were strictly limited in length by Bourne, complaint was made of the insufficient time permitted, and Shubotham remarked: 'You shall have a whole day's praying on Mow some Sunday!' Later this promise found fulfilment. Soon afterwards Shubotham gave a corner of his garden as a site for a chapel, and at considerable personal expense Bourne undertook its erection. Although the revival was nominally Methodist, it proceeded without direction or oversight from the Burslem circuit authorities. Classes were formed, and Bourne preached, although his name did not appear on the circuit plan. The situation was irregular, and not until 1802, and even then under pressure, were the classes acknowledged, when the chapel received a supply of preachers. In 1804 a further revival broke out and extended to Tunstall, largely owing to the visits to Congleton of revivalists from Stockport; this revival was particularly noteworthy for the conversion of William Clowes.

William Clowes,[80] born in Burslem in 1780, presented a great contrast in personality to Hugh Bourne. A man of rich emotional nature, of fluent utterance, and gifted with social qualities, he possessed a magnetic personality. In his unregenerate days his great pursuit was pleasure, and while working as a potter in Hull he fell through his own foolishness into the hands of the press gang, to be released only by the intervention of a friend. In 1805 he returned to Tunstall in the middle of the revival and entered into a dynamic spiritual experience, in which he made rapid progress. He discharged his debts, drew up rules for holy living, became active in tract distribution, a class-leader, and appeared on the circuit plan as an exhorter.

---

[80] See *The Journals of William Clowes* (London 1844); John Davison, *The Life of the Venerable William Clowes, one of the Founders of the Primitive Methodist Connexion* (London 1854); William Garner, *The Life of the Rev. and Venerable William Clowes, One of the Patriarchs of the Primitive Methodist Connexion* (London 1868); John T. Wilkinson, *William Clowes 1780–1851* (London 1951).

At the end of 1805 an eccentric American evangelist, Lorenzo Dow,[81] paid a visit to Britain and laboured extensively in south Lancashire and east Cheshire with great success. In April 1807 Dow preached the farewell sermons of his tour at Congleton. Bourne and Clowes were present and purchased two pamphlets, one being *Defence of Camp Meetings*, by S. K. Jennings, the other by Dow himself, and both giving an account of the camp meeting movement in America. On 31 May 1807 the first British camp meeting was held. Four preaching-stands, made from stones from the hillside, were erected, and the people numbered several thousands, many of them finding conversion. The die had been cast, and it was published abroad that similar meetings would follow. Official opposition now arose and the circuit preachers put out bills against camp meetings, in the light of which some hesitated to give support. Moreover, a legal issue arose, since the Conventicle Act was still in force against unlicensed preachers. The future of camp meetings hung in the balance and the issue depended almost entirely on one man – Hugh Bourne. A second meeting was held on Mow Cop on 19 July 1807, and a still more important one on 23 August at Norton in the Moors for the purpose of counteracting the evil influence of the local wakes. This third camp meeting was crucial in its importance. In July the Burslem preachers had brought the whole matter to the Conference at Liverpool, when an adverse judgment was passed.[82] The enforcement of this decision by the preachers on their return naturally diminished the number of active supporters of the movement, but, answering the demand of his own conscience, Bourne went forward with the Norton meeting, which proved highly successful. It was the turning-point.

The consequence of the Norton meeting was the expulsion of Hugh Bourne by the Quarterly Meeting of June 1808; this was ostensibly on the ground that he had not attended

[81] G. Herod, *Biographical Sketches* (London 1855), pp. 17–240.

[82] *Minutes*, 1812 edn, ii (1807), 403: 'It is our judgment, that even supposing such meetings to be allowable in America, they are highly improper in England, and likely to be productive of considerable mischief. And we disclaim all connexion with them.' Two things help to explain this decision: reports of excesses associated with the American meeting, and the serious fissure in Methodism which had occurred in 1797 under Kilham.

class, but its real reason was later declared to be that 'he had a tendency to set up other than the ordinary worship'. Bourne's attitude was exemplary; he uttered no complaint but paid up his class-money and went on with his work. Shortly afterwards he relinquished his secular calling in order to give himself wholly to the work of evangelism. The measure of this commitment can be known only by a reading of his Journals.

Bourne's followers soon became known as The Camp Meeting Methodists, and societies were established. Determined that there should be no secession, he urged his converts to join the Methodists and in particular asked the Burslem Circuit to take over the society at Stanley, but the offer was refused. Bourne wrote in his Journal: 'Here necessity is laid upon us and we are obliged to go on in the work without them.'[83] The time of crisis had come and in March 1810 the Camp Meeting Methodists had become a distinct community.

In June 1810 William Clowes suffered similar expulsion, being deprived of his plan, and in the following September his ticket of membership was withheld on the ground that, contrary to Methodist discipline, he had participated in camp meetings. Unwilling to depart from their leader, many of the members of his classes chose to share his exile. A refuge was found in the home of Mr Smith, of Tunstall, where for some two years meetings for prayer and preaching had been held, and because of attendance at this meeting James Steele also was deprived of his office as school superintendent and class-leader. This expulsion deprived the Methodist society of many who went out voluntarily. The house having become too small to accommodate the Clowesites – the name given to the group locally – they moved to a warehouse, and before long preparations were made for the building of a chapel in Tunstall. As the small group was not certain of its strength or ultimate survival, the chapel was built structurally so that it could be turned into four cottages if found necessary. It was opened on 13 July 1811.

On 30 May 1811, a joint meeting was held between the Camp Meeting Methodists and the Clowesites; union was

[83] *Journal*, 23 May 1810.

agreed upon and arrangements were made for class tickets to be printed. These bore the date 'May 1811', and the text was significant: 'But we desire to hear of thee what thou thinkest: for as concerning this sect, we know that every where it is spoken against.' On 26 July, James Steele was elected as circuit steward of the newly-formed circuit; James Crawfoot,[84] of Delamere Forest, who had been employed by Bourne as an evangelist, and William Clowes were made preachers, and some two hundred members were recorded as constituting the new denomination. On 13 February 1812 a third meeting was held and there is a significant entry in Bourne's *Journal* for that date:

> We called a meeting and made plans for the next quarter and made some other regulations. In particular we took the name of the society of the Primitive Methodists.

Bourne is silent as to any reason for the adoption of this name for the new community, neither was he responsible for the selection of it. Not until many years afterwards, it seems, did its precise origin become known. In 1790 James Crawfoot had heard Wesley's farewell address to his preachers in Chester, and in a moving appeal concerning the preaching of the gospel he declared:

> Fellow labourers, wherever there is an open door enter in and preach the Gospel: if it be to two or three, under a hedge or a tree, preach the Gospel; go out quickly into the streets and lanes of the city, and bring in the poor and the maimed and the halt and the blind. . . . *and this is the way the primitive methodists did.*[85]

'Twenty-two years later at the Tunstall meeting' Crawfoot arose and recalled the incident; he 'remarked that he thought this was the particular emphasis of the new enterprise: so the designation was immediately adopted'. Thus a new Methodist denomination had come into being, 'undesigned of man'.

The number of preaching places had now reached thirty-four and there were in all twenty-three preachers; printed

[84] G. Herod, op. cit., pp. 241–72.
[85] John T. Wilkinson, *William Clowes 1780–1851*, p. 92; F. F. Bretherton, 'Wesley's Last Visit to Chester', in *W.H.S. Proc.*, xxvi (1947–8), 76–9.

plans were now issued in place of the written plans which had
been previously supplied.

The new denomination did not spread widely or rapidly.
For the next four years the Connexion consisted of no more
than the Tunstall circuit. The scattered population of the
moorland countryside was partly the cause, and unfortunately
Crawfoot withdrew from his evangelistic labours after about
a year. More important was the fact that the majority soon
moved towards adopting a policy of consolidating existing
societies rather than one of extension. To Bourne this 'Tunstall
non-mission law' was disturbing, for he firmly believed in
aggressive evangelism as the very principle by which the
work had begun. Nevertheless, he acquiesced and prepared a
draft of rules for the government of the societies, which,
after consideration throughout the societies themselves, was
adopted in January 1814.[86] Bourne gave reluctant consent to
being 'General Superintendent'; he also formed a Tract
Society and began the institution of Sunday Schools.

In the same year the door to extension was re-opened
through John Benton's ignoring of the Tunstall 'non-
mission law'. With a thousand copies of Lorenzo Dow's
hymn-book he missioned across the borders into Derbyshire
and brought into being a small circuit, which he handed over
to Bourne. One of the places entered was Belper and it was
there that, because of their singing in the streets, the early
Primitive Methodists received the nickname of 'Ranters'.

For some time Bourne had been concerned about the
decline of camp meetings, and in June 1816 one was held at
Mercaston, in Derbyshire. Out of it sprang the great revival
which took place in 1817–18 and by means of which, by the
preaching of a woman itinerant, Sarah Kirkland,[87] the work
spread to Nottingham where a strong society was established.
Another camp meeting, held in Nottingham Forest, was
attended by some twelve thousand people and from it the
work advanced into Lincolnshire and Leicestershire, where
Loughborough became the centre of a third circuit in 1818.

[86] These Rules are printed in the *Primitive Methodist Magazine* (1822).
[87] W. F. Swift, 'The Women Itinerant Preachers of Early Methodism', in *W.H.S.
Proc.*, xxix, 79–82.

The plan of 1822 shows forty-two places in five counties. This remarkable revival led to the abandonment of the principle of consolidation and thrust the Connexion out once more to open-air evangelism. It should be noted that this was the period of the ravages of the Luddites and Levellers, the 'Radical Reformers' whose outrages took place largely in the region where this revival arose and proved a timely visitation.[88]

The year 1819 was important, and in some sense decisive. It was increasingly recognized that the wide development of the Connexion demanded organization. A 'Preparatory Meeting' therefore was held in August, at Nottingham, to formulate outlines of Connexional policy and to prepare for the first Conference, to be held at Hull in May 1820. Preachers' allowances were fixed; plainness of dress was urged upon them and none was to be allowed to enter upon business. In the main the system of administration was framed upon the Methodist pattern. It was determined that Conference should consist of 'delegates' from the circuits in the proportion of two laymen for each travelling preacher – and this feature remained unchanged, being eventually incorporated into the Deed Poll.

The years 1819–24 were also years of immense advance. It was in 1819 that William Clowes entered Hull, and this was soon to be the centre of the fourth circuit, marking the beginning of a period of forward thrust up the Yorkshire coast and westward to Leeds, eventually crossing over into Cumberland and Westmorland. By 1824 Hull had created seventeen circuits and a total membership of 7,660. As early as 1822 Clowes wrote: 'Our circuit extends from Carlisle in Cumberland to Spurn Point in Holderness, an extent of more than two hundred miles.'

Tunstall also developed its work in Manchester, south Shropshire and Cheshire and on to Liverpool. Nottingham expanded its work into Lincolnshire, and northward into west Yorkshire. The seventy-two circuits by now in existence became grouped into four districts, and from this time district

[88] R. F. Wearmouth, *Methodism and the Working-Class Movements of England 1800–1850*, pp. 30–3.

representation took the place of circuit representation in the Conference.

In 1819 the Connexional membership was 7,842, by 1824 it had reached 33,507: such was the strength of the evangelistic urge, fulfilled by the preachers, both itinerant and lay, at great cost and at times much suffering, for persecution was by no means unknown, not only from a hostile populace but from both magistrates and clergymen.[89] Mostly recruited from country folk, the preachers had no scholarship, yet they knew the Scriptures and were men of intense prayer, and for the most part they came into those areas where Wesley and his preachers had not laboured. Behind the whole movement lay the organizing ability of Bourne himself, not least in his efforts to train the preachers through various treatises which came from his pen, and in the publication of the *Magazine*, of which he was editor from 1819 to 1842.

The years 1825–28 brought a period of crisis.[90] Slender increases and one heavy decrease in membership, together in some cases with financial difficulties, largely arising out of the existing social distress of the time and therefore deeply affecting the infant societies, were disconcerting; so much so that the preparation of the Deed Poll was postponed. The fact was that greater discipline was needed, and with great insight Bourne examined the situation and became the unflinching advocate of stern measures. He recognized that many of the societies were composed of those whose experience of church affairs was small; in addition there were cases of unsuitable persons who had gained admission into the ministry.[91] In 1824 he had issued anonymously 'A Private Communication'[92] to the preachers and officials, his authorship of which was soon discovered and brought him bitter reaction. The outcome was the creation of new regulations, behind which his influence is apparent. Thirty preachers were induced to leave the Connexion, and by 1827 the sifting process had begun to take

---

[89] Thomas Church, *Gospel-Victories: or Missionary Anecdotes of Imprisonments, Labours, and Persecutions, Endured by Primitive Methodist Preachers, between the Years 1812 and 1844* (London/Edinburgh 1851).

[90] John T. Wilkinson, *Hugh Bourne 1772–1852*, Chap. 8.

[91] *Minutes of Primitive Methodism* (1827).

[92] John Walford, op. cit., ii, 132–5.

effect; by 1828 there came an upward trend. Bourne had rendered great and distinguished service in a time of severe testing. At the Conference at Scotter in 1829 it was decided that the Hull and Tunstall circuits should combine to send missionaries to the United States,[93] and in the same year the Deed Poll was ordered to be executed.

Despite the crisis the advance of the Connexion continued, particularly in East Anglia, Essex and Huntingdonshire, notwithstanding the serious social unrest in the region, for these were the days of the rick-burners on the farmsteads. In Wiltshire, Berkshire and Hampshire persecution was the most severe, and the experiences of these early years burnt themselves deeply into the memory of the denomination. Still further progress was made in the southern counties, reaching into Cornwall and South Wales. In this period the importance of female itinerants should not be overlooked, together with the labours of female local preachers, for these were widely successful. A further factor which contributed to the success was the exceedingly popular early Hymn-book, largely the work of Bourne; the measure of its influence is seen in the large number of pirated editions which were produced.[94]

The year 1842 brought the superannuation of Bourne and Clowes. Both had served the Connexion with unflagging zeal, each in his own particular way. Never ceasing to be an evangelist, Bourne had become the administrator and organizer in Connexional affairs, ever striving for the development of a centralized unity. Clowes had fulfilled his ministry as a flaming evangelist, with eloquent and penetrating appeal wherever he preached. Not only between the two men, however, but also between Bourne and his other brethren there were times of tension. Bourne could be peremptory and severe, even to bluntness, though he was utterly innocent of self-seeking. One recurrent source of difference concerned 'particularism', the tendency of districts to be self-contained and self-determining.[95] It was under the stress of his labours in his later years that Bourne proved difficult, but his Journals

[93] *Minutes of Primitive Methodism* (1819), p. 324.
[94] J. T. Wilkinson, op. cit., pp. 195-7.
[95] John T. Wilkinson, *William Clowes 1780-1851*, pp. 88-101.

bear testimony to his tremendous zeal and dogged perseverance. It should be remembered that even after his superannuation he went over, in obedience to the call of his spirit, to America to superintend the societies – no mean venture for a tired man in his seventy-third year. Even on his return for the remaining years until a few weeks before his death on 11 October 1852 he went to and fro 'confirming the churches'. The *Journals* of William Clowes, largely written from memory and published in 1844, also bear eloquent witness to his power as a preacher of the gospel. He died on 2 March 1851.

At the close of the period now under consideration Primitive Methodism at its twenty-first Conference recorded a membership of 104,762, with 519 travelling preachers and 8,524 local preachers. There were 5,170 Connexional and rented chapels.[96]

IV

The thirty years from 1827 to 1857 proved a period of intense conflict within Methodism. Almost exclusively concerned with the issues of church-government, they were marked by three distinct secessions, in 1827, 1835 and 1849. The controversies related to a principle held by them all, and ultimately they coalesced into a single Methodist community – the United Methodist Free Churches.[97]

On the one hand, there was the Methodist Conference, still composed exclusively of ministers and determined to hold on to its authority, to be exercised in the Church as a whole through circuit superintendents; on the other hand, there was increasing opposition to ministerial absolutism, determined to secure a Connexional authority which should allow a real measure of self-government within the circuits and churches, together with a controlling Conference which should be composed of elected representatives, ministerial and lay. Looking back, it is clear that reform was essential and that protest was entirely justified, but there is little question that

[96] *Minutes of Primitive Methodism* (1850).
[97] There are only two comprehensive histories of the movement: Joseph Kirsop, *Historic Sketches of Free Methodism* (London 1885); Oliver A. Beckerlegge, *The United Methodist Free Churches: A Study in Freedom* (London 1957).

despite undoubted sincerity upon the part of both contenders, their methods and sometimes their spirit were open to criticism.

The first secession took place in 1827, and the group concerned was originally known locally as 'Nonconforming Methodists', becoming designated finally as 'Protestant Methodists'.[98] The immediate cause was the proposal to erect an organ in Brunswick Chapel, Leeds. A number of trustees desired its installation, but the majority of the leaders, members and local preachers in the circuit were against it on the ground that it would spoil the freedom, warmth and simplicity of the customary Methodist worship. The old prejudice against the organ as 'a popish instrument' had not yet died out. Fulfilling Conference regulations[99] originally intended as a safeguard for the societies, the trustees appealed to the District Meeting, which rejected the application. Unfortunately it left the door open for the trustees to appeal to the Conference, which granted the desired permission. This decision not only overruled the District Meeting but was contrary to the desire of the majority in the Brunswick Circuit. The blame for it was laid upon Dr Jabez Bunting, and it was regarded as 'an act of arbitrary and unjustifiable power' because it was held that Conference had acted contrary to its own regulations. A local preacher, Matthew Johnson, at once took the initiative in a systematic agitation, and called together the local preachers of the two Leeds circuits in meetings which, according to Methodist rule, were irregular. For this action he was suspended from his office for three months, and several other Leeds local preachers chose to share the silence imposed upon him. A Special District Meeting was called, and this was regarded by some as unconstitutional.[100]

[98] J. Barr, *A Statement of Facts* . . . (Leeds 1827). The designation 'Wesley Methodist Nonconformists' was printed on the first class-tickets in 1827.

[99] *Minutes of Wesleyan Conference*, 1812 edn, v (1820), 146: 'Organs may be allowed, by Special Consent of the Conference: but every Application for such Consent shall be first made at the District-Meeting; and if it obtain their sanction, shall be then referred to a Committee at the Conference, who shall report their opinion as to the propriety of acceding to the request, . . .'

[100] The people in Leeds would doubtless be aware of the regulation passed at the Leeds Conference of 1797 regarding the power of the Chairman as indicated in the concessions then made: *Minutes*, 1812 edn, i (1797), 379.

Amongst those present was Dr Bunting, though not as President of Conference, as the regulation allowed, but as Secretary. This meeting approved the suspension of Johnson, but as it had no administrative power the matter was left to the verdict of the Leaders' Meeting, which, under the pressure of the superintendent, proved adverse.

The result was the loss, either by expulsion or secession, of a thousand members, and these formed the beginnings of the Protestant Methodists. Although the controversy had its centre in Leeds its repercussions spread far beyond.[101] The issue went much more deeply than the question of permission to install an organ; it was a 'protest'[102] 'against submitting any longer to the unscriptural domination of the Methodist preachers . . . executive power being virtually exercised by the travelling preachers only'.

The new denomination held its first service in the Methodist New Connexion Chapel, Ebenezer Place, Leeds, on Christmas Day 1827; eventually, after meeting in various places, it found a disused Baptist Chapel in St Peter's Street, and by March 1828 this building, now called 'Stone Chapel', was re-opened for worship. Though mainly centred in the Leeds area, societies were formed in other towns – Burnley, Barnsley, Keighley, Preston and Sheffield, and also in London. An Annual Assembly was held until 1836, when, with a membership of several thousands, the denomination united with the Wesleyan Association,[103] the rise of which we are now to consider.

This second controversy had far more serious consequences than those arising from the Leeds case. It originated in a proposal to found a Theological Institution for the training of young preachers for the itinerancy. The 1833 Conference appointed a committee to work out a scheme, and in 1834 it

[101] B. Gregory, *Side Lights on the Conflicts of Methodism*, Chapter III, 'The Leeds Case and its Sequences'.

[102] A series of 'protests' is given in *Wesleyan Protestant Methodists* (Leeds: 27 August 1828).

[103] In 1839, James Sigston, a Leeds schoolmaster who had been Matthew Johnson's colleague, was President of the Wesleyan Association; Johnson himself was four times its Secretary.

issued its report,[104] signed by twenty preachers including Dr Bunting and Dr Samuel Warren. This group went so far as to nominate Bunting as 'President of the Theological Institution' and as Theological Tutor, thus increasing the number of offices already held by him. The Conference of 1834 approved the nomination, and this was at once regarded by many as a breach of the Leeds Concessions (1797) that no new regulation should be confirmed until a year had passed, thereby giving opportunity for discussion by the societies.[105]

Dr Samuel Warren, superintendent of the Manchester circuit, at first favourable to the proposed Institution, now led the opposition – a change of attitude on his part arising, it would appear, out of the proposed appointment 'which would increase power in the hands of a few individuals'. He attacked the proposal in a pamphlet[106] which circulated widely, and for which he was suspended from the superintendency by a Special District Meeting. He sought restitution by a legal suit in Chancery which he lost (1835).[107] Since the approval of the scheme by the Conference in 1834, opposition had become widely organized, and laymen had been expelled in many circuits. In November 1834, a meeting was held in Manchester and the 'Grand Central Association' was constituted. In February 1835, over seventy officebearers and members of the Rochdale circuit prepared an address[108] to be presented at the Conference, declaring that the sole remedy for existing grievances was the admission of the laity to a share of power in the matters of legislation

---

[104] *Proposals for the Formation of a Literary and Theological Institution* (London 1834).

[105] *Minutes*, 1812 edn, i (1797), 376, 378.

[106] Samuel Warren, *Remarks on the Wesleyan Theological Institution for the Education of the Junior Preachers: together with the Substance of a Speech delivered on the Subject in the London Conference of 1834.* This was answered by Jonathan Crowther, *A Defence of the Wesleyan Theological [Institution] . . . in Reply to the 'Remarks' of Dr. Warren* (1834). In the course of his legal proceedings, Dr Warren discovered that neither the Plan of Pacification nor the Leeds Concessions had been inserted in the Conference Journals. The omission, though probably accidental, was widely published, and fanned the flame of revolt; cf. M. Baxter, *Memorials of Free Methodism* (London 1865), p. 218. It has been estimated that nearly a thousand pamphlets were issued in connection with this controversy.

[107] *Wesleyan-Methodist Magazine* (London 1835); *The Order, Unity and Stability of the Constitution of Wesleyan Methodism Vindicated* (1835).

[108] M. Baxter, op. cit., pp. 211–17; amongst the signatories was John Petrie (1791–1883), a distinguished Methodist and the friend of John Bright and Richard Cobden.

finance and discipline. In the following April nearly a hundred delegates from Manchester met in Sheffield at the time of the Conference, remained there for a week in the hope of their address being received, and later were joined by the Rochdale representatives; but they were refused. It is true that Robert Eckett, who three weeks earlier had been suspended along with others in London for declaring their interest in reform, was heard by the Conference Committee, to which he presented an appeal bearing a hundred signatures of trustees and class-leaders, and small concessions were allowed.

Although the issue of the Theological Institution played but a minor part in their statement of grievances, a strong group in Liverpool[109] aligned themselves with the agitation, and many laymen suffered expulsion from their societies. They voiced their views in *The Watchman's Lantern*, a periodical issued locally which was countered by the Wesleyans in *The Illuminator*, though both journals were short-lived.

It was at the Conference of 1835 that Dr Warren, along with others, was expelled.

The first assembly of the Wesleyan Association[110] was held in Manchester in August 1835, with Dr Warren as its President. It was composed of representatives, both ministerial and lay, freely elected by the circuits; eighty-four delegates were present and five itinerant preachers. In 1837 at the Liverpool Assembly the broad outlines of a constitution, drafted by the first Assembly, were now worked out more fully. A crucial issue arose as to the membership of the Assembly. Dr Warren and others with him pressed the principle of the Methodist New Connexion, namely, that each circuit should send one minister and one layman; others, under Robert Eckett of London, stood for free representation, without *ex officio* privilege, and this was carried.[111] In October 1837, Dr Warren resigned from the Association and entered the ministry of the Church of England.

The Association grew by accretion. Almost eight thousand members in all seceded or were expelled from the Methodist

---

[109] cf. 'The Wesleyan Methodist Association in Liverpool, 1834–5', in *W.H.S. Proc.*, xxxv (June 1966), 142–8.

[110] The addition of the word 'Methodist' to the designation was made in 1839.

[111] M. Baxter, op. cit., pp. 437–8; *Minutes of Wesleyan Methodist Association* (1837), p. 9.

societies. In 1836 the Protestant Methodists and the Independent Methodists of Scarborough united with the Association, and in 1837 the Arminian Methodist Connexion[112] did likewise, adding about a thousand members. In 1836 several Wesleyan societies in Jamaica also came into the Association, together with groups in Hobart Town and Nova Scotia.[113] There was also the accession of an Independent Wesleyan group in Wales. In the succeeding years other groups were added, partly arising out of continued and considerable emigration. Missions were begun in Ireland, in Hamburg and Australia (1839), in Prince Edward Island (1841), New Brunswick (1842) and Wisconsin (1845).

By 1838 the membership of the Association had reached 26,521, with 67 travelling preachers and 946 local preachers. Chapels and preaching places numbered 663. In 1839 the United Methodist Churches in Scotland joined the Association and in 1840 a 'Foundation Deed' was adopted, for which Robert Eckett was largely responsible.

The Association repeatedly expressed a desire for closer unity with other dissenting sections of Methodism, and in 1844 specific approach was made to the Methodist New Connexion but without success. Later movement towards unity was frustrated by criticism of the Association which appeared in the Jubilee volume of the Methodist New Connexion in 1849.[114]

The Association continued its work and witness until 1857, when, by union with the Wesleyan Reformers, consummated in Exeter Hall, London, on 14 May, there came into being the United Methodist Free Churches.

The most serious secession suffered by Methodism was in the 1840s, culminating in the formation of the Wesleyan Reform movement. This movement, resting upon a growing demand for constitutional reform, centred especially around

[112] A small group in the neighbourhood of Derby, and hence for some time styled 'Derby Faith Methodists', holding Sandemanian views as to the nature of faith and therefore constituting a secession from Methodism on doctrinal grounds; cf. *N.H.M.*, i, 427, 520.

[113] *Minutes of Wesleyan Methodist Association* (1838).

[114] R. Eckett, (1) *A Vindication of the Wesleyan Methodist Association*; (2) *A Refutation* (1849). *Minutes of Wesleyan Methodist Association* (1849), pp. 34–5.

the personality of James Everett, who at the time of his expulsion, along with others, in 1849, was a minister of forty years' standing. As far back as 1839 an anonymous volume of which he was the supposed, and eventually the admitted, author had come from his lively pen; it had created excitement amongst the preachers, and had been condemned by Conference. This was *Wesleyan Takings: or, Centenary Sketches of Ministerial Character, as exhibited in the Wesleyan Connexion,* and was marked by biting satire and humour. Further anonymous writings began to appear in 1844 and the years following, and with shattering results. These *Fly Sheets from the Private Correspondent* bore neither printer's nor publisher's name. Each concluded with the words: 'By Order of the Corresponding Committee for detecting, exposing and correcting abuses: London, Manchester, Bristol, Liverpool, Birmingham, Hull, Leeds, Glasgow.' Printed in Birmingham, the first of these (1844) was headed: 'On Location, Centralization, Secularization'; the second (1846): 'The Presidential Chair, the Platform and Connexional Committees'; the third (1847), a miscellaneous tract concerning 'Anonymous Publications', 'Reclaimed Ground', 'Reasoning and Resolve', 'The Core and Cure of Misrule'; the fourth (1848) and fifth (1849), after the expulsion, a recapitulation and re-emphasis of the earlier issues concerning reform. These pamphlets contained pointed attacks upon important personalities, but chiefly upon Dr Bunting, as the key personality in the 'metropolitan hierarchy'. The writings were caustic and even abusive. Sent at first to ministers only, and post-paid, they were eventually disseminated far and wide. The Conference retaliated with the anonymous *Papers on Wesleyan Matters,* first published in 1849, which were indeed as intemperate and unworthy as the publications they censured. Without doubt the writers of these papers 'only aggravated the evils they were intended to remove'. The whole matter now became a bitter party conflict.

Eventually it was determined that every effort should be made to discover the authorship of the Fly Sheets, and Dr George Osborn was allowed to send a 'Declaration'[115] to all

---

[115] R. Chew, *James Everett: A Biography* (London 1850), p. 366, gives the terms of the

ministers as a 'test' of their opinions, with the purpose of discovering those who had made no contribution to the Fly Sheets and had no sympathy with their contents. When the Conference assembled in Manchester in 1849, it was found that, despite repeated pressure, thirty-six ministers had declined to sign the Declaration. To deal with so many recalcitrants was obviously difficult, and it was decided to interrogate only a few.

Suspicion fell chiefly upon Everett, who was summoned to the Conference, but, along with others, he declined to answer the indictment as to the authorship.[116] After a short interval he suffered final expulsion.

Everett has never been proved to be the author of the Fly Sheets, either in whole or in part. The wording of the official sentence passed upon him, that he was under 'the strong and generally prevalent suspicion', points to him, and the suspicion was not without some plausible foundation. Despite the defence of his admirers in the last century, who believed his authorship was never proved, it is difficult to deny it.[117]

Two others under suspicion were Samuel Dunn (1797–1882) and William Griffith (1806–1883), both of whom suffered a similar fate. Dunn had started a monthly periodical, The Wesley Banner, in January 1849, and in the interests of reform challenged the attempt to silence minorities and strongly protested against the legality of Dr Osborn's 'Declaration'. William Griffith, criticized for his contribution to The Wesleyan Times, the newspaper which was the champion of liberal ideas, was likewise interrogated on the question of the authorship of the Fly Sheets. The Conference recommended that both ministers should remain within the ranks, the former if he would pledge the discontinuance of The Wesley

Declaration as follows: 'We, the undersigned, agree to declare that we regard with indignation and abhorrence the annonymous [sic] attacks on the motives and character of our brethren that have recently appeared in certain clandestine publications; that we have never intentionally communicated with the authors of those publications, with a view to afford information or assistance; . . . Wesleyan Takings: or, Centenary Sketches of Ministerial Character, as exhibited in the Wesleyan Connexion, during the First Hundred Years of its Existence, II (London 1851), xi.

[116] B. Gregory, op. cit., p. 452.
[117] Oliver A. Beckerlegge, The United Methodist Free Churches, pp. 32–3.

Banner, the latter if he would agree to send no further contributions to *The Wesleyan Times*. With these conditions they refused to comply, and so were expelled from the Connexion.

No reader of the Fly Sheets can fail to see how sinister were their caustic and abusive comments, but the bitterness of the conflict is further measured when it is remembered that *The Watchman*, the newspaper supporting the Conference position,

> exceeded far in coarseness and vulgarity anything which had discoloured the *Fly Sheets*. This certainly deserved the epithets applied to the *Fly Sheets* – 'slimy and disreputable'.[118]

The expulsion of these three ministers caused widespread sensation. The London *Times* declared that the Conference had

> taken that step which smacks more of the Inquisition than a British tribunal . . . and we pronounce them at once a gross outrage on all our old English principles of fair play.[119]

Shortly after the expulsions a large meeting was held in Exeter Hall, London, the first of a series of meetings throughout the country. It is estimated that during the year these three ministers addressed some one hundred and forty meetings, attended by 170,000 people. Widespread sympathy was expressed and a fund was raised to support them and the cause of reform. On the other hand many circuit superintendents acted with complete arbitrariness in stripping classes of their membership where sympathy with the movement was discovered. Extraordinarily bitter feeling was manifested, and in five years expulsions or secessions from societies reached more than a hundred thousand, almost one-third of the Wesleyan membership. While many never found their way into another Christian community, it would be difficult to estimate how many joined other denominations.[120]

Eight months after the Conference of 1849 four hundred delegates from groups of reformers met in Albion Street Independent Chapel, London, and sought by deputation to

[118] B. Gregory, op. cit., p. 436.
[119] Quoted in R. Chew, op. cit. (London 1885), p. 408.
[120] O. A. Beckerlegge, op. cit., p. 37.

approach the President of Conference, but were refused on the ground that their petitions were from meetings not legally constituted. For seven years (1850-6) the delegates met in this way at the same time and place as the Conference, and addressed it by letter. They requested that the expelled should be reinstated; that the laity should be represented in the church courts; that the Leaders' Meetings should control the admission and exclusion of members; and that while the Connexional principle should still be maintained there should be local independence in matters of internal economy. In the hope of reconciliation they held off from any attempt to organize a separate community, but year after year they were repulsed. Meanwhile expulsions and secessions continued in the circuits, sometimes even with violence.[121]

In 1854 the delegates moved in the direction of negotiation with other non-Wesleyan groups in the hope of union. The Bible Christians and the Primitive Methodists delayed their answers. An approach was made to the Methodist New Connexion[122] but proved unsuccessful, though a few societies of the Reformers became incorporated in the older body. The Wesleyan Methodist Association, however, having expressed a desire for wider union with Methodists of liberal opinion, responded to the invitation. It was found that only few and minor differences existed, and only slight modification of the constitution of the Association was required, and so a basis of union was agreed in 1855. On 14 May 1857 the union was completed and the united community held its first Assembly in the Baillie Street Chapel, Rochdale, on 29 July, when the name chosen was 'The United Methodist Free Churches'. James Everett was its first President and Robert Eckett its Secretary. The combined membership was 39,968 with 110 preachers and 769 chapels, towards which numbers the Reformers brought 19,113 members and 500 chapels, along with several preachers. The Foundation Deed of the Association (1840) was taken as setting forth the constitution of the new denomination.

[121] R. C. Swift, 'The Wesleyan Reform Movement in Nottingham', in *W.H.S. Proc.*, xxviii, 74-9.
[122] *Minutes* (Methodist New Connexion), (1854), p. 40.

Most of the Reformed societies joined with the Association to create the new body, but some remained outside the union, still continuing separately to protest against any measure or pattern of Conference authority. In 1859 these formed themselves into the Wesleyan Reform Union.

V

The group known eventually as the Independent Methodists[123] had its origins in unusual circumstances at the close of the eighteenth century. In 1796 the Methodist society at Warrington was a society largely self-contained, there being no resident minister. The circuit town of Northwich was twenty-five miles distant, and in the neighbourhood Methodist societies were few. Although the society in Warrington made no complaint of its isolation, its inevitable tendency was to rest upon its own resources both for its administration and for its spiritual maintenance. A feature peculiar to this society was the holding of cottage meetings, but these were looked upon with disfavour by the Methodist authorities, and in 1796 an official demand was made that they should cease. In one of these meetings at Warrington some were unwilling to comply; though not formally leaving the Methodist society and convinced that good work was being carried on, they continued to meet, and so in this way they grew into a separate society, making provision for its own sustenance. So far as is known, there was no open or bitter controversy. As yet they were without a name to distinguish them.

It was given to one, Peter Phillips (1778–1853),[124] a chairmaker of Warrington, to fashion the character of the new movement. In his labours he was eminently supported by his wife, Hannah Phillips (1780–1858), a notable woman preacher. Though at this time Phillips was but a youth of nineteen, he had become convinced by his study of the New Testament that a separated and salaried ministry was without scriptural

---

[123] There are two histories of this movement: (i) *A Short History of Independent Methodism* (Wigan 1905); (ii) J. Vickers, *History of Independent Methodism: Sketches of Worthies; Origins of Circuits; Expositions of Principles and Polity* (London 1920).

[124] J. Vickers, op. cit., pp. 23–31; A. Mounfield, *The Quaker Methodists* (Nelson, Lancs. 1924), pp. 22–9.

foundation, and this principle has throughout its history been a distinctive feature of Independent Methodism. His memorial tablet[125] records that as a preacher for more than fifty years he 'travelled more than thirty thousand miles and preached upwards of six thousand times'.

In the early days of the movement the little meeting in a room in Bridge Street, Warrington, was strengthened by the addition of some Quakers, who in concern for the decline of their own fellowship and having a natural affinity with this offshoot of Methodism, began to follow the example of the cottage meetings, and at the home of one Peter Wright of Stretton in Cheshire, established a second meeting place. Although as yet the societies were unconcerned about their name, a designation was found for them from outside, and they became known as 'Quaker Methodists', and the union developed an interchange of qualities: the Methodists adopted Quaker plainness in dress[126] and speech, and the Quakers became noted for their singing; they sang along the streets on their way to their meetings and on funeral occasions, and were sometimes styled 'The Singing Quakers'. By 1801 three new meetings had been formed,[127] all of them in Cheshire. In the following year the first chapel, a plain square building, was built at Friars Green, Warrington. Erected out of the slender resources of shoemakers, shopkeepers and candle-makers, it stood for fifty years, during which time it was twice enlarged.[128]

The time came when, after consultation in Manchester, it was decided to unite these societies of various origins, on a federal basis, and in 1806[129] the first Annual Conference was held at Macclesfield. It would appear that shortly afterwards the name 'Independent Methodist' was taken.[130]

[125] In Friars Green Chapel, Warrington.
[126] An interesting picture of Peter Phillips is given by his grandson: 'He wore a suit of Quaker's garb, an ample skirted coat, white kerchief, knee-breeches and blue knitted stockings with low shoes' (A. Mounfield, op. cit., p. 25).
[127] At Stretton, Whitley Reed, and Statham, the last transferred later to Lymm.
[128] It was demolished in 1859.
[129] Vickers (op. cit., p. 9) regards the meeting in Manchester in 1805 as the *first* Conference, and so dates the origin of the denomination. Of neither the 1805 nor the 1806 meeting are any records extant.
[130] There were societies in Macclesfield, Manchester, Warrington, Stockport and Oldham; the last-named had described itself as 'Independent Methodist', whereas the

Two further factors in their early history should be noted. The first was the significance of a visit from Lorenzo Dow,[131] the American evangelist, who, at the invitation of Peter Phillips, visited Friars Green in 1805 and was not only the instrument of a great revival but also contributed to a greater cohesion between the societies. The second was the association with Hugh Bourne, a lifelong friend of Phillips, who in the first preachings of Primitive Methodism visited the societies frequently and included the Rizley society on his own first preaching plan. Bourne declared: 'I was very fond of their way.' Many of the Quaker Methodists had attended the early camp meetings, and it is noteworthy that Bourne himself attended the Conference of 1808 at Macclesfield, by invitation, listened to a discussion concerning the ministry of women, and on request 'agreed to write an answer to the propositions', which he eventually published as a tract.[132]

The constitution of the Independent Methodist Churches was distinctive and still remains so. These Churches have no authority but what is conferred upon them by their members, each Church being a separate entity, yet associated with other Churches of like persuasion for mutual help. The seat of all authority is in the Church and without any restriction as to franchise or as to sex, for any office including that of minister. The Annual Meeting of the Connexion is therefore not a legislative but a deliberative assembly, and cannot intervene in the affairs of any Church without its consent. There is no distinction between ministers and laity, and each Church is entirely self-governed. The Annual Assembly has no power of coercion. Ultimately, however, circumstances necessitated some form of organization, but not until 1860 was a Model

---

Manchester society called itself 'Methodist Independent'. It may be that some of the societies had an earlier origin than the year 1796. The total membership of the societies was recorded as 1,219 (Vickers, op. cit., p. 10). In 1833 the societies agreed to call themselves 'The United Church of Christ'; in 1841 the title, 'United Free Gospel Churches', was tried, but to the dissatisfaction of those who wished to keep clear their association with the Methodist tradition. In 1898 the name 'Independent Methodists' was resumed.

[131] See above, p. 306.

[132] For Bourne's *Remarks of the Ministry of Women*, see John T. Wilkinson, *Hugh Bourne 1772–1852*, pp. 59–60. It seems that Bourne was responsible for the entry of Hannah Phillips into the work of preaching.

Deed adopted, and this was not enrolled in Chancery until 1894. This looseness of organization led to many losses, but the necessity for self-reliance enabled a number of societies to survive and grow.

The growth of the denomination was slow, but by 1821 societies had been established in south Lancashire and Cheshire, in Manchester, Liverpool, Sheffield, Bedford, and as far north as Yorkshire, Newcastle upon Tyne, Gateshead, Paisley and Glasgow; there was an outpost in Wales. These were served by more than a hundred preachers. Aggregate statistics are not available for the early years, but even as late as 1864 – the first reliable figures – the Churches only numbered 46, with 188 ministers and 2,730 members.

VI

It remains to give some brief account of a movement which developed in north-east Lancashire in the first half of the nineteenth century, and which has received less notice than it deserves. This was the Methodist Unitarian Movement (1806–57),[133] which

> owed little to the aggressive propaganda of Priestley and his school, whose determinist philosophy it deliberately rejected. It was still less indebted to the Liberal Independents and Arian Presbyterians of the eighteenth century, . . . the enlistment of laymen in the ranks of the ministry, the poverty of its members, and the establishment of societies in hamlets and villages far removed from large centres of population emphasised the isolation of the Methodist Unitarian Movement, and tended to preserve it apart from the organised Unitarianism which, at the beginning of the last century, inherited the prestige and traditions of a cultured and opulent Dissenting interest.[134]

The founder of the movement was Joseph Cooke (1775–1811), who became a Methodist itinerant preacher in 1795, and served until his expulsion on doctrinal grounds by the

[133] H. McLachlan, *The Methodist Unitarian Movement* (Manchester 1919); also 'Methodist Unitarians and the Beginnings of the Co-operative Movement in Rochdale in 1844', in H. McLachlan, *Essays and Addresses* (Manchester 1950), pp. 213–29.
[134] H. McLachlan, *The Methodist Unitarian Movement*, pp. 1–2.

Conference of 1806. The agitation associated with the Kilhamite movement undoubtedly left its mark on Cooke's mind; his co-operation with laymen in the organization of which he became the founder was based upon principle as well as expediency.[135] The ground of complaint against Cooke was his doctrinal position as expressed in two sermons which he preached in Rochdale in 1805,[136] and which under pressure he afterwards published. Being asked to reconsider his doctrinal position, he was removed to Sunderland, and requested to refrain from any preaching that might result in agitation. He violated the agreement, however, and on the ground of 'bad faith', in addition to his erroneous doctrinal position, he was expelled by the Conference in 1806.

If Cooke did not arrive at the doctrinal position of Unitarianism within his few remaining years – he died in 1811 – at least he moved in that direction, and the Methodist Unitarian Movement was 'the logical sequence of the operation of his spirit and the application of his method in the study of the Scriptures'.[137]

Returning to Rochdale after his expulsion, he was enthusiastically received by some of his former hearers; subscriptions were raised and a large building – Providence Chapel – was erected, and at the opening service Cooke made further declaration of the rational and scriptural principles by which he was animated. Large congregations continued to attend.

At Newchurch, in Rossendale, John Ashworth, a member of the Methodist society, became convinced of the rightness of Cooke's position and reluctantly, with about thirty others, left the society and began a separate group. After the death of Cooke in 1811, Ashworth was to become the virtual leader of the Methodist Unitarian Movement.

[135] It may also be noted that services in the 'Cookite' chapels were held during church hours, and that lay preachers administered the Communion.

[136] Joseph Cooke, *On Justification by Faith and the Witness of the Spirit* (Rochdale 1806). In 1807 he published in *Methodism Condemned by Methodist Preachers; or, A Vindication of the Doctrines Contained in Two Sermons, on Justification by Faith, and the Witness of the Spirit; For which the Author was expelled from the Methodist Connection* [sic] (Rochdale 1807) and in *The Hasty Sentence Arrested; or, Genuine Methodism Fairly Examined, in a Letter to the Author of Genuine Methodism Acquitted, and Spurious Methodism Condemned* (Rochdale 1807) certain correspondence, in which he challenged the accusation brought against him of breaking faith. See *N.H.M.*, i, 415.

[137] H. McLachlan, *Essays and Addresses*, p. 16.

The ministrations of Cooke and his colleagues began to move to neighbouring populations – Padiham, Burnley, Todmorden and Haslingden – and the new sect became known by the name of 'Cookites', a designation which did not disappear until after Cooke's death. Cooke died at the early age of thirty-five on 14 March 1811. He had been a friend and pastor to more than a thousand people. It is not easy to define precisely his doctrinal position, but it is clear that theologically he had steadily moved away from a Trinitarian position, and might fairly be called a Sabellian. It is also true that Ashworth and his fellows were unacquainted with Unitarianism at the time of Cooke's death; indeed, it is probable that they were unaware of the doctrinal error into which they had fallen.

The majority of those whose names appeared on the circuit printed plan were prayer-leaders; their functions were similar to those of the Methodist class-leaders, and many of the places of meeting were their homes. The introduction of the Cookites to organized Unitarianism arose through the preachers supplying occasionally the services of the Elland Unitarian Chapel, and eventually this brought them within the reach of financial assistance for their cause. One occasion in particular, when the Rev. John Grundy, of the famous Cross Street Chapel, Manchester, was the preacher at Newchurch, was probably the first assembly to be properly styled 'Methodist Unitarian', and the first Annual Meeting of the Methodist Unitarian Association was held at Rochdale in 1818. The work expanded, but twenty years later the organization, never fully co-ordinated, began to dissolve into Independency. There had been no periodical movement of preachers, as was the normal Methodist pattern, and so the circuit preacher tended to be regarded as the minister.

The passing of the early disciples of Joseph Cooke really marked the end of the distinct Methodist Unitarian Movement, and there was a steady absorption into organized Unitarianism. It should be emphasized that, according to the convictions of those associated with it, the Movement derived its doctrine from the Scriptures, and their piety and zeal were derived from Wesley himself. The general structure of the Association and the circuits composing it bore a clear resemblance to the

Methodist pattern. Its characteristic features were a lay ministry with regular exchange of preachers in the area, a profound love of prayer, and a zeal for Sunday School work; its congregations were for the most part composed of working men, weavers, colliers, artisans, whose means were slender indeed.

It is not surprising that a distinctive feature of the Movement was its concern for social and political ideals, against the background of the conditions of the time, urgent as they were for constitutional reform and social betterment. John Fielden (1784–1849), of Todmorden, who was elected Member of Parliament for Oldham, was an ardent crusader for factory reform, the founder in 1832 of the Society for Social Regeneration and a leader in the anti-Poor Law cause. In Parliament he moved the second reading of the Ten Hours Bill (1846). He was the main figure in the Methodist Unitarian cause in Todmorden. The outspoken radicalism of the leaders of the Movement is evidence of their position, and many Chartists and social reformers belonged to the community. At least half of the original twenty-eight members of the Rochdale Equitable Co-operative Society were Methodist Unitarians. In its social and political ideals Methodist Unitarianism stood for principles which made for independence of thought and action, sobriety and brotherhood in service.

INDEX

Page 247. Local preachers & ministers.